Building the
CANADIAN WEST

Building the
CANADIAN WEST

THE LAND AND COLONIZATION POLICIES
OF THE CANADIAN PACIFIC RAILWAY

by JAMES B. HEDGES

PROFESSOR OF AMERICAN HISTORY
BROWN UNIVERSITY

NEW YORK / RUSSELL & RUSSELL

FIRST PUBLISHED IN 1939
REISSUED, 1971, BY RUSSELL & RUSSELL
A DIVISION OF ATHENEUM PUBLISHERS, INC.
L. C. CATALOG CARD NO: 74-139928
PRINTED IN THE UNITED STATES OF AMERICA

PREFACE

THE pages which follow are the outgrowth of the author's earlier studies of the influence of the railway upon the settlement of the Northwestern States of the United States. Those investigations aroused his interest in the rôle played by that same agency to the north of the 49th parallel, where in the Prairie Provinces approximately one-fifth of the total land area alienated by the Dominion Government was granted to the Canadian Pacific and its subsidiaries. The scale of that company's operations, combined with the completeness of its records, seemed to offer an unusual opportunity for a study of the railway as a colonizer.

The term "Canadian West" is here used to denominate the Provinces of Manitoba, Saskatchewan and Alberta in which the Dominion subsidy lands of the Canadian Pacific were located. Only incidental attention has been given to British Columbia, where the Company at various times owned subsidy lands obtained from the Province, but where its work of promoting agricultural settlement was much less notable than on the Prairies.

The work has been projected against the background of the American frontier and American experience. Parallel and contrasting developments on the two sides of the imaginary boundary line have been kept constantly in mind and it is believed that events in each area take on a new significance when viewed in the light of those in the other.

Grateful acknowledgment is made to various officials of the Canadian Pacific who facilitated the search for materials, and especially to Mr. Ashley Edwards, whose unflagging interest and indefatigable energy proved equal to every obstacle; to Mr. H. E. Hume, formerly Chairman of the Dominion Lands Board of the Department of the Interior, Ottawa, who placed his vast fund of information at the author's disposal; to officials of the Parliamentary Library, Ottawa, for numerous courtesies; to the Harvard University Press for permission to use in Chapters II and III material which appeared in the writer's *Federal Railway Land Subsidy Policy of Canada* (Cam-

v

bridge, 1934); to the Social Science Research Council for grants-in-aid which made possible the gathering of the material for the volume; to my colleague, Professor Robert H. George, for helpful suggestions with respect to the maps; and to Miss Louise Waitt who has repeatedly typed large portions of the manuscript.

JAMES B. HEDGES

PROVIDENCE, RHODE ISLAND
August, 1939

CONTENTS

MAPS

Building the
CANADIAN WEST

I

THE BACKGROUND

IT HAS been said that "the most important feature of the economic life in a colony or newly settled community is its commercial connection with the rest of the world. Upon this more than
on any other circumstance depends its prosperity. . . . The history
of modern colonization does not show a single case where a newly
settled country has enjoyed any considerable economic prosperity,
or made notable social progress, without a flourishing commerce
with other communities."[1] This means that ordinarily the prosperity
of the colony must depend on an export staple. While the author of
the statement had particular reference to overseas colonies, his
generalization is equally applicable to those pioneer communities
which formed on the grasslands of interior North America, communities which in a sense were "colonies" of the older portions of
the United States and Canada. These communities, too, must have
an export staple to serve as the basis of "a flourishing commerce"
with other parts of the same country or with the outside world.
Their staples were, of course, agricultural products, whose chief
markets were at a distance. Access to those markets presupposed
adequate transportation facilities, and in the interior plains of
North America these could be provided only by the railway.

When the railway first came to the Canadian prairie it had already
played a vital and indispensable part in the development of the
prairie and plains portion of the United States. There, between
1850 and 1880, a railway network had formed which crisscrossed
the treeless expanse between the Great Lakes and the Rocky Mountains, broke down the isolation of those regions, and paved the way
for the occupation of this "last American frontier." In much of that

---

[1] G. S. Callender, *Selections from the Economic History of the United States*
(Boston, 1909), p. 6.

area the railway and the settler had advanced together. Sometimes the railway jutted out into the unsettled districts in anticipation of the farmer who was to come; sometimes the pioneer built his sod hut on the lonely plain in the confident assurance that the railway would soon follow. But regardless of whether railway or settler led the way at the moment, there would have been little permanent settlement without the railway, actual or potential. The railway was one of the prime factors in the growth of that vast region.

A series of significant maps recently published shows that in western Canada, too, the onward rush of the pioneer and the railway went hand in hand.[1] And while the conclusion to be drawn from those maps is that much of the time railway building lagged behind settlement, communities of homesteaders formed at a substantial distance from the railway only in the knowledge that where they went the railway soon would follow. The railway, then, became *ipso facto* a colonizer. And if by chance it happened to be endowed with a land subsidy it had a double interest in promoting settlement. Only through the occupation and development of the country could it hope for a profitable traffic or for the sale of its land.

As the pioneer railway of western Canada and as the one possessed of the largest land subsidy, the Canadian Pacific undoubtedly played the major rôle among the companies which helped to people the prairie provinces. The importance of its work has long been understood. It has sometimes been referred to as "The Great Colonizer," in recognition of its long-sustained efforts in the cause of western land settlement. Thus far, however, this recognition has rested upon nothing more permanent than oral tradition handed down from the generation which witnessed the failures and the successes of those who worked so tirelessly to settle the Northwest. Of books about the Canadian Pacific there have been many. General histories, of both the substantial and the romantic variety, have appeared. Biographies of Van Horne, of Donald A. Smith, of James J. Hill have been written. But nowhere has more than casual attention been given to the history of the company's land subsidy.

The land and settlement policies of the railway can be understood, of course, only when projected against the background of

[1] W. A. Mackintosh, *Prairie Settlement, The Geographical Setting* (Toronto, 1934).

physical and economic conditions prevailing in the Northwest.[1] Even before Confederation, it was apparent that the province of Canada had virtually reached the limits of agricultural expansion. On the west the path was blocked by the Great Lakes; on the north the Laurentian Shield was an effective barrier. Although efforts were being made to push back the agricultural frontier in that sector, such efforts were largely foredoomed to failure. The all-important question, then, was whether the great Northwest was susceptible of settlement and development.

Except for the Selkirk settlement, established in the valley of the Red River in 1812, the fur trader had held undisputed sway in this region. As late as 1870 all but a handful of its scanty population were half-breeds. Settlement throughout the Northwest was confined to the shadows of the trading posts. In the fifties, however, both the British and the Canadian Governments had taken steps indicating an increasing interest in the future of the prairie country. In 1857 a select committee of the House of Commons, after taking exhaustive, if contradictory, testimony as to the possibilities of the country, recommended its cession to Canada. In the years 1857-60 Captain John Palliser, under the auspices of the colonial office, made extensive explorations of the region between Lake Superior and the mountains. Captain Palliser classified the territory between the Laurentian Shield and the Rockies into two large areas, the "fertile belt" and the semi-arid country. The "fertile belt" embraced the valleys of the Red and the Assiniboine, together with the park-like regions in the valley of the North Saskatchewan. This belt, he thought, offered distinct natural advantages for agricultural settlement. "The lakes and rivers provided an abundance of fish, which would provide part of the food for the colonists while he was establishing himself. There was a good supply of rich pasture and natural hay sufficient to provide for cattle throughout the year. Sufficient areas had been cleared by fires that the settler might begin to cultivate his land immediately. There was ample timber for the construction of buildings, and wood and coal for fuel."[2] The semi-arid region, the treeless or "true prairie," situated in the upper val-

[1] In the first part of this chapter I have relied largely upon the pioneer work of W. A. Mackintosh, *op. cit.*
[2] Mackintosh, *op cit.*, pp. 33-34.

leys of the Souris and the South Saskatchewan, Captain Palliser considered unfit for settlement.

Meanwhile, in 1857 and 1858 the government of the province of Canada sent out exploring expeditions, of which S. J. Dawson and Professor H. Y. Hind were the most important members. Generally speaking, their findings corroborated those of Captain Palliser. Hind and Palliser agreed that the semi-arid belt was unsuited to settlement. Both agreed as to "the fertility of the Park Belt and the adjacent wooded sections, and as to the fitness of that area for settlement: they both saw the necessity for improved transportation: neither looked for rapid settlement."[1] Even in those restricted portions of the West which Professor Hind regarded as suited to settlement, he greatly underestimated the area of good arable land. His estimate was 11,000,000 acres, with an equal area adapted to grazing. In those areas alone, according to the 1926 census, the improved land amounted to 22,000,000 acres, with 37,000,000 acres occupied.

Neither the inconclusive character of the evidence presented before the select committee of the House of Commons nor the modest prospects painted in the reports of Hind and Palliser could stem the tide of opinion demanding that Rupert's Land be ceded to Canada. The growing trade between Minnesota and the Red River settlement, with the resulting fear of annexation to the United States, the increasing discontent with the fur monopoly, the unsatisfactory nature of the Hudson's Bay Company government in the territory all pointed to the need of a new dispensation in the Northwest. Basically, however, the acquisition of Rupert's Land was the result of the conviction within the new Dominion that "the agricultural possibilities of the country were too great to admit of its being reserved any longer for the fur trade." In short, the Dominion of Canada was embarking upon "a clean-cut experiment in agricultural colonization." The Rupert's Land Act of 1868 authorized the Dominion Government to purchase the territory of the Hudson's Bay Company. On July 15, 1870 this vast area formally came into the possession of the Dominion.

The region thus handed over to the Dominion is really the northern portion of the interior plain of North America. With a base of some 800 miles along the international boundary, it sweeps

[1] Mackintosh, *op. cit.*, p. 39.

northward, bounded on the west by the Rocky Mountains and on the east by the Laurentian Shield. Its southern part presents great variation, ranging from the level, fertile Red River Valley, with its average level of 800 feet, through the second prairie level of 1,600 feet, terminating at the Missouri Coteau, to the third prairie level, which attains an altitude of as much as 4,000 feet in the foothills of the Rockies.[1] The entire area, therefore, slopes eastward and northward, with an average fall of 5 feet per mile from the mountains to Lake Winnipeg. This southern part of the Canadian plain is a treeless area, with diminishing rainfall from east to west.

North of the treeless area stretches the crescent-shaped Park Belt, from Lake Winnipeg through the Swan River district, Prince Albert, and Battleford to Edmonton. This is essentially the "fertile belt" described by Palliser and Hind, and was early recognized as a region well suited to settlement.

Throughout the West rainfall is scanty. While in most sections there is normally enough rain for the growth of drought-resisting crops by moisture-conserving methods, the specter of drought has always hung over the region. "Rainfall deficiency is perhaps the most important single fact in the life of the Canadian plains. It divides the history of settlement into 'good' and 'bad' years. It has been the chief conditioning factor of agricultural practice."[2]

The essential point with respect to rainfall, however, is not so much the total precipitation as the degree to which it is concentrated in the growing season. In general, in the regions of scanty rainfall, the proportion coming in the spring and summer is large. Thus while at Winnipeg the annual rainfall is 20.4 inches, 12.4 inches fall during the growing season. At Medicine Hat, however, 8.3 inches out of the 12.8-inch total fall between April and August inclusive. This vagary of the climate has somewhat tempered the hazard of drought.

If drought has been a constant threat in the southern portions of the Northwest, frost has been no less a menace in the North. Fortunately, another climatic peculiarity has tended to minimize this danger. "The climatic axis of the Northwest lies along a belt extending approximately from southwestern Manitoba to the Yukon

[1] Mackintosh, op. cit., pp. 7-8.
[2] Ibid., p. 14.

Territory. Along this axis, making allowance for local variations, summer temperatures are considerably higher than at points of similar latitude on either side of it, and winter temperatures are considerably lower."[1] It is this northward swing of the summer isotherm which has made it possible to push the agricultural frontier into the Peace River country. There spring comes as early as in Winnipeg, although winter begins somewhat earlier. "Agricultural settlement on the Canadian plains has followed the isotherms west and northward."[2]

The settler coming into the Canadian Northwest from eastern Canada, from Great Britain, from northern Europe, or from many parts of the United States faced an unaccustomed situation, a country wholly unlike any he had known before. The comparative absence of trees was both a blessing and a curse. If it simplified the task of preparing the soil for planting, it complicated the pioneer's fuel problem. Light rainfall and extremes of temperature, drought and frost rendered farming precarious in many instances. Could the settler "find a livelihood and security? Could the resources of this new country support agricultural settlement; or should the country . . . be left to the buffalo and the fur trader? Much thought was given to these questions before the decision to colonize was reached. The questions continued to be asked long after settlement had been undertaken."[3]

Fortunately for the Canadian settler these same questions had been asked years before with respect to the prairie and plains regions of the United States, and answered. As a result, a technique of prairie pioneering was at hand for the farmer in the Canadian Northwest. This technique was the product of the experience of the American pioneer in settling the treeless areas of the neighboring republic. There, in the thirties and forties of the nineteenth century, the settler with a forest background dating back for generations found himself confronted by environmental conditions wholly new to him. He who came of western European stock which for ages had carved homes out of the wilderness now for the first time sought to tame the prairie. Many were the questions which he asked him-

[1] Mackintosh, *op. cit.*, p. 12.
[2] *Ibid.*, p. 13.
[3] *Ibid.*, p. 26.

self: Could a soil barren of trees produce crops? What of timber for building, for fuel, for fencing? Where would he obtain water? How would he transport his staple to market? These and many other questions he put to himself. The traditional instruments for coping with the forest situation had been the ax, the long rifle, the boat, and the wooden plow. The ax and the long rifle were of diminishing importance in a treeless country; the boat was of doubtful value on a land-locked prairie; the wooden plow would not cut the tough prairie sod. The settler then began the long and painful process of adapting his technique to changed conditions. He gained valuable experience in the oak openings of Michigan and the small prairies of northern Indiana and Illinois. John Deere's steel plow, introduced in the late thirties, was proving invaluable. Having conquered the small prairies by the fifties, the farmer was prepared for the assault on the Grand Prairie of central Illinois, where the railway came to his assistance. Soon the advance guard of settlement had arrived at the semi-arid country west of the 98th meridian. Here the march was halted for a season while a new weapon, new tools, new methods of cultivation, new laws for land and water were evolved.[1]

The long rifle was now definitely discarded in favor of the six-shooter, which made possible the subjugation of the mounted Plains Indians. Barbed wire made its appearance as the answer to the problem of fencing a country without trees. Soon the fenced-in squares on the checkerboard replaced the open range and transformed the cattle kingdom into a farming frontier. The wind was harnessed and made to pump the water available only at great depths. The English common-law doctrine of riparian rights was modified to suit the conditions of the semi-arid country. The homestead unit of 160 acres quickly proved inadequate on the Great Plains. Where it did not bring grief and disaster to the settler, the unscrupulous made a mockery of it. When too late, it, too, was modified.

A new system of tillage was evolved to meet the needs of the semi-arid environment. In Utah and California in the fifties and sixties settlers had worked out, by the trial and error method, the

---

[1] For the adjustments necessary for the conquest of the plains, see Walter P. Webb, *The Great Plains* (Boston, 1931).

technique of dry farming, based upon the principle of conserving the moisture in the soil. Summer fallowing came to be an essential element of the dry farming practice, and it spread over the plains country. Few there were who saw that the constant cultivation entailed by summer fallowing would ultimately result in soil drifting and dust storms.

Invention came constantly to the aid of the farmer. Improved farm implements and labor-saving machinery speeded the occupation of the area between the Mississippi and the Rockies. The level, treeless country placed a premium on the machine process. Oliver's chilled steel plow, introduced in the late sixties, was a milestone in the advance across the prairie. "In 1878 the invention of roller milling had converted the hardness of the spring wheat from a blemish to a virtue."[1] The mechanical grain elevator revolutionized the methods of storing and grading grain and it was destined "to become as characteristic a feature of prairie landscape as the native vegetation."

These methods, these tools, this new technique awaited the settler on the Canadian prairie. He merely needed to import them across the 49th parallel. Important as they were, however, they were not enough. The growing season in the Northwest is short. To avoid frost damage to his crop, the settler must have an early-maturing variety of wheat. Here the Canadian was forced to rely on his own ingenuity and he proved himself resourceful in the extreme. Beginning with Red Fife, he bred successive types of wheat which made possible the persistent northward migration of that plant.

But there were other essential requirements which had to be met before the Northwest of Canada could come into its own. Only when good land at low cost was no longer to be had in the United States could Canada hope for a substantial diversion of that great human stream which for decades had poured into the western and northwestern states. When that time came, other factors being favorable, this historic movement of people would push across the international boundary into the Canadian prairie.

Of paramount importance to the settlement of the Northwest was adequate transportation. This meant, in the first analysis, a railway across the country, but it meant more than that. Combined with the cheaper and more efficient transport service offered by the rail-

[1] Mackintosh, *op. cit.*, Introduction, p. xii.

way, there must be cheap ocean rates, made possible by the steel hull of the steamship and the improvement of the marine engine. As a result of these developments the ocean freight rate on wheat from Montreal to Liverpool declined from 18 to 20 cents per bushel in 1874 to 2 cents in 1904.[1] Between 1886 and 1906 the combined ocean-rail rate from Regina to Liverpool declined from 35 cents per bushel to 21 cents. In conjunction with rising wheat prices at the close of the century, these cheaper transport costs made for profitable wheat production in the West.

A converging of all these factors—the new technique of prairie and plains farming, early maturing wheat, improved transportation, and the exhaustion of the better land in the United States— was ultimately to inaugurate a new era in the Canadian West.[2] But this new day was not even in sight in 1870; and it seems likely that the statesmen of the young Dominion who assumed the task of trying to settle the country had scant appreciation of the complexity of the problem.

The plan of the Dominion Government to settle the Northwest with farmers required something more than new tools and instruments and new agencies of transportation. It required also a policy for the administration and disposal of the land which had come into the possession of Ottawa.[3] In surrendering its title to Rupert's Land, the Hudson's Bay Company had imposed upon the Dominion the condition that it might "claim in any township or district within the fertile belt in which land is set out for settlement, grants of land not exceeding 1/20 of the land so set out," the land to be selected by lot. If the West were settled and developed, the Hudson's Bay Company intended to obtain some of the profit. By the Dominion Lands Act of 1872 provision was made that the company should receive section 8 in each township, section 26 in each township whose number was divisible by five, and the southern half and northwest quarter of section 26 in all other townships. In this way 6,313,900 acres passed into the hands of the Hudson's Bay Company. From this area it has enjoyed the unearned increment resulting

[1] Mackintosh, op. cit., p. xi.
[2] The importance of these factors is developed admirably and in great detail in A. S. Morton, History of Prairie Settlement (Toronto, 1938).
[3] For a detailed discussion of the land policy of the Dominion Government, see Chester Martin, "Dominion Lands" Policy (Toronto, 1938).

from the efforts of others. Having little incentive to push the sale of its land, the company largely sat tight in the assurance that land values would surely rise.

The government promptly adopted the rectangular system of survey in vogue in the United States. The land was surveyed in ranges of townships extending north from the 49th parallel, each township being 6 miles square and containing 36 sections, each 1 mile square. The sections, in turn, were subdivided into quarter sections of 160 acres. No more satisfactory system of survey could have been devised. It obviated conflicting or overlapping claims and it made for ease of administration.

In the Act of 1872 Canada took over the homestead policy adopted in the United States just a decade earlier. A quarter section was granted free to the settler on condition of three years' residence and cultivation. By subsequent amendment, provision was made by which a person homesteading 160 acres might also obtain a 3-year option to purchase an adjoining quarter section. This right of preëmption, as it was called, gave assurance to the settler that while he was perfecting title to his homestead the occupation of adjoining land by homesteaders would not prevent the subsequent enlargement of his farm. In a region where summer fallowing was to occupy a conspicuous place in farming practice this provision for the later acquisition of a second quarter section seemed to have much to recommend it.

The privilege of preëmption, however, was susceptible of abuse. It served to scatter settlement. Many who filed preëmption claims were never able to take them up. To others preëmption was merely an opportunity for speculation on a small scale, and the quarter sections were useless while thus tied up. Frequently a homesteader was unable to pay for his preëmption at the appointed time. Rather than relinquish it he was tempted to mortgage his homestead, to which he had obtained his patent. As a result he all too often lost both the preëmption and the homestead. The growing realization of these conditions gave rise to a demand for the repeal of preëmption, which was finally done in 1890.

Armed with a liberal land policy, Dominion officials worked out plans to advertise their lands in the British Isles and on the continent of Europe. Immigration propaganda became an important activity of the Canadian Government, in sharp contrast to the United States, where the encouragement of settlement devolved upon the states and upon individuals and corporations. During the seventies a considerable number of farmers from the eastern provinces, especially Ontario, disposed of their holdings to avail themselves of the homestead policy of the West. Together with Scottish farmers they settled in the Red River Valley and in southern Manitoba generally, where the two classes formed "the effective backbone of Manitoba."

Rather more spectacular was the Mennonite immigration of 1874. Mennonites had been settled in southern Russia since the days of Catherine the Great. About 1870 their pacific views brought them into conflict with the government of Alexander II. A general exodus followed in which several thousand of them found their way to the Kansas prairies, where they quickly established prosperous settlements. In March, 1872 the Canadian Government was advised by the Colonial Secretary that certain groups of Mennonites in South Russia were contemplating emigration to Canada. They desired information as to whether they would be exempted from military service and from the ordinary form of oath, and whether land grants and other inducements would be offered them. The Dominion Government in reply invited the Mennonites to send delegates to Canada at the expense of the Department of Agriculture. At the same time a Canadian immigration agent in Germany was sent to Russia to confer with the Mennonites. Delegates visited the West in 1872-73 and selected land in the Red River Valley as the site of their proposed settlement. An Order in Council of March, 1873 set aside a reserve of eight townships, which provided a large compact block of land. In July the Mennonites were finally promised exemption from military service and from oaths; a free grant of land, their own religious schools, low rates from Hamburg to Winnipeg, to continue through 1876, and provisions for the immigrants while en route completed the list of inducements.

The first of them arrived in 1874 and by 1879 some 6,000 had settled on the Manitoba prairie. The early arrivals were fairly well-to-do, but many of the late-comers were so impoverished that special arrangements were necessary to move them. On the security of property pledged by their co-religionists in Waterloo County, Ontario, the Dominion Government advanced the sum of $96,400 to enable the immigrants to establish themselves on the land. By 1892 the entire sum had been repaid with interest.

While not the most progressive and productive of farmers, the well-known thrift and frugality of the Mennonites provided a guarantee of the success of their venture. Although they occupied a very fertile area they were not known as skilled farmers. They were, however, a stable and dependable community. Their village type of social organization, combined with their indifference to governmental and civic affairs, naturally set them apart from the society in which they lived. All in all, they were welcome settlers on the prairie at a time when farmers were all too few.

Another foreign group who located in Manitoba in the early years were the Icelanders. Driven from their homeland by the pressure of overpopulation, they began to arrive in the West in 1876. Through an erroneous idea as to their usual occupation, the first groups were sent to the west shore of Lake Winnipeg, where they were expected to support themselves by farming and fishing. Founding the settlements of Gimli and Icelandic River, they experienced many difficulties before their success was finally assured. Those arriving later were sent to Greenborough in southern Manitoba, where they quickly succeeded as farmers. Unlike the Mennonites, the Icelanders were quickly assimilated to the life of their adopted country. While retaining their own language, they learned to speak English, participated in the political life of the province, and in other ways became full-fledged citizens of the Dominion.

The seventies abounded in schemes and plans for colonizing the West, but most of them came to nothing. Numerous organizations and societies, some of them of a philanthropic nature, were formed with a view to settlement, but most of them were stillborn. The figures for homestead entries show how meager were the accomplishments of the decade, apart from the Mennonite and Icelandic settlements. From 1874 to 1880 inclusive the homestead entries amounted to 10,988 as compared with 5,903 cancellations, a net gain of 5,085.[1] Assuming that all of these became *bona fide* farmers and that each one represented a family of five, they would account for the addition of some 25,000 people to the population of Manitoba and the

[1] *The Canada Year Book* (1926), p. 923.

Northwest territories. These were slender results of a decade of hope and relentless effort.

To those gifted with foresight, it would have been evident in 1880 that many things must happen before the successful settlement of the Canadian West could be achieved. To all, however, it was apparent that one indispensable condition must be met before substantial results could be expected. This was a railway by which the staples of the prairie could find their way to market. That railway was soon to come, and it quickly became a foremost agency for the promotion of settlement.

II

THE ORIGIN OF THE LAND SUBSIDY

THE significance of governmental land policies in the settlement and development of the American and Canadian West is well understood. In outward appearance and general form, the land systems of the two countries have several points of similarity. Both governments rejected the revenue point of view in administering their public domains and, through the adoption of the homestead idea, committed themselves to the use of the land as an instrument of national development. Yet at the very moment that they were giving land directly to the individual settler, they were also giving it to railway companies in the form of subsidies. These two lines of action were distinctly at cross purposes, for the grants to the railways removed vast areas from the reach of the homesteader and forced the farmer to pay tribute to the corporation. The justification of these contradictory policies lay, of course, in the generally accepted belief that the building of railways increased the value of the settler's acres sufficiently to compensate for the few extra dollars which he paid for them. Of the soundness of this contention in many instances there can be little doubt. But in both the United States and Canada, before the race for railway subsidies had run its course, millions of acres of the finest lands available were in the hands of the transportation companies; and, whatever the merits or defects of carrying the principle of governmental aid to railways to this extreme conclusion, the subsidies themselves and the manipulation of them by the various companies became important adjuncts of the general land policies.

The subsidy system of the United States has been the subject of frequent investigation, but that of Canada has been less thoroughly examined. This is unfortunate, for the colonization of the western lands of the two countries, which was the by-product of their land grant practices, was, in reality, one great movement rather than two. Settlers in search of desirable lands knew no boundary lines; Americans migrated into Canada and Canadians moved into the United States. The great transcontinental railway companies north and south of the border were managed with the same ends in view, sometimes by men who had been railway promoters on both sides of the 49th parallel. A study, therefore, which assembles the essential features of the Canadian subsidy policy, and attempts to show not only its more obvious similarity to that of the United States but also the numerous points of striking contrast, may help to serve as part of the basis for a coördinated story of the westward movement in a major portion of the North American continent.

Adopting the land grant idea in the middle of the last century, when the pioneer had but recently crossed the Mississippi, the United States during the next 20 years granted approximately 150,000,000 acres of land to western railways. So great was the popular enthusiasm for railways in this period that no price would have been thought too high for their construction, and it was easy enough to be lavish with land of which there seemed to be an unlimited supply. Aside from the national importance of the projected lines, which was alleged in support of the grants to the Pacific railways, the chief argument in favor of land subsidies to railways in general was that which represented the government as a private landowner wishing to secure the largest possible return from his domain.[1] Much of the government land, however, was far from the settled portions of the country and would not sell unless the country could be developed. If a portion of this were given to a railway which would render the remaining lands salable, the government would be acting in the enlightened manner of any intelligent landowner. To emphasize this idea, the grants were to be made in alternate sections, with the price of the remaining lands doubled, so that the gain to the government would be in direct and in exact proportion to the amount of the land granted.

As the building of the railways progressed and settlement advanced, the various transportation companies developed exploitive

---

[1] J. B. Sanborn, *Congressional Grants of Land in Aid of Railways* (Madison, 1899) is the standard work on the origins of the land grant policy in the United States.

tendencies which irritated and alarmed the people of the West and culminated in the Granger movement. A general feeling of hostility toward the railways displaced the former manifestations of friendliness, and no amount of argument could convince the rebellious settler of the justice of the land subsidy policy. In the face of this opposition, grants of land to railways became less frequent and by 1871 the practice was discontinued.

The year 1871, which marked the end of the subsidy era in the United States, began it in Canada. In that year the Conservative Government of Sir John Macdonald sponsored a proposal that a railway to the Pacific should be built by private enterprise, assisted by the government with generous grants of land as well as of money. Recent developments had brought the importance of a Pacific railway very much into the public mind. The acquisition of Rupert's Land by the Dominion was quickly followed in 1871 by the entrance of British Columbia into Confederation. But British Columbia came in only at a price. Led by the redoubtable Alfred Waddington, the 10,000 inhabitants of that western province had demanded the construction of an overland highway to the Pacific. A greater challenge to a young nation of 4,000,000 souls could scarcely be imagined. To build a railway through the forbidding waste north of Lake Superior, across the uninhabited prairies, and over the Rocky and Cascade barriers to tidewater was no mean achievement. As in the United States, the greatest asset in the accomplishment of such an undertaking was the land, and thus the origin of the land bounty system in Canada was inseparably bound up with the plans for the railway across the continent.

The proposal of the Macdonald Government provided, in addition to the grant of land, that construction should begin within two years and be completed within ten, a provision designed to satisfy the demands of British Columbia for the prompt construction of the railway. While the land grant idea was accepted by the Opposition, they protested that the country was unequal to the task of completing the enterprise in so short a period. But the government refused to yield this point, although it did agree that the building of the road should not entail an increase in taxes in the Dominion.[1]

[1] *Journals of the House of Commons of the Dominion of Canada*, Session 1871, pp. 197, 203, 264, and 268. The House resolved that the railway should be "con-

This stipulation carried with it the implication that land was to be given on a large scale, since in no other way could an increase of the tax burden be avoided.

The Act of 1872,[1] which incorporated this proposal into law, provided for a grant of land not exceeding 50,000,000 acres to be appropriated in aid of the railway to the Pacific. The lands were to be located in alternate blocks of not more than 20 miles in depth, and not less than 6 nor more than 12 miles in frontage on the railway, the blocks to be so laid out that each one granted to the company on one side of the railway should be opposite a block of like width reserved for the government on the other side of the railway.[2]

The conveying of lands in large tracts was a distinct departure from the American practice of locating railway lands by alternate sections. Although open to the objection that it almost certainly would lead to a less equitable division of the good and bad land between railway and government, it was thought to be better suited to the conditions prevailing in the Canadian Northwest than the alternate section method. Under the latter system, it was said, there would be such a dispersion of homesteads in a given township as to retard community development and render difficult mutual assistance among the settlers, especially during the years prior to the sale of the intervening railway sections.[3] With large blocks available for homestead, however, compactness of settlement would result in the areas reserved for the government.

While predicated upon Sir John Macdonald's original plan that the railway be built by private enterprise, the act carried with it no definite provision for the actual construction of the road. If Canada had little of means and less of experience upon which to draw for such an undertaking, that was not true of the United States. American capitalists, with governmental bounties, had completed one

structed and worked by private enterprise . . . and that the public aid to be given . . . should consist of such liberal grants of land, and such subsidy in money, or other aid, not increasing the present rate of taxation, as the Parliament of Canada shall hereafter determine."

[1] Entitled "An Act respecting the Canadian Pacific Railway." *Statutes of Canada,* 35 Victoria, Cap. 71, assented to June 14, 1872.

[2] *Ibid.*

[3] As late as 1880-81 this argument was employed against the alternate section method. See *Debates of the House of Commons,* 1880-81, p. 331.

railway to the Pacific and were projecting others. The enormous profits attending their efforts made them quick to recognize chances for similar fortunes elsewhere.

But while the Macdonald Government was not averse to accepting the aid and experience of American capital, political expediency demanded that Canadian interests be equally represented. One of the most prominent Canadian business men of the time was Sir Hugh Allan, who controlled the Allan Steamship Line. Although primarily interested in water transportation, he had recently entered the railway business through his promotion of the North Shore road along the St. Lawrence, in competition with the Grand Trunk. If the assistance of Jay Cooke and his Northern Pacific associates, who had already indicated an interest in the undertaking, could be secured in coöperation with Sir Hugh, the question of American domination might be less of an issue. The negotiations between the Canadian and American capitalists moved smoothly enough, but before plans could be definitely shaped, strong opposition developed within the Dominion.

In Ontario, the presence of Sir Hugh Allan as one of a company to build the new railway meant that the terminus would be in Montreal rather than in Toronto. Moreover, in this province any suggestion of a possible affiliation with the Northern Pacific group was regarded with extreme suspicion. People there had no faith that the American promoters would not deliberately hamper the building of this Pacific railway to check competition with their own line. In Quebec, Sir George Cartier, a Cabinet member with a strong following among the French-speaking element, used his influence against Sir Hugh. As Cartier was closely associated with the Grand Trunk, the reasons for his position were obvious. With plenty of money available for purposes of propaganda, Allan won over Cartier and his supporters. But the opposition in Ontario was made of sterner stuff. A group of Toronto business men organized the Interoceanic Railway Company and petitioned the government for a charter and aid for building a line of railway to the Pacific. They felt that their future security and prosperity were too closely interlocked with the Pacific railway to allow the building of it to fall into unsympathetic hands. All attempts which the government made in the way of mergers and adjustments between the two contending groups were unsuccessful. After the Conservatives were reelected in 1872, an entirely new company, known as the Canadian Pacific, was organized, with a board of directors drawn from the various provinces and with the American capitalists excluded. Of this company Sir Hugh Allan was elected president.

Important to the story of the evolution of the Canadian land subsidy policy are some of the outstanding features of the charter granted to the Allan company.[1] Thirty million dollars and 50,000,000 acres of land were offered in aid of the railway, on condition that no American interests should be admitted. The land was to be conveyed in the alternate blocks of the dimensions described in the Act of 1872, with an added provision to the effect that the company "shall not be bound to receive any lands which are not of the fair average quality of the land in the sections of the country best adapted for settlement."[2] This was the first appearance of the idea that railway subsidy lands were to be of a certain designated quality, an idea which, as subsequent discussion will show, was to grow into a most important factor in the Canadian bounty system. Another clause of the charter, in regard to the price of the alternate blocks retained by the government, stated that "unless the Company shall sell lands granted to them at a lower price, or shall otherwise agree, the Government shall for and during the term of twenty years . . . retain the upset price of such alternate blocks at an average price of not less than two dollars and fifty cents per acre."[3] It was openly charged in the Canadian Senate at the time that the Allan charter was copied from that of the Northern Pacific.[4] While this statement cannot be justified when applied to the charter as a whole, there can be no doubt that the plan proposed in the clause just quoted was borrowed from the Northern Pacific. It is noteworthy, however, that while in the United States it was the government which insisted upon the double minimum as a justification for the land grant policy, in Canada the railway company imposed the condition as a means of preventing the government from underselling it.

[1] For the charter, see *Sessional Papers* (No. 13), 1873.
[2] *Ibid.*
[3] *Ibid.*, p. 20.
[4] See *Debates and Proceedings of the Senate of Canada,* First Session, 2nd Parliament, 1873, p. 113. Statement by Mr. Campbell, April 18, 1873.

But the terms of the Allan charter were never put into effect. As soon as the charter was granted, with its specific rejection of American participation, rumors purporting to come from disgruntled railway promoters in the United States were circulated to the effect that all was not strictly fair and aboveboard in the negotiations. There were those in Canada who did not quite believe it wholly fortuitous that Sir Hugh Allan was elected president of the new company, and who were willing to give credence to any sort of story. A steady undercurrent of dissatisfaction prevailed, and when the private correspondence of Sir Hugh was stolen and published, everyone was prepared to believe the worst.[1] The correspondence revealed that Cartier and Macdonald had made liberal use of Allan's money before the election of 1872. Out of this discovery grew the charge that the charter was the reward for services rendered, and that even the high office of prime minister had been degraded to this end. A political storm of the first magnitude resulted, and interest in all other issues was lost in the turmoil. A later and calmer survey of the whole affair reveals great indiscretion surely on the part of the Conservative leaders, but nothing much more than that. Sir Hugh had been a regular contributor to Conservative election funds for years. Moreover, he really gained nothing by the Conservative victory and the resulting charter except the assurance that the work in behalf of the railway would continue. Sir John Macdonald's indiscretion, too, was tempered by the very clear indication that he felt he was acting in the best interests of the Dominion.[2] But neither the Allan company nor the Conservative Party was able to hold out against the attack at its height. The company gave up its charter and the party went down to a smashing defeat at the hands of the Liberal Party, under the leadership of Alexander Mackenzie.

No government could have made its debut under more inauspicious conditions than that of Mackenzie. A country torn by political dissension and burdened with financial depression offered little of promise to railway promotion, yet the government showed no disposition to relax its efforts in that direction. As an inducement to

[1] For this correspondence, see *Journals of the House of Commons*, Session 1873, Vol. VII.

[2] For Sir John Macdonald's defense of his position, see Joseph Pope, *Memoirs of Sir John Macdonald*, Vol. II, pp. 174-89.

private capital, Mackenzie offered $10,000 in cash and 20,000 acres of land per mile, in alternate blocks of 20 square miles, each block to have a frontage of not less than 3 or more than 6 miles on the line of the railway.[1] Regardless of terms, however, private capital seemed unavailable and every offer went begging.

Discouraged in his efforts to interest a private company in the construction of the railway, Mackenzie resolved that the line should be built by the government itself. The plan which he formulated with that end in view called for the completion of the links between navigable waterways, the abandonment, for the present at least, of the difficult portion north of Lake Superior, and British Columbia's consent to an extension of time for the finishing of the project. Mackenzie was completely unsuccessful in his attempts to win concessions from British Columbia, but he did make substantial progress in the location and construction of the road.

When the Conservatives were returned to power in 1878, Sir John Macdonald went forward for a time with the policy of government construction. In pursuance of this plan, Parliament adopted resolutions in 1879 appropriating 100,000,000 acres of land in aid of the railway.[2] These resolutions provided that all ungranted land within 20 miles of the railway should be used in satisfaction of this appropriation. If the lands adjoining the line of railway were not "of fair average quality for settlement," a substitute acreage was to be reserved in other portions of the prairie. The lands were to be vested in appointed commissioners, who were authorized to sell the land from time to time, and to invest the proceeds in government securities to be held for meeting the expenses of building the railway.

Beyond these very general provisions the resolutions of 1879 did not go, and it remained for the Department of the Interior to formulate a complete scheme for describing, setting aside, and selling this immense domain. Sir John Macdonald, in outlining such a plan, made direct reference to American policy, and used it as the basis of his proposal for handling the Canadian grant. In a memorandum of June 25, 1879,[3] after explaining the details of procedure in the

[1] *Statutes of Canada,* 27 Victoria, Cap. 14, assented to May 26, 1874.
[2] *Debates of the House of Commons,* 1879, pp. 1895-96, for the resolutions. For the vote on them see, *ibid.,* p. 1979.
[3] This memorandum is to be found with *Order in Council* No. 976, June 28, 1879. (These are cited hereafter as *O. C.*)

United States, he expressed the belief that "a system somewhat similar . . . would be most convenient to adopt in administering the land grant of our own Railway." He would discard the large blocks, contemplated in earlier Canadian legislation upon the subject, in favor of the alternate sections of the United States, and would scrap the idea of reserving exclusively for sale all the lands along the railway, in favor of a system of free grants or homesteads distributed through the railway belt. Such free grants would not only silence the charges of land monopoly, but would also conduce to the sale of the intervening railway lands.

Sir John estimated that in Manitoba and the northwest territories there were, within 110 miles on either side of the railway, 125,000,000 acres of land, 100,000,000 for the railway and the remainder for free grants. Land on each side of the railway he would divide into five belts: Belt A to extend back from the railway for 5 miles; Belt B for 15 miles beyond Belt A; Belts C and D, each, for an additional 20 miles; and Belt E stretching out for another 50 miles. In Belt A, all lands were to be sold at not less than $6.00 per acre. In the other belts, four 80-acre homesteads were allowed in the even-numbered sections, the remaining lands in such sections to be sold as preëmptions at $1.00 to $2.50 per acre.[1] The odd-numbered sections in those belts were railway lands, ranging in price from $5.00 per acre in Belt B to $1.00 per acre in Belt E.[2] Thus, except for Belt A, where all lands were reserved for the purpose of the railway, the alternate section idea was to prevail: odd-numbered sections for the railway, even-numbered for the government.

This plan had scarcely been formulated, however, when a change in the American policy led to material modification of the Canadian regulations. Congress had increased from 80 to 160 acres the amount of land which could be homesteaded or preëmpted within the limits of a railway land grant. This change was believed to require "a corresponding alteration in the area of Dominion lands proposed to be homesteaded within the zone embracing Canadian Pacific

[1] *O. C.* No. 976, June 28, 1879, gave approval to the plan set forth in the memorandum of Sir John Macdonald. With the same Order in Council are to be found the detailed regulations for carrying the plan into effect. The title is "Regulations respecting the disposal of certain Dominion Lands for the purposes of the Canadian Pacific Railway," dated July 9, 1879.
[2] *Ibid.*

Railway lands, otherwise the manifestly superior advantages of the
United States over the Canadian policy would result in securing to
the Western and Northwestern States and Territories of the American Union all European and other immigration for years to come."[1]
The need for change was considered the more urgent in view of
the exceedingly liberal conditions of sale offered by the Northern
Pacific and the St. Paul, Minneapolis and Manitoba companies in
the Northwest of the United States, whose territory was in direct
competition with that through which the Canadian Pacific was to
be built. As the Deputy Minister of the Interior expressed it, "a
rebate of one-half the purchase money is made to persons who may
have placed half the land purchased, or in that proportion, under
cultivation within three years of the date of purchase, thus evi-
dencing the value which the Railway Companies attach to actual
settlement. It is presumed that the loss in abatement of the purchase
moneys under this system is considered by the Companies as more
than compensated for by the additional traffic which the rapid
settlement of the country would bring to their roads."[2] In view of
these facts the government increased from 80 to 160 acres the homestead and preëmption areas within the limits of the railway belts,
and allowed in Belt A the same proportion of homesteads and
preëmptions as in the other belts.[3]

The resolutions of 1879 and the resulting regulations introduced
significant changes in the land subsidy policy of the Dominion. The
idea of the alternate section became definitely a part of the Canadian
system, supplanting the original provision for large blocks. These
regulations were devised with the assumption of continued governmental construction of the railway, but before they had received
an adequate trial the plan for completion by the government was
abandoned in favor of another effort by private enterprise.

There were those in the government, and out of it, who had not
abandoned hope of having the railway built by capitalists. Sir

1 "Memorandum (confidential) by J. S. Dennis, Deputy Minister of the Interior,
to Sir John Macdonald, Minister of the Interior," July 3, 1879, with Ref. 20,088
on 18,909, Dominion Lands. The manuscript material used in this and the following chapter is to be found in the Dominion Lands Branch of the Department of
the Interior, Ottawa.

2 O. C. No. 1422, October 9, 1879; also O. C. No. 1461, October 24, 1879.

3 Ibid.

Charles Tupper, the Minister of Railways and Canals, was one of these, and it was he who urged the government to turn to a remarkable group of men who seemed to possess precisely the requirements needed for building the railway to the Pacific. These men, George Stephen, James J. Hill, Donald A. Smith, R. B. Angus, and John S. Kennedy, working together, had succeeded in converting the bankrupt St. Paul and Pacific road, in the United States, into a going concern. They had built this line to the Canadian boundary and had negotiated a traffic arrangement beyond to Winnipeg. In addition to this interest in an American company, several of the men were associated with important enterprises in Canada. This combination of successful railway promotion in the United States with a general understanding and knowledge of Canadian business and railway affairs was an ideal one. And the American venture had been a highly profitable one. If, reasoned Sir Charles Tupper, these men were planning to reinvest their profits, it was the part of wisdom for the government to seek some sort of agreement with them. Tupper's counsel was heeded, negotiations were begun and carried through to a successful conclusion, and on October 21, 1880, the Syndicate Contract, under the terms of which the Canadian Pacific Railway was finally to be completed, was signed.

In December of the same year the contract was placed before Parliament for approval. Besides receiving the lines under construction by the government, the company, in return for building about 2,000 miles of railway, was to have a cash subsidy of $25,000,000 and a land grant of 25,000,000 acres.[1] The government promised freedom from rate regulation until the annual earnings on the capital expended in the construction of the railway reached 10 per cent,

[1] For the provisions of the contract, see *Statutes of Canada*, 44 Victoria, Cap 1 (1881).

It should be noted that whereas the railway land subsidies in the United States were granted in pursuance of a general policy of using the public domain to encourage the construction of railways, the land subsidy of the Canadian Pacific was one of the stipulations in a definite contract which the Dominion Government entered into with the Canadian Pacific. The land subsidy, therefore, was part of the price which the Dominion paid to the Canadian Pacific Syndicate for the construction of a railway to the Pacific, which other private agencies, and even the government itself, had not succeeded in building. The land grant to the Canadian Pacific was not regarded in 1881 as part of a larger Dominion policy of encouraging railway building through the use of land. The grant, however, became a precedent for subsequent grants to other companies.

with exemption from tariff duties on construction materials, from taxes on lands in the northwest territories (unless sold or occupied) for 20 years, and from dominion or provincial taxation of the railway and railway property, as well as of the capital stock of the company forever. As a guarantee against encroachments by rivals, no competitive lines connecting with the western states were to be chartered for a period of 20 years.

The terms of the contract were indubitably very favorable to the company, but neither that fact nor the right and duty of the Opposition to oppose can justify the unreasoning attack which the Liberals launched against every provision of the agreement. So largely did the question become a political issue that it was impossible to consider any individual clause on its merits, and the unanimous disapproval of every item by the Liberals was the signal for an equally unanimous defense by the Conservatives.

Led by Edward Blake, the Opposition lost no opportunity for arousing the country against the contract. Another company, headed by Sir William Howland, was hurriedly organized. This group offered to construct the road for $3,000,000 and 3,000,000 acres less than the Syndicate Contract required, and, as evidence of the genuineness of the offer, deposited a guarantee of $1,400,000. As further indication of good faith, it was prepared to pay duty on construction materials, and to waive the monopoly clause, the exemption from rate regulation, and the exemption from taxation. While the seemingly less onerous character of the offer of this company served as a strong talking point for the spokesmen of the Opposition, the government professed to believe that the Liberals had organized the company solely for political purposes. They could safely bring it forward at the eleventh hour, when there was no possibility that the government would break the contract already signed.

Among the most pointed of the Liberal criticisms of the contract were those directed at the monopoly clause, which did so much to estrange the West from the East, and the exemption from taxation, which placed such a heavy burden upon the impecunious settlers in the West, a burden made heavier by the interpretation which rendered the lands exempt for twenty years after the issuance of the patent. If the freedom from regulation until ten per cent had been earned seemed unduly favorable to the company, it had been anticipated in a clause of the General Railway Act, while the exemption from duties on construction materials was justifiable, even if not consonant with the "national policy" which the Conservatives had recently adopted.

Probably no feature of the Liberal attack upon the contract consumed more time or occasioned more bitterness than their denunciation of the alleged extravagance of the government in trafficking away the resources of the Dominion, and in this connection it is the debate on the land subsidy which chiefly interests us. Discussion on this subject began formally on December 13, 1880, when Sir Charles Tupper moved that the House go into Committee of the Whole on the following Tuesday to consider resolutions affirming the expediency of granting the $25,000,000 and the 25,000,000 acres of land provided for in the contract.[1]

The Liberals immediately trained their guns upon the excessively generous provisions of the land subsidy. Blake and his followers emphatically challenged the validity of the Conservative boast of an advantageous bargain with the syndicate. Pointing out the disingenuous nature of the government's claim to a saving of from 25,000,000 to 75,000,000 acres, compared with former land grant proposals, the Liberal leader asserted that if the value, rather than the amount, of the land were considered, the subsidy was princely in its proportions. The significant thing, in Blake's estimation, was the location of the land, not the area. Since the company was entitled to the alternate sections within 24 miles on either side of the railway, the value of its land was far in excess of any similar area elsewhere in the West. Ridiculing the Conservative estimate of $1.00 per acre as the value of the land, Blake used their own earlier prices to prove that the figure was absurdly low.[2] In terms of the land regulations instituted by the Macdonald Government in 1879, the bulk of the Canadian Pacific land grant would fall in Belts A and B, where the prices were $6.00 and $5.00 per acre respectively.[3] It was the land 60 miles or more from the railway which those regulations had priced at $1.00 an acre.

Continuing their attack, the Opposition made much of the con-

---

[1] *Debates of the House of Commons*, 1880-81, p. 48.
[2] *Ibid.*, p. 79.
[3] *Ibid.*, p. 80.

trast between the enormous area the Canadian Pacific was to receive and the much smaller grants made to the railways in the United States. One Liberal member had computed the average grant to the American railways, exclusive of the Pacific roads, to be 3,790 acres per mile, while the syndicate was to have almost 13,000 acres for each mile of construction.[1] Even the Northern Pacific, the most generously endowed of the lines in the United States, might not obtain more than 15,000,000 acres of arable land.

Nor did the Liberals fail to stress the adverse effects which such a large subsidy would have upon the whole course of settlement in the West. Canada, it was observed, must compete with the United States for immigrants, which it could not hope to do successfully unless able to "offer conditions at least equal to those offered by the United States."[2] On this point the contract contained no clause satisfactory to the Opposition. Without any reservation whatever, it ceded to the syndicate 25,000,000 acres of land, the most fertile and best situated in the Northwest. Because of the alternate section plan, not only the railway lands, but the Crown lands as well, would be at the mercy of the company. Fifty million acres, more than could possibly be sold within a quarter of a century, would be subject to the arbitrary whim of a private syndicate.[3] The latter would have it in its power to paralyze the efforts of the government to settle and develop the West. If, for purposes of speculation, or for other reasons, the company should withhold its lands from sale, the government would be powerless to sell and colonize its own lands. In each of the government sections within the railway belt there were to be two homesteads and two preëmptions—in other words, two settlers.[4] Should the railway section not be sold, the occupant of the government section would be forced not only to "keep up his roads and his fences, but the roads and fences of the neighboring lot," and he would be obliged "to pay double municipal and school taxes." As the Opposition viewed the situation, few would be disposed to occupy the government sections unless those of the railway were sold at the same time, and the surest way to expedite sales by the syndi-

[1] *Ibid.*, p. 792.
[2] *Ibid.*, p. 738.
[3] *Ibid.*, p. 738.
[4] It was assumed that the homesteader would buy the adjoining preëmption lot.

eate was to set a time limit for the disposal of its lands, thereby rendering it impossible for sections to be deliberately held in the hope that the expenditure of labor and capital by the settler on the Crown lots would enhance the value of the adjoining railway land.

Fortunately for the Liberal argument, there seemed to be ample precedent for the establishment of such a time limit for the sale of railway lands. The Conservative Government having adopted the Union Pacific Railroad in the United States as a standard for the construction of the Canadian Pacific, there was no reason why the Opposition should not employ the same road as a criterion of land subsidy practice. Accordingly, they seized upon the clause of the Union Pacific charter which required that subsidy lands not sold within ten years after the completion of the road should be open to occupation and preëmption like other lands at not less than $1.25 per acre.[1] The fact that this clause had not been enforced against the Union Pacific in no way diminished its effectiveness as an argument against the land subsidy. But, while making much of the absence of such a guarantee in the Canadian Pacific contract, the Liberals attempted no inclusion of a definite time limit in the document. Instead, they sought to achieve the same end by other means. The Opposition insisted it was only fair that the government should officially place a price on the land, in order that the entire country might know definitely the monetary value of the aid extended to the syndicate.[2] If a value of $1.00 per acre were assigned the land, in accordance with the estimate of the Minister of Railways, then the company ought to be forced to sell at that maximum. In the event the company was unwilling to sell the land for less than $2.00 to $3.00 an acre, it would be the duty of the government either to give a considerably "less amount than 25,000,000 acres, or take before Parliament and before the people the responsibility of giving to the syndicate lands valued by the syndicate and by the government at $50,000,000 or $75,000,000."[3] The Liberals sponsored an amendment, therefore, requiring that a maximum price be placed on the land, thereby depriving the company of every incentive to

[1] *Debates of the House of Commons*, 1880-81, p. 739.
[2] *Ibid.*
[3] *Ibid.*

retard the settlement of the West by holding the land for appreciation in value. But, like all other attempts to change the contract,
this was voted down by a strict party vote of 49 to 118.[1]

If the Opposition was unable to see anything good in the terms
of the agreement, the Conservatives were equally incapable of finding any defects in it. On their side, much of the burden of defending
the provisions of the contract devolved upon Sir Charles Tupper.
As Minister of Railways and Canals, it was his duty to expound the
document to the House, and, in this case, to expound was but to
justify its every clause. Tupper largely anticipated the objections
of the Liberals, and he very cleverly sought to confound them out of
their own mouths. By presenting an imposing array of their earlier
statements in regard to land and land grants, utterly inconsistent
with their current comments, he made their criticisms appear
patently captious, partisan, and void of sincerity. Replying to Liberal
assertions as to the great value of western lands, he quoted Blake
as having in 1875 ridiculed the idea that land for the Georgian
Bay branch was worth $2.00 an acre.[2] Blake had then thought that
$1.00 per acre was more reasonable. Very appropriately, Tupper
could point out that during the 6-year interval nothing had happened to increase the value to $3.18 per acre, the value the Opposi-
tion was now attaching to the land in the West. Tupper made
equally effective use of earlier speeches of Alexander Mackenzie
expressing the belief that the competition of the free lands of the
United States would prevent the sale of the Canadian lands at more
than $1.00 per acre.[3]

No less inconsistent were the Liberal complaints in regard to the
amount of land granted by the contract. As the Conservatives pointed
out, the Allan charter had called for a grant of 50,000,000 acres,
while the Mackenzie Government in 1874 had offered 54,000,000
acres to any company which would build the railway. Thus, as
compared with the Opposition proposal, the terms of the contract
actually saved the country 29,000,000 acres. Far from being extrava-
gant, the Conservatives were husbanding the resources of the
Dominion. The resolutions of Parliament in 1879 had pledged

[1] *Ibid.*, p. 740.
[2] *Ibid.*, p. 63.
[3] *Ibid.*

100,000,000 acres in support of the railway; the government was using just one quarter of this amount.[1]

Liberal fears of a great land monopoly in the West, the Conservatives alleged, were wholly groundless. Instead of "locking up" 54,000,000 acres in large blocks, as the Liberals had sought to do under the Act of 1874, the contract locked up but 25,000,000 acres in alternate sections. While under the Allan charter the government was obliged not to sell its lands for less than $2.50 an acre, the syndicate agreement made it possible to give away the remaining lands if the public interest so required.[2] "No policy," Tupper said, "did the Syndicate press more strongly upon us than that of settling the land as fast as we could. They say we should be only too glad to plant a free settler upon every acre belonging to the government."

Nor would the company withhold its lands from sale for speculative or other reasons. The surest guarantee against such a course was the zeal which the members of the syndicate had displayed in settling the lands of the St. Paul and Pacific in Minnesota. Fortunate it was for Canada that the experience gained there would now be brought to the colonization of the Canadian prairies. The entire history of railway land subsidies, the Conservatives asserted, was a refutation of the land monopoly charge of their opponents. The company must sell the land and bring a population into the country in order to sustain the road. The land grant railways of the United States had incurred large expenditures in promoting the sale of their lands, the Atchison, Topeka, and Santa Fe having spent 88 cents per acre for that purpose.[3] The "glass cases and jars containing wheat, corn and other products of the Western States," which were on exhibition at every railway station, were the work of the railways, not of the United States Government. Surely nothing less was to be expected of the men who were to build the Canadian Pacific through an uninhabited wilderness. The company would expend from nine to ten millions in the cause of immigration, which, in turn, would relieve the Dominion Government of that expense.

After weeks of debate, in which the contending forces exhausted

[1] *Ibid.*, p. 70.
[2] *Ibid.*
[3] *Ibid.*, p. 537.

every argument, and in the course of which the twenty-three amendments offered by the Liberals were voted down with monotonous regularity, the contract with the syndicate was finally approved by a straight party vote. With that vote, the Canadian Pacific Railway approached one step nearer to reality, while the railway land subsidy policy of the Canadian Government became a fact rather than a theory.

One who compares the political aspect of railway land subsidies in the United States and Canada cannot fail to be impressed by two important differences. Canada was not troubled by the constitutional issue which proved so vexatious in the United States. In the Dominion there could, of course, be no question as to the constitutional right of Parliament to vote land subsidies in aid of railways. In the United States, on the other hand, there were those who had genuine doubt as to whether the Constitution warranted such grants by Congress, and there were many more who seized upon the constitutional argument as a means of cloaking base and selfish motives. In Canada, likewise, the debates attending the adoption of the land grant policy fail to reveal the sectional cleavage which bulked so large with her neighbor to the south.

In one respect, however, the political history of land subsidies in the two countries is similar: in neither was the principle of railway land grants a party issue. While it was a Conservative Government which signed the contract with the syndicate, the subsidy idea had been adopted years before, and the Mackenzie Government in the seventies had been committed to that principle. And, despite the opposition of the Liberals to the Syndicate Contract, their quarrel was with the specific provisions of the grant rather than with the principle. That the Howland Company, which the Opposition supported, offered to build the railway for 22,000,000 acres of land represents a difference in degree rather than in kind.

III

LOCATING THE LAND

AFTER ten years of discussion and political controversy, a definite plan for the handling of land subsidies had been formulated and the Canadian Pacific Syndicate, fortified with a promise of 25,000,000 acres of land, assumed the tremendous responsibility of completing the transcontinental railway. The land provisions of the Syndicate Contract were the product of various developments. Although there had never been much doubt in Canada as to the wisdom of using the land for the building of railways, there had been considerable uncertainty as to the best manner of using it. Here the basic principle of conveying land by alternate sections, which had been so consistently employed in the United States, was not at first accepted. The earlier proposals made in Dominion councils had contemplated the granting of land in large blocks, a procedure which, had it been put into effect, would have been so complete a departure from the American method as to leave little in common between the two, save the simple fact that both had given land in aid of railways. When the alternate section plan was written into the agreement with the company which was undertaking the building of a railway across the continent, a very significant point of contrast was removed, and the common use by both countries of this method of land conveyance has led to the assumption that the railway land subsidy policy of Canada was "transplanted bodily" from the United States.[1] But to accept a similarity in one feature, however fundamental, as indicating a resulting parallel in growth and development would lead to quite erroneous conclusions, and would leave out of account the more interesting phase of the Canadian land grant system. Granting a railway company 25,000,000

[1] For such a view, see Samuel E. Moffett, *The Americanization of Canada* (New York, 1907), p. 75.

32

acres of land was one thing; locating and selecting it was another. The land bounty had been won only after a sharp political battle, with all the attendant publicity, but the lands were set aside and located through administrative regulations, Orders in Council, and Acts of Parliament, all of which largely escaped public notice. A study of these documents, however, reveals the policy of the Canadians taking unusual departures from American practice and makes of it not a slavish imitation but an original creation, developed along new lines dictated by their own peculiar needs and circumstances.

At the outset, the Syndicate Contract contained a provision which, when put into operation, afforded endless opportunity for the growth of a subsidy policy unique in character. One clause, which became known as the "fairly fit for settlement" clause, read: "If any such sections consist in a material degree of land not fairly fit for settlement, the company shall not be obliged to receive the same as part of the grant."[1] Here was a regulation which, followed to its logical conclusion, meant that the company need not accept any 25,000,000 acres of the wilderness which was then the Canadian West, but that it could, in a sense, pick and choose, a privilege not granted to the subsidized lines in the United States. This "fit for settlement" idea had appeared before in Canadian records. A similar provision had been part of the Allan charter. It had come to light again in the Act of 1874 and in the resolutions of 1879. But there is every reason to believe that the political exponents of the subsidy plan gave scant attention to the real significance of such a clause. It was only when the debate on the Syndicate Contract was approaching an end that reference was made to this stipulation, and then the discussion was in no sense commensurate with the importance of the subject. There is little to indicate that either side regarded the clause with any concern, other than as something to attack or defend in a political discussion. However, the persistence with which the idea had been injected into Canadian land grant legislation is evidence that although the politicians were largely unmindful of its significance, there were others who were not. Sir Hugh Allan's associates were men of the Northern Pacific, while the syndicate group was in control of an

[1] For the contract, see *Statutes of Canada*, 44 Victoria, Cap. 1 (1881).

American land grant railway. Here were men who knew at first hand the workings of land subsidies in the United States, who knew what pitfalls to avoid and what concessions to obtain, and it seems reasonable to suppose that the "fairly fit for settlement" clause was a result of their experience.

Another provision of the Syndicate Contract created an additional problem in locating the 25,000,000 acres to which the company was entitled. The Canadian Pacific was the only railway on the continent which received a fixed area of land, regardless of the length of its line. In the United States, and in Canada, with this one exception, railways received a stipulated area per mile of railway built. In the United States, too, the land was contiguous to the railway throughout its entire length, which made for ease in describing and conveying the subsidy. The adoption of the American practice in Canada, of course, would have required the donation to the railway of land in Ontario and British Columbia. Since the Dominion Government could not do this, in view of provincial ownership of the land, it was compelled to provide the entire Canadian Pacific subsidy from the region lying between Winnipeg and the Rocky Mountains.[1] For the 900 miles of railway to be built across the prairie, the company was to receive its lands in alternate sections within 24 miles on each side of the railway, creating what was subsequently known as the 48-mile or main line belt. But, for the construction of the line through the long stretches of Laurentian rocks and muskeg wastes north of Lake Superior and across the rugged mountain chains of British Columbia, it also was to obtain its reward in the prairie provinces. This provision worked no hardship on the company, as it was in reality an added guarantee of a good selection of land, but it did complicate the problem of locating a large grant already conditioned by the "fit for settlement" requirement. Any railway in the United States would doubtless have welcomed a gift of the fertile lands of Illinois and Iowa in return for pushing a line across the Rockies, but Congressional restrictions allowed no such privileges. Numerous as were the legal loopholes through which the wily American railway promoter might make his

---

[1] *Ibid.* Although in 1871 British Columbia had transferred to the Dominion Government a large area of land to be used in aid of a Pacific railway, the Canadian Pacific Syndicate refused to accept the land as part of its subsidy.

way to greater profits, he found that in this one respect the law could not be easily circumvented. The subsidies in the United States, providing as they did for stipulated amounts of land per mile along the entire length of the line, carried no guarantee as to the quality of the land. All American land grant roads received certain undesirable lands, while the transcontinental lines found themselves in possession of vast areas either totally worthless or valuable only for grazing purposes. The Canadian Pacific, in attempting to avoid the acquisition of lands of such low quality, thrust upon the Dominion Government a heavy burden of responsibility. It was soon to become evident that the administration of the Canadian Pacific grant was not the simple matter of conceding automatically a certain number of acres for each completed mile of rails, as had been true in the United States, but the more difficult one of finding 25,000,000 acres of land, part of it along the railway, part of it elsewhere on the prairie, but all of it measuring up to the company's standard of land "fairly fit for settlement."

The problem was further complicated by the decision of the syndicate to change the route of the railway across the prairie country. Because the investigations of Palliser and Hind had shown much of the treeless prairie to be unsuited to settlement, all the early plans for building the railway, whether by the government or by private capital, had contemplated a northern route through the Park Belt. The Syndicate Contract, therefore, provided for a reservation of land along the railway line from Winnipeg to Jasper House. But the publication of the reports of Sir Sanford Fleming, Engineer-in-Chief of the Canadian Pacific Railway in the seventies, showed that his botanist, Professor John Macoun, dissented strongly from some of the conclusions of Palliser and Hind. He asserted that much of the treeless prairie was susceptible of settlement. He was also one of the first to grasp the significance of the large proportion of annual precipitation falling during the growing season in the West. The revelations of Professor Macoun, the need for the shortest and cheapest route, and the desire to obviate the engineering problems and higher construction costs entailed by the broad rivers and deep valleys of the North, soon caused the syndicate to abandon the Winnipeg-Jasper House plan in favor of the line from Winnipeg to Calgary. This change, of course, had far-reaching effects upon both the country and the railway. It meant that for almost 20 years the course of settlement was to be directed predominantly into the southern portions of the West. It made inevitable the rejection as not "fairly fit for settlement" of much land within the 48-mile belt, thereby rendering more difficult the task of finding the required acreage for the company.[1]

The subsidy was to be administered through the Department of the Interior. The general provisions were simple. For convenience in conveying the lands to the company as portions of the line were completed, the railway was divided into two sections, eastern and central. As each 20 miles of track were laid, the government was to convey the lands at a stipulated acreage per mile according to location in the eastern or central section. The alternate sections tributary to the main line, limited as they were to the prairie, would not satisfy the total amount of the grant. This shortage, according to the contract, was to be made up from other lands on the prairie, between the 49th and 57th parallels. Here the company might, with the consent of the government, select lands in the "alternate sections extending back 24 miles on each side of any branch line or lines of railway to be located by the Company . . . , or of any common front line or lines agreed upon between the government and the Company."[2] The lands so located along branch lines were to be part of the main line subsidy, and it was assumed that in this manner any deficiency could be overcome. In theory, then, all of the lands granted were to be alternate sections directly tributary to either the main or branch lines, but in actual practice the company, in searching for lands "fairly fit for settlement," went far afield and eventually found itself with millions of acres far removed from either main or branch lines, with grants to other companies frequently intervening between these reserves and the company right-of-way.

The work of building the railway was inaugurated very soon after the approval of the contract, and with equal promptness be-

[1] Had the main line extended from Winnipeg to Jasper House, as originally planned, a much larger acreage "fairly fit for settlement" could have been obtained within the 48-mile belt.

[2] *Statutes of Canada*, 44 Victoria, Cap. 1 (1881).

ginnings were made in the formidable task of securing title to the land. The general financial policy of the syndicate group was a conservative one. The directors of the company sought to build their road without resorting to the enormous bonded indebtedness which had characterized most railways on the continent. It was perhaps because of this conservative fiscal program that such persistent and vigorous attention was given to the acquisition of the lands granted to the railway. The ultimate financial success of the venture depended in no small measure on the immense resources which would be gained through the sale and development of the subsidy lands. That vigilance was necessary is attested by the fact that not until 22 years after the contract became law, and 17 years after the completion of the railway, was the last acre finally set aside for the company. The need for alertness was increased with the appearance in the early eighties of numerous smaller railway companies for whom millions of acres were reserved, first for purchase, later as subsidies. As to the soundness of the Canadian Pacific's later contention that these grants violated the spirit of the Syndicate Contract, there may be reasonable doubt; that the wholesale and indiscriminate manner in which Ottawa authorized land bounties to the lesser railways added greatly to the difficulty of finding the land for the Canadian Pacific, and forced the company to adopt an apparently aggressive policy for the protection of its interests, there can, however, be no question.

As the construction of the road moved forward, the company acquired at various times four large land reserves, far removed from the main line belt. The establishment of these reserves was pressed in each case by the railway as part of its consistent effort to protect itself against governmental delay in reserving and conveying the lands. Once land subsidies became the accepted policy, the Canadian Pacific was not alone in petitioning the government, and it was quite possible for much valuable land to be turned to other uses before enough rails could be laid to claim the entire grant.

The first of the land reserves was obtained during the second year of construction. In January, 1882, 161 miles of the main line had been constructed from Winnipeg westward, and the Pembina

Mountain Branch had been located.[1] On the basis of this construction, actual and anticipated, the company requested and secured the location and conveyance of the lands already earned along the main line and along the located branch to the south.[2] A request made at the same time, however, for the reservation of an additional tract of land extending south from the proposed branch line to the international boundary was refused. But the company was not content to accept a first refusal as final. Engineers and surveyors had been at work, and a few convincing figures were at hand. The most generous estimate of land available in the 48-mile belt placed the total at only 6,000,000 acres. Great additional tracts must come from other portions of the West if the entire grant was to be realized. Immigration into the Northwest was too scattered and too uncertain to justify the projection of enough branch lines in that territory to make up the deficit. Against the time when colonization should be more stable and conditions more propitious for railway expansion, the company felt the need of some form of guarantee of land in the North.[3] The government was eventually persuaded of the justice of the company's request, and the first northern reserve was created.[4] (See Map I.) This reserve, between the 52nd and 54th degrees of latitude and the 104th and 116th degrees of longitude, contained some of the finest land in the Dominion. Here, it was estimated, the odd-numbered sections would yield 19,000,000 acres which, after deducting the lands unfit for settlement, would guarantee the company one-half the total grant.[5]

Successful in its first efforts, the company was not slow in making another attempt to secure a reserve in the South. There was more possibility of immediate revenue from land south of the railway, where settlement and development had already begun, than in the lands to the north, whatever their potential value. In requesting this additional allotment the company advanced perfectly plausible

[1] See letter of A. M. Burgess, Secretary, Department of the Interior, to Charles Drinkwater, Secretary, C. P. R. Co., March 14, 1882, File No. 34187-2. In this letter Burgess refers to and summarizes various letters from the C. P. R. on the subject, especially Drinkwater's letter of January 13, 1882.
[2] Ibid.
[3] O. C. No. 2099, October 24, 1882, which relates the view of the company.
[4] Ibid.
[5] Ibid.

arguments. The first estimate of 6,000,000 acres available in the 48-mile belt along the main line had been reduced to a scant 5,000,000 as the surveying proceeded.[1] Moreover, many of the sections from Winnipeg to the western boundary of Manitoba were already privately owned, and therefore not available for the land subsidy.[2] The Minister of the Interior acceded to the company's request that the apparent shortage be made up from lands to the south. Arrangements were made for a reserve of approximately 2,500,000 acres between the original western boundary of Manitoba and the Coteau or Dirt Hills.[3] The land lay between the southern limit of the 48-mile belt along the main line of the Canadian Pacific and the northern limit of a belt previously reserved for the Manitoba Southwestern Colonization Railway.[4] A few months later the reserve was extended to include all of the odd-numbered sections of land still at the disposal of the government, between the 48-mile belt and the 49th parallel, and between the Red River and the original western limit of Manitoba.[5] This enlarged Southern or International Boundary Reserve (see Map II), like the one in the North, was too far from the main line to be directly developed by it. Both were too remote to contribute in a substantial manner to the growth of the traffic of the railway. The two reserves, however, were dependable assets of a company embarking upon an undertaking of great magnitude. They guaranteed the larger portion of the grant, assured the Canadian Pacific of a significant influence in the future development of the country, and afforded a measure of control over rival transportation enterprises.

In the nineties, two additional reserves were obtained in partial satisfaction of the main line grant. The first of these, known as the Lake Dauphin Reserve, was secured ostensibly in connection with the building of a line of railway referred to as the Lake Dauphin Extension of the Selkirk Branch.[6] Projected in 1891, this branch

[1] *O. C.* No. 2152, November 3, 1882, in which these facts are set forth.
[2] *Ibid.*
[3] *Ibid.*
[4] The lands reserved for the Manitoba Southwestern Colonization Railway were to be purchased at $1.00 per acre. It appears, however, that they were not acquired by the railway.
[5] *O. C.* No. 110, January 25, 1883.
[6] *O. C.* No. 414, February 18, 1895, sets forth the facts in connection with this line.

had been "surveyed and located within the meaning of clause 11 of
the original Contract of 1881," which provided for the granting of
land along the branch lines for the purposes of the main line subsidy. Accordingly, the company asked for the odd-numbered sections within 24 miles of the proposed branch line. In addition, it
petitioned for other lands, to be used as reserves against probable
deficiencies in the statutory belt along this line. The fertile and
highly desirable lands in the Swan River district were suggested as
a possibility. It was estimated that some 250,000 acres of land
"fairly fit for settlement" were available there.[1] To the east and
south, between the grant of the Manitoba and Northwestern Railway Company and the belt appertaining to the Lake Dauphin
Branch, was a similar area of suitable land.[2] Prior commitments by
the government, however, made it impossible for the Canadian
Pacific to acquire all of this acreage. Much of the land had been
reserved since 1885 for the Winnipeg Great Northern Railway, one
of the various colonization roads which followed on the heels of
the Canadian Pacific.[3] The government did agree, however, to the
allotment of a smaller reserve, and set aside the odd-numbered
section still at the disposal of the Dominion within a belt of 24
miles on either side of the Lake Dauphin Branch from the point
where it left the western limit of the Winnipeg Great Northern
Reserve to its terminus.[4]

With the way closed to the acquisition of a really large tract of
land in closer proximity to its own lines, the company turned once
again to the far Northwest. In this region the government reserved
for it the odd-numbered sections between the 4th and 5th meridians
of the Dominion land surveys and the 54th and 55th parallels of
latitude.[5] The land, subsequently designated as the Second Northern
Reserve, was situated to the east and northeast of Edmonton, so far
removed from the main line of the railway that there would be

[1] Charles Drinkwater, Secretary, C. P. R. Co., to John R. Hall, Secretary, Department of the Interior, June 27, 1894, File No. 34187-8.
[2] *Ibid.*
[3] *O. C.* No. 414, February 18, 1895.
[4] *Ibid.*
[5] *O. C.* No. 3613, December 18, 1895. Annex "B" to this Order in Council is the
letter from Charles Drinkwater, Secretary, C. P. R. Co., to T. Mayne Daly, Minister of the Interior, asking that these lands be reserved for the company.

slight chance of any real colonization for many years to come. (See Map I.)

These reserves were not administered without many conflicts of opinion between the two parties to the agreements. One long and serious controversy developed which altered materially the character of the original grant. At an early date in the construction of the railway, the company had been forced to borrow heavily from a Conservative Government genuinely anxious lest the project which it had sponsored should result in failure. In 1886 there remained on the company's books a balance of $9,880,912, with interest, on a loan of $29,880,912. Funds were not available to meet this balance, and the company turned to its only tangible asset, the land already given by Ottawa. By an agreement of March 30 of that year, the railway guaranteed to the government the relinquishment of an area of land which, valued at $1.50 per acre, would approximate the amount of the unpaid debt.[1] This reduction of the land grant by 6,793,014 acres was to be effected, in the words of the statute, "by the retention by the Government of land of equal average quality and value with the lands constituting the portion of the Company's land grant not heretofore disposed of by the Company."[2]

For several years no actual steps were taken toward the execution of the covenant. During those years the company worked steadily at the examination of the lands within the 48-mile belt and in southern Manitoba. By January, 1889, it had actually accepted 6,524,000 acres, which it had set forth in detailed schedules, and it estimated, on the basis of available information, that it would eventually find in these two areas enough suitable land to bring the total to approximately 8,350,000 acres. This would leave some 16,650,000 acres to be accounted for. Interpreting the agreement of March 30, 1886 to be merely a reduction of 6,793,014 acres in the total acreage to which they were entitled, the company, by the simple subtraction of that amount from the 16,560,000 acres, arrived at an estimate of the area which remained to be selected. Its

[1] The agreement, together with the Act of Parliament approving it, is to be found in *Statutes of Canada*, 49 Victoria, Cap. 9, assented to June 2, 1886.
[2] *Ibid.*

assumption was that it was free to appropriate this balance of some 9,850,000 acres from the best lands available in its First Northern Reserve. To this end, it projected a series of branch lines into that region, each line to be the means of developing a particular area, and to carry with it the alternate sections to a distance of 24 miles on either side of the road.[1] By thus locating the lands to which it was entitled in the North, the company would be certain of serving them with its own lines, thereby reducing the dangers of competition to a minimum.

But while the government and the company could agree on the efficacy and value of branch lines, on the question of locating land for the railway along these proposed northern extensions they were at loggerheads. Here the interpretation of the agreement of land relinquishment of 1886 became of the utmost significance. Canadian Pacific officials held the view, as previously indicated, that the agreement had effected nothing more than a reduction in the total area to which they were entitled.[2] The government, on the other hand, was equally firm in the opinion that there must be actual relinquishment by the company of lands of quality and value equal to those retained. It is easy to see the advantages which would accrue to the company if its interpretation was accepted.

The government, however, was not easily persuaded. The Minister of the Interior, in a communication to the Cabinet in regard to the controversy, made a clear-cut statement of the government's stand. He recommended "that the Company be definitely informed that the government is not in a position to deal with the Company in regard to the residue of the subsidy to which they are entitled on the basis that the arrangement of 1886 amounted to no more than a reduction of the acreage originally intended to be granted to the Company, and that the government will require in fulfillment of the said arrangement that out of the land that would have been available for the gross subsidy, a portion sufficient to yield to the government for the purpose above mentioned, 6,793,014 acres,

[1] Charles Drinkwater, Secretary, C. P. R. Co., to John R. Hall, Secretary, Department of the Interior, January 17, 1889, File No. 34187-7.
[2] Memorandum by E. Dewdney, Minister of the Interior, March 11, 1890, with O. C. No. 863, May 20, 1890, in which he refers to the discussions and correspondence between the company and the government.

shall be set apart and freed from all claims by the Company in respect of the subsidy promised in the original contract."[1]

In suggesting the basis of an equitable plan for the release of the lands by the Canadian Pacific, the minister referred to the report regarding the amount and value of the lands reserved in the North for the company, which had already been prepared by the Department of the Interior. The report showed that the tract contained the very best land in the territories and that nowhere else in the Northwest could there have been found a block of equal area and fertility. Of 1,057 townships surveyed by the department, 641 were of the finest quality, with only 6 townships totally unsuited for farming. Of the unsurveyed portions of the reservation, the land along the Saskatchewan was fertile, with an abundance of timber; that to the north and east of Battleford was favorably known; while the Carrot River Valley had an excellent reputation. "Everything considered," observed the minister, "a very close approximation as to character and value will be obtained by assuming for the whole of the reservation the same proportions of the several kinds of land as are found in the surveyed districts." On the basis of this assumption, the odd-numbered sections of the Northern Reserve would contain about 19,000,000 acres of farming land, of which almost 12,000,000 would be of the very finest quality.[2] After deducting 10 per cent for water, Indian Reserves, etc., there would remain over 17,000,000 acres "fairly fit for settlement."

The Department of the Interior recommended as a solution of the difficulty that the Northern Reserve be divided into two equal parts, taking the 110th meridian of longitude, which was the 4th meridian in the Dominion Lands system of surveys, as the dividing line.[3] The Canadian Pacific should relinquish to the government that portion of the reserve to the east of this line of demarcation. But, in order to protect the rights of the Dominion and to provide land subsidies for other railways, should such be deemed desirable, there was to be added to this eastern portion the adjoining land to the south of the 52nd parallel, and extending to the South

[1] Memorandum by E. Dewdney, Minister of the Interior, March 11, 1890, with O. C. No. 863, May 20, 1890.
[2] Ibid.
[3] Ibid.

Saskatchewan River and the northern limit of the 48-mile belt of the Canadian Pacific.[1] The added area was likewise to be released from all claims in respect of the land subsidy of the railway company which might subsequently be advanced.[2] This secured an equal division of the land not only from the point of view of area, but also from that of value. The advantage of fertility of soil and proximity to markets and centers of population enjoyed by the eastern part would be counter-balanced by the superior climate and admirable distribution of timber and water in the western part.

By an additional provision, the Canadian Pacific secured a return of approximately 1,000,000 acres of the land yielded to the government. The ultimate attractiveness of the government's portion of the reservation would be enhanced by the completion of the Qu'Appelle, Long Lake, and Saskatchewan Railway, which was then projected northward from Regina. It was deemed desirable from the point of view of public interest that the Canadian Pacific should build a branch from a point on this line, at or near Saskatoon, to the navigable waters of the North Saskatchewan River. To encourage early construction, the government proposed to grant to the company, from the lands just released, a belt of territory stretching from the southern boundary of the reservation, in a northwesterly direction to the 110th meridian, and to a width of 24 miles.[3] Such a block would yield in odd-numbered sections about 1,000,000 acres, which would constitute not an additional subsidy, but rather a portion of the main line grant. A common front line was to be established, as provided by the eleventh clause of the contract of 1881, but the lands were to be reserved to a depth of only 12 miles on either side instead of the 24 miles which the contract had called for. Such an arrangement was considered mutually advantageous. In this way the government would secure railway facilities for this eastern portion of the reservation, without

[1] The precise description of the tract thus added was the area "bounded on the north by the 52nd parallel of latitude, on the east by the 104th degree, and on the west by the 110th degree of longitude, on the south by the South Saskatchewan River from the said 110th degree of longitude till it intersects the northern boundary of the 48 mile belt of the Main line of the C. P. R." *Ibid.*

[2] Since this additional area had not been reserved for the Canadian Pacific, this last provision evidently was designed as a safeguard against any request which the company might make in the future.

[3] Dewdney's memorandum of March 11, 1890, *loc. cit.*

relinquishing its claim to too great an area, while the Canadian Pacific would receive land tributary to a branch line which it would probably build in any event.

By an Order in Council of May 20, 1890, these recommendations of the Minister of the Interior were approved,[1] and on January 7, 1891 were incorporated into an agreement between the government and the Canadian Pacific Company. All lands in the area east of the 110th meridian were released to the government immediately; lands in the western portion of the reservation not selected by January 1, 1892 were to be opened to settlement after that date.[2] The line of railway from Saskatoon to the North Saskatchewan River was to be constructed in return for the 1,000,000 acres reserved for that purpose, the area known thereafter as the Battleford Block.[3]

The company, although forced to yield to the government's interpretation of the relinquishment, accepted the final adjustment as an equitable disposition of the controversy. Perhaps a company less in the public eye might have succeeded in persuading the government of the justice of its point of view. But the political controversy over the original contract had been too heated for the Conservative Party to allow any charges of undue leniency towards the Canadian Pacific to be brought against it.

As a result of the agreement, the proposed network of branch lines through the Northern Reserve was largely abandoned. Development of some of the lands to have been served by these lines was later made possible through the construction of the roads eastward from Lacombe and Wetaskiwin on the Calgary and Edmonton line. But the Canadian Pacific's first thought was to settle and develop the lands which were reasonably close to its main line, and, absorbed in this work, it gave little thought to the Northern Reserve during the nineties. Indeed, during much of the period the movement to the west was so small and the demand for land so slight as to leave even the main line belt and the Southern Reserve largely unsold. Under such conditions there was little incentive to make the out-

[1] O. C. No. 863, May 20, 1890.
[2] For the text of the agreement, see Ref. 255263 on 51724.
[3] Ibid.

lays necessary for construction in the North, and, in the main, the lands were ultimately served by other lines of railway.

The establishment of these land reserves of millions of acres, far to the north and south of the main line of the railway, the logical result of the terms of the Syndicate Contract, which included the "fit for settlement" clause, combined with a flat grant of acreage, made the Canadian policy entirely unique. When the rush of settlers to the Canadian West began, bringing an unprecedented demand for land, the government consistently encouraged the building of competitive trunk lines to the west, and, eventually, both the Canadian Northern and the Grand Trunk Pacific were built through the Northern Reserve. The Canadian Pacific Company was placed in the position, then, of having land not only far removed from its own lines, but actually tributary to rival railways. Railway competition was doubtless a desirable thing, but under such circumstances it did violence to the theory implicit in the system of railway land subsidies—that the railway company receiving the lands would promote settlement as a means of developing traffic for its lines. Every settler placed on the lands in the North meant business for the other companies, not for the Canadian Pacific. There was no reason, therefore, for any special effort to encourage immigration to that region, no urge to build up settlements which would benefit competitors. In fact, if there were an incentive in either direction, it was to delay the occupation of those lands until the cultivation and development of the government land in that area had brought about a sharp appreciation in the value of the railway sections. The zeal which the company displayed in the work of settling the South was largely absent in the North, where ordinary business sense dictated a policy of waiting for the enjoyment of the unearned increment resulting from the labor and capital expended by others. The contrast between the low prices paid by the settler for land in the Canadian Pacific's 48-mile belt and the high prices he was ultimately forced to pay for that in the Northern Reserve is evidence that this waiting policy on the company's part was, from the financial standpoint at least, entirely justified.

In the United States, where there was strict adherence to the principle that lands granted as subsidies must be directly tributary to the railway, most efforts towards holding the land for increased prices would have resulted disastrously. Here the generally accepted practice was for each railway to develop and settle its own lands as rapidly as possible. Even the indemnity lands, located, as they were, not more than 50 miles distant, could be included in such a scheme of development. The transcontinental companies, building through unsettled country where traffic was non-existent, were forced, in their own interest, to make the rapid promotion of settlement one of their primary duties. They were likely to be mindful of the fact that they were first of all transportation companies, and only incidentally land companies, and that their continued existence as transportation enterprises depended upon the increased traffic brought about through the disposal of their lands to settlers.

The policy of granting Dominion lands without regard to distance from the railway was not confined to the main line subsidy of the Canadian Pacific. In the late eighties the government, eager to expedite the settlement of the West, offered additional grants to the company to encourage the construction of branch lines in the South. In 1889 provision was made for a land subsidy in aid of the Souris Branch, which had been located from a point on the main line near Brandon, in a southwesterly and westerly direction for about 185 miles.[1] At the rate of 6,400 acres per mile, the construction of this road would entitle the company to about 1,200,000 acres.[2] Early in 1891 the president of the Canadian Pacific expressed the willingness to extend the Souris Branch to some lignite coal fields, about 60 miles distant, in return for a grant of 6,400 acres per mile.[3] Since this extension would place Winnipeg and the settled portions of Manitoba in direct communication with a valuable supply of fuel, and would provide railway facilities for an excellent wheat producing region, the government readily accepted the proposal.[4] An additional area of almost 400,000 acres was, therefore, added to the original grant, making a total of more than a million and a half acres to which the Canadian Pacific would acquire title on account of the Souris Branch.[5] As in the main line

[1] The history of this grant is to be found in O. C. No. 271, February 7, 1891.
[2] Ibid.
[3] O. C. No. 250, February 7, 1891.
[4] Ibid.
[5] Ibid.

subsidy, the lands were to be "fairly fit for settlement."[1] The company must pay 10 cents per acre to the government to cover the cost of survey, and any *bona fide* settler located on the lands was to have the right to purchase from the company as much as 320 acres at not more than $2.50 per acre.[2]

The insertion of the "fit for settlement" provision in the grant precluded any possibility of finding in the South the land with which to satisfy the subsidy, for, as previously noted, there was not a sufficient amount south of the main line to provide for the needs of the main line grant. Recourse must be had, therefore, to the area in the North, to which the company had earlier relinquished its claims under the agreement of 1886. Accordingly, it was arranged that the company be given the odd-numbered sections in two strips of 12 miles each on either side of the Battleford Block, extending from Saskatoon, through Battleford, and northwesterly to the 4th meridian.[3] The area of approximately 1,000,000 acres thus acquired would be convenient for the Canadian Pacific to administer, since the combined belts would extend 24 miles on either side of this particular line of railway.[4] To satisfy the remainder of the grant for the Souris Branch, there was reserved a triangular tract to the southwest of the Battleford Block, an area of about 900,000 acres in odd-numbered sections, from which it was thought the necessary acreage could be obtained.[5] In 1894, a further grant of 6,400 acres per mile, authorized for the Pipestone extension of the Souris Branch, again presented the problem of finding increased acreage, and again resulted in an additional reservation of land in the North.[6] So, in return for railway construction in southern Manitoba, the Canadian Pacific received lands in what later became central Saskatchewan, an altogether significant commentary upon a very irrational feature of Dominion land subsidy policy.

After the final reserve had been set aside for the Canadian Pacific, a deficiency of some 3,000,000 acres in the main line subsidy

[1] *Ibid.*
[2] *Ibid.*
[3] *O. C.* No. 271, February 7, 1891.
[4] *Ibid.*
[5] *Ibid.*
[6] *O. C.* No. 253, February 10, 1899, gives the history of the grant in aid of the Pipestone Extension.

remained. Ultimate adjustment of the grant had to depend upon agreement with reference to a large area of land in the 48-mile belt which was clearly not "fit for settlement." The company had not neglected opportunities for the development of the sub-humid portions of this belt. Every acre of land which could be brought into the "fairly fit for settlement" category meant an added acre directly tributary to the railway. From Swift Current west to the mountains the main line of the Canadian Pacific traversed a region of deficient rainfall—the home of the range cattle industry of Canada. Here various experiments had been undertaken in the hope that the country might be found suitable for grain farming, and thus provide a greater volume of traffic than that resulting from ranching operations. With a view to determining the agricultural possibilities of the section, the company had established ten experimental farms along the line west of Swift Current,[1] where all sorts of field and vegetable crops had been planted. Although the success of the experiments was strictly limited by the climatic cycle, the farms were continued for a number of years before they were abandoned in the face of a capricious and fickle climate. Indeed, so encouraging were the results first obtained that a large German colony had been established at Dunmore under the joint auspices of the Canadian Pacific and the Dominion Government.[2] But even the sturdy German farmer had at last to admit defeat, and that effort, too, came to nought.

Another very pretentious attempt at the development of this semi-arid region was that of an English gentleman, Sir John Lister-Kaye. It likewise failed, but as an experiment in colonization de luxe it is most interesting. In 1889 he presented to the government a petition setting forth his plan to settle 70 families in each of 20 settlements along the main line of the Canadian Pacific.[3] He asked that he be allowed to purchase at $1.00 per acre the quarter section contiguous to the homestead of each settler, and that he be permitted to buy in connection with each colony 640 acres in the center of the settlement, for the purpose of forming a community

[1] *Manitoba Daily Free Press*, May 30, 1884.
[2] *Ibid.*
[3] The petition is with *O. C.* No. 208, May 27, 1889.

center.[1] Each settler was to be required to have £100 clear, to which Sir John's company would add, by way of a loan, $1,200, the combined sums to be expended in the erection of a "dwelling house, sheds for horses, cows, sheep and pigs; and in the purchase of two mares, four cows, nine sheep, four sows, share of digging a well, purchase of plows, harrows, harness, seed-sower and seed. From this fund we also plough 20 acres, so that when the settler arrives, as we intend him to do, June 1, 1890, he will find his farm stocked and twenty acres in grain. . . . "[2] Thus would most of the difficulties of pioneering be removed! The new arrival would find himself not only warmly housed, but spared the effort of turning the first furrows in his new domain.

The expansive scheme of Sir John appealed to the Canadian officials. The plan to settle 1,400 families at different points in the northwest territories, combined with the prospective expenditure of $1,800,000 in the cause of colonizing the prairies, was too alluring to be resisted, especially in a period when the movement of people to the west had been all too slow. The plan was given official sanction and operations on a large scale were begun almost immediately.[3] The townships for the experiment were to be selected, as far as possible, adjacent to the farms of the Canadian Agricultural Coal and Colonization Company, from Crane Lake west to Langdon.[4]

Whether such an orderly and complete settlement of a new country could have been carried out, even in regions of consistent rainfall, is open to question. But all the optimism of Sir John Lister-Kaye, the coöperation of the government, and the enthusiasm of the early settlers were not enough to carry the project through to success in a section of doubtful weather conditions. The undertaking was a comparative failure and marked the end of large-scale attempts to utilize the semi-arid region, in its natural state, for any form of farming except stock raising.

Land which was suited only for live stock farming could in no sense be regarded as "fairly fit for settlement," and unless some

[1] *Ibid.*
[2] *Ibid.*
[3] *Ibid.*
[4] *Ibid.* This was another organization which had invested extensively in land at some nine or ten points along the C. P. R. main line, in the dry belt.

understanding could be arrived at between the Canadian Pacific and the government with reference to the dry lands, it would be necessary to set aside still another reserve in the North, far removed from the main line. The only kind of agreement which would avail in this instance was one which would seek to adapt the policy of railway land subsidies to the conditions prevailing in that peculiar area. It was at this point that the Canadians developed a feature of their land grant policy which was vastly superior to the American policy, and which constitutes another important difference between the subsidy systems of the two countries.

Probably the greatest single weakness of the land grant policy in the United States was its inelasticity. Once the principle of the grant by alternate sections had been adopted, it had been impossible to depart from it, regardless of conditions. The alternate section idea had been established at the time when the energies of the country were engrossed in the settlement of the humid areas of the Mississippi Valley. There the alternate section was well conceived, and probably constituted the fairest method of dividing land between the railway and the government. But, like the homestead unit of 160 acres, which was also the product of the fertile, well-watered regions of the West, the alternate section grant was totally unsuited to the semi-arid lands west of the 98th meridian. Some of the sub-humid country could have been reclaimed by irrigation, but no railway company could be expected to make the heavy expenditures for such a purpose unless the land was owned in solid blocks. On the other hand, most of the land in the area of deficient rainfall was valuable chiefly for grazing purposes. For efficient ranching operations, however, the 640-acre section was far too small a unit, and when rigorous adherence to the alternate section grant precluded the possibility of legal acquisition of large compact blocks within the limits of railway land grants, the cattleman was driven to the use of illegal means to achieve his objective. But the Congress which had waited 42 years before attempting, in a feeble way, to adapt the homestead unit to the conditions of the Great Plains, was not disposed to bring the land subsidy policy into line with the needs and requirements of that region. In the face of such circumstances the Canadians were much more willing to experiment, and to adjust their policy to the special conditions prevailing in different areas. The Dominion Government had in the decade of the eighties permitted deviation from the alternate section in the dry lands of southern Alberta.[1] Now, at the beginning of the next decade, it seemed that a similarly flexible policy with reference to the main line belt of the Canadian Pacific offered the best chance of effecting a final settlement of the company's land subsidy.

Since such a large part of its land was located at a great distance from the railway, the company was naturally desirous of locating within the 48-mile belt the largest possible portion of the balance due it. With this end in view, it was in the early nineties reëxamining land which it had previously rejected as unfit for settlement.[2] It was evident to the government, however, that unless the alternate sections were abandoned, there was a great deal of the land which the company would not accept. In fact, the investigations of government agents confirmed the views of the railway officials as to the character of the land. Early in 1894 the Deputy Minister of the Interior and the Superintendent of Mines jointly submitted to the Minister of the Interior a report in regard to the dry lands. In this document they placed in writing the recommendations which they had made verbally "with regard to the relatively dry country along the line of the Canadian Pacific Railway which may be described generally as having its eastern boundary at Moose Jaw and its western boundary at Crowfoot Creek, and within which during the past few years the rainfall has been insufficient to permit of the growth of cereal crops with reasonable certainty."[3] Continuing, the report said:

There have been years within the experience of the Department when the rainfall was sufficient for this purpose, but such observations as we have been able to make during the years which have elapsed since the completion of the railway . . . would indicate that the recurrence of these dry periods is so frequent that while the country would in its natural state be well adapted for the grazing of cattle, the growing of cereal crops could only be

[1] This was in connection with the subsidy to the Alberta Railway and Irrigation Company.

[2] See letter of William Pearce, Superintendent of Mines, to John R. Hall, Secretary, Department of the Interior, December 1, 1893, File No. 211000-1.

[3] A. M. Burgess, Deputy Minister of the Interior, and William Pearce, Superintendent of Mines, to T. Mayne Daly, Minister of the Interior, January 29, 1894, File No. 211000-1.

rendered safe and sure by the application of an extensive and scientifically planned system of irrigation. The examination . . . of the physical conformation of the country between Medicine Hat and the 5th Principal Meridian leads . . . to the conclusion that there are large areas in that region which could be satisfactorily and profitably irrigated by the waters of Bow River, and adopting the basis of calculation which experience in regard to irrigation would appear to justify, namely, that for every acre of irrigated land five acres of adjacent land would be rendered specially valuable for grazing and other purposes connected with the keeping and feeding of live stock, we have come to the conclusion that in round numbers about three million acres could thus be reclaimed from comparative aridity and rendered productive for all purposes of mixed farming, having special relation, however, to dairying and cattle raising.

The further observation was made that "in order to induce a company organized on a thoroughly efficient financial and commercial basis to undertake the work of irrigating all or any of these tracts, it will be necessary that the sectional system of survey should be abandoned, that the road allowances provided for in the Dominion Lands Act should be closed up, that the area falling to the school endowment should be provided for in a solid block so situated as to derive reasonable advantage from the irrigation works, generally, and it would also be desirable that the Hudson's Bay Company should, if possible, be induced to . . . . have their proportion of these tracts allotted to them on a similar basis. . . . ."[1]

In other words, for the utilization of those lands irrigation was deemed necessary, and in order to induce a responsible company to undertake to make large expenditures for the purpose, the alternate section system of grants must yield to large, compact blocks. With the opinion of the government agents, Sir William Van Horne, the President of the Canadian Pacific, fully concurred.[2] He added, however, that the company was not in a position to bind itself to undertake to bring the area under irrigation.[3] All it could agree to do was to accept lands *en bloc* and take the chance that they might later be made available for settlement and cultivation by some scheme of irrigation. Within limits, the company was

[1] *Ibid.*
[2] W. C. Van Horne to T. Mayne Daly, Minister of the Interior, February 15, 1894, File No. 211000-1.
[3] *Ibid.*

willing to take this chance. In fact, the directors had passed a reso-
lution authorizing Van Horne to accept lands in the district if
conveyed in blocks. The president would look with favor upon an
agreement binding the company to accept a considerable quantity
of land in large tracts, with the option of taking a larger amount
within a stipulated time. Such action he considered necessary, since
the land would be worthless without water, and time would be required to determine the feasibility of irrigation.[1]

So satisfactory was the progress of the negotiations between the
government and the company that in July, 1894, an Act of Parliament authorized the Governor in Council, with the consent of the
Canadian Pacific Railway Company, to grant "so much of the subsidy lands of the said Company as remains ungranted, wholly or in
part in tracts of such area as he deems expedient, and including
sections bearing even, as well as those bearing uneven numbers,
on that portion of the Main line of the said Company between
Medicine Hat on the East and Crowfoot Crossing on the West, and
within twenty-four miles on each side of the said portion of the
said Company's line of Railway."[2] Sections reserved for the Hudson's Bay Company or for school purposes were not to be included
in the block, unless other public lands of equal extent and value
were provided elsewhere.[3]

It soon developed, however, that the terms of the Act were not
agreeable to the Canadian Pacific. The company alleged that, unknown to it, the provision for granting the lands *en bloc* had been
made applicable only to that portion of the line between Medicine
Hat and Crowfoot Crossing, and stated that after careful investigation it had come to the conclusion that this restricted area would
not supply more than 1,000,000 acres of the deficiency in the main
line grant, which was in excess of 3,000,000.[4] Besides, it had discovered that irrigation on a large scale would be much less costly in
proportion to results, and more efficient, if carried out from the
Bow River in the neighborhood of Calgary than from any point

[1] *Ibid.*

[2] *Statutes of Canada*, 57-58 Victoria, Cap. 7, assented to July 23, 1894.

[3] *Ibid.*

[4] Charles Drinkwater, Secretary, C. P. R. Co., to T. Mayne Daly, Minister of the
Interior, November 26, 1894, Annex "B" to *O. C.* No. 3613, December 18, 1895.

within the limits named in the Act of Parliament.[1] When, a few months later, the railway company formally withdrew its proposition to accept lands in a block, its action was based upon the belief that the powers given to incorporated companies to take water from rivers in or near the territory in question, together with the authority assumed by the government with respect to such waters, rendered it necessary that further details concerning the supply of water available for irrigation should be determined between the government and the company before entering into an agreement.[2] The company suggested, however, that there should be obtained an Act of Parliament giving the government full power to deal with the problem, and expressed complete willingness to discuss the features and details of such an act.

Before an agreement had been reached, however, the Conservative Government was defeated in the election of 1896, and there followed several years of delay, during which no progress was made in the final adjustment of the company's land subsidy. The Canadian Pacific had been, of course, the creation of the Conservatives, and with the advent of the Liberals to power the close contact and understanding between government and company were largely destroyed. During the early period of the Laurier Government the railway made few if any advances toward Ottawa, and certainly did not press for a settlement of the question of the land grant. The Department of the Interior, engrossed in the formulation and execution of a vigorous policy for the promotion of settlement in the West, also gave scant attention to claims of the company upon the government.

The activity of the government in advertising the attractions of the prairies to the farmer in the United States, and the tide of immigration which began to pour into the Northwest at the beginning of the new century, made it the more important that the balance of the company's lands should be located for them before it was too late. By 1901 informal negotiations had been resumed and two propositions had been made by the government to the company: one, that the railway should accept all lands within the 48-

[1] *Ibid.*
[2] Drinkwater to Daly, May 6, 1895, Annex "C" to O. C. No. 3613, December 18, 1895.

mile belt west of Medicine Hat, except Hudson's Bay lands; the other, that the area be extended considerably to the north and south.[1] In that same year the company employed an expert irrigation engineer from the United States, who made extensive investigations into the problem of irrigating the district, and whose favorable report led to a continuation of the informal conferences. Early in 1903 the discussions entered upon their final stage, when the company presented a very vigorous statement of its case. The government, it was charged, had violated both the letter and the spirit of the Syndicate Contract by sponsoring a general policy of railway land subsidies which had made it possible for companies other than the Canadian Pacific to acquire much of the valuable land in the Northwest.[2] This policy had served greatly to restrict the area within which the Canadian Pacific might have made selections of land and needlessly complicated the problem of the ultimate adjustment of the subsidy. Reviewing the history of the land grant, the company set forth in detail the amount of land in the various reserves which came within the classification of "fairly fit for settlement."

	ACRES
1. The Main Line Belt	5,255,870
2. The First Northern Reserve[3]	6,620,000
3. Southern Reserve[4]	2,244,130
4. The Lake Dauphin Lands[5]	400,000
5. The Second Northern Reserve[6]	386,000
Total	14,906,000

[1] Memorandum, William Pearce to R. E. Young, Department of the Interior, August 9, 1901, File No. 34187-14.

[2] Charles Drinkwater, Secretary, C. P. R. Co., to Clifford Sifton, Minister of the Interior, February 9, 1903, File No. 34187-14.

[3] This was the area set aside by the O. C. of October 24, 1882, and embraced the territory between the 52nd and 54th degrees of latitude and between the 110th and 116th degrees of longitude, from which, by the agreement of January 7, 1891, there was released the portion east of the 110th meridian, except for the Battleford block.

[4] The area south of the main line belt, reserved by O. C.'s of November 3, 1882 and January 25, 1883. This was really in two parts. That reserved on November 3, 1882, was situated between the main line belt and the Manitoba Southwestern Colonization Railway reserve, bounded on the east by the original western boundary of Manitoba, and on the west by the Coteau or Dirt Hills. The second part, reserved on January 25, 1883, was located between the main line belt on

Deducting this figure from the 18,206,986 acres to which the subsidy had been reduced by the relinquishment of 1891, there was still due the company an area of 3,300,986 acres. As yet no provision had been made for satisfying this balance. The lands in the 48-mile belt west of Medicine Hat were worthless in their existing state. While it was conceded on every hand that the irrigation of those lands would be of great benefit to both the company and the country, it was estimated that it would cost about $3.50 per acre to bring them under water, which approximately equalled the average price received by the company for its lands up to that time.[1] It could not think of accepting these lands, therefore, unless they were granted in a block. The odd- and even-numbered sections between Medicine Hat and Calgary would amount to about 2,500,-000 acres, which, if accepted, would still leave a balance of 800,000 acres as yet unprovided for.[2]

The company had observed that a considerable portion of the reserve set apart for the land grant to the Manitoba and Northwestern Railway Company was no longer needed for that purpose, owing to failure to complete construction within the specified time. In this reserve there were some 1,200,000 acres in odd-numbered sections at the disposal of the government, from which the Canadian Pacific would probably be able to select the remainder of its subsidy. Its proposal, therefore, was that it take the land between Medicine Hat and Calgary in a compact block and choose the balance from the Manitoba and Northwestern reservation.[3] In submitting this proposition it recognized, of course, that should its scheme for irrigating the arid region prove a failure the lands would be virtually worthless.

Negotiations continued during the months which followed, until by July 24, 1903, Clifford Sifton, Minister of the Interior, and Sir

the north, the Red River on the east, the 49th parallel on the south, and the original western boundary of Manitoba on the west.

[5] Reserved by O. C. of February 18, 1895.

[6] Reserved by O. C. of December 18, 1896, and situated between the 4th and 5th meridians (D. L. S.) and the 54th and 55th degrees of latitude. The region east and northeast of Edmonton.

[1] Drinkwater to Sifton, February 9, 1903, *loc. cit.*

[2] *Ibid.*

[3] *Ibid.* The Manitoba and Northwestern was one of the colonization railways.

Thomas Shaughnessy, President of the Canadian Pacific, had agreed upon the essential features of a settlement.[1] The company was to have practically all the land for which it had asked in connection with its irrigation project. It was to select in the First Northern Block any odd-numbered sections previously rejected but now considered "fairly fit for settlement," and was to claim toward the satisfaction of the main line grant not more than 500,000 acres in the Manitoba and Northwestern reserve.

Within a month the details had been worked out, and by an Order in Council of August 22, 1903, approval was given to the arrangement by which the main line subsidy, together with the grants to two subsidiary companies, was finally closed out.[2] The Canadian Pacific agreed to increase to about 2,900,000 acres the compact area to be included in the irrigation project. For the balance of its main line grant, the company might select not in excess of 642,000 acres in the reserve of the Manitoba and Northwestern.[3] In this way there came into being the Irrigation Block of the Canadian Pacific in Alberta (see Map III), where in the years after 1903 the company undertook to develop perhaps the largest irrigation scheme in North America, as well as a program of assisted settlement and colonization far more extensive than anything which other land grant railway companies had attempted.

While the agreement of 1903 was in final satisfaction of the grants made directly to the Canadian Pacific, brief mention must be made of subsidies, originally voted to other railways, to which the Canadian Pacific fell heir and which were administered under the land policies of the company.

The government in the early eighties embarked upon a policy of granting land subsidies to smaller companies, known as colonization railways, which, it was hoped, would open up to settlement large portions of the West not tributary to the main or branch lines of the Canadian Pacific.[4] The grants to three of these railways were

[1] Clifford Sifton to Mr. Turriff, Department of the Interior, July 24, 1903, File No. 34187-15.

[2] O. C. No. 1434, August 22, 1903. The two companies were the Saskatchewan and Western and the Manitoba Southwestern Colonization Railway.

[3] Ibid.

[4] J. B. Hedges, The Federal Railway Land Subsidy Policy of Canada (Cambridge, 1934), Chapter III.

subsequently taken over and administered by the Canadian Pacific, while portions of the grants to two others were also acquired.

The pioneer of these companies was the Manitoba Southwestern Colonization Railway which was chartered in 1879 and authorized to construct a line from Winnipeg southwesterly to a point near the western boundary of Manitoba. Shortly it was permitted to purchase 3,840 acres of land per mile of railway at the price of $1.00 per acre, an amount which was soon increased to 6,400 acres per mile. This latter figure soon came to be the accepted area allotted to colonization railways. In 1884 Parliament authorized the company to lease its line to the Canadian Pacific, thereby making it a virtual branch of the larger company. In the same year W. C. Van Horne, of the Canadian Pacific, who was also a director of the colonization railway, advised the Minister of the Interior that the road was unable to obtain necessary funds, due to unfavorable reports circulated in Great Britain with respect to the Northwest and the prospects of the Canadian Pacific. In view of the strong popular demand in the West for feeders for the Canadian Pacific, the minister felt that the company must be salvaged. As a result of his recommendation Parliament authorized a free grant of 6,400 acres per mile for 152 miles of railway.

By additional construction the company ultimately earned a total of 1,396,800 acres of land. As in the case of the main line grant to the Canadian Pacific, the problem of locating and describing the land for the Manitoba Southwestern was made more difficult by the "fairly fit for settlement" clause included in the Order in Council providing for the grant. There was set apart for it a large reserve stretching along the 49th parallel between the road allowance separating Ranges 12 and 13 on the east and the Grand Coteau or Dirt Hills on the west. (See Map II.) Prior to 1902 the Canadian Pacific had accepted from this reserve approximately 1,000,000 acres. The balance had to be found elsewhere. About 100,000 acres were set aside for it en bloc in southern Alberta. The residue of some 250,000 acres was provided for in the Manitoba and Northwestern Reserve in the North, where the Canadian Pacific was authorized by the Order in Council of 1903 to select up to 640,000 acres by way of a final adjustment of its main line subsidy and of the grant to the Manitoba Southwestern.

The two smallest of the colonization railways were the Great Northwest Central and the Saskatchewan and Western. The former was authorized to construct a line of railway from a point on the Canadian Pacific main line at Brandon to the Rocky Mountains by way of Battleford. For this it was to receive the usual subsidy of 6,400 acres per mile. It constructed but 50 miles of railway, however, by which it earned a total of 320,000 acres. This subsidy was subsequently acquired by the Canadian Pacific and administered in accordance with its land policies. By building some 15 miles of railway from Minnedosa to Rapid City, the Saskatchewan and Western earned 98,880 acres, later taken over by the Canadian Pacific and sold in a block.

The subsidies to the Alberta Railway and Irrigation Company and to the Calgary and Edmonton Railway were acquired only in part by the Canadian Pacific. The parent companies from which the Alberta Railway and Irrigation Company was descended were the Alberta Railway and Coal Company and the Northwest Coal and Navigation Company. The first of these received a grant of 6,400 acres per mile for a line from Lethbridge to the international boundary; the other was subsidized in like amount per mile for a railway from Dunmore to Lethbridge. The total area of the two subsidies was 1,114,368 acres. When in 1912 the Canadian Pacific assumed control of the Alberta Railway and Irrigation Company it took over the unsold portions of the land grant. The Calgary and Edmonton Company was empowered to build a line between the two towns, with extensions to the Peace River on the north and to the international boundary on the south. The company earned 1,888,448 acres, of which the government retained 407,402 acres until 1912 as security for certain sums advanced by it to the railway. Although the Canadian Pacific leased the railway, it had no control over the land subsidy, except for the security lands which it acquired in 1912. Lands of both the Calgary and Edmonton and the Alberta Railway and Irrigation Company were located in Alberta in reasonable proximity to the railways.

With the obligation of the government to the Canadian Pacific discharged to the last acre, one phase of the Dominion subsidy policy was passed. The fundamental principles and practices which were developed in the handling of this grant for a large project became the generally accepted methods employed in the administration of subsidies for lesser undertakings. The features of the Canadian system which distinguished it from that of the United States were definitely established. The "fairly fit for settlement" clause had, in the main, been the force initiating these variations. The land reserves far removed from the main line of the railway, which resulted from the provision, were not easy to manage. In the United States, where the railway companies were forced to accept lands directly tributary to their own lines, regardless of quality, titles could be secured in a more systematic fashion. If the consequences of Canadian departure from the American policy at this juncture seem not to have been too satisfactory, that was not true in other instances. The system in Canada was adapted and altered to fit particular situations in a way which was quite unheard of south of the border. When the need for irrigation demanded that the alternate section be abandoned in certain localities, the Canadians promptly abandoned it. By being willing to shape special points of a general scheme to specific needs, they avoided, to some extent at least, the difficulties which beset the Americans, who attempted to regulate the public domain from the Mississippi to the Pacific by the same ironclad set of statutes.

IV

BEGINNINGS OF LAND POLICY

WITH the approval of the Syndicate Contract by Parliament in February, 1881, the new company turned, with all the vigor and competency which were ever to characterize its course, to the problem of administering the vast landed estate which it expected to earn through the completion of the road. And while the land and colonization policies of the Canadian Pacific were soon to be marked by the boldness and the imagination of the pioneer, they represented for the moment little more than the fruit of a generation of experimentation in railway land settlement.

As a late comer into the ranks of land grant railways in North America, the company was in a position to take advantage of that wisdom which comes from long experience. Ever since the Illinois Central grant of 1850 the railways of the United States had, by a trial and error method, been evolving a more or less standardized procedure in the administration of railway lands. In the course of this evolution the Illinois Central had, with great advantage to itself, transformed a great prairie waste into an agricultural empire.[1] Perceiving that its future depended upon the early settlement and cultivation of its territory, it had disposed of its lands chiefly in small tracts to actual settlers, at prices which netted the company a very satisfactory return. It had advertised the Illinois prairies on two continents, had built up a well-coördinated organization for the recruiting of settlers, had extended a helping hand to the individual farmer, and had dotted the landscape with colonies of Yankees, Swedes, French-Canadians, and Germans. Through its town-site promotion it had exerted an important influence upon the course of urban development in its territory, while through en-

[1] Paul W. Gates, *The Illinois Central Railroad and Its Colonization Work* (Cambridge, 1934).

62

couragement to improved agriculture it inaugurated a phase of railway activity which later companies were to extend until, in certain instances, they exercised a dominant influence over the trend of agriculture in their sectors.

In the sixties and seventies railways west of the Mississippi were carrying forward the work which the Illinois Central had so well begun. Men trained in land affairs by the latter road sometimes were induced to organize the land departments of the newer companies. In any event, the policies of the Illinois Central were an open secret, from which inexperienced promoters were free to take the best, while avoiding mistakes which the pioneer land grant railway had inevitably made.

Fortified in this way, the Chicago, Burlington and Quincy road duplicated in Nebraska the work of the Illinois Central. In the early seventies this company, through the efficiency of its European organization and its success in attracting settlers to its territory, excited both the admiration and the despair of rival railways. Mennonites and other sects from southern Russia were planted on the Nebraska prairies along with people from western Europe and the older states of the Union. So rapidly did this work proceed that by the end of the eighties the Burlington land grant was sold and settled.

In Kansas there were two important railway colonizers, the Kansas Pacific and the Santa Fe. The former, through the National Land Company, developed one of the most perfect railway organizations for recruiting, transporting, and locating settlers along its lines. Specializing in the establishment of groups and colonies, the land company was instrumental in the founding of a large number of such settlements in Kansas and Colorado, including the famous Greeley colony in the latter state.[1] With the dissolution of the National Land Company, the Kansas Pacific carried forward the work and played a conspicuous part in the evolution of the Swedish colony at Lindsborg, Kansas, one of the most important Scandinavian communities of the Middle West, together with several groups of

[1] J. F. Willard and C. B. Goodykoontz, *Experiments in Colorado Colonization, 1869-1872* (Boulder, Colorado, 1926). Also *Star of Empire*, April, 1870, which reviews the work of the National Land Company in Kansas and Colorado. This paper was the organ of the National Land Company.

German Russians of the Catholic persuasion at various points in Kansas.[1]

The Santa Fe, besides advertising the prairies of central and western Kansas throughout the older states of the Mississippi Valley, waged its campaign on the shores of the Black Sea, where it induced some 15,000 German Mennonites, domiciled in Russia since the days of Catherine the Great, to take up their abode in the valley of the Arkansas, which they transformed into a veritable Garden of Eden, and where they introduced new and hardier varieties of wheat.[2]

In the Northwest the Northern Pacific began the settlement of its country when Jay Cooke launched his campaign of education on two continents, which made his company the best advertised railway corporation in America, and which caused Northern Pacific territory to become famous as "Jay Cooke's Banana Belt." Unhampered by a too strict regard for truth and accuracy, and resolved to attract the attention of both investor and settler, he made the Northern Pacific a household word.[3] While the panic of 1873 severed Cooke's connection with the company before the results of his efforts were fully apparent, the work was ably carried on in the eighties and succeeding decades, first by Henry Villard and afterwards by his successors in control of the Northern Pacific.[4] Endowed with the most pretentious of American railway land grants, the company found the settling of the vast domain from Lake Superior to Puget Sound, with its great stretches of prairie, plain, mountain, and valley, a herculean task which it was never able to complete.

The foremost rival of the Northern Pacific in the colonization of the Northwest was the Great Northern. Beginning as the St. Paul and Pacific, which in the sixties and seventies had made but slight

[1] Alfred Bergin, "Swedish Settlements in Central Kansas," *Collections of Kansas State Historical Society* (1909-10), XI, p. 19 ff.

[2] Glenn D. Bradley, *The Story of the Santa Fe* (Boston, 1920). Schmidt, "Reminiscences of Foreign Immigration Work for Kansas," *Transactions of the Kansas State Historical Society* (1905-06), IX, pp. 485-97.

[3] James B. Hedges, "The Colonization Work of the Northern Pacific Railroad," *Mississippi Valley Historical Review* (December, 1926), XIII, pp. 311-42.

[4] *Ibid.*, also Hedges, "The Promotion of Immigration to the Pacific Northwest by the Railroads," *Mississippi Valley Historical Review* (September, 1928), XV, pp. 183-203. Hedges, *Henry Villard and the Railways of the Northwest* (New Haven, 1930).

progress despite the possession of a valuable land subsidy in the state of Minnesota, the road was in a bankrupt condition when in 1879 it was acquired by a group of Canadian capitalists, and reorganized and renamed the St. Paul, Minneapolis and Manitoba. Not only did the road prosper under the new control, but under the new management, which adopted intelligent policies in the administration of the land grant, it quickly became a most important factor in the settlement and development of central and northern Minnesota.[1]

The men who controlled this road in 1881 were the very ones who composed the syndicate which had just contracted with the Dominion Government to construct the Canadian Pacific Railway. During the debate on the contract in the House of Commons, proponents of the measure commented on the good fortune of Canada in securing the services of men so able and so experienced in the cause of land settlement.

Nor were these high hopes of rapid settlement of the West under syndicate auspices confined to Parliament or to members of the Conservative Party. The leading newspaper of the prairie, the Liberal *Manitoba Daily Free Press*, which yielded to no one in its devotion to the best interests of the Northwest, believed the identification of this particular group of men with the Canadian Pacific augured well for the speedy peopling of the western country. While disapproving of the exemption of the company's lands from taxation, together with other provisions of the contract, the *Free Press* emphasized the primary importance of colonization. As the editor phrased it, "While we condemn the bargain we do not condemn the terms."[2]

Referring to the report that the Howland Company had offered to build the road for smaller subsidies in land and money, the *Free Press* said the vigorous encouragement of immigration and settlement in the West weighed far more heavily than the number of dollars and acres given for the construction of the railway. The group most likely to prosecute that great work with success was obviously the one which should be preferred. It regarded the presence of the St. Paul and Manitoba Railway proprietors in the syndicate as an excellent guarantee of the speedy settlement of the

[1] Joseph G. Pyle, *The Life of James J. Hill* (New York, 1917).
[2] *Manitoba Daily Free Press*, January 13, 1881.

lands of the Northwest on liberal terms. They had "experience, knowledge, intimate acquaintance with the country and with the methods best adapted to further colonization." It doubted whether in all Canada "any set of men could be found as well qualified to undertake the vast work of populating our fertile prairies." A few thousand settlers more or less each year would have a greater effect upon the future of the Northwest than "the granting of a few million dollars or acres more or less to a syndicate."[1] The *Free Press* thought the question of immigration was the more vital and pressing because "the Tory government by its fatuous land policy, its ill-directed, wasted immigration efforts and its general mismanagement of Northwest affairs has driven away many thousands who would otherwise have settled in our midst."[2]

With so much expected from the company, it was inevitable that the formulation of its land policy should be awaited with eager anticipation. Simultaneously with the approval of the Syndicate Contract, and weeks before the formal organization of a land department, rumors were flying as to the nature of this policy. These reports had it that the company was to place a flat price of $2.50 per acre on the land, and that one-half of this would be remitted to the purchaser upon the fulfillment of certain conditions as to residence and cultivation.[3] Since no announcement had as yet been made by the company, these reports obviously were mere conjecture inspired by a knowledge of the policy by which the syndicate members had administered their Minnesota land grant.

After three months of speculation of this sort, there came the announcement of the organization of the Land Department and the appointment of a Land Commissioner. The new official was J. H. McTavish, factor of the Hudson's Bay Company at Fort Garry. That this choice was regarded as an altogether happy one, which promised well for the West, was indicated by the observation of the *Free Press* that

> . . . his well-known business capacity and administrative ability is a guarantee that the affairs of the Company, so far as the land is concerned, will be managed in a way that will conduce to the welfare of the country, while at the same time the interests of the

[1] *Ibid.*
[2] *Ibid.*, January 20, 1881.
[3] *Ibid.*, February 18, 1881.

Company will be faithfully protected. The fact of Mr. McTavish being at the head of the Land Department is a guarantee, not only to the people who have thrown in their lot in this land, but also to those who contemplate coming here to live, that everything which human agency can devise will be done toward developing this great country.[1]

Even after the organization of the Land Department, however, there was a further delay of many weeks before the sale of lands began. This was due in part to the tardiness of the government in conveying the land to the company, but more especially to the difficulty of deciding upon a land policy. In August of 1881 the board of the company convened in Winnipeg, where earnest consideration was given to this problem.[2] The attention of the group was directed in particular to the danger of forestallment of the best lands by speculators who had no intention of occupying the land, and who planned to extract a profit through sale to the *bona fide* settler. The company was naturally desirous of pricing its land at a price sufficiently low to attract the cultivator of the soil, but, should the figure be too low, the speculator would be attracted by the opportunity for making a profit. This was a problem which would tax the ingenuity of the railway officials.

By the end of September, 1881, the land examiners had made sufficient progress with their work to enable the Land Department to proceed with the actual sale of the land. Over 1,500 applications had been received for the purchase of 750,000 acres.[3] The policy adopted for the sale of land was based on the high resolve to sell only to the actual settler or to persons who would agree to cultivate and otherwise improve the land. In this way, as the *Free Press* naïvely expressed it, "the pernicious evil of speculators buying large tracts and locking them up" would be avoided. Yet, whatever chance there may have been of realizing this fond hope was forfeited when the company announced a flat price of $2.50 per acre for the land, regardless of quality or location.[4] This, in effect, was a bid to the speculator to buy the better lands in anticipation of an assured advance in value. The contracts provided for the payment of one-sixth of the purchase price in cash, with the remainder in

[1] *Manitoba Daily Free Press*, May 27, 1881.
[2] *Ibid.*, August 2, 1881.
[3] *Ibid.*, September 23, 1881.
[4] *Ibid.*

five equal annual installments. Improvements upon the premises were to remain, taxes were to be paid by the purchaser, and wood and timber, pending final payment, were to be cut only for fuel, fencing, or building purposes.

As a further safeguard against speculative buying, the purchaser must agree to "bring under cultivation and sow and reap a crop on three-fourths of the land" within four years. Should he erect buildings of an approved character on the land, however, the cultivation requirement would be reduced to one-half of the area purchased. As an added encouragement to the actual settler, a rebate of $1.25 per acre was allowed for each acre cultivated and cropped within the 4-year period.

This policy, indicating such a commendable desire on the part of the company promptly to fill the West with a multitude of genuine "dirt" farmers, met with the complete approval of the *Free Press*, the vigorous defender of western interests. The editor of this journal was convinced that the regulations created an effective foil to the speculator. As he expressed it, "before the actual settlers have enhanced the value of his [the speculator's] land to any great extent, in most instances the time limit of four years will have expired and he will be obliged either to give it up or to break and put under cultivation at least three-fourths of his possessions. It is very likely before going to such expense and trouble that, in many cases, the speculator of the class we are discussing will be only too glad to sell the land at a reasonable and just figure."[1]

The optimism of the *Free Press* would undoubtedly have been somewhat less pronounced had it not overlooked one essential point. The land regulations contained no provision for forfeiture of the land in the event of non-fulfillment of the cultivation and cropping conditions within the allotted time. The one penalty incurred thereby was the forfeiture of the rebate of $1.25 per acre, so that the speculator, for the price of $2.50 per acre, could retain his purchase, even though not a foot of the prairie sod had been turned. Nor could any one doubt that, with the lands priced at such a low figure, the temptation to, and opportunities for, profitable speculation within the 48-mile belt would be substantial.

The Land Department, however, was quick to remove this loophole. Early in 1882 it incorporated in the land regulations a provision

[1] Editorial, *Manitoba Daily Free Press*, September 23, 1881.

whereby, in the event of failure of the purchaser to carry out strictly the conditions of his contract within the specified time, the company reserved the right to cancel the agreement, with resulting forfeiture and reversion of the land to the company.[1] The vendee, however, was to be allowed the value of his permanent improvements, apart from cultivation, to the extent that such improvements had increased the worth of the land for agricultural purposes. The declared purpose of the forfeiture clause was to prevent the lands of the company from falling into the hands of speculators, to the disadvantage of the actual settler.

It is not surprising that these provisions should have occasioned criticism. The forfeiture clause, it was alleged, placed the purchaser too much at the mercy of the company; the arrangement for the erection of buildings satisfactory to the railway carried with it the possibility of pressure upon the farmer; while the requirement of cultivation and cropping of from one-half to three-fourths of the land within four years was unduly onerous.[2] Yet such terms seemed to afford the only guarantee that the avowed objectives of the company—early cultivation and production—would be even approximately achieved. Given the very natural desire of the settler to acquire as much land as possible, irrespective of his ability to cultivate it, drastic measures seemed imperative. Uncultivated and undeveloped land in the hands of the settler was only slightly less objectionable than when held by the speculator. The stringent application of the cultivation clause, under penalty of forfeiture, was regarded, therefore, as the one protection of the company against purely speculative purchases on the one hand, and retarded production by the settler on the other. Nor was it to be forgotten that the ease of preparing the treeless prairie for planting rendered the cultivation requirement less burdensome to the actual settler on the land. In short, as the *Free Press* expressed it, far from being excessively severe, the Canadian Pacific land regulations, compared with any other "promulgated in the Canadian Northwest . . . appear to us most liberal and just."[3]

Looking back over these first formative months it is evident that

[1] Editorial, *Manitoba Daily Free Press*, January 12, 1882.
[2] *Ibid.*, January 13, 1882.
[3] *Ibid.*

the Canadian Pacific Syndicate had as yet made little progress in the actual sale and settlement of its enormous land subsidy. It had made a beginning, however, and had formulated a land policy which was largely a reproduction of that which had worked so well for the Manitoba road in Minnesota. This policy, while praiseworthy in its objectives, was unfortunately conceived in a spirit of hope and enthusiasm not entirely warranted by the cold, unpleasant facts of the existing prairie situation. A policy realistic in the light of the Minnesota setting might well be an idealistic dream when applied to the Canadian Northwest. While the physical features were very similar north and south of the international boundary, the two areas were in essentially different stages of economic development. The pioneer had been settling the Minnesota prairie since 1860. Much of the government land within the limits of the Minnesota company's land grant had been occupied before the Canadian group obtained control of the railway in 1879. From the moment of their acquisition of the road, therefore, there had been an active demand for the railway land which made possible its ready sale under the settlement and rebate conditions which the Canadian Pacific was seeking to apply in its territory. In the Canadian Northwest, on the contrary, settlement had made little progress as yet, with the result that the government sections in the 48-mile belt were still largely available to the settler, who could have little incentive to purchase railway land, even at the low price of $2.50 per acre, with a rebate for cultivation.

In the spring of 1882 the Land Department promulgated a set of regulations more definitely in line with conditions then existing. For the first time it gave formal and official recognition to the fact that there were those who desired to buy land as an investment. Whether called speculators or colonizing companies, these men were both numerous and influential at the moment. Out of deference to them the company adopted a plan providing for a partial deviation from the flat price, and for the sale of lands in quantity.[1] When Parliamentary approval of the Syndicate Contract, plus the vigorous manner in which the company pushed the construction of the road, served notice that the railway to the Pacific was at last to be built, there developed in the West the state of mind which begets

[1] *Manitoba Daily Free Press*, April 4, 1882.

a boom. It was assumed that the settlement and development of the country, which had awaited the coming of the railway, would now go forward with a rush. Enterprising men naturally desired to be in on the ground floor and thereby share in the profits which seemed sure to follow. The spirit of speculation, especially in land, became rampant, and when the government gave encouragement to the speculator the railway could not be entirely indifferent to his ambition.

In December, 1881, the government adopted regulations by which companies might purchase lands remote from the railway for colonization purposes. In return for the privilege of buying the odd-numbered sections at $2.00 per acre, the companies agreed to place two settlers on homesteads on each even-numbered section within the area, each homesteader to be entitled to purchase the preëmption lot attached to his homestead. If, at the end of five years, the company had colonized the even sections, it received a rebate of $1.00 per acre on the odd-numbered sections purchased by it. It was the hope of Sir John A. Macdonald that, with this inducement, the colonization companies would "occupy the place for the present of the numerous railway companies in the United States, which have been proved there to be the best immigration agents—in fact the only immigration agent" in that country. Although many companies were formed to take advantage of this opportunity, the results were disappointing in the extreme. The government actually entered into contracts with 26 companies, covering 2,842,742 acres. Nine of the companies placed no settlers at all on the land, while the others brought in a total of 1,243 settlers. In retrospect, it would appear that the companies were largely predestined to failure because of the distance of their lands from railway lines, existing or projected.

Since these companies were operating outside the railway belt, their success would tend to divert settlement from the areas adjacent to the Canadian Pacific main line. It was important, therefore, that the railway should seek to attract some of these companies to the 48-mile belt along its line. To do so, however, concession must be made to the speculative element involved in them, and this concession took the form of regulations for the sale of land in bulk.

Such lands were to be taken in as compact a form as possible, on both sides of the railway, and in such proportions that the mean distance from the road should not be less than 12 miles. This last provision is the more interesting in view of the requirement of the government that companies colonizing for it should accept lands not less than 12 miles distant from a line of railway. The land was priced at $5.00 per acre, payable one-fourth in cash, and the balance, except as otherwise provided, within 5 years. One-half of the land was to be brought under cultivation, and a crop sowed and reaped, within 5 years from the date of sale. Should the purchasers "by themselves, or their representatives or assigns" faithfully perform the cultivation conditions, they were to be discharged from the balance of the purchase price of $5.00 per acre over and above the initial payment of $1.25 per acre. In short, if the lands were brought under settlement and cultivation, they could be acquired at the price of $1.25 per acre. If, however, the purchasers should fail to carry out the cultivation and settlement conditions, they must pay the balance of the purchase price within 60 days after the expiration of the 5-year period. The essence of this plan, then, was that companies desiring large areas of land for colonization purposes could contract for their purchase at $5.00 per acre. If they or their assigns colonized the land, a rebate of $3.75 per acre was to be granted, which would make the price but slightly in excess of the $1.00 per acre exacted by the government from colonization companies fulfilling the settlement conditions. But, on the other hand, a company which had no plan for bringing the land under settlement and cultivation, and which desired merely to hold the land for appreciation, might purchase it at $5.00 per acre, payable within 5 years.

On the face of it this plan seemed to play directly into the hands of speculators desirous of holding land for appreciation in value. Careful consideration of all the circumstances, however, renders such a conclusion largely untenable. When it is recalled that 20 years later, at the time of the great boom in the West, land companies purchased large tracts of land at $2.75 per acre and less, the $5.00 price set on the land appears as no great concession to the speculator. On the contrary, it was the penalty incurred by failure to comply with the settlement conditions. From the company's viewpoint, the plan was a colonization scheme under which the purchaser earned a rebate of $3.75 per acre by prompt resale of the land to actual settlers. Before the collapse of the boom of 1882 a large area was sold under this policy to several large land companies.

The *Free Press* watched the adoption of this policy with interest and with regret. Having approved so heartily of the earlier plan for the sale of railway lands, it naturally was disappointed with the new departure. Commenting upon the change it said:

> We observe that the Canadian Pacific Company has adopted a plan looking toward the sale in bloc of large areas of land. There is, of course, a very appreciable distinction between the action of a Railway Company in this regard and that of a government and speculative land companies. We can readily conceive that the Company will strongly insist upon the strict fulfillment of the conditions as to settlement or cultivation upon which its sales are based. Its interests are necessarily bound up to a large extent with the speedy increase of population and the speedy cultivation of the land. The transportation of grain will bring much revenue to the coffers of the Company, and that is dependent upon settlement. Yet we shall watch the progress of the Company's experiment with a considerable degree of misgiving as to its final success even under the best circumstances. We only hope the company will be able to reconcile this new phase of its policy to the view of its fine interests we have mentioned above.[1]

The skepticism of the *Free Press* with respect to Canadian Pacific policies was soon to be intensified by further developments. The company was about to depart even further from its original policy of sale to settlers only. The finances of the company being in a precarious state, it became necessary in the spring of 1882 to obtain monetary assistance. Since the chief tangible asset of the railway was its land subsidy, which it was authorized to use as a basis for the issuance of land grant bonds, common sense dictated an attempt to convert a portion of this asset into cash with which to continue construction of the line.

On June 6, 1882 the Canadian Pacific, through President Stephen and Secretary Drinkwater, entered into an agreement with Edmund B. Osler and William B. Scarth of Toronto, and John Kennedy Tod and Oliver H. Northcote of New York, acting in behalf of a group of English and Canadian capitalists, including the Duke of Manchester, who had for some time been considering a large-scale

[1] Editorial, *Manitoba Daily Free Press*, April 5, 1882.

investment in the lands of western Canada.[1] By this contract Osler and his associates covenanted to purchase from the railway company: (1) 5,000,000 acres of land to be set aside for them in sections 1, 9, 13, 21, 25, and 33 in every township in the main line belt; (2) the area of all town and village plots and sites at the railway stations on the main line between Brandon and the eastern boundary of British Columbia; and (3) land grant bonds of the railway to the amount of $13,500,000. The land was priced at $3.00 per acre and was to be paid for in the land grant bonds at a 10 per cent premium plus accrued interest. Thus by providing financial assistance to the railway company through their investment in land grant bonds, the purchasers obtained a substantial discount from the contract price of the land. On July 24, 1882, they transferred all their estate and rights under the agreement of June 6th to the Canada Northwest Land Company, a corporation organized under the laws of Great Britain.

In pursuance of the agreement, the Canadian Pacific, on April 14, 1883, conveyed to the Canada Northwest Land Company 1,500,000 acres of land, for which the latter paid $4,200,000, largely in land grant bonds, but with $275,000 in cash. Meanwhile the purchasers discovered that they had been over-sanguine in regard to their financial prospects. Unable to muster the funds necessary to carry through the original agreement, they asked for a revision of the contract, which the railway consented to on December 20, 1883. By the new bargain the land company reduced its bond purchase to $6,000,000 and the land area to 2,200,000 acres, exclusive of town sites. There now remained 700,000 acres to be located for the company. Of this area, 171,200 acres were provided from the land reserved for the Land Corporation of Canada, one of the numerous colonization companies of the previous year. The balance was to be taken in the reserved sections of the main line belt between Range 33, west of the 1st meridian and Moose Jaw. Should that not suffice, the company could claim land in those townships of Manitoba in which it had already received its 1,500,000 acres.

When the passing years made it evident that the settlement of the West was to be a long, slow process in which large returns from

[1] The various agreements with the Canada Northwest Land Company are to be found in the Office of the Secretary of the C. P. R. in Montreal.

landed investments would not be immediately forthcoming, the ardor of the English investors began to cool. Much of the stock of the company found its way back across the Atlantic where it lodged in the hands of Canadian security holders. As the stock depreciated in value it was accepted at a premium in payment of land, thereby retiring the stock. Soon some 4,000 shares had been cancelled in this way, and the control of the company was rapidly passing into the hands of a small group of insiders. With the growing concentration of stock ownership in Canada there came increasing complaint against administration of the company from England.

In 1893 the original company went into liquidation and a new one, with the same name, was incorporated in Canada to take over the business and property of the organization. Control of the new Canada Northwest Land Company passed into the hands of the Canadian Pacific through its acquisition of 5,625 shares of preferred stock of the land company of the par value of $100 per share and an equal number of shares of common stock of the par value of $25 per share. At a meeting of stockholders in Toronto in September of that year Donald A. Smith, W. C. Van Horne, R. B. Angus, and T. G. Shaughnessy were elected to the directorate, and Van Horne was made president of the company. The Canada Northwest Land Company had become a subsidiary of the Canadian Pacific.

While contemporaneous with the various colonizing companies which contracted for the purchase of large areas from the Canadian Pacific under the regulations of 1882, the Canada Northwest Company was not one of them. Its contract with the railway contained no provisions or requirements with respect to settlement of the land. It paid a fixed price for the land irrespective of whether it located settlers on its holdings. The Canadian Pacific regarded its agreement with the land company not as a promise of early colonization of the land but as a means of obtaining the financial assistance it so sorely needed at the time.

Although not compelled to colonize its lands, the company naturally was not indifferent to the problem of land settlement. In the eighties it actively encouraged the occupation of the intervening government sections as a preliminary to the sale of its own properties. In December, 1882, it advertised 300,000 acres in the districts adjacent to Regina, Qu'Appelle, and Moosomin, that is, in the areas of relatively rapid settlement, where the demand for land ensured satisfactory prices to the company. These lands it offered for sale without settlement or cultivation conditions. Its prices and terms of sale in that period were distinctly less favorable to the settler than those governing the sale of land directly by the Canadian Pacific.

With its acquisition by the Canadian Pacific in 1893, the company's land policies were, of course, shaped by the railway, whose land commissioner served in a similar capacity for the land company. The Land Department of the Canadian Pacific now undertook to obtain buyers and settlers for the land it had first sold in 1882. Wherever possible it arranged for the sale of the company's sections in combination with those of the railway in the same district. Because they represented an initial investment of $3.00 per acre, the Canada Northwest lands were held at substantially higher prices than railway lands of the same quality and location. Sometimes these lands netted a figure which was double that of Canadian Pacific lands. So successful was the land department of the railway in its management of the properties of the Canada Northwest Company that in 1903 and 1904 the latter redeemed the 5,625 shares of preferred stock held by the railway, while in 1907 and 1908 it repaid the capital of 5,625 shares of common stock to the extent of $24 per share.

This agreement to sell more than 2,000,000 acres to the Canada Northwest Land Company was soon to be followed by yet another departure from the original land policies of the railway. Late in 1882 the Land Department completely abandoned the flat price system when it offered for sale the land in the 48-mile belt, at prices ranging from $2.50 to $7.00 per acre, and without settlement conditions.[1] At the same time it placed on the market 2,500,000 acres in southern Manitoba and southeastern Assiniboia, comprising the International Boundary Reserve of the company. Commenting upon this last step, the *Free Press* reported a rush to take advantage of the opportunity offered. "The purchasers embraced all elements in the community from the avaricious speculator down to the peasant

[1] *Manitoba Daily Free Press*, December 16, 1882.

farmer."[1] On the first day, 7,840 acres were disposed of at an average price of $6.50 per acre.

In the opinion of the *Free Press* these new features of the company's policy were "extremely unfortunate for the Government, as it has been their great boast that the Syndicate were selling their land at reasonable figures and on terms requiring its settlement and cultivation. It is still more unfortunate for the country, however, as it is an additional blow at its early and rapid population."[2]

Actually, however, the situation was not as bad as the *Free Press* thought. The company had not abandoned its efforts to attract the *bona fide* settler. In the 48-mile belt it substituted for an ironclad cultivation requirement an inducement to that end in the form of a price differential between lands cultivated and those which were not. Prices ranged from $2.50 per acre upwards with cropping conditions, and from $4.00 per acre without contingent provisions.[3] For cultivation a rebate of one-half the purchase price was allowed on the area cropped, to be applied on the next payment falling due.[4] Land within one mile of the railway and in the vicinity of towns and stations, which had at first been reserved from sale, was placed on the market in April, 1883, with heavy rebates for cultivation. Land grant bonds were accepted in payment for lands at a premium of 10 per cent.

But even these liberal terms brought disappointing results in the face of the depressed conditions of prairie agriculture in the middle eighties. Toward the end of the decade the land department decided that further inducements were necessary to stimulate sales. In 1888 it reduced the minimum price of land in the 48-mile belt to $2.00 per acre, without mention of cultivation or cropping conditions.[5] For actual settlers it extended the time of payment from 6 to 10 years, thereby drawing a distinction between settler and speculator which continued to find expression in the land regulations of the company for the next 20 years. In the same year the Land Department placed on the market, on the same terms, the land grant of the Manitoba Southwestern Colonization Railway along the in-

---

[1] *Manitoba Daily Free Press*, November 22, 1882.
[2] *Ibid.*, December 16, 1882.
[3] *Ibid.*, April 21, 1883.
[4] *Ibid.*
[5] *Ibid.*, January 3, 1888.

ternational boundary. Much of this grant lay in one of the well-settled regions of the West, where the homesteads had long since been taken up. Officials of the company emphasized the fact, therefore, that purchasers of these lands would enjoy the advantages of schools, churches, and municipal organization to a degree unequaled in most places on the prairie.[1] Unlike other areas remote from the Canadian Pacific main line, this land offered the additional attraction of reasonable proximity to secondary railways.

The policy of price reduction was not at this time extended to the great Southern or International Boundary Reserve of the company. As these lands were not yet served by branch lines, there seemed to be no immediate urge to sell them. For this area, therefore, the Land Department maintained a price scale ranging from $4.00 to $10.00 per acre, which, according to the *Free Press*, placed the land beyond the reach of intending settlers. As a result little of the land was sold during the next decade. In fact, it was not sold in substantial amount until the great boom in the West after the turn of the century, when large blocks were disposed of at prices as low as $2.50 per acre.

In the early nineties the company attacked the problem of land sale and settlement with renewed vigor. Except for lands deemed especially valuable because of proximity to stations or for other special reasons, it reduced the price scale on lands in the main line belt and in the Manitoba Southwestern grant. Land previously offered at $4.00 was now priced at $3.00, while $6.00 land was reduced to $4.00 per acre.[2] It was at this time, too, that the company made its first serious effort to sell lands along the main line west of the 3rd meridian and in the great reserves to the north, remote from the railway. In 1892 it returned momentarily to the flat price system when it advertised lands in the Red Deer and Battle River districts at the uniform rate of $3.00 per acre.[3] As nuclei of homestead settlements were forming in those areas, the time seemed auspicious to push the sale of railway land. At the same time it announced an auction sale of Saskatchewan Valley lands to be held at Edmonton on May 3, 1892, a rather unusual procedure in dealing with railway

[1] *Manitoba Daily Free Press*, January 3, 1888.
[2] *Manitoba Evening Free Press and Sun*, January 26, 1892.
[3] *Ibid.*, March 26, 1892.

subsidy lands, whether in Canada or the United States.[1] The land was
to be placed on sale at an upset price of $3.00 per acre and sold to
the highest bidder, without conditions. One-tenth of the purchase
price was to be paid at the time of sale, with the balance in 9
annual installments. Intending buyers might purchase tickets from
Winnipeg at a single fare for the round trip. Should the holder of
the ticket purchase land from the company at the auction, the
amount of the ticket was to be credited on the cost of the land. An
area of 150,000 acres was thus made available for purchase, and
the company emphasized the proximity of the land to the relatively
"old" settlements of Edmonton, Fort Saskatchewan, Sturgeon River,
and St. Albert. The sale was widely attended by land seekers from
all parts of the United States, and resulted in the disposal of some
15,000 acres at prices ranging from $3.10 to $5.60 per acre, which
was considered satisfactory.[2] So encouraged was the company by this
first trial of the auction method that a second sale was held in July
of the same year. While not as successful as the first, it resulted in
the disposal of about 7,000 acres for $30,000, chiefly to large pur-
chasers. These two sales seem to have been the only instances of
the use of this particular means of reaching the land buyer.

Due to a variety of reasons, among them the reduced price of
land, the auction sales, and special efforts to encourage immigration
to the West, the land sales of the company for 1892 exceeded those
of any year since the early eighties. The improvement was but temporary, however, for the next year depression settled upon the country in such extreme form as to bring a sharp decline in sales which
continued unabated until 1896, when signs of improvement foreshadowed the more general recovery which ultimately issued in the
great land boom at the beginning of the new century.

Canadian Pacific land policies in this formative period, which
came to an end in 1896, were not shaped without an eye to the
progress of settlement on government sections within the confines
of the railway's land grants. In the beginning it was the expectation
of company officials that those attracted to the West by railway
advertising and immigration activities would purchase land freely
from the Canadian Pacific. Undoubtedly the extremely liberal char-

[1] *Manitoba Evening Free Press and Sun*, March 26, 1892, also April 21, 1892.
[2] *Ibid.*, May 9, 1892.

acter of the terms under which company lands were first offered
for sale was in part the result of the belief that this would be the
case. The great demand for railway land in 1882 and 1883 seemed
to justify this hope. With the passing of the boom, however, it soon
became apparent that little land could be sold to settlers while
government land was available in abundance for homesteading.
The first duty of the railway, therefore, was to foster the occupation of the government lands. Within a few years the company discovered that its experience was similar to that of land grant railways
in the States, where the first speculative fever was almost invariably
"followed by a heavy falling off in land sales, owing to the presence
of vast quantities of free grant lands."[1] Profiting by this experience,
the company was extensively advertising the free government lands
and making every effort to stimulate their settlement. In 1885 the
directors announced that because of their preoccupation with the
settlement of the government sections within the railway belt and
south of it to the international boundary, they were making little
effort to effect sales of company land.[2]

Soon this avowed policy of the Canadian Pacific attracted the attention of the *Free Press*, which remarked that "the C. P. R. immigration agencies, contrary to the general belief, are not employed in
securing settlers for C. P. R. lands, but devote their energies toward
settling immigrants on government property, the company recognizing the fact that the filling up of the Dominion lands will enhance
the value of their own."[3] By 1888 the free government lands within
the railway belt were sufficiently occupied to encourage the company to believe the time was at hand when its lands would not
only be readily saleable, but would bring higher prices than in the
past.[4]

Higher prices for railway land constituted but one of the benefits
resulting from prior occupation of the government lands. Successful
farmers on homestead or preëmption claims were large potential
buyers of the land of the company. Aside from the areas sold to land
companies, it is probable that sales to homesteaders accounted for

[1] *Annual Report*, 1884, p. 28.
[2] *Ibid.*, 1885, p. 18.
[3] *Manitoba Daily Free Press*, June 18, 1886.
[4] *Annual Report*, 1888, p. 20.

the major portion of the land disposed of by the Canadian Pacific to 1896. According to the Annual Report for 1894, the company's lands were seldom sold to "new immigrants but generally to those who have already established themselves on free homesteads, and who, from their improved condition are able to increase their holdings by the purchase of adjoining railway lands."[1]

By the middle nineties this policy of first pushing the settlement of government land had become so thoroughly established that the company adhered rigorously to it, as in subsequent years it opened up to sale its great land reserves scattered throughout the West. It was evident, however, that the government sections in southern Manitoba and in the main line belt east of Moose Jaw were sufficiently absorbed to ensure the rapid sale of railway lands in those districts once economic conditions in the West became favorable.

No company, of course, could hope to own and administer such a vast landed property as that of the Canadian Pacific without being subjected to bitter criticism at times. In part such attacks upon the railway company resulted from resentment occasioned by the sheer magnitude of its holdings. In part, also, the opposition was directed against certain alleged privileges and practices of the company with respect to its lands. From the beginning there was complaint and controversy in regard to the clause of the Syndicate Contract exempting company lands from taxation for 20 years unless sold or occupied. Soon there arose the question as to the meaning of the word "sold." Were lands which had been under contract for sale but which subsequently reverted to the company "sold" and therefore taxable? Various municipalities, especially that of Cornwallis, supported the affirmative of this question and proceeded to tax such lands. The Canadian Pacific took the negative and in the subsequent litigation, which was carried to the Supreme Court of Canada, the railway won the decision. The lands had not been "sold" and were not taxable.[2]

Another question which the courts were called upon to decide was the time at which the 20-year tax exemption began. Did it date from the signing of the Syndicate Contract or from the issue of the patent to the land? If the former, the entire main line grant would become

[1] *Annual Report*, 1894, p. 16.
[2] For the question of the taxation of Canadian Pacific lands, see 35 *C. S. C. R.*, 551, and 1911 *Appeal Cases*, 328.

taxable in 1901. As the bulk of this land would almost certainly be unsold at that date, a heavy burden would be placed upon the company. Patents to large blocks of land were issued at various times after 1881, some of them as late as 1903 and 1904. The Canadian Pacific interpreted the exemption to begin with the issuance of the patents. Struggling Communities in the West, which were sorely in need of the revenue which taxation of the land would provide, naturally took issue with the company. When the province of Alberta sought to establish the right of taxation there followed litigation in which the Privy Council ultimately sustained the contention of the railway. The exemption began with the issue of the patent.

In the eighties, too, there was much objection, especially by the *Manitoba Free Press*, to what was conceived to be the railway's shielding of the Canada Northwest Land Company from taxation. It will be recalled that, under the agreement of June 6, 1882 the railway reserved for the land company certain stipulated sections in the main line belt. Although the railway conveyed 1,500,000 acres to the company on April 14, 1883, it seems to have withheld for a time the title to the remaining 700,000 acres to which the land company was entitled. In this way, according to the *Free Press*, the company enjoyed the tax exemption accorded to the Canadian Pacific on its lands. When the tax assessor appeared, the lands reserved for the land company were the property of the Canadian Pacific; when the purchaser appeared, these same lands were the property of the Canada Northwest Land Company.[1]

The *Free Press*, after computing at $24,000 the tax loss of four municipalities resulting from this exemption, came to the conclusion that the additional tax burden thereby placed upon the actual settler was a prime deterrent to immigration. Continuing, it observed that ". . . the farmer who labors all the year and pays his own taxes has to pay those of the alien land Company as well. This grasping corporation does not hesitate to take advantage of the enhanced price of its land in consequence of its proximity to schools, churches and roads, the result of the settler's toil. Is it any wonder, then, that the settlers should complain against this grasping and soulless neighbor? Is the concern which thus seeks to load its taxes

[1] *Manitoba Daily Free Press*, December 3, 1886.

upon settlers any attraction to intending immigrants?"[1] The worst thing the *Free Press* could say about the company was that it was even more of an octopus than the old Canada Company in Ontario, in that the latter enjoyed no such freedom from taxation.

The following year the *Free Press* estimated the financial loss to municipalities in Manitoba through such exemption to be not less than $60,000 annually, which did not include Dominion lands not yet alienated and therefore not taxable.[2] This, it asserted, would increase the loss to $100,000 annually, which would completely offset the annual subsidy of $100,000 paid by the Dominion to the province in lieu of its public lands.[3] Soon the agitation conducted by the *Free Press* against the Canada Northwest Land Company was reflected in the Manitoba Legislature, which adopted a resolution offering the assistance of the province to any municipality desiring to test the legality of the tax evasion, but which alone could not afford to come to grips with such a powerful corporation.[4] This threat seems to have produced the desired results and agitation in the public press against this particular privilege of the land company ceased.

It was inevitable that the Canadian Pacific should be charged with holding its lands at excessive prices, with resulting responsibility for wide dispersion of settlement in the West, and with other practices allegedly inimical to the best interests of the prairie region.[5] This feeling of hostility led eventually to the proposal that the Dominion Government should fix a maximum price for railway lands as a means of aiding the settler and checking speculation. This idea, of course, was palpably absurd. The surest way to play into the hands of the speculator was to establish such a maximum. If it were placed at a figure lower than the market price of lands in a particular locality, that would be the signal for the speculator to rush in and buy up large tracts. The proposition was open to the further objection that it would impair the value of the land as security for raising capital for the railway. The *Free Press* was quick to point out the fallacy of the argument employed by proponents of the idea when it said: "It [the railway company] is doubly interested

[1] *Manitoba Daily Free Press,* January 31, 1887.
[2] *Ibid.,* March 10, 1888.
[3] *Ibid.*
[4] *Ibid.,* May 7, 1888.
[5] *Ibid.,* May 15, 1890.

—to get a price for its land and to create traffic. That price can never be an exorbitant or unreasonable one as long as the Company has to compete against free homesteads and government lands at a low figure. If railway lands are sometimes quoted at $4.00 to $10.00 per acre, it is because their situation or some other circumstance gives them that value; if they are not worth it, people will not pay it."[1] It is probable that the agitation for a maximum price on the lands of the railway was a product of the depressed conditions prevailing on the prairie in the eighties and early nineties. With the improved conditions after 1896 the idea seems to have disappeared from public discussion.

Attention thus far has been directed to the agricultural lands of the railway. It possessed, however, town and city properties and grazing lands which required policies for their administration. A railway built through unsettled country exercises a profound influence not only on rural development but also on the growth of towns; it becomes, in fact, the chief promoter of town sites. To this rule the Canadian Pacific was no exception, and, with characteristic foresight, the company planned its towns with a view to obtaining the maximum profit therefrom.

In the planting of towns on the prairie the railway enjoyed the complete coöperation of the Conservative Government. On March 11, 1882, the Department of the Interior withdrew from entry "all even-numbered sections next to and along both sides of the Canadian Pacific Railway and its branches," thereby creating what came to be known as the "mile-belt reserve."[2] All agents of Dominion lands throughout the West were instructed to warn intending settlers to keep out. The purpose back of this move, as interpreted by the *Free Press*, was to withhold those lands from alienation until the town and station sites along the railway had been located, and to prevent the advance acquisition by private parties of government sections on which such towns or stations were to be located. In this way, it was alleged, the railway would be assured of the undivided ownership of the future commercial centers of the West. The *Free Press* charged that the syndicate members were so eager to secure all the increased

[1] *Manitoba Daily Free Press*, May 15, 1890.
[2] Telegram, Department of the Interior to Agents, Dominion Lands, March 11, 1882, File No. 43499, Dominion Lands Branch, Department of the Interior.

value of adjacent lands that they located homesteads in advance of construction at points they wished to reserve, "their squatters being under agreement to surrender their locations to the Company when the latter require them." According to another report they "were prepared to alter the located route in order to secure for themselves alone all the eligible town sites." The railway, it was asserted, had duped the Conservative Government into support of its Machiavellian scheme.

The Canadian Pacific would have been utterly unlike other land grant railways had it not sought to secure for itself the major profits and perquisites which went with the promotion of towns. Actually, however, the plan was not as dark or sinister as the *Free Press* believed. The paper, in its analysis of the situation, overlooked two essential points. First of all the country was in the throes of the boom, with the spirit of speculation running riot. Care was necessary on the part of both the company and the government to prevent the engrossing by speculators of all land in the vicinity of towns and stations. The action of the Department of the Interior was intended to safeguard the government sections against the designs of the speculator. By simply refusing to sell, the railway could protect its own. In the second place the *Free Press* failed to appreciate that the town sites were not always railway monopolies. In numerous instances they were joint enterprises of the company and the government. At division points, where rapid growth was anticipated, towns were laid out on both railway and government land. Thus Regina and Qu'Appelle each included two railway and two government sections, while Virden and Moose Jaw each comprised one railway and one government section. In most cases, however, the towns along the main line were originally provided for by the reservation of one section of railway land.

In the promotion of these towns the Canadian Pacific employed a device frequently used by the railways in the United States, namely, division of the proceeds with a land company which assumed the responsibility of managing the town properties. By the agreement of June 6, 1882, the railway sold to the Canada Northwest Land Company the area of all town and village plots located on the main line between Brandon and the eastern boundary of

British Columbia.[1] The railway was to receive one-half the net proceeds of the sale of the land after deduction of the price thereof and of the cost and expense of managing, administering, and selling the same. The town sites were to be conveyed to a body of four trustees of whom the railway and the land company named an equal number. The first trustees for the railway were R. B. Angus and Donald A. Smith; for the land company, E. B. Osler and William B. Scarth. In accordance with this agreement, 47 towns were established and conveyed to the trustees. Included in the list were such important prairie cities as Regina, Moose Jaw, Calgary, Swift Current, and Medicine Hat. By an agreement of April 13, 1908, this trusteeship was terminated and the unsold town-site properties divided between the two companies.[2]

This coöperation of the Canada Northwest Land Company in town-site promotion was limited to the main line of the Canadian Pacific. As branch line construction proceeded through the West the establishment of new towns became the exclusive prerogative of the Land Department of the railway. First and last it sponsored some 800 village and town communities in the 3 prairie provinces. While it was the fixed policy of the company to locate towns on its own land, it sought, wherever conditions warranted, to secure possession of adjacent government land with a view to the profits resulting from the growth and expansion of the town.

Commenting upon company town sites, the Annual Report for 1888 said:

> The town sites along the line, which have as far as possible been secured for the benefit of the Company, are contributing handsomely to its revenues. The sales from town sites last year were $519,837 and the total sales to the 31st December last year have been $1,399,327. Only a small portion of the Company's interests in town sites have been disposed of, and its receipts from this source will rapidly increase as the country increases in population. . . . From the proceeds of town sites large and handsome hotels have been built and equipped at Banff . . . and at Vancouver.[3]

---

[1] The agreement covered only towns which should be established during the construction of the main line and within one year following its completion between Winnipeg and the Pacific Coast. For the text of the agreement, see the original in Office of the Secretary of the C. P. R. Co. in Montreal.

[2] See original of the agreement in Secretary's Office, Montreal.

[3] *Annual Report*, 1888, p. 21.

The most spectacular, as well as the most profitable, venture of the Canadian Pacific in town-site promotion, however, was at Vancouver, far removed from the land grant received from the Dominion Government. So rapid was the growth of this town that by 1889 the proceeds of town lot sales there exceeded those in all other company towns combined. Returns for 1888 were $483,084, making a total of $868,059 since the town was laid out 3 years before.[1]

Progress in the location of town and station sites along the main line of the railway was sufficiently rapid to enable the Department of the Interior to lift the ban on entries within the mile-belt reserve as far west as the 4th principal meridian on January 1, 1884.[2] On April 30 of the same year the reserve was opened to entry to the western limit of the railway's land grant.[3]

If the company was provident in the administration of its town properties, it was no less so in its policy with reference to grazing lands. Between Swift Current and the mountains the main line of the railway traversed a region well adapted to the cattle industry, where in the early eighties cattle barons were leasing from the government large areas of land. By 1885 some 66 different companies had leased about 3,000,000 acres, some of the leases covering upwards of 100,000 acres.[4] Since many of these ranches lay wholly or in part within the limits of Canadian Pacific land grants, the company promptly took steps to protect its equity in them. While it had not yet accepted the odd-numbered sections within the ranches and might eventually reject certain ones of them, it insisted that the Department of the Interior should collect the rental of 2 cents per acre and place the proceeds to the credit of the company pending final selection. The account was then to be adjusted, the railway receiving the rental for the land ultimately accepted, while that for the rejected lands would be retained by the government.[5] In this way the Canadian Pacific received a revenue from these lands, although many of them were not finally ac-

[1] Annual Report, 1888, p. 21.
[2] P. C. O. No. 2441, November 29, 1883.
[3] P. C. O. No. 937, April 30, 1884.
[4] Sessional Papers (No. 53), 1885, pp. 1-9.
[5] Charles Drinkwater, Secretary, C. P. R., to A. M. Burgess, Deputy Minister of the Interior, March 17, 1886, Sessional Papers (No. 34), 1883, p. 21. Also Drinkwater to John R. Hall, Secretary, Department of the Interior, June 23, 1887, Sessional Papers (No. 25 A), 1888, pp. 46-47.

cepted by it until the adjustment of 1903, in which the company took over the large area *en bloc* in southern Alberta.

To December 31, 1896, the Canadian Pacific had disposed of a net area of 3,623,066 acres from its main line subsidy, and 171,958 acres from the Manitoba Southwestern grant.[1] Sales from the main line grant had been made in large and small amounts. By far the largest single sale, of course, was that of 2,200,000 acres to the Canada Northwest Land Company, which accounted for 60 per cent of the total area sold.

The difficulty of selling land once the boom sentiment had subsided is shown by the fact that the net area disposed of to the end of 1896 was actually somewhat less than the 3,631,640 acres sold to December 31, 1883.[2] This latter figure, reflecting the full effects of the land boom before wholesale cancellations had begun, included 794,240 acres sold to settlers, and 2,837,400 acres to companies.[3] Allowing for the sale to the Canada Northwest Land Company, there remained 637,000 acres sold to colonization companies formed to take advantage of the regulations of 1882 providing for the sale of land in quantity for colonization purposes. Because of the failure of several of these companies to comply with the conditions respecting cultivation and settlement, the railway soon cancelled their contracts. It first moved against the delinquents in 1884 when about 130,000 acres were cancelled.[4] By December 31, 1886, it had cancelled contracts for 696,330 acres, of which 400,000 acres were covered by the contracts of the French Colonization Company and the Land Corporation of Canada.[5] In 1892 the railway effected a settlement with the Ontario and Qu'Appelle Land Company whereby it surrendered 136,495 acres purchased in 1882.[6] These three companies, therefore, account for the cancellation of more than half a million acres.

Not all the sales to companies turned out so badly, however. The Qu'Appelle Valley Farming Company, which purchased more than

[1] *Annual Report*, 1896, p. 19.
[2] *Ibid.*, 1883, no pagination.
[3] *Ibid.*
[4] *Ibid.*, 1884, p. 28.
[5] *Ibid.*, 1886, p. 21.
[6] *Ibid.*, 1892, pp. 16-17.

25,000 acres, made a valiant effort to live up to the terms of its contract with the railway. During the summer and autumn of 1882 it broke 2,700 acres of its purchase, while by the spring of 1884 it had prepared 7,000 acres for seeding. Due to the location of much of its land in the one-mile belt along the railway, it had paid substantial prices for its land, but the increased initial outlay had been partially offset by the generous rebate allowed by the Canadian Pacific on the sections cultivated within the stipulated period of time.

Somewhat less satisfactory was the showing of the Netherlands and American Land Company. This corporation, composed of wealthy Dutchmen, had purchased in the early eighties some 50,000 acres lying along the main line of the railway between Virden and Grenfell, much of it within the mile belt. Despite the favorable location of its holdings the land company had neither cultivated the land nor exerted itself to dispose of it to settlers. On the contrary it had placed a prohibitive price on its holdings. The railway, however, dealt very leniently with this organization. In 1892 the Land Department of the Canadian Pacific, at the request of the land company, undertook the task of selling and settling the land which it had sold 10 years before.[1] By reducing the price of the land to $4.00 per acre, with generous terms of payment, the railway experienced little difficulty in selling this attractive area.

While there were other colonization companies of 1882, such as the Provident Commercial Land Company and Richard Sykes of Stockport, England, which met with some success, these organizations were, generally speaking, complete and utter failures. It is not surprising, therefore, that Canadian Pacific confidence in large land companies revived but slowly at the turn of the century.

But it was not merely the large buyer who found himself in contractual difficulties with the Land Department of the railway. The small fellows were prone either to overreach themselves amid the optimism of the early eighties or to succumb to failure and discouragement. Despite the settled policy of the company to accord "the most liberal treatment . . . to all *bona fide* settlers who appeared to have acted in good faith," it found itself compelled to abrogate many contracts covering smaller areas. To December 31,

[1] *Manitoba Evening Free Press and Sun*, May 13, 1892.

1896, the total cancellations in the main line grant covered 1,284,-652 acres.[1] Of this area, somewhat more than one-half is represented by cancelled contracts of companies, leaving about 600,000 acres covered by contracts held by small purchasers—not an excessive area for 16 years of fluctuating fortune in the Northwest.

In spite of all the difficulties of this early period, however, there were many small purchasers who managed to keep in good standing with the Land Department of the railway. After allowing for all the cancellations and for the completed sales to the Canada Northwest Land Company and other companies, there remains a net area of at least 1,000,000 acres taken in small tracts in the period which closed in 1896. During the 12 months ending October 1, 1888, there were 340 buyers, of whom 59 were from places other than the Canadian West, chiefly from Ontario, but including also England, Scotland, and the United States.[2] Of those who gave prairie addresses the majority were probably resident farmers seeking to enlarge their holdings, rather than new arrivals on the scene. In 1892, the year in which the auction sale of land was introduced, there were 1,632 purchasers, of whom 800 were from Ontario, 450 from the United States, and 154 from England. Settlers from the States purchased 87,680 acres.[3] These figures seem to indicate that a large proportion of the land buyers in that year were new settlers on the prairie, and they undoubtedly reflect both the special effort put forth by the company at that time to stimulate its sales, and the growing scarcity of government lands in districts in close proximity to the railway.

If the land sales of the railway over the 16-year period from 1881 to 1897, apart from the large areas disposed of to the Canada Northwest Land Company and similar organizations, were not all that the Canadian Pacific had hoped for, there is evidence to show that the completion of the railway had beneficial effects upon the West in that period. Compared with the decade 1871-81, there was increased activity along all lines. Immigration, homestead entries, land settlement, the formation of foreign colonies, the growth of population,

[1] Figures compiled from the Annual Reports for those years.
[2] *Sessional Papers* (No. 36 B), 1889, pp. 291-96, for names and addresses of purchasers.
[3] *Annual Report*, 1892, pp. 16-17.

all indicate that developments were proceeding with a quickened pace.

The 47,991 immigrants entering the Dominion in 1881 represented the largest influx of any year, save one, since Confederation.[1] The boom spirit in the country, and especially in the West, fostered by the assurance that the railway was to be built, is reflected in the figures for the following year when 112,458 persons sought new homes in Canada. Jumping to 133,624 in 1883, the number declined to 103,824 in 1884.[2] Not again until 1903 was immigration to reach the 100,000 mark. Through the late eighties and early nineties the trend was in general downward, falling to 16,835 in 1896, the lowest figure since 1868.[3] This sharp decline reflects clearly the extreme depression which held the western world in its embrace in the middle nineties. During the 10-year period 1882-91, approximately 920,000 immigrants entered the country. As the population of the Dominion increased by only 508,429 in the decade 1881-91 it is apparent that the bulk of the new arrivals either failed to remain in the country or were offset by the exodus of Canadians to the United States.

Homestead entries tell much the same story. The 2,753 entries of 1881 jumped to 7,483 the following year, with 3,485 cancellations, a net gain of 3,998.[4] In 1883 the net result was even more favorable. Compared with the 6,063 homestead claims filed, there were but 1,818 cancellations. For 1884 the figures were 3,753 entries and 1,330 cancellations. The net entries for the 3 years 1882-84, therefore, were 10,666.[5] The years of large immigration were precisely the ones of more rapid occupation of the government lands. Between 1885 and 1896 inclusive the largest number of entries for a single year was in 1892 when 4,840 claims were filed. In that year Canadian Pacific and Dominion agents made a special effort to move farmers from the middle western states to Canada, which may explain in part the relatively large amount of land occupied under homestead. Thereafter entries declined until in 1896 there were but 1,857. For the years 1881-96 the total homestead entries were 56,520 with

[1] The Canada Year Book (1918), p. 30.
[2] Ibid.
[3] Ibid.
[4] Ibid. (1926), p. 923.
[5] Ibid.

16,326 cancellations, a net gain of 40,194.[1] While this 16-year total seems insignificant compared with the 30,000 net entries for the single year 1906, it is not unimportant when contrasted with the meager results of the decade which preceded.

Between 1881 and 1891 the population of Manitoba and the northwest territories increased from 118,706 to 251,473, a growth which accounted for more than one-fourth of the total gain in Dominion population in the same period.

In the period prior to 1896 settlers occupied the area in Manitoba tributary to the main line of the Canadian Pacific and pushed into the Qu'Appelle Valley in Assiniboia. Much government land in southern Manitoba served by branch lines was also taken up. In the late eighties a group of Mormons from Utah located in southern Alberta where they established the community of Cardston, developed irrigation sufficient for their needs, and formed a nucleus of further settlement in that part of the West. A ranching population, largely English and Scottish in origin, was attracted to Alberta by the call of the open range. Settlers from the British Isles found their way into the districts adjacent to Edmonton and Prince Albert, old Hudson's Bay Company posts. The completion of the Calgary and Edmonton line in the early nineties attracted substantial numbers of non-English immigrants to that area. Scandinavians settled at Wetaskiwin, Battle River, and Red Deer Lake. West of Edmonton, east of Leduc, and at Stony Plain Germans and Austrians located. The country around Egg Lake and Beaver Lake was occupied by Austrians and Russians. Icelanders were drawn to the region west of Innisfail and Red Deer. French and German settlers had gone into the grazing country around Leduc. The formation of these settlements pointed to the urgent need for the further construction of railway lines into the country north of the Canadian Pacific main line. Within the next decade such lines were to be built, partly by the Canadian Pacific, partly by other companies.

Throughout this period, as later, the Canadian Pacific, by virtue of its large land ownership in the West, exercised an important influence and fairly effective control over the trend of land values generally on the prairie, which tended to fluctuate as the railway

[1] Compiled from *The Canada Year Book* (1926), p. 923.

increased or reduced the price of its lands. While other land and railway companies in the main sold on less favorable terms than did the Canadian Pacific, they could not disregard the price system of the latter company. When in the late eighties, therefore, it made a sweeping reduction in its price scale, other organizations quickly followed its example. When the emergence of the West from periods of business recession into the optimism of better times found expression in an increase of speculative activity, it undoubtedly was the policy of the company to encourage the speculative spirit within reasonable bounds. It sold land for speculative purposes, but never in excessive amounts. By a careful watch over developments in the West, by reading aright the signs of the times, and by gauging its policies accordingly, the Canadian Pacific was a force making for conservatism in land affairs and for restraint upon unbridled speculation.

During the years 1881-96 the Canadian Pacific had formulated a land policy based originally upon the high purpose to sell its land only to actual settlers, at a flat price, with a generous rebate for cultivation of the land. The flat price it was forced to abandon because it was unsound and failed to take account of the elements of fertility and location in determining land values. The resolve to sell only to actual settlers proved wholly impracticable. It was an unrealistic approach to the problem of land sale. There were times when the financial necessities of the company dictated another course. On occasion the railway found that to sell land at all it must sell to speculators. After a thorough trial, the land department abandoned the rebate for cultivation in favor of preferential treatment for the actual settler, either in the form of a more extended period for payment or a price differential in his interest. Despite strenuous efforts to sell and settle its lands the company had achieved a very indifferent success in the face of very adverse conditions. It had gained valuable experience, however, and had perfected an organization which would enable it to deal with the increased demand for land which was soon to come.

V

ADVERTISING THE WEST

AS THE largest private owner of land in the West, the Canadian Pacific Syndicate assumed, with the Dominion Government, the leading rôle in the promotion of immigration to the prairies, and just as the land policy it first adopted showed the influence of American experience, so its early immigration work was based in part on the example of American railways. Although no less an authority than the *Free Press* deemed the success of the syndicate members in promoting settlement in Minnesota to be their chief qualification for building the Canadian Pacific, there is little evidence as to the particular views they entertained on the matter of recruiting settlers for the Canadian West. Their knowledge of American conditions, however, seems to have told them that for the moment no important movement of settlers from the United States could be expected. The middle western states were as yet immigrant-consuming rather than immigrant-producing areas. This fact, combined with the natural desire of a Canadian syndicate to people a British Dominion with British people, caused them to concentrate upon the British Isles and eastern Canada as the chief fields in which to seek the pioneers who were to build the West.

Little time was lost in launching an advertising campaign in Great Britain. By the autumn of 1881 an attractive publication, *The Great Prairie Provinces of Manitoba and the Northwest Territories*, had been issued there, setting forth in interesting form the advantages offered to settlers in the Canadian West.[1] A year later there was available in London for the prospective pioneer evidence more tangible than the written word. He could now behold with his own eyes magnificent displays of prairie products attractively arranged in the company's offices, together with sam-

[1] *Manitoba Daily Free Press*, October 24, 1881.

ples of soil taken at different depths and at various points in the territory through which the Canadian Pacific was building.[1]

By that time the immigration department of the company in Great Britain and Europe had been organized under the able and energetic direction of Alexander Begg, General Emigration Agent of the railway, and the form and direction which he gave to this work continued without material modification for several years. In May of 1884 Begg submitted to George Stephen, President of the Canadian Pacific, a report of the work of his office for the winter and spring of 1883-84, and the account which he gave constitutes not only the most complete statement of this activity but also our chief source of information in regard thereto.[2] Intended as it was for the perusal of the high officials of the company, and not for publication, it may be regarded as a faithful summary of the efforts which the railway was then making to arouse British and Continental interest in Canada.

Folder maps and pamphlets prepared in the London office had been published in English, German, French, Dutch, Danish, Finnish, Norwegian, Swedish, Welsh, and Gaelic, and were being distributed through thousands of agencies in Great Britain, and through over two hundred centers in northern Europe. The volume of this literature, advertising "free homes for all," amounted to over a million pieces within a period of six months. Through the London office the company advertised regularly in 167 journals in Great Britain and in 147 continental papers. While the office force answered the thousands of inquiries concerning Manitoba and the Northwest which this propaganda elicited, "travellers" carried the good word into the countryside. They canvassed the remote corners of England, Scotland, Wales, and the North of Ireland, displaying poster maps at hotels, railway stations, and other public places. The islands and highlands of Scotland had been the object of the special attention of a representative "thoroughly conversant with the Gaelic people and their ways." Work of the "travellers" was supplemented by special lecturers, equipped with a new device

[1] *Manitoba Daily Free Press*, December 21, 1882, quoting from an account contained in the *London Morning Advertiser*.

[2] *Report on the work of the Emigration Department of the Canadian Pacific Railway Company, in London, England during the winter and spring, 1883-1884.* This manuscript report is found in the archives of the railway in Montreal.

for the conduct of railway immigration propaganda, the lantern slide. When not used by the employees of the company the lanterns were freely loaned to independent lecturers desirous of advancing knowledge of the Dominion.

In the autumn of 1883 Begg inaugurated a plan for supplying the press of Great Britain and Ireland with the latest Canadian news. These items were carefully collected and compiled each week from the Canadian press and "from clippings received from the Montreal office," and distributed to about 500 leading journals, a large portion of which made regular use of the material. In London a complete record was kept of all publications pro and con with reference to Canada, which enabled Begg's staff "to meet and counteract misstatements." *Along the Line,* a monthly publication carrying the latest items of interest with reference to Canadian Pacific territory in the West, was supplied to the principal hotels and reading rooms and was widely distributed through the company's offices in Great Britain. The *Canadian Gazette,* specifically dedicated to the advancement of knowledge in regard to the Dominion, the railway officials scattered broadcast over the United Kingdom, with results which were very encouraging. Stands of produce from the Canadian Northwest were supplied to about 30 leading exhibitions and agricultural shows during the season 1883-84, while small samples of Canadian grain were actually placed in the hands of representative farmers in attendance at the fairs.

One device introduced by Begg to advertise the Canadian West anticipated a method employed by Clifford Sifton at a later time and for which Sifton has received the credit. With the waning of the initial enthusiasm engendered on the prairies by the assurance that the syndicate was prepared to go forward with the construction of the Canadian Pacific, there followed a reaction in which optimism as to the future of the West gave way to deep gloom. In the middle eighties slanderous statements about the Northwest were being published both in eastern Canada and in Great Britain. Crop failures, droughts, early frosts, in fact all the vagaries of weather and climate were widely featured, to the distress of those who were trying to people and develop the country. With a view to combating this insidious campaign, Alexander Begg prepared in 1885 two pamphlets bearing respectively the titles *Plain Facts* and *Practical*

Hints from Farmers in the Canadian Northwest.[1] They consisted
of answers to definite questions which had been put to some 250
settlers in that country, together with the names and addresses of
the farmers in full. The contents of these publications would seem
to indicate that Begg was seeking to convey an accurate impression
of the country to the public, and that, while refuting slanderous
statements, he was making no attempt to conceal or minimize the
difficulties which beset the pioneer. He was desirous of attracting
to the West those persons who were likely to make a success of
the venture, who would benefit themselves as well as the Canadian
Pacific Railway. For farming, an initial capital of £100 to £150 was
strongly recommended. As the *Morning Post* expressed it, "Mr.
Begg has made no attempt to deceive or mislead. He has given
accurate information from which intending emigrants can draw
their own conclusion. . . . All the answers of Mr. Begg's correspondents . . . are more or less favorable, although in one case we
are told of wheat sown on May 20th being frozen."

These publications were soon followed by another effort in the
same direction, but of a more elaborate and comprehensive character. With the coöperation of the Dominion postal authorities,
Canadian Pacific officials sent to every postmaster in the Northwest
a circular asking their aid in disseminating among the farmers of
the prairie a detailed set of questions concerning their experience
in the new land.[2] The replies to the questions, together with the
names and addresses of the settlers, were then collected and forwarded to Begg in London, who incorporated them in a new pamphlet under the title *What Settlers Say about Manitoba and the
Northwest Territory.*[3] The questions asked for hints to newcomers,
data on capital requirements, climate, summer frosts and storms,
soil, water, fuel, cattle raising, cost of preparing land, dates of
plowing, seeding and harvest, farm houses and fencing, first season's crop, growth of flax, mixed farming, price of provisions, sheep
raising, sport in the Northwest, success of settlers, and "how do
you spend your winters." The replies to these questions as set forth
in the new publication were in general of a satisfactory nature and

[1] *Manitoba Daily Free Press*, August 28, 1885, quoting London *Morning Post.*
[2] *Ibid.*, September 14, 1885.
[3] *Ibid.*, April 22, 1886.

were widely distributed throughout the British Isles. Believing that the farm women of the old country were desirous of seeing the West through feminine eyes, Begg promptly obtained and published testimonial letters from four hundred women living on prairie farms.[1]

In the opinion of Begg the testimony of settlers in the West offered the most efficacious means of promoting a desirable kind of immigration and he strongly urged that the company should maintain an official in the Northwest for the primary purpose of gathering such evidence. As he thought, "a regular supply of favorable letters sent over from settlers to me and judiciously and regularly published here and there throughout Great Britain would disarm the sting of unfavorable criticism and the complaints of grumblers. The latter in the face of the experience of successful and contented settlers would go for naught."

In the conduct of his work in Great Britain Begg had maintained an active correspondence with the St. Lawrence steamship companies, had supplied them with poster bills advertising the West, and had arranged with them for the distribution of Canadian Pacific publications bearing their advertisements. But while these relations with the steamship companies had been very beneficial, the Canadian Pacific was handicapped in its efforts to settle the Northwest by its inability to secure a satisfactory through rate to western Canada by way of New York. This was the more serious, of course, because of the obstruction of the St. Lawrence route during the winter season. Begg recommended, therefore, that while using the all-Canadian route in summer, the company should establish a practical working arrangement with the New York lines for other seasons of the year.

Immigration work of the Canadian Pacific in Continental Europe was carried on by H. H. Toe Laer, under the supervision of Begg's London office. During the winter of 1883-84, Toe Laer had visited 30 important immigration centers in the countries of northern Europe, appointed 196 corresponding agents throughout the continent, and answered 4,000 inquiries concerning Manitoba. This last form of activity was made the more significant as well as more onerous by the prohibition upon the circulation of emigration

[1] *Manitoba Daily Free Press*, February 4, 1886.

literature by agents in Norway and Sweden. Although Toe Laer spoke hopefully of the prospects on the Continent, he, too, felt handicapped by the lack of satisfactory inland rates from New York to the Canadian Northwest.

While in no sense unmindful of the difficulties and the keen competition to be encountered in the promotion of emigration to Canada, Begg was convinced that the work was now well organized, that the country was becoming favorably known in England and on the Continent, and that the tide was certain to run more strongly in the future. He observed that while the company had been working mainly in the interest of the Northwest, it had also rendered a valuable service to the entire Dominion. He believed the time was at hand when the railway should devote its efforts almost exclusively to the West, leaving to the government the larger Canadian field.

In the late eighties and nineties the work which Alexander Begg had organized was expanded and perfected under the direction of Archer Baker. Fortunately, Baker, in 1894, submitted to President Van Horne of the Canadian Pacific a comprehensive statement of the work as it was then carried on, and this report constitutes our chief source of information for that period as Begg's account does for the earlier years.[1]

The emigration propaganda was now carried on from handsome new headquarters in London, which, as the report stated,

. . . for advertising purposes . . . is on the finest site in London; taking all the pros and cons into consideration, less people would see it if positions were exchanged with the Bank of England, Mansion House or Royal Exchange. Ask any four persons in the country who have come up to London, say on an excursion ticket, whether they know the C. P. R. London office, and the chances are that three of them will either know the office by that name or as the Canadian Emigration Office near London Bridge. Southern Railway terminals, Tower Bridge, Tower of London, the Monument, Electric Railway, London Bridge, Billingsgate, St. Paul's Cathedral, all playing [sic] into our hands and tending [sic] to direct a stream of persons past our windows either on foot or in vehicle as it would be impossible to parallel anywhere else in the world. No government, corporation or individual interested

[1] Archer Baker, *Report on British and Continental Emigration to Canada, 1885 to 1894.* This manuscript report is in the archives of the company in Montreal.

in colonization occupies an office in a similarly commanding situation, owing partially to official ideas of respectability, to the great expense which would be involved, and partially to the fact that such positions are rarely obtainable at any price.

The large window space in these quarters, containing exhibits of grain and minerals, and photographs of Canadian scenes, varied from month to month, provided a never ceasing attraction to the throngs of passersby, estimated at three-quarters of a million per day. In the language of the report, it was a misnomer to refer to the London "Office"; it really was a shop whose windows were arranged for the attraction of would-be emigrants and in this respect it differed from "the Canadian Government offices in the different towns, which necessarily are located in comparatively unfrequented portions of the City." From morning until night a constant stream of enquirers demanded attention. Books singly and in packets were supplied when asked for, the ordinary distribution in this way and by post amounting to some 2,000 per day. Within the offices a commodious waiting room, equipped with oil paintings and photographs of Canadian scenes, together with files of Canadian newspapers, was so alluring that "it would be difficult to find a better known or more widely talked about Emigration Agency" in any part of the world. The company maintained a branch office in the West End of London, together with well-located quarters in Liverpool, Manchester, and Glasgow.

Correspondence necessarily engaged much of the attention of the London office. About 200 letters were received daily, many of them being merely preliminary enquiries. In order to deal with them satisfactorily and at the same time avoid the clerical work of writing a separate letter to each person, "five seductive standard letters were written and set up by our printers so as to resemble ordinary typewritten letters, leaving us to merely type in the name and address of our correspondent and the date." This work had been systematized to the point where it was impossible to give information about any one Canadian Pacific service without advertising all the others. Nothing was left to the imagination of the enquirer and no opportunity was offered to him to "cool off."

The friendly relations established by Alexander Begg with the 5,000 steamship agents in Great Britain had been maintained and strengthened by Archer Baker's regime. With a profound respect for the influence of these agents in the agricultural areas, it had been his policy to further their interest in, and knowledge of, Canada. He constantly supplied them with Canadian Pacific books, pamphlets, and show cards, on which the agent's advertisement was stamped at the railway's expense. They were regularly visited by the travelling agents of the company; many of them had been privileged to visit Canada, at the expense of the Canadian Pacific, with a view to attaining a first-hand acquaintance with the country. Baker believed that once the desire to emigrate was aroused in the individual, his destination was largely determined by the influence brought to bear upon him. It was important, therefore, that Canada should be well and favorably known to the steamship agents in order that they might be disposed to exert themselves in its behalf. In the London office careful record was kept of all persons booked by the agents for Canada, with a view to detecting and preventing subsequent diversion of emigrants to rival routes and countries.

The London office was equally careful to coöperate with philanthropic emigration agencies in Great Britain, such as the Children's 'Aid Society, the Society for the Promotion of Christian Knowledge, and the Self-help Emigration Society. Emigrants from these organizations had been directed to Canada with "great success."

A large collection of Canadian paintings and photographs was kept in constant circulation about the country through agents, mechanic's institutes, hotels, reading rooms, agricultural fairs, and other centers where they were viewed by the agricultural classes. Local agents traced their Canadian bookings in many cases to the "harvesting scenes" supplied by the London headquarters.

Special importance attached to the advertising conducted by means of photographs at the Imperial Institute, whose "Canadian section should rather more properly be called the Canadian Pacific Section." But the institute was used in other ways to promote the cause of emigration. Since many of those making enquiries at the Canadian Pacific headquarters in London were not willing to accept as "gospel" all that was said to them about Canada, it was convenient to be able to refer the skeptics to the Imperial Institute, where they could secure confirmation of the spoken word through the magnificent exhibits of Canadian products there maintained.

Another means of bringing Canada to the attention of the emigrating classes was through the lecture platform, which provided the principal excitement in the long winter evenings of the countryside. In this work professional lecturers were used to a certain extent, but in the main it was carried on by clergymen and other local notables who in many instances had visited Canada with the aid of Canadian Pacific generosity. So great was the interest in this type of work that numerous sets of lantern slides were kept in constant use throughout the winter season. At these meetings the distribution of pamphlets and other forms of literature made possible the reinforcement of the camera's impression by the printed word.

Convinced that the school child of today is the emigrant of tomorrow, Baker lost no opportunity to propagate the Canadian faith in the schools of the mother country. The Board Schools, some 5,000 in number, were so many centers for filling the youthful mind with information with respect to Canada. They were unceasing in their requests for descriptive literature, which was abundantly supplied by the Canadian Pacific organization. In many cases the better types of such literature were bound by the master and either awarded as prizes or used as "unseen readers," the term applied to unlicensed books.

Because of the belief that an initial interest in Canada could best be stimulated in other ways, it was not Baker's policy to advertise promiscuously in newspapers. Nevertheless, it was recognized that this was the only practicable means of reaching certain classes of people, and could not, therefore, be dispensed with. In the aggregate, the newspapers were extensively used, the advertisements being carefully varied to suit the needs of the class most likely to see them. The preferred papers, of course, were those read by the small farmers, the group from which emigrants were largely recruited.

The clergy were utilized in ways other than as lecturers. Mindful of their prestige among their flock, the company periodically mailed to them descriptive literature, accompanied by lithographed letters urging them to use their influence in the interest of Canada and announcing that similar publications would be sent to their parish-

ioners upon request. The effect of this was to make of every minister a more or less active propagandist in favor of the Dominion.
Not only did he use his good offices with his congregation but also
with his immediate family and relatives. In this way there was
maintained a fairly steady flow of clergymen's sons to the Canadian
Northwest.

Important as were the various advertising media thus far discussed, they all left something to be desired, so far as the appeal
to certain classes was concerned. Printed material descriptive of the
West could be obtained by all elements of the population without
difficulty. Thousands examined specimens and samples of Canadian
products at the London and provincial offices, at the leading exhibitions, and at the more important agricultural fairs. But there
were other thousands of potential emigrants in the more inacces-
sible portions of the country who were unable to travel to the
scene of these exhibits. The exhibits must, therefore, be carried to
them, and for this purpose the Canadian Pacific devised a method
which appears not to have been employed in Great Britain by any
emigration agency, public or private, up to that time.

This innovation in the art of propaganda was the Travelling Exhibition Van, which, figuratively speaking, carried Canada to the
most remote corners of the British Isles. The precise date of its
introduction is not clear, but in 1894 it had been in use for several
years and had become a familiar sight along the country roads of
England. In the words of Archer Baker:

. . . the system followed is to be present at the various towns on
market days, wherever possible. Handbills are sent on a few days
in advance to ministers, and for display in hotels and public
houses, announcing the day on which the Van will arrive. On arriving at a town or village a place on the market (if there be one)
is obtained. If there is no market the most prominent position
available is secured. The Van is opened out and publications are
distributed to applicants.

The Travelling Passenger Agent mixes with the crowd, which
very speedily gathers, answering questions and explaining the
samples. The pamphlets are accepted with the greatest avidity,
and, after the largest distribution, it would not be possible to find
a single copy mutilated or thrown away. They are undoubtedly
taken home to the country farm houses where literature of any
kind is by no means plentiful, and there preserved or lent about.

The valuable character of the Van's work is fully appreciated by the Local Agents, who are the best judges of what is likely to promote emigration in their own districts. Applications for a visit are far too numerous for speedy compliance; but those into whose neighborhood the Van has already been, have shown great activity in following it up, and taking the fullest advantage of its presence by distributing their own advertisements and identifying themselves with it. They very rightly anticipate a harvest of enquiries and bookings as a result of the visit. The newspapers regularly chronicle the movements of the Van and have spoken in the highest terms of the quality of the produce exhibited.

While the primary purpose of the van was to enable the rural folk to obtain a first-hand acquaintance with Canadian products, the capable attendants accompanying it served to clear up misconceptions as to climate. Sometimes returned "ne'er-do-wells" were encountered and had to be silenced, since such men would soon prejudice a whole countryside. During 1893 the van visited 513 different places, travelled 1,825 miles, and was inspected by 1,750,000 people.

So convinced was Baker of the efficacy of the van as an advertising medium that he urged the importance of placing additional ones in operation in Great Britain. Because the van must of necessity proceed slowly in order to permit adequate examination of its samples by the rural classes, only an increased number would make possible visits of the frequency which the situation required. The other prime need in connection with emigration work in the British Isles was an increased supply of literature, which Baker thought should be provided by the Dominion Government. Although the annual circulation of such material was well in excess of a million pieces, approximately double that amount was needed adequately to supply the five thousand steamship agents alone. Since the Canadian Pacific was bearing "well nigh the whole burden and heat of the day in this respect," it seemed reasonable that the added cost should be borne by the Ottawa authorities.

Emigration work on the Continent was carried on within limits imposed by restrictions of the various governments. In Germany, due to the prohibition upon advertising and other open forms of solicitation, activity was confined largely to the sending of publications by post to addresses coming into the possession of company officials. Friendly relations were cultivated with Hamburg steamship agents whose efforts in behalf of Canada were also circumscribed by law. Conditions in Scandinavia, however, were somewhat more favorable. In Göteborg, the Canadian Pacific office was situated within close proximity to the emigrants' lodging houses. The agent corresponded with, visited, and supplied publications to the various steamship agents, arranged for the publication of newspaper articles in the Christiana papers, and obtained addresses of relatives and friends of emigrants already booked by the different steamship agencies, with a view to forwarding literature to them by post. The various posting houses and tourist hotels, numbering some three hundred, were regularly provided with illustrated maps and books, as were the rural storekeepers in whose shops the farming classes gathered in the evenings. Special attention was given to the publication by the press of articles written by Scandinavians who had visited Canada through the facilities of the Canadian Pacific. Prospective emigrants were advised that upon application to the Göteborg office information relative to the West would be supplied by men who had actually farmed in Manitoba. In Holland, Canada was at a disadvantage by virtue of the paucity of agents representing the St. Lawrence lines. While Belgium was more adequately supplied with agents of these lines, little could be done there because the prosperity of the country militated against emigration.

Reference has been made to delegates of prospective settlers sent to Canada at the expense of the railway company to examine the West and to report their impressions to their friends and neighbors. The complement of this procedure was the use of "return men," natives of the old country who had emigrated to the West and become farmers. By reason of their longer experience with prairie conditions these men were supposed to speak more authentically of Canada than the "delegates" whose impressions were formed during hurried trips through the country. As early as 1891 the Canadian Pacific began the experiment with the "return men." In that winter seventeen settlers from the Northwest were sent by the company to London, where they placed themselves in the hands of Archer Baker to be used as his discretion might determine.[1] Much was expected from this departure, but the results seem to

[1] *Manitoba Evening Free Press and Sun,* January 30, 1891.

have been disappointing. Great discrimination was necessary in the selection of the men. Many were glad to offer themselves for service for no other reason than to obtain a holiday in the home land without cost to themselves, and a trip made in this spirit was likely to be barren of results. Nevertheless, the experiment was continued in England for four years before the company finally decided the accomplishments were not commensurate with the expense involved.[1]

Despite the abandonment of the practice in Great Britain, Archer Baker believed that "a judicious system of return men" promised satisfactory results on the Continent, where emigration propaganda was restricted by law to the less obtrusive forms. Under such conditions quiet, personal work by the "return men" in the communities from which they had emigrated would serve as an acceptable substitute for the more open advertising campaigns carried on in Great Britain. The peasant farmer of Europe was likely to be more receptive to the idea of emigration when presented in his own tongue by an old acquaintance with a first-hand knowledge of Canadian conditions.

The organization of immigration work and the methods by which it was conducted in Great Britain and on the Continent changed but little between 1894 and 1903. In the latter year, however, the company acquired added facilities for directing people of the Old World toward Canada. Traffic arrangements between the Canadian Pacific and the Atlantic steamship lines had never been entirely satisfactory. Both Begg and Archer Baker had felt their work was hampered by this fact. In 1902 President Shaughnessy announced that the Canadian Pacific had offered to establish steamship service from Liverpool to a St. Lawrence port in summer, and to Halifax during the winter months. Realizing the delays which would attend the negotiations with the British and Dominion Governments, however, he proceeded to feel out the existing Canadian steamship lines with a view to purchasing one of them. The result was that early in 1903 the company acquired the Elder Dempster fleet of fourteen vessels. The importance of this venture of the railway into the trans-Atlantic steamship service was cogently expressed by an official of rival interests: "This gives the Canadian Pacific the inside track

[1] *Manitoba Morning Free Press*, December 16, 1895.

over all other steamship companies and railways. This new arrangement will make Montreal a railway port, instead of a general port as at present."[1] For immigration activities of the company it had a special significance. From the beginning, land grant railways in America had depended largely upon the agents of steamship lines to recruit settlers in the various countries of Europe. The Canadian Pacific, however, became the first and only railway to possess the special facilities for immigration promotion which steamship lines alone could offer. From this time forward the interest of the Canadian Pacific in immigration was two-fold: it was interested as a railway engaged in the settlement of the West; it was interested as a steamship line drawing a profit from the immigrant traffic.

While cultivating the European field so diligently, the Canadian Pacific did not lose sight of the fact that there were those in the older provinces of the Dominion who could be transplanted to the prairie setting. Although the company came ultimately to feel that, as a transportation system extending from coast to coast, it was bad policy for it to move settlers from one part of the country to another, officials of the railway were restrained by no such feeling in the early days. When the problem was to create settlements in the West which would provide traffic and the rudiments of a settled society around which increasing numbers of farmers might gather, the place whence the settlers came was a matter of secondary importance. In the eighties and nineties eastern Canada undoubtedly supplied a major portion of those who settled in the West, and since the Dominion Government, the other agency chiefly interested in promoting western settlement, could not openly encourage the movement of people from Ontario or the maritime provinces to the prairie, this work devolved almost entirely upon the Canadian Pacific.

Until the completion of the line north of Lake Superior, however, even the railway company was handicapped in its efforts to move people from the eastern provinces to Manitoba. In the absence of an all-Canadian line it was necessary to detour the immigrants through Detroit and Chicago to St. Paul, whence they could be carried to Winnipeg. Unless the resolve to retain Canadian resi-

[1] Quoted in John Murray Gibbon, *Steel of Empire* (Indianapolis, 1935), p. 359.

dence and nationality was robustly developed in the settler, though, the chances were that he would never see the Canadian Northwest. The American railways, then actively engaged in promoting the settlement of their own territory, naturally subjected the Canadian farmer to persuasive arguments in favor of the northwestern states, and all too often he succumbed to their allurements. Nevertheless, the Canadian Pacific promptly began campaigning in the East and it is evident that some of those destined for the Winnipeg sector actually withstood all the blandishments of American interests.

Besides the ordinary forms of emigration propaganda in which the Canadian Pacific engaged in the eastern parts of Canada, certain new devices were employed to arouse interest in the West. By the middle eighties the railway exhibition car had established itself as an essential feature of the work. Equipped with samples of products gathered along the line between Calgary and Winnipeg, this car penetrated into all portions of the eastern provinces which had railway facilities.[1] The exterior of the car was sufficiently gaudy in appearance to attract the attention of the curious and lure them to the railway stations where it was on exhibition. Once within the car, the prospective settler found the exhibits, conveniently and tastefully arranged, impressive evidence of the possibilities of the new land.

"Return men" from the prairie were sent "down east" to "preach Manitoba" to the people. In order to lend dignity and impressiveness to this work, local government officials from the West frequently served in this capacity. The reeve of Shoal Lake, writing from Teeswater, reported the prospects for emigration from that quarter as excellent, while the reeve of Lansdowne, from his station at Pictou, in Nova Scotia, was less enthusiastic, because of bad crops in the Maritimes and the fear of Canadian Pacific monopoly in the Northwest.[2] Still another dignitary, working in the vicinity of St. Thomas, found the people of western Ontario grossly ignorant of the advantages of Manitoba but well informed by agents of American railways as to the unbelievable misery and suffering caused there by the winter's blizzards. While such men were not

[1] For reports of the travels of this car, see *Manitoba Daily Free Press*, January 10, 1886 and March 11, 1887.
[2] *Manitoba Daily Free Press*, January 23, 1888.

paid by the railway for this work, the company was, of course, glad to provide them with free transportation.

The most efficacious method of inducing emigration from the eastern provinces was one whose use in England and Continental Europe was virtually impossible. With the completion of the line north of Lake Superior, the home-seekers' or land-seekers' excursion quickly took its place as the surest means of educating eastern farmers to the attractions of the West. Conducted in the early spring and late summer of each year, these excursions were largely patronized from the first. While many doubtless availed themselves of the excursions merely as a means of seeing the country at low cost, or to visit friends or relatives already living in the West, large numbers of the excursionists were *bona fide* farmers who came to the Northwest in search of new opportunities.

The first of these to receive attention in the public press of Winnipeg was that of August, 1887, which was jointly organized by the Canadian Pacific and the Manitoba and Northwestern railways. Many of the excursionists were reported to be people of considerable means, some of whom were seeking locations for themselves, while others desired places for their sons.[1] The following August the tide was running more strongly. It was then necessary to run the excursion from Ontario in two sections and a total of 657 farmers were represented.[2] During the season of 1888 the Canadian Pacific carried into the Northwest by special colonist trains over 3,000 persons and more than 300 cars of settlers' effects.[3]

At first the company relied on newspaper and poster advertisements to recruit the necessary prospects for the excursions. When this was found to be inadequate, colonization agents were appointed to carry on intensive work among farmers in different localities in the older provinces. In addition to permanent employees of the railway engaged in this activity, the company was glad to avail itself of others for shorter periods of service.[4] One of the most successful merchants of Manitoba, with large interests in the southern part of the province, was commissioned to work the

[1] *Manitoba Daily Free Press*, August 23, 1887.
[2] *Ibid.*, August 11, 1888.
[3] *Ibid.*, February 22, 1889.
[4] *Ibid.*, January 26, 1889, March 1, 1889, February 13, 1890, February 28, 1890, April 2, 1890, for mention of work of different agents.

district north of Toronto, along the Toronto-Bruce division of the Canadian Pacific, the region in which he had lived as a youth.[1] The railway coöperated with the people of the Prince Albert and Batoche districts, not served by the Canadian Pacific, when they sent lecturers and delegates to Ontario to sing the praises of their localities.[2] Increasing interest in the West was reflected in enlarged patronage for the excursions. Soon as many as a thousand farmers went West on a single trip.[3] The home-seekers' excursion idea was carried to its logical conclusion when the company organized cheap excursions from the prairie to the eastern provinces and back.[4] As a result of the missionary work of the excursionists, a large number of desirable settlers, especially from Ontario, accompanied them on their return to the West.

Before many years had passed there was a labor shortage on the prairie at the harvest season. Here again the Canadian Pacific took the lead in the solution of the problem. Through the local station agents along the main and branch lines east of Moose Jaw, the Land Department ascertained the labor needs of each locality. As soon as this information was assembled in the Winnipeg office, the colonization agents in the East were instructed to obtain the desired number of harvest workers. When the agents had recruited the full quota of laborers, the company conducted harvesters' excursions on which the workers were carried to the West without charge. The first year these excursions were in vogue about 3,000 harvesters were taken to the wheat fields, 1,300 arriving in Winnipeg in a single day.[5]

The *Free Press*, whose earlier hostility to the Canadian Pacific had now been disarmed by the abrogation of the company's monopoly privileges in Manitoba, was inclined to chide the government for its failure to show something of the commendable alertness and enterprise of the railway. Referring to the harvesters' excursions it said: "The C. P. R. Company did a wise thing in its own interest in organizing those laborers' excursions for the harvesting

[1] *Ibid.*, February 13, 1890.
[2] *Ibid.*, May 9, 1890.
[3] *Ibid.*, April 2, 1890.
[4] *Sessional Papers* (No. 6), 1891, p. 87.
[5] *Manitoba Evening Free Press*, July 10, 1891, and *Manitoba Daily Free Press*, August 7, 1891.

of the Northwest crop. . . . If it pays the C. P. R. to carry laborers
into the Northwest free, to work in the harvest fields and perhaps
remain to have harvests of their own, it will also pay the nation—
the government—to send them in free." The generosity of the company was enlightened self-interest. It enjoyed the freight of the
grain which would have perished without the harvesters, and there
was the chance that many of the latter would become prairie
farmers.

Through the nineties the harvest excursions assumed an ever-
increasing importance as a means of advertising the West. Where
a thousand or two workers occasioned comment at first, by the end
of the decade the arrival of ten thousand harvesters from the East
caused no surprise, but elicited from the *Free Press* the observation
that "the visitors, a large number of whom are in the West not
merely for the purpose of making a few dollars in the harvest field,
but with the intention of inspecting the country with a view of
taking up homesteads are certainly seeing the country at its best.
. . . In the crowds are farmers from all parts of eastern Canada,
and in inducing such a large number of people to come West at
this time the C. P. R. . . . have secured an advertisement for the
West that is sure to be far reaching in its effects."[1]

It was in this same period that the company came to appreciate
the important rôle which the gentlemen of the press could play in
publicizing the West. Cordial relations with them were established
and maintained in every conceivable way. It was evident, though,
that however favorably disposed newspaper men might be toward
the Canadian Pacific territory, they could hardly be expected to
wax enthusiastic about it until they had seen it with their own
eyes. From the beginning it had been the policy of the company to
provide free transportation and other facilities for examining the
country to individual journalists and other writers who might
spread the good word. But this was not enough. Editors must be
taken to the prairie in groups and, since regional editorial associations were numerous, why should not editors' excursions be organized and conducted through the Northwest at the expense of the
Canadian Pacific Railway? By the middle nineties such jaunts were
recognized as one of the most practical ways of making known the

[1] *Manitoba Morning Free Press*, August 26, 1899.

attractions of the country. Editors as a class were not averse to travel, and after enjoying the hospitality of the company on a holiday trip, they could not well refuse to boost its territory.

The *Free Press* was greatly pleased and impressed by this phase of Canadian Pacific policy. Commenting upon the excursion of the Western Canada Press Association, it said:

> The Canadian Pacific Ry. Co. have apparently regarded themselves as controlling a national highway, and have thought it due to the country to cooperate with those various bodies to enable them to see what it is the West has to offer. For this ever ready willingness to bring into this country parties large and small, transportation free, whose members were in every respect in a position to benefit the country and to advertise it, the Company is entitled to credit, and as a great deal of this important work has been done within the past two years and some of it being done at the present moment when the Canadian Press Association are being taken over the C. P. R. western system, it is only right to acknowledge, as the Western Canada Press Association has done, the splendid service of the railway and the extreme courtesy and kindness of the Company. If the Company benefits in the future by the additional settlement which this advertising is calculated to induce, no one will regret it, and certainly the country benefits and benefits largely. It is satisfactory to know that the C. P. R. regards itself as liable to extend all reasonable facilities to visitors of the class mentioned, and in individual cases where the same results are to be obtained all possible facilities are given to hundreds of persons every year from all parts of the world. Where so much fault is found with the C. P. R., it is a pleasure to be able to endorse this part of their policy as national in its character.[1]

Because of the vast area of land available for settlement in the Middle West of the United States, little if any effort was made by the Canadian Pacific to induce emigration from those states for almost a decade after the syndicate assumed control. In the eastern states, however, the situation was different. Those states were still sending their children to the West and there was a chance that some of them might be turned in the direction of Manitoba. In New England, moreover, there were considerable numbers of French-speaking Canadians who, it was hoped, might be induced to repatriate themselves in western Canada. With a view to attract-

[1] *Manitoba Morning Free Press*, August 16, 1899.

ing these people, the railway exhibition car, with its samples of prairie produce, made extended trips through that section, some of them consuming more than three months' time. While this served to arouse an initial interest in the country, follow-up work was necessary in order to crystallize sentiment in favor of emigration. For this work French-speaking persons, some of them Catholic priests, were frequently used.

With the beginning of the nineties the company gave increasing attention to Michigan as a promising field for the recruiting of settlers. Prior to the coming of the railway the great waste north of the Great Lakes had prevented the normal expansion of Ontario to the west, thus forcing an exodus of Canadians into the neighboring states, especially into Michigan, which lay directly across the path of westward migration from Ontario. These expatriates now became the special object of the attention of immigration workers. Here, unlike in eastern Canada, the railway enjoyed the coöperation of the Dominion Government. Agents of the latter engaged actively in personal solicitation in the rural areas. While they found that many farmers were desirous of moving to the Northwest, few were willing to sacrifice their live stock to obtain the means necessary to cover the cost of transportation. Low excursion rates were required to meet this situation. When the matter was called to the attention of the Canadian Pacific officials a flat rate of $5.00 was established from the Soo to all points in the West.[1] The government agents thereupon advertised cheap excursions of which there were four within a period of two months, and which were liberally patronized.

An important adjunct in this work was the exhibition car or van, jointly operated by the Canadian Pacific and the government, which travelled the highways and country roads, much after the fashion of the van used in England by the railway company. The car was in charge of L. O. Armstrong, an effective speaker who represented the railway. Armstrong has supplied us with a description of the daily routine of this agency of western settlement:

We rise about 6:30 A.M., as we need a good amount of time to get the exhibition ready, to write the name of the hall and

[1] *Sessional Papers* (No. 13), 1893, p. 97. Report of work in Michigan by M. V. McInnes.

place where the car and lecture are to be on all the small bills, to look after the horses, etc. The car leaves for the next place, whenever possible, in the morning. . . . On the way an envelope, of which I enclose a sample, is thrown out at every door after some occupant has been brought to the window by the blowing of a horn. The team arrives at noon. After dinner the horses are saddled in turn, one goes in one direction, the other in the opposite, so that we have reached the farmers in the four cardinal directions. The result is a good attendance at the car and at the lecture. The car advertises the lecture and the lecture the car. . . . The lecture begins at 8 P.M. and lasts 1½ hours. At 10:30 we are packed up and about eleven we begin the sleep of the just.[1]

During this same period a special effort was made by the company to inaugurate a movement from the Dakotas to the West. In 1890 a government agent travelling in Dakota and Minnesota observed the widespread depression and dissatisfaction which there prevailed. Following a report of his observations to Canadian Pacific officials and to the Dominion Department of Agriculture, he was called to Ottawa for a conference with authorities of the Canadian Pacific and the Manitoba Northwestern railways. This resulted in the provision of free transportation for a group of delegates from Aberdeen, South Dakota, to the Canadian Northwest and also of a loan which would enable farmers leaving South Dakota to secure the release of their chattels.[2] A favorable report by the delegates, combined with free transportation, induced 24 heads of families to settle on the prairie.[3] Encouraged by this auspicious, if small, beginning, the railway redoubled its efforts the next year. The difficulty, however, seemed almost insurmountable. The impoverished condition of the Dakota farmers was not the only complication. Loan companies, banks, American railways, and the press of the northwestern states sought to prevent their emigration to Canada. To thwart the efforts of Canadian agents, Dakota newspapers launched a campaign of slander against Manitoba and the Northwest. They were pictured as "a sandy, sterile waste, where vegetable growth was impossible," and where snow and ice covered the ground for nine months of the year.[4] Spies were sent to the

[1] *Sessional Papers* (No. 13), 1895, p. 4.
[2] *Ibid.* (No. 6), 1891, pp. 169-70.
[3] *Ibid.*
[4] *Ibid.* (No. 7), 1892, pp. 195-99.

prairie "for the purpose of decrying it, and their statements were sworn to and their affidavits published in full." After consultation between government agents and Canadian Pacific officials, it was decided that the best means of combatting this propaganda was for the railway to provide free transportation to enable an increasing number of delegates from Dakota farming communities to visit western Canada and report back to their constituents. During the year 1891 about 150 delegates were thus able to inspect the country.[1] Their opinions in writing, over their own signatures, and printed on the reverse side of letter paper used by agents, were given widespread circulation throughout the Dakota country. This was supplemented by two columns of Canadian material appearing in every weekly edition of the *Aberdeen Star*, as well as by pamphlets, maps, etc., sent to every farmer in South Dakota. In May the first party of settlers, chiefly former Canadians with a minority of Germans, arrived in Winnipeg, thanks to free transportation arranged by the railway. This group settled some 40 miles west of Yorktown. In September they were followed by other contingents of one-time Canadians lured to Dakota years before by the "misrepresentations and false reports" of American railways, only to suffer from "exorbitant rates of interest, high taxes, drought, frost, hail, hot winds, cyclones, and bad government." The total number of arrivals during the year was estimated at 2,000.

Meanwhile the work was being pushed into other states. The government and the Canadian Pacific joined hands in the preparation of 5 articles on Canada for publication in more than 1,200 papers in the western states. They printed the testimony of delegates in pamphlet form for wider dissemination, and the Canadian Pacific offered free transportation to delegates from all parts of the United States.[2] The importance of this last provision as a means of acquainting the agricultural classes of the Middle West with the Canadian prairie is indicated by the increasing number of delegates sent by middle-western groups to examine and report upon the country. In 1892 a total of 182 such delegates were sent from North Dakota, of whom 156 located on either government or railway

[1] *Ibid.*
[2] *Ibid.*

land.[1] In the same year 42 of the 72 Nebraska delegates located on land in the West.[2] With the aid of more favorable economic conditions throughout the continent, this increased interest of American farmers in the prairie country might well have developed into a strong tide of emigration. The business situation, however, was to become worse rather than better. In 1893 the panic broke with its devastating avalanche of business failures, accompanied by falling prices for agricultural products. Thousands of farmers were plunged so deeply into the economic mire that all thought of emigration had to be abandoned. Even the announced readiness of the Canadian Pacific to provide free transportation, not merely for delegates, but for all settlers and their effects, availed nothing in the face of the business stagnation which enveloped the land.[3] The fulfillment of the promise of the early nineties was thus deferred to a later time.

Enough has been said to indicate the far-flung character of the Canadian Pacific organization and activities for acquainting the world with the opportunities awaiting the settler in the Northwest. In Great Britain, on the continent of Europe, in the eastern provinces of Canada, and in the United States every conceivable medium had been employed to focus attention on the West. Large sums of money had been expended in the cause of immigration but, in the main, the period which closed in 1896 was void of results at all commensurate with the effort and means employed. It was discouraging business, this settling of a frontier country. Many times the temptation to relax their efforts must have been strong among officials of the company. The railway, however, must stand or fall, prosper or decline with the settlement and development of its country, and there could be no turning back. And, insignificant as are the results of this period when compared with those which the railway and the Dominion achieved later, a substantial beginning had been made in peopling the country. Nor is it quite fair to contrast the great tide which poured into the prairie in the years after 1897 with the mere trickle of the depression years 1893-96 which immediately preceded. To appraise accurately and ade-

[1] *Sessional Papers* (No. 13), 1893, p. 144.
[2] *Ibid.*
[3] *Manitoba Morning Free Press*, March 3, 1895.

quately the achievements of the period 1881-96, they should be contrasted with what preceded rather than with that which followed. This tribute of the *Free Press* to the work of the company, though paid in 1889, is equally pertinent if the period be extended to 1896.

In addition to the sale and settlement of railway lands, it is the policy of the Company to assist in the settlement of government free grant lands, and large sums of money have been annually expended towards that object. Round trip explorers' tickets are sold at Winnipeg to those coming here in search of land, and if the holder purchases railway land or settles upon government land the cost of the ticket is refunded by the railway company. This enables the prospector to examine the land free of cost before making a selection.

The efforts of the C. P. R. in the matter of settling Manitoba and the North-West has been as great, and probably more methodical, than the government's. It has sent its agents into all parts of Western Europe, through the Eastern Provinces and also through the northern and western states of the neighboring Republic, and its immigration department has been the direct means of settling thousands of people on these northwestern plains. The Company has expended thousands of dollars in advertising the country and exhibiting its products, and is still carrying on the good work. Several colonies of Europeans have been established by the Company in different parts of the country, and nearly all of them are flourishing. Foreign immigrants regard it as an additional inducement to be able to settle among their fellow-countrymen, as they dislike settling among people who do not understand their language or customs, so the Company adopted the plan of forming colonies of the different nationalities, and now the Germans, Swedes, Icelanders, etc., may immediately upon their arrival, go among their own people to take up land. . . .[1]

Early Canadian Pacific policy with respect to colonies of the various nationalities was radically different from that of American land grant railways. The latter, while glad, of course, to have such colonies occupy government land within their territory, were especially eager to have them purchase and settle upon railway land. The establishment of such colonies on railway land constituted one of the outstanding features of the immigration work of railways in the United States. To be convinced of this one needs but to think

[1] *Manitoba Daily Free Press,* December 21, 1889.

of the Santa Fe's Mennonite colonies in Kansas, the Northern Pacific's English colony in Minnesota, or the Great Northern's Irish colonies within the same state. There is no evidence, however, that in this early period the Canadian Pacific made any effort to induce colony settlement on its own lands. Eager and ready it was to aid in the establishment of such groups, but on government homesteads. Where both railway and government sections were desired by the colonists in the interest of compactness of settlement, the railway company gladly relinquished its sections in return for units of equal area and value elsewhere. This policy resulted in part from the well established practice of the company to encourage settlement of government lands in advance of the sale of its own lands, and in part from the impecunious condition of the various colony groups settled on the prairie in this period. The Mennonites brought large sums of money with them to Kansas. The colonies in western Canada, on the contrary, were so poor that in most instances they required financial assistance even to settle on homesteads. Consequently there could be no thought of purchase of land from the railway.

Among the earliest of the foreign colonies were two settlements of Hungarians from the anthracite coal regions of Pennsylvania. In the spring of 1885 Canadian Pacific agents in the United States discovered a Hungarian nobleman, Count Paul O. Esterhazy, who had long desired to rescue his compatriots from the "hopeless life in the mining towns" of Pennsylvania.[1] Upon invitation from the company he visited Canada, made a tour of inspection of the country tributary to both the Canadian Pacific and the Manitoba and Northwestern Railway (now part of the Canadian Pacific system), and promptly became an enthusiastic advocate of Hungarian settlement on the prairie. Finding that the railway companies would exchange their sections for government land in adjoining townships, he requested the Dominion authorities to set aside reserves for his proposed colonies. His plan was to establish 100 families on the line of each of the railways.

The first of the colonies to materialize was that on the Manitoba and Northwestern line. A contingent of 38 families left Hazleton,

[1] Andrew A. Marchbin, "Early Emigration from Hungary to Canada," *Slavonic Review*, XIII, pp. 129-30.

Pennsylvania, on July 30, 1885, to be followed a month later by a group of 12 families. Upon arrival in Winnipeg the settlers were received by company officials and located on homesteads some 18 miles from Minnedosa. Christened "Hun's Valley," this settlement was fortunate in its location. The fertile soil, the good grazing land, and an abundance of timber provided an admirable setting for the colony, whose leader, G. Döry, made the most of the opportunity which awaited him. He not only understood the psychology of his heterogeneous flock, composed of Magyars, Slovaks, Ruthenians, Czechs, and South Slavs, but he possessed the knowledge of agriculture which enabled him to teach his people how to "break the land and level the forest." The third important element in the success of the colony was the helping hand of the Manitoba Northwestern Railway, whose officials established "a most liberal credit system, by the operation of which our settlers were promptly put in possession of the necessary farming cattle, and of all such requisites which are indispensable at the start of a new colony, so far removed from the centers of civilization. It is readily admitted that without the aid thus afforded the Hungarian settlement near Minnedosa could not have been accomplished in so short a time."

Later in the summer of 1885 a group of 95 families proceeded from Pennsylvania to Toronto, whence the Canadian Pacific provided free transportation to Winnipeg. Many in this party found employment for the winter with the Canadian Pacific construction crews, but with the understanding that in the spring they should be located on homesteads. This colony was established on the Canadian Pacific main line, near Whitewood in the Qu'Appelle Valley. It was named Esterhazy, in honor of the Count, and, allowing for the inevitable misfits to be found in such an undertaking, it experienced a steady and satisfactory development. An agent of the Dominion Government, inspecting the settlement in 1888, reported that it was "remarkably prosperous," that it produced the finest wheat in the entire countryside, and that its stock of cattle was being rapidly augmented. His one criticism was that in the beginning too much money had been put into "costly dwelling houses" costing $250, and not enough into cattle. As a result of the favorable reports of the settlers a group of 60 additional families were joining the colony. Another Dominion agent who visited the colony in

1891 found that in "all branches of agriculture the prospects, advantages and progress of this colony are simply marvellous" and that "their great industry and perseverance, together with a good location, have already placed them in comparative wealth in cattle, in crops, in household goods and farm implements."[1] The Hungarian pioneers had demonstrated beyond doubt the great possibilities of the Qu'Appelle Valley as a farming region. But the development of the colony was not to be measured solely in terms of material things. The settlement possessed two post offices, Esterhazy and Kaposvar, a common school and a Catholic school, an English church and a Roman Catholic church.

If the Hun's Valley settlement owed its success to the assistance of the Manitoba and Northwestern Railway, the Canadian Pacific's subvention had played a no less vital rôle in the launching of Esterhazy. Not merely did the company abide by Sir William Van Horne's promise of free transportation for all Hungarian immigrants from Toronto to Winnipeg, but through the kindly interposition of George Stephen, then president of the railway, financial assistance to the extent of $25,000 enabled the colonists to equip themselves with the cattle and implements necessary to begin farming operations.[2]

A third Hungarian colony was established through the combined aid of the Dominion Government and the Manitoba and Northwestern Railway. Beginning with but 17 families, it experienced a steady, if slow growth. By cultivation of the soil in summer and the cutting of firewood in winter, with which they supplied the neighboring town of Nepawa, they accumulated enough within a 6-year period to pay most of the loans extended to them by the railway company.[3] The chief deterrent to an extension of the cultivated area had been the wooded character of the uplands within the reservation set aside for them.[4]

The success of the Hungarian colonies inspired the Canadian

[1] Sessional Papers (No. 7), 1892, p. 200. Joint Report on Hungarian Colonies by G. Döry and R. S. Park.
[2] Sessional Papers (No. 12), 1887, pp. 237-38. Report of Count P. O. Esterhazy on Hungarian immigration and colonization.
[3] Sessional Papers (No. 7), 1892, p. 201. Joint Report on Hungarian Colonies by G. Döry and R. S. Park.
[4] Sessional Papers (No. 15a), 1889, pp. 6-7.

Pacific, the Allan Line, and the Dominion Department of Agriculture to send Theodore Zboray to Hungary in 1888 to recruit settlers for western Canada. Although Zboray's mission was rendered abortive by his arrest for conducting emigration propaganda, the glowing reports which the Esterhazy and Hun's Valley pioneers sent back to their native land, combined with the quiet, unobtrusive efforts of Count Esterhazy, largely achieved the same purpose. Western Canada was becoming well and favorably known to the various nationalities of the Austro-Hungarian Empire, whether domiciled at home or in the United States. The Hungarian colonies established in the West in the eighties were the precursors of the large Ruthenian immigration to the prairie which began in the nineties.

Another colony of homesteaders aided by the Manitoba and Northwestern was that of the Church Colonization Society in Townships 22 and 23, Ranges 32 and 33, west of the 1st principal meridian.[1] This settlement was regarded by a Dominion Government agent as one of the less successful experiments in prairie colonization. While some of the pioneers were appreciative of the assistance extended by both the society and the railway, and were doing their utmost to help themselves, others who had "done but little for themselves were outspoken fault-finders." Settlers who had received as much as $600 from the railway were still without a shelter for their stock. The close association of the church society and the railway company in this project is shown by the fact that A. F. Eden, Land Commissioner of the latter, served as agent of the church organization.[2]

Near Langenberg was the German colony of Hohenlohe, established by D. W. Riddle, who was in charge of German immigration work for the Manitoba and Northwestern.[3] Located immediately on the line of the railway, the settlers, with characteristic German energy, had within a few years made substantial progress along all lines of agricultural development. They were learning to cope with the rigors of the climate, and a government inspector could observe with satisfaction that but four of them had reported frost damage to their wheat. Enlargement of the colony through further immigra-

[1] *Ibid.*, p. 4.
[2] *Ibid.*
[3] *Ibid.*, p. 6, and *Sessional Papers* (No. 12) 1887, p. 75.

tion of Germans from the United States and Germany was expected. To encourage the development of a well-rounded community, the railway offered free lots in the town site to those who would open stores.

Even more rapid had been the development of the Icelandic colony at Thingvalla, on the line of the Manitoba and Northwestern. Of the 52 who had homesteaded within the settlement, only 8 had received loans from the railway.[1] The colonists had built unpretentious, but comfortable, log houses, and while they had done little in the way of grain farming, they had been surprisingly successful with cattle and sheep, for which the abundance of hay and water was well suited.

One of the most successful colonies established under the patronage of the Canadian Pacific was a Scandinavian settlement in Townships 18, 19, and 19a, Ranges 2 and 3, west of the 2nd principal meridian.[2] Begun with financial assistance extended by President George Stephen, the members of this group were considered by Dominion agents to be among the finest on the prairie. By 1888 the project was regarded as an assured success. Blessed with a congenial soil and with wood for building purposes, the pioneers had built comfortable log houses and brought a considerable area under cultivation. So favorable were their impressions of the country that they had induced a substantial number of their fellow Swedes from the old country to make plans to join them the following year.[3]

In December of 1889 the *Free Press* thought the work of foreign colonization then in progress in the Northwest of such significance that it published a long article on the subject under the title of "Land Companies."[4] Naturally the Canadian Pacific claimed the bulk of the attention, and the description of the company's work in promoting the formation of such settlements merits brief recapitulation. During the current year activity in Manitoba had been confined largely to the Icelandic settlements at Gimli and Greenboro, and to French colonists at Oak Lake, St. Alphonse, and Rat River. In the northwest territories, among other colonies aided

[1] *Sessional Papers* (No. 15a), 1889, p. 6.
[2] *Ibid.*
[3] *Ibid.*
[4] *Manitoba Daily Free Press,* December 21, 1889.

by the company, were New Stockholm, a Swedish settlement north of the Qu'Appelle River, near Whitewood Station, which then numbered 250 souls, and a Roumanian group at Balgonie which had received loans from the railway and now comprised some 250 persons. Rosenthal and Josephsburg, south of Dunmore, were German settlements. Although the 32 original homesteaders had been forced to borrow $3,000 from the Canadian Pacific, the settlers had prospered and increased to a total of 400 persons. Other colonies were Wapella, a center of Russian Jewish settlement; Fleming, another Swedish group; New Finland, the Finnish community north of Whitewood; a German colony north of Grenfell; and the Icelandic group at Medicine River north of Calgary, numbering 200 persons.[1] All of the colonies in the Northwest, on Canadian Pacific lines, were reported to have been assisted by the company, though some of them were not founded by it. Two years later all of these colonies were said by a Dominion agent to be in a flourishing state, except for the German groups south of Dunmore, which had failed because of adverse weather conditions encountered in the dry belt. The company, thereupon, financed the removal of these people to new locations in the Wolseley and Grenfell districts.[2]

In view of the close relations existing between the Canada Northwest Land Company and the Canadian Pacific, the immigration and colonization work of the former deserves a word in this connection. The executive head and spokesman of the organization in western Canada was W. B. Scarth, who had long been interested in settling Scottish people in the Dominion. At the same time, Lady Cathcart, in Scotland, was desirous of getting rid of the surplus population on her estates. In the course of propaganda carried on in Scotland by the land company, negotiations with Lady Cathcart were begun which resulted in a plan which attempted "to combine sound finance and genuine, clear-eyed philanthropy."[3] Some 50 families were brought over, met at Quebec by an agent of the land company, and accompanied to Moosomin, where another representative of the company had assembled cattle and implements, seed and provisions, which were then distributed among the settlers who

[1] Ibid.
[2] Sessional Papers (No. 6), 1891, pp. 88 and 101.
[3] Manitoba Daily Free Press, January 31, 1885.

were located on homesteads in that vicinity.[1] This assistance, of course, was not charity. The company secured itself by a lien on the homesteads, and hoped and prayed for the success of the enterprise. At the same time its interest in and concern for the undertaking was not that of the ordinary mortgage company. Its own large holdings of land in that district must remain unsold, pending the occupation of the government land. In assisting the Scots it was guided by the intelligent selfishness of the prudent business man.

This was merely the beginning of a Scottish migration to the West which was to grow with the passing of time. Within 2 years about 200 families representing 1,000 souls had been established in new homes.[2] Of these a considerable proportion were Crofters from the islands off the Scottish coast. Their former landlords advanced £50 per family and the Canada Northwest Land Company loaned an equal sum. Besides the original settlement at Moosomin, colonies were formed at Wapella, Burrows, and in the bluffs near Qu'Appelle.[3] To educate the colonists in the ways of prairie farming, so different from those of Scotland, the land company maintained in the various settlements inspectors who carefully supervised the work of the newcomers.

In addition to the colonies, of diverse nationality, established or aided directly by the Canadian Pacific and affiliated companies, there were numerous other group settlements in which the railway company played a contributory rôle of a less direct character. Typical of these were the French communities which owed their inception largely to the zeal and activity of the Reverend Father J. B. Morin. This cleric, with indefatigable energy, travelled the length and breadth of the United States, doing missionary work among his French-Canadian brethren, with a view to repatriating them in the Canadian West. The Edmonton area, due probably to fertility, combined with an abundance of wood and water, was chosen by him as the region in which to settle the *habitants*. By 1896 he had located in the colonies of Morinville, Saint Albert, Edmonton, Fort Saskatchewan, Beaumont, Rivière qui Barre, Saint Pierre, Vegreville, and Stony Plain a total of 483 families, of whom 327 had come from

1 *Ibid.*
2 *Ibid.*, October 6, 1887.
3 *Ibid.*

the United States.[1] While one might suppose that New England, with its large French-Canadian population, would have supplied the bulk of these repatriates, the greater portion of them seem to have come from the western and northwestern states. Kansas and Minnesota appear to have been particularly important sources of this migration.[2] That Father Morin would have been powerless to effect this important work without the assistance of the Canadian Pacific is indicated by his statement that "the C. P. R. Co. has shown kindness to me and my friends which I am glad to acknowledge. Free tickets for delegates, tickets in favour of numerous families, reduced tickets for needy colonists, advances of money, etc. I have always been fortunate in my requests for favours and for this I cordially thank the officers of the powerful company."[3] The coöperation of the railway in this work of Father Morin is the more significant since his colonies were far removed from the main line and would not contribute directly to its traffic. They were tributary, however, to the Calgary and Edmonton Railway, leased by the Canadian Pacific, and connecting with its main line at Calgary. The officials of the railway, therefore, were taking a broad and long-term view of the problem of western development, with the realization, of course, that the first essential was to start an important stream of migration to the West, of which all portions of the Northwest would ultimately receive their share.

When this formative period in the settlement of the Canadian West came to an end in 1896, numerous colonies dotted the prairie areas tributary to the Canadian Pacific. In the main these settlements were small as yet, but, nevertheless, they served as so many nuclei about which larger communities were in time to grow; and every group which survived the discouragements of the depressed nineties supplied proof of the country's potentialities. In fostering the founding and growth of these colonies the Canadian Pacific had played a leading rôle in the development of the West. But, notable as these settlements were in relation to the subsequent course of events, their existence could in no way remove the fact that fifteen years of constant effort by the Canadian Pacific had produced results which fell far short of the original expectations of company officials.

[1] *Sessional Papers* (No. 13), 1897, p. 57.
[2] *Ibid.*, 1895, pp. 82-83, and 1896, pp. 48-49.
[3] *Ibid.*, 1896, p. 49.

VI

THE LAND BOOM ON THE PRAIRIE

IN THE history of the settlement of the Canadian West the year 1896 will ever occupy a conspicuous place. It marked the termination of one era and the beginning of another. It brought to a close a long period of Conservative domination in the Dominion and it inaugurated a term of liberal ascendancy which was to last until 1911. It saw the country reach the depth of the depression of the nineties and emerge again on the threshold of a period of prosperity and expansion. It witnessed the transition from the day of hesitation and uncertainty with respect to prairie settlement to that of rapid occupation of the western domain. It was the date when the government itself began to assume an increasingly vigorous and aggressive attitude toward the problem of filling up the open spaces on the prairie. Without question the creation of a new society in the three prairie provinces was the outstanding feature of Canadian development in the years between 1896 and 1914.

It was in the years immediately following 1896 that certain basic conditions essential to the successful settlement of western Canada became favorable.[1] The first of these was a railway or, more specifically, a "favorable ratio between the price of wheat and the cost of transportation." Although the Canadian Pacific was completed in 1885, it was not until the late nineties that the advance in the price of wheat and the decline in the cost of transportation produced this favorable ratio. The second requirement was a variety of wheat adapted to the short growing season in the West, thereby obviating the recurring damage from frost which had brought sorrow and discouragement to the settlers in the eighties. By 1896 the planting

[1] W. A. Mackintosh, "Some Aspects of a Pioneer Economy," *Canadian Journal of Economics and Political Science*, November, 1936, p. 460. For a fuller discussion see A. S. Morton, *History of Prairie Settlement*.

of Red Fife wheat on the prairie was general. The third essential was the introduction of farming methods suitable to the prairie environment with its light rainfall. By the close of the century the dry farming technique, developed in the Great Plains area of the States, had crossed the border into Canada. "Just before the turn of the century a coincidence of these favorable circumstances" within the West set the stage for the scene which was to follow.

Fortunately these developments within Canada were contemporaneous with a world-wide economic expansion. Late in 1896 the depression which for several years had gripped the world began to lift. There came an upturn in the price of wheat. New discoveries of gold in South Africa and in the Klondike, combined with the cyanide process for extracting gold from low grade ores, brought a sharp increase in the world's gold supply. As prices advanced, business confidence was restored. The Spanish American War of 1898 produced a short boom in the neighboring republic, whose effects were quickly felt elsewhere. Large demands abroad for American agricultural products brought a marked improvement in the situation of the farmer in the middle western states.

Economic recovery and expansion, combined with rapid technological changes, resulted in far-reaching dislocations among the industrial and agricultural workers of Europe. Better transportation facilities gave to these classes a new mobility and western Canada beckoned to them. Although the United States continued to be the chief beneficiary of this exodus from Europe, the Dominion attracted increasing numbers of the land-hungry folk of the Old World.

But the movement was not merely one between hemispheres. Within the New World itself the migratory tendency was accentuated. People from the Maritime provinces and from Ontario poured into the West of Canada in increasing numbers. Emigration from the middle western states to Canada, hitherto a mere rivulet, broadened into a tide.

There were special reasons for this exodus of farmers from the Mississippi Valley states to the prairies of Canada. Due to the improved price of farm products, to increased settlement and development of the country, and to the fact that the choicest lands had been alienated and occupied, land values in those states steadily appreciated at the turn of the century. Over large sections of the country good farm land sold at $50 to $75 per acre, which rendered it increasingly difficult for young men to embark upon a farming career. The farmer found it hard to provide for his sons. The temptation was ever stronger, therefore, for him to sell this high-priced land and to try his fortunes elsewhere. The proceeds often sufficed to purchase land to serve the needs of both father and son, with a cash balance for buildings and necessary improvements. Thousands of American farmers were disposed to move. Their destination was uncertain. Marginal land was abundant farther west in the States. And there was western Canada about which the American farmer knew little, most of which was wrong. He was frankly skeptical of the country to the north, but he was not unwilling to be convinced of its merits. Here was an opportunity for the proper authorities to sell Canada to him: to educate him in regard to the advantages and opportunities which the prairie offered, and to disabuse him of the misconceptions which interested parties in the States had helped him form with respect to it.

With this happy conjunction of auspicious circumstances, within and without Canada, making possible the large-scale settlement of the prairie provinces after 1896, agencies conducting immigration propaganda could now hope for success where before they had largely failed. And there was no dearth of media for advertising to the world the opportunities of the Canadian West. Land companies, the Canadian Pacific Railway, and the Dominion Government were quick to seize the chance which awaited them. In eastern Canada the Canadian Pacific made known the possibilities of the West. In Great Britain and Continental Europe both the railway and the Dominion Government carried on the good work. In the United States, government and railway officials enjoyed the coöperation of a multitude of land companies which were then exploiting large tracts of fertile prairie land.

The advent of the Laurier Government to power in 1896 coincided so closely with the dawn of better times for the West that strong partisans of the Liberal Party have seen a causal relationship between the two events. Sharp contrasts have been drawn between the alleged lethargy and indifference of the Conservatives with respect to western settlement and the vigorous methods adopted by the Liberals. Yet the policy of the Conservatives was all that conditions of the time would warrant. Herculean efforts in the early nineties must, of necessity, have been unavailing. The Conservatives deserve no censure for their failure; the Liberals merit no special praise for their success. Candor compels the admission, however, that Laurier and his associates made the most of a good opportunity.

The policy of the Laurier Government for the development of the Canadian West was a dual one—a program of railway expansion and the energetic encouragement of immigration and settlement. While the Conservative Government in the eighties had sponsored the various colonization railways in the West and voted extensive land subsidies to them, the function of these lines was limited to opening up to settlement areas not reached by Canadian Pacific lines, and to serving as feeders for the latter. Although these small railways had interfered somewhat with the plan of the Canadian Pacific for branch line construction on the prairie, they had in no sense threatened the position of the older company as the one great artery of commerce between East and West in Canada. It remained, therefore, for the Laurier regime to promote the construction of two new trunk line railways across the Northwest with a view to providing the competition which the government believed was so much needed.

One of these new highways was the outgrowth of colonization railways. In 1889 the Dominion Parliament had chartered the Lake Manitoba Railway and Canal Company, granted it a land subsidy of 6,400 acres per mile, and authorized it to build from Portage la Prairie to Lakes Manitoba and Winnipegosis. Incorporated anew in 1892, its charter was acquired in 1895 by Mackenzie and Mann, the two most spectacular railway promoters that Canada has produced. Four years later they combined this road with the Winnipeg Great Northern, another of the colonization railways projected a decade earlier. In 1901 the Canadian Northern, as the new company was known, absorbed the Manitoba and Southeastern which had built from Winnipeg in a southeasterly direction toward the international boundary. Through these three sources the Canadian Northern found itself in possession of a land grant of substantial proportions.[1] By 1902 Mackenzie and Mann had acquired the former Manitoba lines of the Northern Pacific, and had built lines from Gladstone to Lake Manitoba, from Gladstone to Winnipeg, and from Winnipeg to Port Arthur.

William Mackenzie and Donald Mann were now fairly launched on their remarkable careers as railway builders. Natives of Ontario, they had progressed by way of the lumber camp to the dignity of railway contractors. Working individually, they had engaged in construction work for the Canadian Pacific and then in 1889 formed the partnership of Mackenzie and Mann. During several years of close association as railway contractors in various parts of the Dominion, they developed special aptitudes which supplemented each other admirably and fitted them for their subsequent careers in railway promotion. Mackenzie became skilled as a financier, Mann as a manipulator of politicians.

After 1902 they expanded their Canadian Northern Railway to the east and west. By 1911 they had extended it through the fertile valley of the North Saskatchewan to Edmonton, occupying essentially the route originally contemplated for the Canadian Pacific. They had also engaged extensively in the building of branch lines on the prairie. In that year, through the Dominion Government's guarantee of the bonds of the company, the construction of the Canadian Northern entered upon its final stage. The line was pushed east from Port Arthur to Montreal and west from Edmonton across the mountains to Vancouver. By means of money subsidies from the government, by the sale of bonds guaranteed by the government, and by issuing to themselves virtually all the common stock of the company, Mackenzie and Mann had achieved the construction and control of "ten thousand miles of railway without themselves investing a dollar."

Meanwhile another transcontinental was in the making through the expansion of the Grand Trunk Railway into the Canadian West. In pursuance of an agreement of 1903 the government built a line from Moncton, New Brunswick, to Winnipeg, which it leased for fifty years to the Grand Trunk Pacific, a subsidiary of the Grand Trunk Railway. The western section of this transcontinental, the

[1] For the history of the land subsidy of the Canadian Northern see J. B. Hedges, *The Federal Railway Land Subsidy Policy of Canada*, pp. 107-14.

Grand Trunk Pacific, was built by the company with Dominion guarantee of the bonds of the railway.

While this reckless building of competing lines of railway was in no way justified by the population and resources of the Dominion, it unquestionably served to foster the rapid settlement of the Northwest. Not only were the habitable portions of the prairie brought into touch with railway facilities, but the orgy of construction attracted laborers and immigrants in large numbers, many of whom subsequently exchanged the pick and shovel for the plow. Thus railway building was closely linked with immigration and prairie settlement.

The Laurier Cabinet was particularly fortunate in its Minister of the Interior, who then had charge of immigration as well as Dominion lands. A resident of the West, thoroughly conversant with its needs and the opportunities it offered, a capable organizer, and a vigorous and forthright personality, Clifford Sifton was well equipped to direct a campaign in behalf of the rapid settlement of the prairie with a class of enterprising farmers. While Sifton's ideas on the subject were not as original as his biographer would have us believe,[1] there can be no doubt that he employed the ideas and methods of others with an energy which was productive of significant results.

Sifton recognized that Canadians would naturally prefer to settle the West with British immigrants, but, in view of the limited number of agriculturists available in Great Britain, no great tide of immigration could be expected from that quarter. Nevertheless, an organization in the British Isles was created, agencies were established at strategic points, and successful western farmers, of English birth, were appointed as agents.[2] Other Englishmen, with prairie experience, returned to their native land to devote the winter season to missionary work in behalf of western Canada.

On the continent of Europe Sifton found the opportunities for effective immigration promotion distinctly limited. Germany was practically closed to such activity, while in the Scandinavian countries Canada was unable to compete with the United States.[3] Little

[1] John W. Dafoe, *Clifford Sifton in Relation to His Times* (Toronto, 1931).
[2] *Ibid.*, p. 138.
[3] *Ibid.*, pp. 141-42.

could be hoped for from Belgium and even less from France. As the European country with the largest proportion of farmers, Austria-Hungary seemed to offer the best field for the recruiting of settlers. It was the more clearly indicated by the fact that a substantial beginning had been made through the coming of Galicians or Ukrainians to Canada in the early nineties. Sifton now gave added encouragement to these people. The recruiting of them he turned over to the North Atlantic Trading Company, which received from the government $5.00 for each head of a family and $2.00 for each individual member. As a result of this aid the Galician immigration assumed large proportions and this element came to constitute one of the chief foreign groups in the entire West. While not the most intelligent farmers in the country, they were industrious and thrifty, and played an important part in the ultimate conquest of the prairie. Their essential honesty is shown by the fact that, to the great surprise of Sir William Van Horne, they reimbursed the Canadian Pacific for the free transportation with which it supplied early contingents of them from the port of debarkation to their destination in the West.[1]

Important as was immigration from Europe after 1896, it was undoubtedly the large movement from the United States to the Canadian West which attracted chief attention. If one were to believe his biographer, Sifton deserves the credit for originating the idea of cultivating the American field with a view to securing settlers. To use Mr. Dafoe's words, "From the very beginning Mr. Sifton had his eye on the United States as a field from which desirable settlers could be drawn. This was wholly original with him; it had not occurred to anybody else that from the United States, to which the landless of the world were trekking, immigrants for Canada could be obtained."[2] This clearly is an overstatement. As pointed out above, government agents, in conjunction with the Canadian Pacific, had worked earnestly in the early nineties to start an exodus of middle western farmers to the prairie, only to see their efforts largely nullified by the adverse economic conditions of that time. In the face of these conditions a more pretentious campaign could have been neither justified nor efficacious. In the United States Sifton

[1] *Manitoba Morning Free Press,* May 24, 1899.
[2] Dafoe, *op. cit.,* p. 140.

merely revived an earlier policy, with renewed vigor and on a more elaborate scale. Nor were his methods anticipated merely by Canadian agencies. American railways, American states, and American land companies had long been engaged in the work of land settlement, and few were the tricks of the trade which were not known to them. Sifton's rôle, therefore, was not that of a pioneer in the work, but rather that of the organizer who applied old methods in a large way at a favorable juncture.

At Sifton's suggestion, the Department of the Interior in 1897 established 9 state agencies in the United States, the number being gradually increased until at the outbreak of the World War there were 21 of these general agencies. In charge of these offices were salaried agents who appointed in their territory an array of sub-agents who worked on a commission basis. In this way the government propaganda in its various ramifications was spread into every part of the neighboring republic.

Government agents in the United States operated behind a barrage of newspaper advertising and general publicity. The first essential was to attract the attention of the prospective settler and to elicit an inquiry from him, which in turn would pave the way for personal solicitation by the agent. Extensive advertising in the press was begun immediately and by 1902 advertisements were appearing regularly in some 7,000 agricultural papers in the United States, with an aggregate circulation of more than 7,000,000. The advertisement occupied about 2 inches of space, at a cost of 4 cents per inch. The papers carried also small notices regarding crop conditions in western Canada, sent out by the Department of the Interior from time to time. Care was taken to revise the list of papers yearly with a view to eliminating those which had not been productive of results. Advertising in the press was indulged in only during the slack season on the farm, when the pressure of farm work relaxed sufficiently to admit of the luxury of reading. Careful thought and consideration were given to all advertisements, which were attractively worded and artfully displayed. From July to October inclusive advertising was omitted and inquiries declined almost to the vanishing point. With the renewal of the effort in the late autumn, however, the inquiries quickly increased until they reached a total of 1,000 or more per day at a given agency. From time to time this paid advertising was supplemented by the inclusion of long news stories which local editors accepted as a result of personal visits by government agents.

In a widespread advertising and publicity campaign the good will of the gentlemen of the "Fourth Estate" was, of course, of the greatest importance. To establish and cultivate friendly relations with the newspaper fraternity, the Department of the Interior appointed a press agent in the United States. It was the duty of this official to travel through the states, making the acquaintance of newspaper editors and arousing and stimulating their interest in the Canadian West. He soon discovered that rural editors, especially in the Middle West, were strongly addicted to organization into county, state, or even larger associations for a variety of purposes, including an annual holiday excursion. Taking advantage of this predilection on the part of the editors, Clifford Sifton and Sir William Van Horne, President of the Canadian Pacific, extended a joint invitation to the Minnesota editors to take a trip through the West in the summer of 1898 as the guests of the Dominion Government and the railway. The invitation was accepted and on the resulting jaunt every attention was given the visitors by the agents of the Department and the Canadian Pacific officials. The *Free Press* referred to the excursion as a "happy thought" and expressed the belief that splendid results were to follow.[1] Later in the summer a similar trip was taken by the Wisconsin editors, who formally expressed their gratitude and appreciation to the railway for the courtesies extended them.[2] Both groups of editors saw the West at its best, with bountiful crops, and they returned to their homes in a mood to do full justice to the country through the columns of their papers. Ventures of this sort were convincing proof of the partnership between Ottawa and the Canadian Pacific in the cause of advertising the attractions of the West.

So flattering were the accounts carried in the papers of many of the excursionists that the material was multigraphed and used extensively as immigration literature throughout the middle western states. Believing that the excursion experiment of 1898 had been a thoroughgoing success, Dominion and Canadian Pacific authorities

[1] *Manitoba Morning Free Press*, July 27, 1898.
[2] *Ibid.*, August 24, 1898.

sponsored for 1899 a trip by the National Editorial Association of
the United States.[1] The 600 members of this organization, representing over 1,000 papers, produced a profusion of editorials and
articles which made the Canadian prairie a household word
throughout the States. Henceforth the editorial excursion became
an accepted medium for advertising the West. It seemed to be particularly well adapted to use as a preliminary to the more intensive
form of immigration activity carried on through the personal solicitation of agents. A visit to the West by editors in a given state
afforded an excellent background for organized propaganda in that
area. Thus the excursion idea was extended from state to state, as
the immigration organization was expanded. As a preparation for
the establishment of a general agency in Pennsylvania, the editorial
association of that state, 175 strong, visited the prairie provinces in
1906.[2]

Once the interest of the press had been enlisted by means of the
editorial excursions, and the attention of the prospective settler
arrested through the newspaper advertising and publicity, there was
need for literature of the illustrated sort to convey to the individual
farmer a more definite idea of the prairie. Such material was supplied in vast quantities, both by mail in response to inquiries, and
in person by the agents and sub-agents who scoured the country in
search of settlers, and who visited fairs and other public places
where farmers congregated in large numbers. While applied psychology and super-salesmanship may have been less well developed
then than now, a casual examination of the titles of the booklets
which Dominion agents scattered with a lavish hand through the
farming regions of the United States indicates that the Canadian
press agents were no mere novices in their field.

The pamphlet which was published and republished year after
year, and was distributed most widely, bore the alluring title: *The
Last Best West*. What more effective appeal could have been made to
those Canadian farmers who, finding their pathway to their own
West blocked by the Laurentian barrier, had detoured south of the
Great Lakes into the American Middle West where they had
sojourned for a time? To the American farmer, with the spirit of the

[1] *Sessional Papers* (No. 13), 1900, Appendix No. 1, p. 178.
[2] *Ibid.* (No. 25), 1907, p. 79.

West in his blood, and with a century-old tradition of migration toward the Pacific, the words of this title must have suggested that the Canadian prairie was the natural extension of the American frontier. To the Scandinavian immigrant, who had homesteaded in a sod house in Dakota, there was the promise of a chance to repeat the performance on a new frontier. And to combine in one appeal the idea of the West with the implication that here was the last stand for all westward migration was to win attention for the pamphlet, quite regardless of its contents.

There were other pamphlets and circulars, not so widely distributed, but bearing on the same idea, and written for much the same group of people. *Home Building in Canada, The Wondrous West, Canada, Land of Opportunity, Prosperity Follows Settlement,* and *Evolution of the Prairie by the Plow* were typical titles. The annual circulation indicates roughly the measure of success achieved by each new pamphlet. Some titles reappeared from year to year, while others gave way, after one edition, to another effort along the same line.

These publications were, of course, couched in language of a general character. To substantiate the promise which they held out to the prospective settler, the Department of the Interior was at pains to provide him with information of a more precise and definite nature. Each year there appeared thousands of copies of the *Atlas of Canada,* published not only in English but in several foreign languages as well. This, as its title suggests, was designed to supply accurate information about Canada; to educate the public generally in regard to a country of which they were really appallingly ignorant. Another bit of informative literature was *One Thousand Facts about Canada.* Appearing originally in 1906, it was expanded in 1911 into *Five Thousand Facts about Canada. Canada in a Nutshell, The Country Called Canada,* and *Canadian West* were other pieces of the same character.

Factual and statistical information about Canada as a whole was supplemented by that dealing especially with the West or particular portions of the prairie region. Typical of these were *The Story of a Manitoba Farmer, Peace River Trail,* and *Canada, the Land of the Prairies.* As settlement of the West progressed attention was called to the opportunities for special types of farming in the prairie provinces. In the early years of the century a special effort was made to boom southern Alberta as a winter wheat growing region. The pamphlets *Winter Wheat and Alberta Red Winter Wheat* were notable contributions to this campaign.

It was natural that the aggressive manner in which the Dominion advertised itself in the republic to the south should call forth from the American press from time to time statements of a derogatory nature with respect to the Canadian West. To American attempts to minimize the net gain from American migration to Canada, the Department of the Interior replied with *The Truth about Canadian Immigration*. Slanderous reports with respect to the severity of the winter on the prairie were answered in the little booklet *Canadian Winter*, which appeared in 1914.

While the advertising and publicity thus given to western Canada served to focus the attention of the middle western farmer on the country, there was in the beginning a robust skepticism about, if not an active prejudice against, the prairie, which had to be counteracted before any substantial movement of settlers was possible. The best way to dispel doubts, of course, was to let the farmer see the country with his own eyes. With this in view, the Department of the Interior revived a practice which it and the Canadian Pacific had employed in the early nineties. At that time farmers in a given locality were asked to name representatives or "delegates" who visited the West as the guests of the government and the railway, and who reported their impressions to their friends and neighbors back home. Although this method had produced no large results when the depression of 1893 brought immigration activities in the States to a standstill, it had showed sufficient promise to warrant its use once more at the close of the decade.

Selected with a view to the widest possible distribution over the states of the Middle West, these delegates went annually to the West by the hundreds, reaching a maximum of 465 in 1902.[1] Not content with the delegate's oral report to his own community, the government generally had him record his impressions in writing, for publication in newspapers and in pamphlet form. This material, circulated widely throughout the States, was considered one of the most effective forms of propaganda in behalf of the West.

[1] *Sessional Papers* (No. 25), 1903, Part II, p. 111.

If the views of the delegates were important, that was no less true of the experiences of farmers already settled on the land in the West. In 1897 the Western Immigration Association communicated with some 5,000 farmers who had achieved a reasonable success on the prairie, sending to each a list of questions to answer. This effort elicited about 2,000 replies, giving information which served as the basis for the pamphlet, *A Few Facts*. The appearance of this publication, of which 30,000 copies were distributed the first year, was unusually timely, and contributed largely to the gathering momentum of the movement to the Northwest.[1]

The idea back of this questionnaire method was neither new nor original. Alexander Begg had used the same method in the British Isles for the Canadian Pacific in the eighties. The new refinement which the Department of the Interior gave to it was the use of the facsimile of the settler's letter in order to impart a more realistic touch to the procedure. Clifford Sifton wrote to Sir William Van Horne that "the idea was to impress the ordinary farmer with the sense of reality, in contrast with the usual advertising methods in which glowing statements are printed while there is no guarantee of their genuineness. The letters and statements are all *bona fide*; they have been selected from several thousand which were available. Care has been taken, moreover, to see that the statements which have been selected are fair samples, not too favorable."[2]

Work of the Dominion general agents in the United States naturally conformed to a standardized pattern, with variations occasioned either by conditions peculiar to a particular territory or by the personal views or predilections of the individual agent. The agent at Kansas City soon decided that personal solicitation was not productive of substantial results. As a substitute he held street meetings on Saturday nights in the towns and villages, where the farmers congregated to mingle business with pleasure on the festive occasion of the week. The purpose of such meetings was to effect an organization among the rural folk with a view to the distribution of literature and the dissemination of information with respect to western Canada. The agent succeeded in forming a large number of such associations, which became known as "County Free Land

[1] *Sessional Papers* (No. 13), 1898, p. 113.
[2] Dafoe, *op. cit.*, p. 139.

Clubs," the secretaries of which became for all practical purposes sub-agents in their communities.

The resourcefulness of this same agent made the opening of the Kiowa-Comanche Indian Reservation in Oklahoma to homestead entry the occasion for effective missionary work for Canada. The announcement that 14,000 homesteads were available naturally attracted the land hungry far in excess of the supply of land to be had. By establishing exhibitions of Canadian grain products at two points of concentration, the agent aroused such interest among the disappointed land-seekers that he was able to persuade many of them to try their fortunes in western Canada. In the main, however, the story of the activities of one of the general agents is the story of all, so that a consideration of their individual methods and policies is unnecessary.

The importance of the propaganda of the Dominion Government agents in giving stimulus and direction to the exodus of American farmers to the Northwestern provinces of Canada cannot be emphasized too strongly. No opportunity was overlooked in an effort to educate the rural folk of the middle western states with respect to the country to the north. Yet it is not too much to say that the campaign of the Ottawa authorities in the United States would have been largely unavailing without the complete coöperation of the Canadian Pacific in the work. That this coöperation was merely enlightened self-interest on the part of the railway in no way diminishes the significance or the vital necessity of its participation in the work which the Department of the Interior was carrying on. In a very real sense the railway and the government were in partnership in the promotion of settlement in the West; had the Canadian Pacific withdrawn from the partnership, the Dominion effort would have collapsed.

We have seen that the Department of the Interior and the Canadian Pacific had jointly served as sponsors and hosts of the various excursions made by American editors into the Northwest with a view to enlisting the interest and support of the press in the movement to the prairie. Seldom did a report of a Dominion agent in the United States fail to attest his indebtedness to the railway company for manifold forms of assistance. Thousands of delegates, representing American farming communities, were enabled to make

tours of inspection of the Canadian West through the free transportation which the railway always stood ready to grant to men on
such a mission; and admittedly these delegates were among the
most important means of influencing Americans to move. Once the
favorable report of a delegate had dispelled the doubts of his friends
and neighbors, there still remained for them-the difficult problem
of making a decision. Among the important factors entering into
this decision was that of cost of transportation to the new country.
At this point the Canadian Pacific stood ready to aid the farmer and
to facilitate the work of the immigration agent by granting extremely low rates for the moving of the settler, his family, and his
chattels. By an understanding between the government and the
railway company, dominion agents in the United States were empowered to issue to the *bona fide* settler "Canadian Land Seekers'
Certificates" which, when presented to station agents of the
Canadian Pacific, entitled the holder to travel at the rate of one
cent per mile. The annual reports of the government representatives
indicate that thousands of these certificates were issued annually to
the farmers of the Middle West. In fact, so generous were the
Dominion agents in the issuance of them that the Canadian Pacific
later charged the officials with granting them to men bent on pleasure jaunts to the West. But regardless of its susceptibility to abuse,
the certificate device proved to be an important means of fostering
the migration from the western states.

Railway coöperation assumed yet another form. From time to time
home-seekers' excursions were conducted with a view to enabling
people to visit the West in substantial numbers. Those availing
themselves of this opportunity were under no obligation to settle in
the country. Back of the excursion was the theory that, regardless
of the motive prompting people to make the trip, at least some of
the excursionists would settle permanently on the prairie. The
Dominion agent stationed at Detroit in 1897 reported that he had
organized special excursions to western Canada every month during
the summer and harvest season, "when the country is seen to the
best advantage." He added that "these excursions, which I advertize
liberally, proved very satisfactory, the greater number of them
returning to get ready to move their families next spring."[1] In 1902

[1] *Sessional Papers* (No. 13), 1898, p. 70.

four such excursions were run from Minneapolis and St. Paul over the Soo Line, a Canadian Pacific subsidiary.[1] The Dominion agent reported that most of the excursionists were *bona fide* settlers. The following year the same agent arranged for six excursions from the twin cities by way of the Soo Line.[2]

The campaign of the Dominion Government was just one of the influences directing the stream of population which was pouring from the middle western states into the Canadian Northwest. In the aggregate, perhaps, the land and colonization companies which were formed to exploit railway lands in the western provinces were quite as important a factor in prairie settlement. It was in 1901 and 1902 that the colonization companies made their appearance on the scene. The term, however, was not a new one in western Canada. In 1882 they had sprung as a noxious growth from the prairie soil. They were fired with the ambition to colonize both government and railway lands. Products of the brief boom, they were largely ephemeral and ineffective. They had come twenty years too soon. The West was not ready for them and the part they proposed to play. The new crop of colonization companies which came just after the turn of the century found conditions more favorable. The time was opportune for them.

But there was another and more fundamental difference between the new organizations and their earlier prototypes. The companies of 1882 were Canadian and English, and they aimed to settle the West with British people. The new companies were predominantly American, largely financed by American capital, and resolved to colonize the country with settlers from the United States. And, whether American or Canadian, they employed methods which have come to be regarded as characteristically American. Their technique of land selling had been worked out in the states of the Northwest, where many of them had sold and settled lands for American railways in the late nineteenth century. Many of them had sold land for the Northern Pacific and their methods differed widely from those previously employed by that and other railways. Where the latter had advertised, scattered literature liberally, sent agents to work among foreign groups, and entrusted the sale of the land to

---

[1] *Sessional Papers* (No. 25), 1903, p. 144.
[2] *Ibid.* (No. 25), 1904, p. 146.

the conventional small town real estate agent, in the hope that somehow a sale would follow, the new companies were much more systematic in their attack. They recognized that while the fertile, humid lands of the Mississippi Valley had largely sold themselves, the sub-humid and marginal lands on the plains could be sold only with pressure. They organized the territory in which they sought their buyers, divided it into districts, and filled them with agents and sub-agents. What was more important, the agents were active and aggressive. They energetically sought the buyer and, once they had contacted him, they spent money freely in an effort to "sell" him. They paid his travelling expenses, accompanied him to the land, explained in person its advantages, and allowed him scant opportunity to escape until he had been "sold." Extreme aggressiveness, high-pressure salesmanship, real estate-boosting methods, and a highly perfected organization were the distinguishing features of these companies. Their technique was poles removed from that which the Northern Pacific had employed in Minnesota and Dakota in the seventies. This technique they now brought across the 49th parallel into Canada. Its novelty to Canadian eyes is well attested by the comment of the land commissioner of the Canadian Pacific. "These companies," he said, "work on different lines altogether from any of the real estate agents here with whom we have hitherto done business. They go after their purchaser, pay railway fares, accompany them to the land, personally conduct them over it and stay with them, eat, sleep and drink with them if necessary until a sale is made or they fail in the attempt."[1] He might have added that they frequently built hotels or lodging houses for the accommodation of buyers and provided free livery service for examination of the land.

Because of their effectiveness, and because of the generous expenditure of money which their methods involved, the land commissioner of the Northern Pacific ordinarily sold land wholesale to the companies at a figure $2.00 below the retail price. If the railway thus made an initial sacrifice it was spared the expense of selling the land, and it secured the sale and settlement of areas which otherwise would have remained unsold for years. In the face of the

[1] F. T. Griffin to E. B. Osler, Vice-President, Canada Northwest Land Company, February 21, 1902.

growing scarcity of land in the states of the Northwest, these land men were now prepared to bring their capital, their organizations, their machinery, and their experience to bear on the Canadian situation. With new names for their companies, suggested by the Prairie scene, they appeared in large numbers late in 1901.

One of these companies at least was formed with the blessing of Clifford Sifton and the Laurier Government and was engaged in the colonization of Dominion as well as railway lands. Among the so-called colonization railways which were beneficiaries of the Canadian land subsidy policy was the Qu'Appelle, Long Lake and Saskatchewan Railway and Steamboat Company. Incorporated in 1883 and projected from Regina in the direction of Prince Albert and Battleford, this company by its construction earned a land subsidy of 1,625,344 acres, for the satisfaction of which the Department of the Interior at various times reserved approximately 4,500,000 acres.[1] The men associated with this railway entertained an exalted conception of lands "fit for settlement," and to a greater degree, probably, than other companies, were determined to drive a hard bargain with the government. In order to interest the banking house of Morton, Rose and Company in the projected railway, its promoters, the well-known firm of Osler, Hammond and Nanton, had assured the banking syndicate that the railway "would get a good selection of lands, and that the government would treat the Company very liberally in the matter."[2] According to the bankers, they had been assured that they would be allowed "to select only such lands as we might consider favorable, both as regards quality and location."[3] Having made such glowing promises to their London correspondents, Osler, Hammond, and Nanton were firm to the point of insistence in pressing their claims in regard to the land grant.

Up to 1893 the company had accepted only 377,000 acres out of almost 3,000,000 acres which had been then reserved for it. Deter-

[1] For legislation with respect to the grant, see *Statutes of Canada*, 46 Victoria, Cap. 26 (1883) and 48-49 Victoria, Cap. 60 (1885). For the various reservations of land by the Department of the Interior, see *O. C.* No. 234, February 4, 1891; *O. C.* No. 1635, June 10, 1892; and *O. C.* No. 1240, August 1, 1902.

[2] R. B. Osler to Edgar Dewdney, Minister of the Interior, April 1, 1890, File No. 65383-3.

[3] John R. Hall, Secretary, Department of the Interior, to A. M. Nanton, April 21, 1893, File No. 65383-4.

mined to protect its interests, it requested the reservation of additional areas in the fairest portions of the prairie, despite their remoteness from its line of railway. Inspection of the rejected lands by William Pearce, a government official who yielded to none in his knowledge of conditions in the Canadian West, indicated that more than 1,300,000 acres were "fairly fit for settlement."[1] When the Minister of the Interior refused to accede to the company's demands and stood steadfastly by Pearce's report, it seemed that litigation was inevitable. Before recourse to the courts had been taken, however, the Conservative defeat in the election of 1896 somewhat changed the situation. Despite the fact that E. B. Osler, the most persistent spokesman of the company, was a prominent Conservative who could have no particular influence with the Liberal Government at Ottawa, he renewed his efforts to arrive at a satisfactory agreement with the Department of the Interior. In 1900 Clifford Sifton offered more favorable terms which the railway promptly rejected before beginning litigation. While the decision of the legal issue was still pending, however, there appeared a group of American capitalists and speculators organized as the Saskatchewan Valley Land Company, who offered to purchase from the railway company the lands which the latter had rejected.

The members of this land company were men of wealth and large experience in land and colonization affairs. A. D. Davidson, of Minnesota, President of the company, and F. E. Kenaston, the head of the Minneapolis Threshing Machine Company, had been identified with a syndicate which had purchased 1,000,000 acres of land from the Northern Pacific.[2] Walter D. Douglas, of Cedar Rapids, Iowa, President of the Quaker Oats Company, and Robert Stewart, of Chicago, one of the largest stockholders of the latter organization, were also prominently connected with the land company, Douglas being vice-president. George F. Piper and E. C. Warner, of Minneapolis, together with G. C. Howe and A. D. McRae, of Duluth, were also among the important stockholders. A. J. Adamson of Rosthern and D. H. McDonald of Qu'Appelle were the only resident

[1] A. M. Burgess, Deputy Minister of the Interior, to T. M. Daly, Minister of the Interior, June 11, 1894.
[2] See the proposal signed by these men, dated April 12, 1902, File No. 695-671-1. Also *Manitoba Morning Free Press*, May 14, 1902.

Canadians interested in the project, but the other men named, Douglas and Piper excepted, were natives of Canada who had emigrated to the United States. The interest of those residing in the United States had been aroused through samples of grain forwarded by Adamson and McDonald, through information supplied by General Colonization Agent Speers, of the Dominion Government, and through the natural attraction which the splendid cereal crops of western Canada had for the Quaker Oats Company officials. Organized with a capital of $3,500,000, the Saskatchewan Valley Land Company purchased 839,000 acres of the land grant of the Qu'Appelle and Long Lake Company at $1.53 per acre, thereby giving evidence of its faith in a region whose reputation was so unsavory that it had been shunned and avoided by the settler.[1] But it was not merely the railway lands which had been neglected; the intervening government sections were equally in disfavor, until finally the desolate aspect of the tract had become a matter of concern to Ottawa.

On April 10, 1902, J. Obed Smith, the Dominion Commissioner of Immigration in Winnipeg, wrote to Clifford Sifton, the Minister of the Interior, calling attention to the urgent need for the prompt settlement of this area. Smith thought the land might be of interest to Americans, and since colonization agents from the United States were seeking tracts of land on which to locate farmers, some special inducement might be offered them. As he expressed it, ". . . the government would be justified in making almost any concession to colonization agents from the United States and elsewhere who would undertake to settle the free homestead lands within the said tract."[2]

It seems likely that the Saskatchewan Valley Land Company had been in communication with Smith, and his letter to Sifton appears to have been designed to pave the way for the proposition of the land company. This latter proposal bears the date of April 12, 1902, and on the 25th of the same month C. W. Speers, the General Colonization Agent of the government, submitted the company's offer to the Department of the Interior.[3] He thought that this neglected area, stretching along the line of the Qu'Appelle, Long Lake and

---

[1] *Debates of the House of Commons,* 1904, p. 7056, statement by Clifford Sifton, Minister of the Interior.

[2] File No. 695671-1.

[3] *Ibid.*

Saskatchewan Railway for a distance of 115 miles, discredited the whole country. Speers reported that he had interested some American capitalists and manufacturers of linseed oil, experienced in colonization work, who believed they could grow flax to advantage on the land, and who, according to Speers, were prepared to bring from 800 to 1,000 frugal German families into the district. But the land company desired to acquire a compact block of land, which was not possible through the mere purchase of the railway lands. It proposed, therefore, that it be allowed to purchase 250,000 acres of government land, which would give it a large area *en bloc*. Following some counter proposals by the government, an agreement was arrived at on April 30, 1902.

According to the contract entered into by the two parties, the government was to sell not more than 250,000 acres in even-numbered sections within the limits of the railway land grant, the price to be $1.00 per acre.[1] A deposit of $50,000 in scrip was made by the company to be applied on the last 50,000 acres earned by it. In return for the privilege of purchasing this area of land the company assumed certain obligations. Interspersed among the 839,000 acres of railway land which it had acquired was an equal area of government land in even-numbered sections, of which it was purchasing only 250,000 acres. The company must place 20 settlers on free homesteads in these sections retained by the government in each township, and 12 settlers per township in the even sections purchased from the government.[2] As a guarantee against undue delay by the company, the terms of the contract were to be completed within 5 years—two-fifths within 2 years and one-fifth each year thereafter. Thus, in its relations with the government the Saskatchewan Valley Land Company was not unlike the colonization companies of the early eighties. By colonizing homestead lands for the government, the company earned the right to purchase the remaining government lands within the railway subsidy limits.

The work of the company was carried on with the greatest vigor. No time was lost in the creation of a vast organization, especially in

[1] *O. C.*, May 24, 1902. File No. 695671-1.

[2] The O. C. authorizing the sale to the company did not take into account the fact that the company could not sell these twelve quarter-sections because they had not earned them. This was discovered later.

the United States, and in the summer of 1904 it had 2,200 agencies scattered over 10 different states.[1] It built two hotels within the colonization district, operated them without cost to the prospective settler, and supplied free livery service to enable people to inspect the land. During its first season the company spent nearly $40,000 for advertising and conducted an excursion of some 200 representative men from the middle western states into western Canada.[2] At the Minnesota State Fair in September, 1902, agents of the company distributed 30,000 copies of the *Minneapolis Journal*, containing a 2-page account of the advantages and opportunities which the Northwest offered to American farmers. A similar work was performed at the state fairs in Michigan and Illinois. In February, 1903, advertisements of the company were being carried in 24 newspapers in Iowa, 56 in North Dakota, 20 in South Dakota, 83 in Minnesota, 12 in Wisconsin, 15 in Nebraska, and 112 in Illinois. Many of these were full-page advertisements.[3]

In the face of this publicity the land which had previously been considered worthless, and on which there had been but one or two settlers, soon became highly desirable. Within a few months the company had sold 100,000 acres of the railway land to a German Catholic colony from Minnesota, and this same colony had taken up some 800 free homesteads beyond the limits of the tract covered by the agreement with the government. Before the expiration of the time specified in the contract, 1,682 settlers had been placed on the even-numbered sections, or 59 in excess of the number required by the government.[4]

The company sold at $8.00 to $12.00 retail the railway land for which it had paid $1.53 per acre, and the government land purchased at $1.00 per acre. At wholesale, in blocks of 10,000 acres, the land was priced at $5.50, subject to a discount of $2.50 an acre for cash. When sold on time, a down payment of $1.25 was required on the large blocks, while in the case of retail sales the company received one-fifth in cash and the balance in 5 annual installments at 6 per cent interest. In all cases the purchaser must pay a survey fee of

[1] *Manitoba Free Press*, July 22, 1904.
[2] A. D. Davidson, President, Saskatchewan Valley Land Company, to James Smart, Department of the Interior, February 21, 1903. File No. 695671-1.
[3] *Ibid.*
[4] *Ibid.*

148   BUILDING THE CANADIAN WEST

10 cents per acre. Commissions were paid to agents at the rate of $1.00 per acre retail, and 25 cents per acre wholesale.[1] The precise number of settlers brought to the lands, railway and government, it is probably impossible to determine. At the end of the first year's operations the president of the company expressed the belief that 3,000 heads of families would be a conservative estimate of the work of his organization.[2]

Naturally, such a spectacular venture in land settlement was not unattended by complaint and criticism. One of the charges frequently brought against the company was that its agents took unfair advantage of settlers by telling them that in order to secure free homesteads they must also buy land from the company. The latter steadfastly denied the accusation but admitted that real estate men engaged in retailing blocks of land purchased from the company were guilty of such methods.[3]

The Conservative opposition in the House of Commons found much to criticize in the agreement between the government and the Saskatchewan Valley Land Company. Notwithstanding the fact that a Conservative government had authorized the land grants to the colonization railways, had sponsored the plan for the sale of land to colonization companies in the eighties, and had accorded unusually favorable terms to these companies in the face of their failure, the Conservative leaders could find nothing in the Saskatchewan company of which they could approve. They charged not only that the government was giving credit to the company for those who had voluntarily settled in its territory, but also that a large portion of the entries reported by the company were fictitious, and made by persons having no intention of occupying the land.[4] The government, so the Opposition alleged, had made a very bad bargain. It had sold at $1.00 per acre land which the company was retailing at $5.00 to $10.00 per acre, and, what was worse, it had accepted payment largely in scrip instead of cash.[5] Nor had it escaped the attention of Conservatives that A. J. Adamson, prominently identified

[1] File No. 695671-2.
[2] Davidson to Keyes, Secretary, Department of the Interior, September 2, 1903, File No. 695671-2.
[3] *Ibid.*
[4] *Debates of the House of Commons*, 1904, p. 7036.
[5] *Ibid.*, pp. 7039-40.

with the land company, was a Liberal candidate for the House of Commons. One Opposition member questioned the propriety of this candidacy, forgetting that E. B. Osler had been a Conservative member of Parliament when more than one company with which he was identified had received largess from a Conservative government, and that among the Osler companies thus aided was the very one from which the Saskatchewan Valley Land Company had purchased its railway lands.

Upon Clifford Sifton, the Minister of the Interior, largely fell the burden of repelling the Conservative attack. Replying to the Opposition criticism of the low price paid for the land, he pointed out that the lands would have been homestead lands had they not been sold to the land company; that by virtue of their sale the government was just $250,000 ahead; and that payment in scrip was of no consequence in view of the obligation of the government ultimately to redeem the paper.[1] Continuing, Sifton contended that

> As to the general features of the transaction, the operations of the Saskatchewan Valley Land Company, resulting from the acquisition of this tract of land, have been of immense benefit to the Northwest. If we had given the land to it for nothing, we would have received benefits ten times over in return. This Company has been exceedingly efficient as a colonizing agent. It has placed a lot of valuable settlers not only on this tract but on the remainder of its tracts. I can recall no feature of our colonization policy in the Northwest which has been attended with greater success than the efforts of this Company. Every one familiar with the district will bear me out in what I say, that on this land which was tenantless for many years, we have a very large and thriving settlement which bids fair to grow not only in numbers, but in wealth. . . .

On another occasion Sifton said, "the coming of this company was the beginning of the great success of our immigration work in the West."[2]

While Liberal members of the House of Commons were engaged in the refutation of the charge of their opponents, the leading Liberal newspaper in the West could, with pardonable pride, draw an invidious comparison between the pathetic failure of the coloniza-

[1] *Debates of the House of Commons,* 1904, p. 7041.
[2] Dafoe, *op. cit.,* pp. 306-8.

tion companies twenty years before and the conspicuous success achieved by the Saskatchewan Valley Land Company. Although it is undoubtedly necessary to accept the enthusiastic appraisal by Clifford Sifton, as well as the company's own contention that it was the most important influence in starting the American invasion of the prairie, with some reservation, there can be no doubt that it played a significant part in directing the tide of settlement which was running so strongly at that time.

The success of the Saskatchewan Valley Land Company in its initial effort in the West made its leading spirits eager to exploit other lands in a similar manner. Under the name "Saskatchewan Valley and Manitoba Land Company" they began in 1903 the sale and settlement of the land grant of the Canadian Northern Railway. They were advertising for sale the "best wheat and flax lands in Western Canada" at from $5.25 to $7.25 per acre.[1] While the company announced that it had purchased the land subsidy of the railway, William Mackenzie, the President of the Canadian Northern, said the agreement "is not so much a sale as an arrangement to sell, to make sales. It is an aggressive system for colonization purposes. The idea is to place the land in the hands of actual settlers. The people mentioned in the dispatch handle land on a fixed basis but I suppose it would scarcely be considered a sale until sold."

Regardless of the basis on which the company handled Canadian Northern lands, there can be no doubt that it pushed the sale of them with all the vigor which had characterized its disposal of the lands of the Qu'Appelle and Long Lake Railway, and of the government. By the spring of 1904 it had secured control of over two hundred town sites along the Canadian Northern, involving an investment of $1,000,000.[2] In 1905 the company was running land-seekers' excursions regularly to the Carrot River and Big Quill Lake plains, and was advertising free homesteads in those areas.[3] Along with its redoubled efforts in Canada went a corresponding increase in activity in the United States, Scotland, and England, where additional agencies were established.[4]

[1] *Manitoba Free Press,* June 8, 1903.
[2] *Ibid.,* April 23, 1903.
[3] *Ibid.,* April 1, 1905 and July 15, 1905.
[4] *Ibid.,* April 23, 1904.

Although the home-seekers' excursions revealed a laudable interest of the company in the "dirt farmer" upon whom the prosperity of the West must so largely depend, one should not infer that it was averse to selling to the smaller land companies. The lands were disposed of in large and small tracts, to the settler and to the speculator. Some of these speculative purchasers, in turn, conducted their land business on a large scale and took their toll from the *bona fide* settler. Thus the Canadian Northern Prairie Land Company, for example, was in 1906 selling at $9.50 per acre land which had once belonged to the Canadian Northern land grant.[1]

Another important source of land which was being offered for sale was the land subsidy to the Manitoba and Northwestern Railway. This company, later absorbed by the Canadian Pacific, had constructed 235 miles of railway, which entitled it to 1,501,376 acres of land.[2] Early in its history the company adopted the practice of issuing land warrants good for 160 acres, to be located on the lands reserved for it. The province of Manitoba, individuals, and corporations who gave financial assistance to the railway accepted these land warrants as security. In this way the bulk of the land subsidy of the company was acquired by a mere handful of large holders. Seven parties held a total of 1,378,720 acres. The Manitoba and Northwestern Land Corporation had 295,360 acres, the Winnipeg Western Land Corporation, 426,400 acres, and the Manitoba Government, 542,560 acres.[3]

The rush of settlers to the West at the beginning of the century provided an admirable opportunity for the sale of this land. In 1901 the Manitoba Government disposed of 102,294 acres of Manitoba and Northwestern lands at an average price of $3.10 per acre.[4] As the tide of settlement increased in volume, the sales were correspondingly augmented. In 1902 the provincial government sold 202,776 acres at an average price of $4.00 per acre.[5] Some of this land

[1] *Debates of the House of Commons,* 1906, p. 3109.

[2] See Memo by A. M. Burgess, Deputy Minister of the Interior, to Clifford Sifton, February 27, 1897, File No. 377232. In this Burgess recounts the history of the land grant.

[3] Memo by R. E. Young to Mr. Rothwell, Department of the Interior, March 16, 1905, File No. 91700-8.

[4] *Manitoba Morning Free Press,* February 25, 1903.

[5] *Ibid.*

doubtless was sold in small tracts to actual settlers, but the bulk of it seems to have gone to speculative land companies. Among these organizations was the Eastern and Western Land Corporation, a Toronto concern, whose managing director was the Honorable George E. Foster, one-time Dominion Minister of Finance. With a capital of $1,000,000, this company secured an option on 125,000 acres of land in the Big Quill Plains district. It advertised not only the fact that the land had formed part of the land grant of the Manitoba and Northwestern Railway, subsequently acquired by the province of Manitoba, but also that it had been three times selected: first by the railway, then by the Manitoba Government, and finally by the land company itself.[1]

The ink on this advertisement was scarcely dry when the Eastern and Western Land Corporation sold the entire block of land to an American land company.[2] This company in turn had interested a large German Catholic colony near St. Cloud, Minnesota in the land. As thousands of homesteads were available in the alternate sections of government land, a large compact area could be formed for the location of the colony. By May, 1903 several hundred persons had already moved to their new home, the vanguard of a movement which was expected to aggregate not less than 10,000 souls.[3] Having realized a handsome profit from this transaction in an amazingly short time, the Eastern and Western Land Corporation promptly reorganized as the Ontario and Saskatchewan Land Corporation and laid its plans to repeat the performance elsewhere in the West.

Another company which invested heavily in Manitoba and Northwestern Railway lands held by the provincial government was the Manitoba Land and Investment Company. This corporation purchased about 200,000 acres north and west of Langenburg and Yorkton, which it in turn sold to a group of Minnesota speculators.[4] This group then recruited in the states of the Northwest the settlers who were finally to occupy and develop the land.[5] In cases such as this the land reached the farmer by a long and devious route, and then only after several different parties had taken their profit. The

[1] *Manitoba Morning Free Press*, January 7, 1903.
[2] *Ibid.*, April 11, 1903.
[3] *Ibid.*, May 14, 1903.
[4] *Ibid.*, March 8, 1902.
[5] *Ibid.*

margin of profit derived by the various hands through which the land passed varied greatly. One group might immediately dispose of its holdings *en bloc*, without appreciable expenditure of time and money, while those who sold to the actual settler must incur the expense of advertising and administering their domain.

The colonization companies thus far discussed were of the active, aggressive type. Buying land in large blocks, they either sold it quickly to other speculators or secured actual settlers who would purchase it in small tracts. There was, however, the other and more conservative type which conducted no campaign looking toward prompt settlement of the land and which was not greatly interested in early sale of its holdings. Such a company was quite content to advertise in the press. It trusted that the purchaser would come to it; it seldom actively sought the buyer. This passive policy had the distinct advantage of enabling the company to reap the benefit of enhanced prices resulting from the sale and settlement of adjacent lands.

An excellent example of this kind of organization is offered by the firm of Osler, Hammond and Nanton, one of the best known business houses in the Dominion. As bankers, brokers, and promoters they had had their hands in the launching of several of the colonization railways, including the Calgary and Edmonton, Manitoba and Northwestern, and the Qu'Appelle, Long Lake and Saskatchewan. Later they served as agents for the sale of the land which the railways earned. In 1903 the land department of Osler, Hammond and Nanton was offering for sale lands owned by the Winnipeg Western Land Corporation, the Ontario and Qu'Appelle Land Company, the Calgary and Edmonton Land Company, and the Qu'Appelle, Long Lake and Saskatchewan Land Company.[1] The lands of the Winnipeg Western Land Corporation had originally belonged to the Manitoba and Northwestern Land subsidy. Obviously none of these land companies represented by Osler, Hammond and Nanton was conducting an active campaign for the sale and colonization of its lands. Moreover, the relation of Osler and his associates to the Calgary and Edmonton Land Company was an anomalous one. They were connected with the railway company which received the land subsidy; they were associated with the

[1] *Ibid.*, March 30, 1903.

land company, organized to exploit the land subsidy of the railway; and they acted as agents for the sale of the holdings of the land company.

The lands offered by Osler, Hammond and Nanton were situated in the best districts on the Calgary and Edmonton Railway, and in the Yorkton, Beaver Hills, Qu'Appelle Valley, Prince Albert, and Carrot River districts. In 1904 they advertised a total of some 800,000 acres, of which 600,000, located in Alberta, formed a part of the Calgary and Edmonton subsidy. They administered these lands in a thoroughly conservative manner. They were in no haste to sell; and their policy was that of the land company, interested chiefly in the financial return, rather than that of a railway company, desirous of the traffic resulting from rapid sale and settlement of the land. Not only did they hold the land at a higher price than Canadian Pacific lands of the same quality, but they sold them on terms distinctly less liberal than those governing the sale of Canadian Pacific land to settlers.[1]

Of the various colonization railways receiving land subsidies from the Dominion, only the Alberta Railway and Irrigation Company pursued a vigorous policy for the sale and settlement of its lands. Not only was it a pioneer in irrigation development in southern Alberta, but it was largely instrumental in the location of Mormon settlements in that area. In 1903 it announced that it had 1,000,000 acres for sale. Of this area, 350,000 acres were classed as irrigable, and were for sale in small parcels of 160 acres at prices ranging from $10 up. The balance consisted of grazing lands available in blocks up to 50,000 acres at prices from $3.50 per acre.[2]

The land and colonization companies, no less than the Dominion Government, depended upon the hearty coöperation of the Canadian Pacific for the success of their work. Low rates and special rates were essential to both, and the railway never failed them. Thus, Osler, Hammond and Nanton were at pains to feature, in the large folders advertising their various landed properties, the announcement that settlers destined for Calgary and Edmonton or Qu'Appelle, Long Lake and Saskatchewan lands could obtain from the Canadian Pacific "all special rates, stop-over privileges, etc.,

[1] *Manitoba Free Press*, April 30, 1904.
[2] *Ibid.*, June 6, 1903.

granted by the C. P. R. Co. to intending settlers on their own lands."[1] Settlers coming from the United States were advised to apply to the nearest Canadian Pacific agent for a Canadian land settlement certificate, which enabled the holder to travel at the special immigrant rates over Canadian Pacific lines to any point in the West.

That the propaganda of these land companies in the United States served in a significant degree to supplement the efforts of the Dominion Government and the Canadian Pacific to promote prairie settlement is hardly open to question. As indicated by the discussion above, many of the companies not only sought buyers for their land, but they organized homestead settlement on a large scale. The throngs of Americans who milled about the streets and hotels of Winnipeg in the early years of the century included, along with the homesteader, countless men of capital, seeking from the large companies land for settlement or speculation. This aspect of the American invasions of the West was well illustrated by the *Free Press* when it observed that

> . . . numbers of strangers may be seen around the city hotels at present wearing broad-brimmed, grey felt hats, fierce mustaches and goatees, strange cuts of chin whiskers and other characteristics which stamp them as denizens of the neighboring republic. These are land buyers and speculators and delegates from intending colonists from the states of the Union. They hail from the Dakotas, Minnesota, Iowa, Ohio, Missouri and other sovereign states and are forerunners of what will probably be a big movement of emigration from those places. These land buyers, it is said, will purchase large quantities of the provincial lands and will hold them for sale to the people whom they will induce to come up here from the South. The land is not being purchased in homesteads, but *en bloc*, and the buyers and delegates have already been out looking over the lands which they propose to buy. They have also had one or two conferences with local cabinet ministers on the matter and are being taken over the country by government agents. The colonization behind this scheme is said to be a large and important one.[2]

It was in the midst of this atmosphere of feverish activity in the selling of land that the Canadian Pacific was called upon to formu-

[1] See Osler, Hammond and Nanton folders in File No. 5240, Department of National Resources, Calgary. Hereafter referred to as D. N. R.

[2] *Manitoba Morning Free Press*, April 19, 1901.

late its policy with respect to its own lands. As the largest private owner of land in the Dominion, the railway obviously could not be indifferent either to the general state of land settlement in the West or to the measures adopted by other large landowners in the sale of their land. To a degree, therefore, Canadian Pacific procedure was determined by the conditions prevailing around it. Yet, by virtue of its immense landed estate, the railway contributed significantly to the determination of those very conditions. Canadian Pacific policy influenced, and was influenced by, the larger prairie setting.

Late in 1896 the land department of the railway adopted a measure designed to ease the burden of the purchaser and thereby facilitate the settlement of the land. *Bona fide* settlers were to be allowed two years in which to make the first payment on the land.[1] As the *Free Press* remarked, the immigrant ordinarily found it sufficiently difficult to survive the first two or three seasons without the added strain of meeting the installments on his purchase. The new regulations of the railway, therefore, were calculated to relieve the pressure during that difficult and trying period.

It is not easy to determine the precise effects, if any, which this provision had upon the land sales of the company. If one were to restrict sufficiently his angle of vision, he might readily conclude that the result had been almost immediately beneficial. Sales of company land for the year showed a sharp increase over those for 1895, and, what is more significant, the gain occurred in the last two months of the year, after the new policy had gone into effect. In that 60-day period sales were over 300 per cent in excess of those for the corresponding period of the previous year.[2]

Doubtless the new regulations were not without their influence in producing this sharp increase in sales. It is probable, however, that the more optimistic tone resulting from the steady advance in the price of wheat in the autumn of 1896 was mainly responsible for the improved showing. It is well known that news of the failure of the Indian wheat crop in August of that year arrested the further decline in the price of the product and started a persistent appreciation through the remainder of the year. The last week in August wheat sold in Chicago at 53 cents per bushel; by the first week in November

[1] *Manitoba Morning Free Press,* October 27, 1896.
[2] *Ibid.,* January 1, 1897.

it had risen to 90 cents. Alexander Dana Noyes has long since appraised the effect of this advance on the outcome of the election of 1896 in the United States. It was the matured judgment of Land Commissioner Hamilton that the rise in the wheat market explained the increased demand for the company's lands.[1]

In 1896 the land department of the Canadian Pacific took over the administration of the lands of the Canada Northwest Land Company. Partly because of the increased vigor with which the railway pushed the advertising and sale of these lands, partly because of the excellent location and selected character of them, and partly because of the upturn in the price of wheat, sales of the land company's holdings for the year showed an increase of more than 400 per cent over the previous year. While for statistical purposes the sale of this land was not credited to the Canadian Pacific, every acre thus disposed of was of direct benefit to the railway and to its officials, who now controlled the destinies of the land company. Because of the close proximity of this land to the main line of the railway, its early settlement was of prime importance to the Canadian Pacific. Its sale by the land department of the company constituted an integral part of the colonization campaign which the railway was then waging.

The improved conditions, so clearly indicated by the increased sales of company lands during the closing months of 1896, continued throughout the following year. The area disposed of exceeded that of the preceding year by about 140 per cent. In this improved showing the speculative element had for the moment been reduced to a minimum. The land had been bought by 1,261 different purchasers who had taken an average of 158 acres each, a modest area for the prairie and plains region.[2] Of the total number of buyers, 239 came from Great Britain; 74 from other parts of Europe; 95 from the United States; and 844 from Canada.[3] The preponderance of Canadians undoubtedly reflects not only the results of Canadian Pacific efforts to move people from the eastern provinces to the West, but also the tendency of resident farmers on the prairie to increase their holdings by the purchase of an adjoining area of

[1] *Manitoba Morning Free Press,* January 1, 1897.
[2] *Ibid.,* January 1, 1898.
[3] *Ibid.*

railway land. The attractive lands of the Canada Northwest Land Company were also in demand as shown by the fact that the area disposed of was almost double that of the previous year.[1]

This same satisfactory state of affairs continued through the next 2 years. In 1898 the total number of sales aggregated 1,506, with small parcels again predominating. The land-selling season of 1900 opened auspiciously. As the *Free Press* stated, "the very good harvest of the last year, the excellent prices paid for cereals and produce, the active agents in foreign countries, and the untiring advertising of the C. P. R., coupled with the faithful accounts sent by Westerners to friends in other parts" were all having their effect.[2] Even more significant was the increased proportion of sales to settlers from the United States. For these people the Soo Line, a subsidiary of the Canadian Pacific, entering the Dominion at Portal and making connection with the parent company at Moose Jaw, offered a convenient highway into the new homeland. They purchased and settled extensively in the North Portal and Weyburn districts, where they formed the advance guard of the greater influx which was to follow from the states of the Northwest. At the same time settlers from various quarters of the world were buying the lands of the Canada Northwest Land Company in the Moose Mountain, Regina, and Moose Jaw country.

In the spring of 1901 Winnipeg was fairly swarming with land buyers from the United States, and by the autumn of the same year the Canadian Pacific had definitely embarked upon a policy of selling land in substantial tracts to them. In May of that year the press reported the presence in Winnipeg of 60 delegates from Dakota, Iowa, and Minnesota. These men contemplated making large purchases from the Canadian Pacific with a view to inducing farmers from their neighborhoods to emigrate to the prairie.[3] By October the rush of American buyers had assumed unprecedented proportions. Within a single day 20,000 acres of Canadian Pacific land was purchased by them.[4] During the first 18 days of the month, speculators from Iowa, North Dakota, and Missouri purchased 130

[1] *Manitoba Morning Free Press*, January 1, 1898.
[2] *Ibid.*, April 7, 1900.
[3] *Ibid.*, May 10, 1901.
[4] *Ibid.*, November 2, 1901.

sections, aggregating 83,000 acres. These lands were located in the vicinity of Milestone, Raeburn, Drinkwater, and Yellow Grass, as well as in the region south of Regina.[1] For the month of October the total sales amounted to 150,000 acres at an average price of about $3.00 per acre. While much of this area was obviously bought by actual settlers, the greater portion went to American speculators who planned to retail it to settlers.

As a result of the very active demand for land throughout the season of 1901, the land department decided upon an increase in prices for the following year. Manitoba lands, together with those in Assiniboia east of the 3rd meridian, were priced at $3.00 to $6.00 per acre, while those west of the meridian, except where special conditions dictated otherwise, were offered at $3.00 per acre.[2] Despite increased sales to speculators, the company still indicated its desire for prompt settlement of the land by distinguishing between the settler and the speculator. The latter was required to pay for his land within 6 years, while the former was allowed 10.

Between January 1, 1897, and June 30, 1901, the Canadian Pacific made net sales of 1,123,524 acres from its main line grant and 367,011 from the Manitoba Southwestern, a total of 1,490,535 acres.[3] As speculation did not run riot until the autumn of 1901, this large area represented chiefly sales to actual settlers, new and old, who were encouraged to buy because of the marked improvement in the business situation in those years.

The speculators who bought so eagerly from the railway during the latter part of 1901 were almost wholly of the smaller variety, who purchased from 1 to 10 sections. Fourteen Dakota buyers bought 70,000 acres, an average of 5,000 acres per person.[4] Not until the very end of the year did the large colonization companies come forward with their proposals to purchase large blocks of land. Recalling with some bitterness their experience with the companies of 1882, Land Commissioner Griffin, William Whyte, ranking official of the Canadian Pacific in the West, and Sir Thomas Shaughnessy, who had recently succeeded Sir William Van Horne as president,

[1] *Manitoba Morning Free Press*, October 19, 1901.

[2] *Ibid.*, January 22, 1902.

[3] Figures compiled from the Annual Reports of the Canadian Pacific for those years.

[4] *Manitoba Morning Free Press*, October 19, 1901.

were skeptical with respect to the advances of the American land men. The ultimate decision to sell to them was the result of several important considerations.

First of all, it was apparent that if the Canadian Pacific refused to deal with them, the American colonization companies would obtain large areas elsewhere in the West, which they would sell to American settlers recruited by their organizations in the States. This would divert settlement from the company's lands and retard their sale. The alternative was to build up in the States a Canadian Pacific organization, which would be both costly and time-consuming. Although the railway had advertised extensively south of the boundary, it had never established there land-selling machinery of the elaborate nature possessed by the colonization companies. A further factor of importance was the pending decision with respect to the proposed irrigation block in southern Alberta. If the company were to undertake to develop and colonize that district, it would need promptly to relieve itself of the large area in southern Manitoba and Assiniboia.[1] Probably the most important consideration was the uncertainty of the land department of the company with respect to the saleability of some of this land, combined with the calm assurance of the colonization companies that they could sell and settle it. Although well served by branch lines of railway and situated in one of the older districts of the West, settlement had made little headway in portions of this tract. In places not even the government sections had been taken up. Settlers obviously had their doubts with regard to this land. But American colonization companies, accustomed to risk-taking and experienced in the sale, by high-pressure methods, of the marginal lands of the northwestern states, had no such fears. Their confidence led Land Commissioner Griffin to remark with regard to the proposed sale of a large tract of doubtful value to one of the American syndicates: "If the results are anything like [the colonization company] hopes for—the immediate effect will be to increase the price of all our Canadian Pacific lands in Southeastern Assiniboia south of the Company's main line to $5.00 per acre, and it is easy to see what this will mean to the Canada Northwest Land

[1] In 1905 the district of Assiniboia became part of the new province of Saskatchewan.

Company as well as to the Railway Company."[1] In short, it was good business to give increased value to the better lands of the Canadian Pacific by letting the American land syndicates colonize the less desirable tracts. The speculative fever was running high and the railway would have been the prime loser had it assumed an air of superior virtue with respect to it at the moment.

The first of the colonization companies to make an extensive purchase of Canadian Pacific lands was that of Beiseker, Davidson and Martin, three North Dakota business men and land speculators, whose energy and success in the colonization of lands in their home state had attracted the attention of Griffin, the land commissioner of the Canadian Pacific. Confident that they would achieve an equal success in the Canadian West, Griffin urged the high command of the railway to enter into a contract with them. On December 3, 1901, the Executive Committee of the Board of Directors of the Canadian Pacific convened in Montreal, gave formal approval to such an agreement, and on December 13 the contract was signed. Beiseker and his associates purchased 170,297 acres in townships 11 to 15 inclusive, on the Pasqua Section of the Canadian Pacific line in eastern Assiniboia.[2] The price was $2.75 per acre, to be paid in 9 equal annual installments.

Beiseker and his fellow speculators then created the Canadian-American Land Company, with headquarters in Minneapolis, for the exploitation of their purchase. The land company coöperated in every conceivable way with agents of the Dominion Government in the United States. Its representatives followed in the wake of government agents in an effort to transform every favorable impression into a sale. Personal solicitation was supplemented by circulars and other printed materials sent to prospects whose names the Dominion officials supplied. Within five months the land company had retailed the entire area to settlers from the United States. The success attending their efforts to colonize these lands, combined with the generally satisfactory character of their relations with the rail-

[1] F. T. Griffin to E. B. Osler, February 21, 1902, in Secretary's Office, Montreal. This significant letter shows in detail the considerations which influenced the Canadian Pacific to sell to the land companies.

[2] The minutes of the meeting of the Executive Committee, together with a copy of the contract, are in the Office of the Secretary, C. P. R. Co., Montreal.

way, caused Beiseker and Davidson later to be singled out as the ones to launch the sale of irrigable lands of the Canadian Pacific in Alberta.

Another important purchaser of Canadian Pacific lands was J. H. Haslam, who had for some time been largely interested in fostering the movement of land seekers into southeastern Assiniboia. In December, 1901, Haslam contracted to purchase at $2.50 per acre 82,584 acres of railway land adjacent to the village of Halbrite, south of Weyburn on the Soo Line.[1] He had already established extensive connections with agents in the United States and he promptly built up a far-reaching organization in the middle western states, especially in Iowa and Illinois.

The most important of the colonization companies dealing in Canadian Pacific lands in that portion of Assiniboia was the Northwest Colonization Company. Although it enjoyed the financial support of a group of Minneapolis bankers and capitalists, this company was under the management of O. A. Robertson and F. B. Lynch, two of the best known land men of the entire Northwest. Late in 1901 Robertson opened negotiations with Land Commissioner Griffin of the Canadian Pacific for the purchase of a large area tributary to the Soo Line. While eager to avail himself of the experience and capital of Robertson and his associates, Griffin felt that any agreement with them must also safeguard the interests of the Canada Northwest Land Company, whose holdings were scattered among the railway lands. Since the land company's sections were held at prices considerably higher than the $2.50 per acre which Robertson proposed to pay for Canadian Pacific land, they could not be included in the area which he proposed to buy. After careful consideration by the various parties, an arrangement was effected which was satisfactory to all concerned. On April 8, 1902, Robertson signed a contract for the purchase of 337,090 acres of Canadian Pacific and Manitoba Southwestern lands at $2.50 per acre.[2] The interests of the Canada Northwest Land Company were protected by the inclusion in the contract of a clause requiring Robertson to re-sell the lands to settlers at not less than $4.00 per acre. With this guarantee,

[1] See copy of the contract, Secretary's Office, Montreal.

[2] The extensive correspondence between Robertson and Canadian Pacific officials is preserved in the Secretary's Office, as is a copy of the contract.

Griffin could be reasonably certain that the 227,000 acres of Canada Northwest Land Company land included in the tract could soon be sold to settlers at a sufficient price. Subsequent purchases in December, 1902, on the account of Robertson and of the Northwest Colonization Company covered an area of 412,859 acres, bringing the total of Robertson and Lynch to approximately 750,000 acres. They lost no time in advertising their holdings as "The Garden Spot of Canada." As they said, "with millions of acres to choose from, and with long, practical experience," they had naturally selected the "very best to be had."[1] Soil, location, drainage, water, railway, and elevator facilities were described as all the farmer could desire. While the roseate picture painted by Robertson is hard to reconcile with the doubts which Canadian Pacific officials had once entertained regarding this tract, the high-pressure methods of the colonization company brought astounding results. By the spring of 1905 the entire area had been retailed to settlers from the United States.

The sales to Haslam, to Beiseker, Davidson and Martin, and to the Northwest Colonization Company thus account for 1,000,000 acres disposed of in southeastern Assiniboia in the years 1901-3. This area, together with the 2,200,000 acres sold to the Canada Northwest Land Company, represents 3,200,000 of the 8,500,000 acres contained in the main line belt in Manitoba and eastern Assiniboia, and in the southern reserves of the Canadian Pacific and the Manitoba Southwestern.

Other large sales to colonization companies between 1902 and 1906 included 76,765 acres to the Union Trust Company of Toronto; 150,055 acres to the Ontario and Saskatchewan Land Corporation; 200,004 acres to the Great West Land Company; 116,483 acres to the Alberta Central Land Corporation; 127,200 acres to the Alberta and Saskatchewan Colonization Company; 500,000 acres to the Western Canada Land Company; and 102,510 acres to the Luse Land Company of St. Paul.[2] The lands acquired by the last four of these companies were located in northern Alberta and represent the first serious effort of the Canadian Pacific to sell and settle that portion

[1] *Manitoba Morning Free Press,* July 23, 1903 and May 6, 1905.
[2] These data were compiled from the land records of the Canadian Pacific in the Department of Natural Resources, Calgary.

of the West. As in the case of the other companies, these organizations seem to have sought their settlers chiefly in the United States. Although the early sales to colonization companies were made at the modest figure of $2.50 per acre, the price gradually increased as land values in the West advanced. Thus the Luse Land Company in 1906 paid $6.00 per acre for its land. In the main no settlement conditions were attached to the sale of these large tracts, but the contract with the Luse Land Company contained the interesting clause "that the purchaser shall within one year of purchase place upon each half section a bona-fide settler, not heretofore a resident of Canada and induced to move to Canada by the purchaser."[1]

Between December, 1901 and July, 1906 sales to 13 different colonization companies accounted for 2,300,000 acres or somewhat more than one-fourth of the net area sold by the Canadian Pacific between 1897 and 1906. Besides the tracts, ranging upwards from 40,000 acres, sold to well-organized companies, the railway disposed of a large area in units of a few thousand acres to speculators of the smaller variety who lacked the capital necessary to the conduct of a vigorous colonization campaign. The turnover of lands in the hands of these men was much less rapid than that held by the great companies.

Although the propaganda of American land companies selling Canadian land in the United States served as an important supplement to that carried on by the Dominion Government and other agencies, such uncoördinated activity led to useless expenditure and duplication of effort on the part of the different companies. With a view to obviating this situation there was held at Minneapolis in January, 1904 a convention of United States land men interested in the Canadian Northwest. Among the leading spirits were A. D. Davidson of the Saskatchewan Valley Land Company, and O. A. Robertson and F. B. Lynch of the Northwest Colonization Company.[2] As a result of the meeting the "Western Canada Immigration Association" was formed. The association was to be the medium for pooling the funds of the different companies and for the placing of their advertising in the States. Theodore A. Knappen, the Secretary of the Association, was the one-time Associate Editor of the *Minne-*

[1] A copy of the contract is in the Secretary's Office, Montreal.
[2] *Manitoba Free Press*, January 27, 1904 and January 30, 1904.

apolis Journal, where he had made a specialty of western Canada. The land department of the Canadian Pacific, ever eager to encourage any step designed to promote the development of the prairie region, promptly appropriated the sum of $5,000 to the war chest of the organization.[1]

This show of aggressiveness in behalf of western Canada soon led to a counter-thrust by those pushing the sale and settlement of lands within the states of the Northwest. Meeting in St. Paul in March, 1904, they formed "The American Immigration Association of the Northwest."[2] This seems to have been one of the first expressions of American concern over the exodus to the Canadian West and it presaged a series of organized counter-moves which were to continue to the outbreak of the World War in 1914, and which ultimately were supported by governors and state legislatures as well as by landowners and chambers of commerce.

Important as were the sales to speculators, large and small, in the years 1901 to 1906, the bulk of the land disposed of by the railway in the decade 1897 to 1906 went to actual settlers in the prairie provinces. Sales to settlers numbered 26,241, covering an area in excess of 6,000,000 acres.[3]

This rush of land buyers and settlers to the West after 1902 prompted the Canadian Pacific to revise upward periodically the price of land in small units. In July, 1903 land east of the 3rd meridian was priced up to $10 per acre, according to location. While the company naturally sought to maintain prices on a par with those charged by other companies selling land in competition with it, it seems clear that the terms governing the payments on its lands were more liberal than those offered by competitors. That settlers found these terms satisfactory is indicated by the small number of cancelled contracts covering land sold in this period.

Besides the large area of railway land sold in this era, the land department also disposed of more than 750,000 acres of Canada Northwest Land Company land at prices averaging substantially higher than those realized by the railway company for its land. In

[1] *Manitoba Free Press,* March 17, 1904.
[2] *Ibid.,* March 18, 1904.
[3] Compiled from the report of William Pearce, 1921, in archives of the Department of Colonization, Montreal. Pearce based his report on an analysis of the land records of the company in Calgary.

1902 large areas of this land were sold to colonization companies, but thereafter sales were made chiefly in small tracts to actual settlers.

By 1905 the best of the railway's lands in the south were gone. The main line belt east of Moose Jaw, as well as the large reserves in southern Manitoba and southeastern Assiniboia had been sold and largely settled. An important chapter in the history of the company's land policy had been completed and new ones were about to be written to the west and north.

So much has been said about the American migration to the Canadian West at the turn of the century that it is easy to lose sight of the fact that there was contemporaneously a substantial movement to the prairie from the older provinces of the Dominion itself, especially from Ontario. While the American invasion was actively encouraged by the Dominion Government and the various land companies, as well as by the Canadian Pacific, the exodus from eastern Canada was chiefly stimulated by the railway company. In the absence of government propaganda, the Canadian Pacific employed certain well-defined methods of interesting farmers from Ontario and Maritimes in the prairie regions. It continued the practice, introduced earlier, of operating home-seekers' excursions, especially in the spring of the year. Thus the *Free Press* of April 1, 1898, recorded the arrival in Winnipeg of 400 people via the weekly excursion of the Canadian Pacific, while the issue of March 24, 1899, told of the arrival of 3 train loads of Ontario settlers. During March and the first week in April, 1902, over 3,600 settlers went west from Ontario by way of these excursions, taking with them 600 car loads of settlers' effects.[1] This was the largest movement ever recorded in an equal period of time. In March of the following year trains in 3 sections were necessary to accommodate the Ontario home-seekers, while in June, 1904, a special train brought 364 Ontarians.[2]

At certain seasons of the year, especially at Christmas time, the railway ran excursions from the prairie to the East, to enable settlers to visit friends and relatives in their old homes. Realizing that these visits afforded an opportunity for the farmer to do some missionary work in behalf of the West, the land department of the company

[1] *Manitoba Morning Free Press*, April 8, 1902.
[2] *Ibid.*, March 13, 1903 and June 17, 1904.

sought to supply an incentive for him to speak in support of his adopted country. In 1899 the department offered a commission of $10 per quarter section to excursionists selling Canadian Pacific lands to actual settlers who would establish themselves within 12 miles of the excursionist's residence.[1] The results achieved that year were deemed sufficiently satisfactory to warrant a repetition of the experiment in 1900.

The home-seekers' excursions, widely advertised in the eastern provinces, were supplemented by the work of agents. Sometimes these men were chosen because of their nationality or linguistic equipment. Thus one Klaus Peters of Rosthern was indicated as a logical choice for work among Germans and Mennonites in Ontario. In 1902 he worked among Germans in Waterloo County and was instrumental in starting an important movement of these people to Altona, Gretna, Winkler, Regina, and Rosthern.[2]

The generally improved situation following 1896 is easily illustrated by the statistics of immigration and homestead entries. The 16,835 immigrants entering the Dominion in 1896 increased to 21,716 the following year, and to 31,900 in 1898.[3] A recession in 1900 preceded an upturn in which the numbers mounted steadily until 1906 when 189,000 new arrivals were recorded. With some fluctuations the trend continued upward for the next few years, reaching an all-time peak of 402,432 in 1913.

Of the total for various years, the percentage coming from the United States varied greatly. In 1897 the States accounted for 11 per cent, as compared with 52 per cent from the United Kingdom and 37 per cent from "other countries." In 1902, the year in which the land and colonization companies were so active south of the 49th parallel, 39 per cent came from the United States, 26 per cent from the United Kingdom, and 35 per cent from "other countries." The 103,798 who entered Canada from the neighboring republic in 1910 represented 50 per cent of the total immigration for the year. Statistics abundantly confirmed the current impression of an "American invasion" of the Canadian West.[4]

---

[1] *Manitoba Morning Free Press*, November 26, 1900.
[2] *Ibid.*, April 8, 1902.
[3] *The Canada Year Book* (1918), p. 30.
[4] *Ibid.*

Of the 49,149 immigrants of 1901, some 25,000, or slightly more than 50 per cent, were destined for the prairie regions of Canada.[1] Of the 402,432 persons entering the Dominion in 1913, somewhat more than 137,000 or 34 per cent were bound for that part of the country. From 1901 to 1905 inclusive more than half of all immigrants gave the prairie provinces as their destination. Between 1906 and 1914 inclusive, those provinces never attracted as many as 50 per cent of the total. Allowing for the inevitable westward drift of population within the Dominion, however, it is probable that the prairie provinces ultimately received a majority of the newcomers.

The 1,857 homestead entries of 1896 were the smallest number since 1878. A slight increase in 1897 was more than offset by cancellations. Then there began an upswing which continued for several years. The 7,426 entries of 1900 mounted to 14,633 in 1902 and to 31,383 in 1903.[2] In 1906 there were 41,869 entries, with 11,637 cancellations, the net entries for the year constituting an all-time record. After that year the ratio of cancellations to entries increased materially. In 1911 there were 44,479 entries and 22,122 cancellations; in 1913 the figures were 33,699 and 17,101 respectively.

The growth of population on the prairie, so clearly reflected in the figures of immigration and land alienation, quickly led to the rounding out of the political framework of the Dominion. By 1905 settlement in the northwest territories had increased sufficiently to warrant the creation of the two new provinces of Saskatchewan and Alberta, with seats of government at Regina and Edmonton respectively. In characteristically frontier fashion these towns quickly emerged from the raw and callow aspect of pioneer communities into the more settled state of burgeoning cities, and the trading post soon yielded to stately government buildings.

[1] *Ibid.* (1926), p. 174.
[2] *Ibid.*, p. 923.

VII

LAUNCHING THE IRRIGATION PROJECT

THE strong tide of settlement pouring into the Northwest at the beginning of the new century made it desirable from the point of view of both the Dominion Government and the railway that the Canadian Pacific lands should be definitely located and the unclaimed land in the great reserves of the West opened up to the settler. The result was the agreement of 1903 by which the railway accepted *en bloc* the large area of dry land tributary to its main line, and stretching from Medicine Hat to Calgary. Having disposed of the bulk of its lands in Manitoba and southern Saskatchewan through the large sales of 1902, the Canadian Pacific was now in a position to concentrate its attention upon the development of its proposed irrigation block.

In finally accepting this area, originally rejected as not "fairly fit for settlement," the officials of the railway were guided by a definite and intelligent plan. They could, of course, demand satisfaction of their claims in the more humid lands of the North, where the settler would contribute little to the traffic of the road, or they could accept the semi-arid lands, incur the great expense incidental to their irrigation, and develop the region to the point where its volume of traffic would far excel that of any similar area in western Canada. Enlightened self-interest plainly dictated the latter course. There was, besides, something appealing about the idea of converting this cattleman's kingdom into a region of intensive agriculture which would contrast sharply with the more extensive grain farming so characteristic of other portions of the West.

Irrigation was not a new thing in that portion of the Canadian prairie.[1] As early as 1879 a feeble beginning had been made toward

[1] The beginnings of irrigation development in southern Alberta are fully dis-

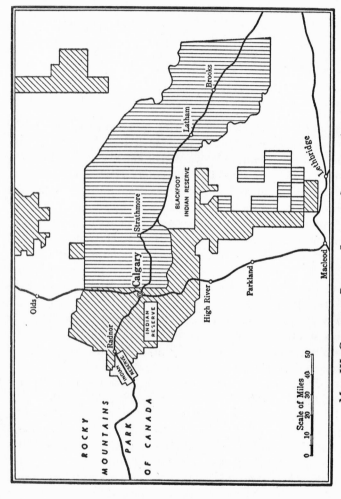

MAP III. CANADIAN PACIFIC LANDS IN SOUTHERN ALBERTA.

The diagonally-hatched areas are those in which the Railway, for the most part, owned the
alternate sections. In the vertically-hatched areas the Railway, for the most part, owned both
the odd- and even-numbered sections. The large area thus hatched is the Irrigation Block.

irrigating land south of Calgary, while three years later an irrigation ditch was constructed near Lethbridge. Further impetus resulted from the settlement of the Mormons at Cardston in the late eighties. Long accustomed to irrigation in Utah, they were quick to perceive the opportunity for developing it in their new home, where they practiced it on a small scale. In the same period occurred the beginnings of two companies which, when ultimately combined to form the Alberta Railway and Irrigation Company, became a major factor in the growth of irrigation in the West. One of these, the Northwest Coal and Navigation Company, constructed a railway line from Medicine Hat to the coal mines on the Belly River; the other, the Alberta Railway and Coal Company, built a line from Lethbridge to Coutts. As both companies received a land subsidy, the Alberta Railway and Irrigation Company found itself in possession of a land grant of more than a million acres.[1] In December, 1891, the company entered into contracts with two influential Mormons, Charles Ora Card and John W. Taylor, for the sale of something more than 700,000 acres on terms calling for a rental payment of 2 cents per acre for a period of 4 years, followed by the payment of $1.00 per acre, spread over a period of 8 years.[2] With a view to facilitating the efforts of Card and Taylor to settle the land, application was made to Parliament for the enactment of a law authorizing the construction and operation of irrigation canals in Alberta, south of the 50th parallel. The passage of this act in April, 1893 was followed by the formation of the Alberta Irrigation Company, which was to be the agency for the settlement and irrigation of the land. But the inability of the two Mormon promoters to interest capital in sufficient quantities to carry out their plans led to the cancellation of their contract in 1895. Their efforts, however, had not been wholly in vain. Their failure made clear the fact that the alternate section method of granting railway subsidy lands was

---

cussed in the manuscript study by Sam G. Porter and Charles Raley, *A Brief History of the Development of Irrigation in the Lethbridge District.* This document is in the archives of the Department of Natural Resources of the Canadian Pacific in Calgary.

[1] For the origin and development of the Alberta Railway and Irrigation Company and its land grant, see J. B. Hedges, *The Federal Railway Land Subsidy Policy of Canada,* pp. 85-92.

[2] Porter and Raley, *op. cit.,* p. 18.

172   BUILDING THE CANADIAN WEST

a formidable obstacle to irrigation. This difficulty was removed when, after repeated representations by the Alberta Railway and Irrigation Company, Clifford Sifton, in 1896, arranged to consolidate the holdings of the company into a solid block.[1]

Meanwhile, the Dominion Government was giving increasing attention to the problem of irrigation. In 1893, J. S. Dennis, Chief Inspector of Surveys in the Department of the Interior, was commissioned to visit the western states of the United States for the purpose of studying and reporting on the irrigation laws and practices of that country.[2] The following year his report was submitted to Parliament, where his recommendations were made the basis of the Irrigation Act passed by that body in July, 1894. That law has been the legal basis of all subsequent irrigation legislation and development in Canada.

With the enactment of this legislation and with the removal of the alternate section hindrance, the Alberta Railway and Irrigation Company addressed itself anew to the problem of irrigation. In 1897 George G. Anderson, an eminent irrigation engineer of Denver, Colorado, was engaged to report on the feasibility and cost of an irrigation system to serve the company's lands.[3] His investigation indicated the practicability of diverting water from the St. Mary's River. The following year the actual construction of the irrigation system began, under Anderson's supervision. The chief contractors for the work were the President and High Council of Latter Day Saints—the Mormon Church—while the sub-contractors, laborers, and teamsters were principally Mormon farmers who came to settle in that part of the Canadian West. These men were paid one-half in cash and one-half in land, the land with water rights being valued at $3.00 per acre. It was to the settlement of these people that the communities of Sterling and Magrath owed their inception.[4]

Among those who followed the construction of this project with friendly interest were various Canadian Pacific officials, especially President Shaughnessy. Connecting with the Canadian Pacific main line at Dunmore, the Alberta Railway and Irrigation Company was

[1] Porter and Raley, *op. cit.*, p. 17.
[2] *Ibid.*, p. 2.
[3] *Ibid.*, p. 18.
[4] *Ibid.*

potentially an important feeder for the former road. Its future was a matter of genuine concern to the Canadian Pacific. In 1898, therefore, Shaughnessy offered in behalf of his railway a bonus of $100,-000, to be earned by the Alberta Railway and Irrigation Company, according to the number of settlers and the amount of traffic which it brought.[1] Later, on account of the difficulty of determining these items, the Canadian Pacific changed the bonus to an outright grant of $5,000 every 6 months, until the total amount had been paid.[2] Shaughnessy's company thus became an important patron of the first large-scale irrigation undertaking in western Canada.

Financial assistance was also forthcoming from the town of Lethbridge. Fearing that the canal would pass it by, this community contributed $30,000 to guarantee the delivery of water for the irrigation of some 20,000 acres within a radius of 10 miles from the center of the town. Construction of the irrigation system progressed steadily. Water reached Lethbridge on July 4, 1900, and Magrath and Sterling in July of the following year.

With the completion of the project, there remained the more difficult problem of settling the lands of the company. Aside from the Mormon farmers who had occupied the land adjacent to Sterling and Magrath, there were few settlers and slight demand for irrigable land. Although parties of prospects were brought from all the border states, sales were disappointing. The offer of irrigable land at $8.00 to $10.00 per acre on liberal terms failed to attract the immigrant. Even the inducement of the free use of the land for 2 years, with the option then to purchase, availed little.[3] The elements seemed to have conspired against the company. Throughout the period of construction the rainfall had been abnormally heavy. Clients brought to view the land were prone to remark that the country needed drainage rather than irrigation. That the region was in the midst of one of the periodic wet cycles, culminating in 3 distinct floods and a total precipitation of 28 inches in 1902, the potential settler did not appreciate. That this period of abundant rainfall beginning in 1895 was certain to be followed by a dry cycle, as the favorable sea-

[1] *Ibid.*
[2] *Ibid.*
[3] For a discussion of the difficulties encountered in the sale and settlement of the land see Porter and Raley, *op. cit.*, pp. 25-30.

sons of the early eighties had preceded the droughts of the late eighties, he also failed to realize. The dry years at that time had supplied the initial impulse to irrigation in the West and to the enactment of the legislation by Parliament in the nineties. A recurring dry cycle would dispel all doubts as to the need of irrigation in the Lethbridge district. Despite initial discouragements the company worked faithfully during the years 1902-12 and had achieved substantial results in land settlement when it was taken over by the Canadian Pacific in the latter year.

While the Alberta Railway and Irrigation Company struggled to make a success of its venture, the Canadian Pacific was launching its irrigation project on a scale which promised to dwarf all similar undertakings in Canada and, perhaps, in the United States. With a compact block of something more than 3,000,000 acres, an area in excess of that of Connecticut, the company was to attempt to develop diversified farming under the more certain conditions which irrigation seemed to guarantee. Here, it was hoped, wheat would yield to alfalfa, stock growing, and intensive farming.

The problem confronting the Canadian Pacific was almost unique in the annals of railway colonization. Not only must it colonize irrigable lands but it must colonize them alone and unaided. Where railway lands were scheduled in alternate sections they in a measure sold themselves. The forces and agencies which drew settlers to the government sections attracted them also to those of the railway. Purchases by farmers living on government lands accounted for large areas sold by the railways. Within the irrigation block, however, where the railway owned both the even- and odd-numbered sections, there were no government lands to draw colonists, no agencies, public or private, engaged in publicizing the region. The progress of settlement must depend upon the efforts of the Canadian Pacific alone. The company must bring the buyers to Alberta, sell them the land, and teach them to farm.

This block of land was situated between the Red Deer River on the north and the Bow River on the south, and extended from the eastern boundary of Range 11, west of the 4th meridian to the 5th meridian, about one mile east of Calgary.[1] Its maximum extent from

[1] In order to have the lands in a compact block the Canadian Pacific purchased 101,823 acres of Hudson's Bay Company sections within the irrigation block.

east to west was about 180 miles, and it was void of settlement except for the village of Gleichen, a shipping point for the cattle interests.

The Canadian Pacific promptly established in Calgary headquarters for the development of the irrigation project and placed J. S. Dennis in charge, as Superintendent of Irrigation. Dennis had long and varied experience in the West, in the service of both the Department of the Interior and the Hudson's Bay Company. A firm believer in the efficacy of irrigation and possessed of very definite ideas as to how the irrigation block should be developed as an asset to the company and the Dominion, he was well fitted for the task he was about to undertake.

For convenience in administration and construction, the company divided the irrigation block into three sections, Eastern, Central and Western, each comprising about 1,000,000 acres.[1] It was the original hope of the company officials that approximately half of the total area of the block, or 1,500,000 acres, would prove to be irrigable. The company planned, however, to complete the western section of the block before proceeding to the construction of the remaining sections. In 1904 the main canal leading from the Bow River east of Calgary was located and placed under construction, and in 1905 secondary canal A was located. The plans called for a main canal 18 miles in length, with 150 miles of secondary canals, and distributing ditches aggregating about 800 miles. According to the original estimates about 300,000 acres in the western section were irrigable.[2]

In designing the system it was the aim of the company to provide a maximum number of combination farms with an approximately equal area of irrigable and non-irrigable land. The company classified as irrigable only those lands lying at a lower elevation than the point of delivery, whereas the general classification of irrigable land in other systems comprised all land at a lower level than the distributing canal from which the water was drawn.[3] As a result, in the western section a large area was classed as non-irrigable which in other systems would have been regarded as irrigable. This method

[1] Dennis to Charles Drinkwater, Secretary, C. P. R., August 15, 1905. File No. 336, D. N. R.
[2] Ibid.
[3] Leo G. Denis and James White, "Water Powers of Canada," Commission of Conservation—Canada. Ottawa, 1911, pp. 299-300.

of classification theoretically made possible a maximum of combination farms.

As soon as construction of the western section was under way, the officials gave their attention to the question of the temporary use to be made of the land in the central and eastern sections, pending the extension of the canal system to those areas. This region constituted the last remaining refuge of the range cattle industry in Canada. In 1903 there were within the confines of the irrigation block 152 ranches leased by the Department of the Interior for grazing purposes.[1] Such leases, covering both odd- and even-numbered sections, were in great demand by the cattlemen, the more so in view of the fact that government land in other parts of the West was subject to homestead entry. When the Canadian Pacific agreed to accept the land in the irrigation block, it was naturally besieged by the ranchers who desired leases from the company.

Eager as was the Canadian Pacific to obtain whatever revenue it could from this land, the procedure to be adopted required careful consideration. Thought had to be given to the question as to whether the leasing of the land would render it liable to taxation under Section 16 of the syndicate contract of 1881. After prolonged discussion of this point, it was finally decided that the company might safely lease the lands, provided the lessee was given the opportunity to purchase the land when it was placed on sale. In the spring of 1907 a total of 721,000 acres within the irrigation block were held under lease at 4 cents per acre.[2] While this tenure of the cattlemen was insecure, and could last only until the company was prepared to extend irrigation to the land, it represented the last stand of a vanishing industry in the face of the advance of the agricultural frontier.

As the classification of land in the western section of the irrigation block proceeded, increased attention, of necessity, was given to the formulation of policies governing the sale of the land. Within a few months Dennis was able to report that some 98,000 acres in Ranges 28 and 29 west of the 4th meridian were of greater elevation than the irrigation canal and, therefore, could not be irrigated. Upon his

[1] File No. 441, D. N. R.

[2] *Ibid.* According to statement by Dennis to Charles Drinkwater, August 15, 1905, 700,000 acres were covered by grazing leases at that time. File No. 336.

recommendation, these lands were placed on sale as grazing lands, at prices ranging from $4.50 to $5.00 per acre.[1] Payment was to be made one-sixth in cash and the balance in 5 equal instalments at 6 per cent interest. As an inducement for the cattlemen to stock the land, an extension of 1 year was allowed for the second payment, when the purchaser placed on the land at least 1 head of cattle for each 20 acres purchased.[2]

Although within a year about 45,000 acres had been sold in small tracts on these terms, the company soon resorted to methods of sale which it regarded as more advantageous to it. Since the Middle West of the United States, as well as western Canada, fairly teemed with land companies which habitually acquired large areas of land to retail to actual settlers, it was natural that the company should turn to them. Elsewhere in the West it had sold land wholesale to such organizations, and it now adopted a similar policy with respect to land in the irrigation block.

Among the land companies with which the railway had done business was a Dakota syndicate which functioned under various names at different times, but of which one A. J. Sayre was a leading member. This company had not only engaged extensively in the colonization of Canadian Pacific lands in the High River district of Alberta, but it had also settled a large area of the railway's land along the Soo Line in the Weyburn and Milestone sections of southeastern Assiniboia. Early in 1905 these men, under the name of the Calgary Colonization Company, purchased about 54,000 acres in the irrigation block, at the price of $5.00 per acre.[3]

Although Dennis had originally regarded these lands as primarily suited for grazing purposes, it was the plan of the colonization company to retail them as agricultural lands to actual settlers; and, under a favorable climatic cycle, plus the influence of the "dry farming" idea, the land was disposed of to prospective wheat farmers. As an inducement to the colonization company to resell to those who

[1] Dennis to Sir Wm. Whyte, Assistant to President, November 11, 1903, File No. 301, D. N. R. Also extract from minutes of the Board of Directors. C. P. R., December 14, 1903, File No. 301, D. N. R.

[2] Ibid.

[3] See the contract, bearing date of January 2, 1905, File No. 208, Section 2, D. N. R.

would improve the land, it was to receive a rebate of 25 cents per acre on each section retailed to an actual settler.[1]

The colonization company promptly established headquarters in Calgary and called to its service the extensive agency organization it had previously built up in the middle western states. The Canadian Pacific, on its part, coöperated in the work by providing free transportation for the agents of the colonization company who were bringing in settlers from beyond the border. So successful were Sayre and his associates that within a few weeks they increased their purchases to some 80,000 acres, while by June of 1905 they sought to purchase all the non-irrigable land outside the irrigable district tributary to secondary canal A at $6.00 per acre on a 10-year contract. In recommending the sale of this tract of about 100,000 acres, Dennis commented favorably upon their agencies in the States, and observed that they were selling on an average of 5 sections per week to actual settlers from the United States, "many of whom have already commenced extensive improvements on the lands purchased." In the opinion of Dennis it was fortunate for the Canadian Pacific that the Sayre group had interested themselves in Alberta lands.[2]

The optimism of Dennis was not entirely shared by Sir William Whyte, Vice-President, in charge of western lines at Winnipeg, who thought the railway company should proceed more slowly and cautiously. Whyte thought that, in any event, no action should be taken upon this latest request until more complete reports were at hand in regard to the work accomplished thus far by the colonization company.[3] Such reports were soon forthcoming and revealed that, of the 80,000 acres purchased, the company had sold 72 sections to actual settlers; that sales had averaged three-quarters of a section per person, the largest single sale being 2 sections. The cost of selling the land, including advertising and commissions to agents, was $3.00 per acre. On the lands thus far sold the colonization company had realized about $11.00 per acre, giving it a net profit of some $3.00 per acre. Western Canada was indeed a paradise for the land speculator!

With reluctance Whyte finally consented to the sale of the new

[1] Ibid.
[2] Dennis to Whyte, June 21, 1905, File No. 225, Section 1, D. N. R.
[3] Telegram, Whyte to Dennis, Nov. 9, 1905, File No. 436, D. N. R.

acreage, but when the contract was finally drawn up it was found that but 65,000 acres were available in the tract. By the terms of this agreement the colonization company received a discount of 50 cents per acre for each section sold to an actual settler. By a further purchase of about 10,000 acres in March of 1906 the total taken by the company within a period of 15 months was brought to almost 160,000 acres.[1] Undeniably the irrigation block was becoming well and favorably known, especially in the United States. This was at the cost, however, of an enormous tribute which the colonization company was exacting from the settler. A price of $11.00 per acre for raw lands, incapable of irrigation, seems difficult to justify for that time. Yet, to the railway, the necessity of starting a movement of people into the district and, to the colonization company, the desire for speculative profit seemed to be a sufficient reason for exorbitant retail prices.

Thus far our discussion has been confined to the arrangements made by the Canadian Pacific for the sale of non-irrigable land in the irrigation block, but so situated as to be unsuitable for use with irrigable land in so-called "combination" farms. Meanwhile Dennis, Whyte, and Shaughnessy were grappling with the problem of determining the means by which the irrigable land was to be sold. This was a subject which called for the most careful consideration. Since irrigation farming required a knowledge of a special technique, common sense seemed to dictate that a special appeal be made to people familiar with that technique. On the other hand, people already established as successful irrigation farmers were not likely to move in large numbers. History does not record mass migrations of farmers from successfully irrigated areas. In the end the company was forced to colonize the land chiefly with farmers inexperienced in irrigation, and to provide the necessary instruction in farming under new conditions.

Once the railway company had decided on the kind of people it was to seek, there remained the question as to methods by which it should endeavor to attract them. It could build up its own special sales force and agency organization in various quarters of the world, or it could avail itself of existing organizations and agencies which

[1] Memorandum by J. S. Dennis, March 28, 1906, File No. 208, Section 2, D. N. R.

would guarantee to the railway a minimum price for its irrigable land. If the latter method offered the advantage of relieving the railway of an added burden and responsibility, it was no less open to the objection that it exacted a needless toll from the very farmer it sought to establish on the land, and thereby increased the hazard under which he labored. Despite its undeniable shortcomings, however, this was the method which the Canadian Pacific first tried.

In June of 1905 Dennis received a proposition from T. L. Beiseker and C. H. Davidson, two North Dakota land men who in 1902 had purchased large areas from the Canadian Pacific in southeastern Assiniboia. They offered to join with A. J. Sayre in forming a company for the sale of irrigable and non-irrigable land served by secondary canal A. This area comprised 110,000 acres of irrigable land and 30,000 of non-irrigable land. They were prepared to net the Canadian Pacific $11.00 an acre for the irrigable land, and $6.00 per acre for the non-irrigable, and, as evidence of their good faith, offered to deposit $10,000 to be forfeited by them in the event of failure to carry out the terms of the contract.[1]

The reaction of Dennis to this proposal was wholly favorable. These men had made such an excellent record in colonizing Canadian Pacific lands in eastern Assiniboia as well as in the irrigation block, were prepared to invest money so freely in the Calgary district for the construction of grain elevators and other improvements, and were so well known in the United States, that, in his opinion, their proposition had everything to recommend it.[2] The railway should capitalize on the experience and efforts of these men instead of attempting to build up a rival organization of its own.

As usual, Sir William Whyte was less favorably impressed by the proposal. He observed that other land companies selling railway land guaranteed a minimum price to the railway and shared with it everything in excess thereof.[3] He was troubled, too, by the $11.00 guarantee for irrigable land when the Alberta Railway and Irrigation Company was receiving as much as $18.00 per acre for its land.[4] In an effort to resolve Whyte's doubts, Dennis could reply that the

[1] Beiseker, Davidson and Sayre to Dennis, June 20, 1905, File No. 355, Section 1, D. N. R. Sayre was at the head of the Calgary Colonization Company.
[2] Dennis to Whyte, June 21, 1905, File No. 355, Section 1, D. N. R.
[3] Telegram, Whyte to Dennis, June 24, 1905, *ibid.*
[4] Telegram, Whyte to Dennis, July 5, 1905, *ibid.*

irrigation project of the latter company was older and better known than that of the Canadian Pacific; and that its demonstrated success enabled it to obtain higher prices for its land. Dennis was convinced that very large expenditures would be required to start a movement to the irrigable lands of the Canadian Pacific, and that for the first year at least the Dakota syndicate would be unable to net anything above the $11.00 guaranteed to the railway.[1]

Whyte, however, remained obdurate. After consultation with President Shaughnessy, he suggested that the contract should cover not more than 30,000 acres; that if the group were successful in the sale of this area, a further agreement could be made for them to handle a larger tract. He added that "we must always bear in mind too that, as business men, we expect to receive profit not only on the irrigation investment but on the lands themselves, or in other words, the profit on the money put into the irrigation canal must be in addition to the value in themselves of the lands affected by irrigation, and then there will be the value to be received for non-irrigated lands."[2]

Meanwhile, Beiseker, Davidson, and Sayre were proceeding with the organization of their new company in anticipation of the acceptance of their terms. Taking the name Canadian Pacific Irrigation Colonization Company, they had arranged for the establishment of a large experimental or demonstration farm at Gleichen, which was to be brought to a high state of cultivation in 1906, and to which prospective land buyers could be taken in order that they might observe the possibilities of irrigation farming. Another demonstration farm was to be established at Langdon. They had engaged the services of one of the best land men in the United States to serve as superintendent of their land agency in Calgary at a salary of $12,000 per year.[3]

Dennis now wrote to Whyte that these men were unwilling to undertake the sale of 30,000 acres; that they contemplated a large initial expenditure for establishing agencies, issuing literature, bringing in delegates, and for demonstration work; and that they would

[1] Dennis to Whyte, June 26, 1905, *ibid.*
[2] Whyte to Dennis, July 18, 1905, File No. 355, Section 1, D. N. R.
[3] Sayre to Dennis, August 9, 1905, *ibid.*

make no profit on the first 30,000 acres.[1] They must, therefore, have the larger acreage originally asked for. Dennis reiterated that the group were prepared to invest a million dollars in the irrigation block, a fact of great significance in the development of an important project.

The importunity of Dennis eventually convinced Whyte, who, in turn, won Shaughnessy over to the idea, and on September 1, 1905 the Executive Committee of the Canadian Pacific Board authorized that a contract for the larger area be entered into. A point which weighed heavily in favor of the approval of the committee was the activity of the company in building elevators "to induce and meet the requirements of settlement."[2]

While the Canadian Pacific officials regarded the sale of lands in the irrigation block as a business proposition in which the railway would realize on both the land and the irrigation investment, they were none the less primarily interested in the colonization of the land and the development of a producing area rather than in land sales as such. The sale of the land at a satisfactory price was not of itself enough; if sold only to speculators, the great objective of the railway would be defeated. This concern for prompt and successful settlement and cultivation of the land is clearly shown in a letter of Dennis to the C. P. I. C. Co., in which he said, "Our desire is that as far as it is possible to do so, each quarter section of irrigable land should have at least a quarter section of non-irrigable land attached to it. . . . Every effort should be made to dispose of all non-irrigable land in a district in conjunction with sales of the irrigable land. I would also point out that in our opinion no one individual should be encouraged to undertake to farm more than 160 acres of irrigable land. Irrigation farming requires a great deal of labor and a quarter section will, it is thought, prove to be big enough for the ordinary farmer to handle, particularly if he has an additional quarter section of non-irrigable land to look after."[3] This same concern for the successful combination of irrigable and non-irrigable land is found in the contract which was finally entered into between the Canadian

[1] Dennis to Whyte, August 14, 1905, *ibid.*

[2] See extract from minutes of meeting of Executive Committee of Board of Directors of C. P. R. Co. held in Montreal, September 1, 1905, File No. 355, Section 1, D. N. R.

[3] Dennis to C. P. I. C. Co., November 29, 1905, *ibid.*

Pacific and the C. P. I. C. Co. on November 1, 1905. The contract covered 110,000 acres of irrigable land "and such non-irrigable lands as may be grouped with and attached to the irrigable lands by the railway company." This contract did not provide for the sale of the land to the C. P. I. C. Co. By it the railway company merely constituted the colonization company its "sole and exclusive agent for the term of three years from the 31st day of December, 1905," for the sale of the specified lands. The purchaser of land through the C. P. I. C. Co. entered into a contract with the railway company. The function of the Beiseker-Davidson group was to obtain purchasers of Canadian Pacific land, to guarantee to the railway $11.00 and $6.00 for irrigable and non-irrigable land respectively, and to retain as profit all proceeds in excess of those figures. One-tenth of the purchase price must be paid by the buyer at the execution of the contract, the balance in not more than 9 equal annual installments, with interest at 6 per cent.[1] By the terms of the contract full power was reserved to Dennis, as Superintendent of Irrigation, to maintain strict oversight of the work of the company and to terminate the agreement upon 15 days' notice in the event of dissatisfaction with its methods or results.

The C. P. I. C. Co. was essentially one of the many colonization companies which were then operating extensively in the Canadian West. Some of these organizations bought land outright, while others merely served as selling agents, as did the Beiseker-Davidson Company in this particular instance. The company naturally arranged to establish an organization in the United States, Great Britain, and Canada. The usual procedure was to select one general agent in a given territory, who in turn organized a force of sub-agents. The general agency was ordinarily held by a prominent real estate or land company, with an abundant experience in land selling campaigns. Beiseker and his associates seem not to have appreciated the fact that in attempting the sale of irrigable land they were undertaking a task essentially different from that which had confronted them and other land companies in the past. One might have supposed that they would concentrate more especially on those portions of the American West where knowledge of irrigation was common. Instead, they proceeded as if selling humid lands.

[1] For contract, see File No. 355, Section 1, D. N. R.

By May of 1906 the company had 90 general agents in Minnesota, Michigan, Illinois, South Dakota, Nebraska, Kansas, Utah, Iowa, North Dakota, California, Ohio, Missouri, Idaho, Oklahoma, Wisconsin, and Massachusetts, together with several in the provinces of Canada.[1] The best results had been obtained in Minnesota, Iowa, and Idaho, of which only the latter was an irrigation state. In August the company reported that the movement of land seekers from the United States had been delayed by the harvest season, but that arrangements were being made for tourist cars to transport groups of buyers to Calgary. In Colorado two such parties were being formed. The Nebraska agents, of whom there were now upwards of 50, reported excellent prospects and promised to forward groups of buyers every week through the autumn season. Equally sanguine were the reports emanating from Utah. It was the belief of the company that 30,000 acres of irrigable land would be disposed of before the season closed. With a view to facilitating the actual occupation and cultivation of the land, the company was operating steam breaking outfits in the Gleichen district, so that the land would be ready for spring planting by the settler.[2]

Whatever the prospects of the company may have been at this time, Dennis was far from pleased with the way things were going. He was dissatisfied with everything from the front office to the agency organization. He found fault with the quantity and character of the advertising, the area of land sold during the previous six months, and with the demonstration farms which were supposed to provide object lessons in the art of irrigation.[3]

A short time later Dennis centered his fire upon other features of the company's policy. A flat price had been placed upon both the irrigable and non-irrigable land, $25.00 for the former and $15.00 for the latter. Non-irrigable land was being sold without an attached area of irrigable land, a practice which Dennis feared would render difficult the sale of the irrigable land at a later time.[4] Dennis rejected the contention of the company that buyers who were really inclined to purchase irrigable land would invest at $25.00 per acre as readily

[1] C. H. Davidson, President, C. P. I. C. Co., to Dennis, May 5, 1906, File No. 355, D. N. R.
[2] C. H. Davidson to Dennis, August 3, 1906, File No. 355, Section 1, D. N. R.
[3] Dennis to C. P. I. C. Co., August 4, 1906, *ibid.*
[4] Dennis to Davidson, September 15, 1906, *ibid.*

as at $20.000, and he disposed with equal dispatch of the argument in favor of the flat price, namely, that it was the practice of land companies generally, and that after the best lands had been sold at that price the remaining ones were then offered at a lower figure. Dennis believed the land should be priced according to quality, location, proximity to the railway, etc., and he suggested that for the present the maximum prices should be $20.00 and $10.00 respectively for irrigated and non-irrigated land. In his opinion land sales were proceeding so slowly that price reductions were necessary in order to stimulate greater activity on the part of land buyers. Such action was the more necessary in view of the failure of the company to develop adequately the demonstration farms which had been promised.

In September, 1906, the criticisms of Dennis resulted in the employment of a new and capable manager of the C. P. I. C. Co., C. W. Peterson, who coöperated readily with Dennis with a view to correcting some of the existing evils. At the suggestion of Dennis, Peterson devoted the next few months to the advertising and sales departments, to a revision of existing agencies and the creation of new ones, and to the employment of capable travelling agents. By the following spring reorganization of the agencies was completed and was described in detail by Peterson in an interesting report to Dennis, a document of sufficient significance, as a description of the organization employed by the large colonization companies then active in western Canada, to warrant careful examination.

In Great Britain the company's chief representative was A. E. Moore, who later entered and long continued in the service of the Canadian Pacific in the British Isles.[1] Moore's entire time was devoted to the perfecting of the organization in Great Britain and Ireland. Headquarters of the agency was in Dublin. Three general agencies were located in eastern Canada: the Union Trust Company of Toronto, Telfer and Osgood in Montreal, and the Trust and Guarantee Company in Toronto. The Union Trust Company had appropriated $12,000 for general agency and publicity work in connection with the irrigation enterprise and it had agreed to devote the entire attention of its land department to the sale of lands in the

---

[1] The agency organization of the company is described in detail in the letter of C. W. Peterson, General Manager, C. P. I. C. Co., to J. S. Dennis, April 29, 1907, *ibid.*

irrigation block. It employed 5 men on salary and expense for soliciting purposes. In the province of Quebec Telfer and Osgood were devoting their entire time to the work. Nor was western Canada neglected, in view of the 3 general agencies in British Columbia.

East and south of the Ohio River, in the United States, agencies were located at Port Chester, New York, Boston, Beaver Falls, Pennsylvania, and Lexington, Kentucky. Due to the factor of high transportation costs, less effort had been made to cultivate this field than others. In the Old Northwest the general agency was that of Strong, Nichols & Covell of Chicago. This firm maintained a salaried force of 6 men who devoted their undivided attention to the work. In addition, there were more than 100 sub-agencies actively engaged in this area.

The Canadian Pacific Irrigation Colonization Company maintained an inspector of agencies in Iowa on salary and expense, together with a large number of general and local agencies. Brubaker and Kirkwold of Minneapolis, the general agents for southern Minnesota, were exclusively concerned with the irrigable lands. Besides their 104 sub-agencies, they maintained a corps of sales solicitors on the road. Walsh and Law, of Cookston, were in charge of northern Minnesota, with 3 members of the firm solely identified with the sale of Alberta land, and with a large list of sub-agents.

North and South Dakota each counted 3 general agencies, while a general agency and 27 sub-agencies were located in Montana. There was also a salaried agent at Butte whose special duty it was to canvass the Deer Lodge Valley, a potentially fertile field from which to draw irrigation farmers. Nebraska, Kansas, and Missouri constituted the territory allotted to the Shedd Realty Company of Omaha, which, to date, had been the most successful agent of the C. P. I. C. Co. Five members of the firm gave all their time to the work, while they at the same time maintained a force of field men and 50 sub-agents.

As a leading irrigation state, Colorado had received special attention. Four general agencies were exclusively engaged in the work, with 12 men in the field, travelling incessantly. There were also 2 salaried men in the state who served as organizers of new agencies. A general agency in charge of the work in Idaho and Utah had the assistance of 2 salaried travelling agents. In the Pacific Northwest

2 men were giving their whole time to organization work. The Ferrier-Brock Company of San Francisco were the general agents for California. They maintained 4 travelling agents and a Canadian Land Department for the sole purpose of pushing the sale of land in the Calgary area. Some 25 new agencies were to be established in the Pacific Coast area.

Realizing the importance of establishing foreign colonies in the irrigation block as nuclei of further growth and development, the company had not neglected this important opportunity. It had opened a special agency at Buffalo for the purpose of conducting a campaign among Polish and German settlements in the eastern states. Arrangements were also being made to open an office near Castle Garden in New York, with a view to interesting newly-arrived immigrants in the possibilities of irrigation farming. While one must applaud the impulse which prompted this interest in foreign colonies, one may well question the judgment which dictated the choice of the eastern states as the particular field for the expression of this interest. Under ordinary conditions much more was to be hoped for from foreign colonies recruited in the middle and far western states, where farming conditions were not unlike those in Alberta.

At that time the C. P. I. C. Co. was expending $1,700 per month in salaries for travelling inspectors of agencies. The staff members of the general agencies and sub-agencies in the United States, all operating on a commission basis, numbered 50 and 600 respectively. All told, this was an imposing organization, covering completely the areas from which prospective settlers must come. Of its efficacy as a means of advertising southern Alberta there could be no question. Whether the results in actual buyers and settlers would be commensurate with the effort, only time could tell.

This far-flung agency system, however, represented merely one aspect of the campaign which was being waged for immigrants. In considerable measure the function of the army of agents was to follow up and cultivate an interest which had already been aroused through the advertising and publicity efforts which were directed from the head office of the C. P. I. C. Co. in Calgary. During the year 1906 the company had spent $26,548 for advertising, and in April, 1907, it had advertisements under contract involving an additional expenditure of $16,554, a total of $43,000 in some 15 months.

Advertisements of the company appeared regularly in 37 American papers and 9 Canadian, all chosen because of their circulation among the farming classes who constituted the potential immigrants. Descriptive literature and pamphlets came from the press in large volume, to be mailed to those whose curiosity had been aroused by the advertisements and to be scattered broadcast by the agency organization.

To reinforce the printed and spoken word with evidence of a more substantial nature, the two demonstration farms, with which Dennis had at first been so displeased, had been revamped under the direction of expert irrigationists from the United States. Crops of all kinds were to be raised by irrigation, affording the desired object lesson to the would-be settler, and guaranteeing the necessary instruction to those who actually settled in the irrigation block.

In order to make certain that the clients rounded up by the agency organization in the United States did not fall prey to the wiles of rival land interests, the company had provided two private tourist cars, operating from Chicago and Denver, in which the land seeker travelled to Calgary in charge of a company agent. Two additional cars were to be installed, one in Ontario and the other on the Pacific Coast. Business was expected to justify fortnightly trips by the four cars.

That the company was sparing no expense was shown by the fact that within a period of 15 months it had expended $220,000 in an effort to sell the land.[1] Of this sum, $67,000 represented commissions paid to agents; salaries and travelling expenses accounted for $41,000; and the cars and their operating expenses had cost about $30,000.[2] In the same period of time the sales of irrigable land had aggregated slightly less than 23,000 acres, while those of non-irrigable amounted to 14,000 acres, indicating clearly that the plan of Canadian Pacific officials for the association of the two kinds of land in combination farms had not been entirely realized.[3]

To appreciate the difficulty of stimulating a demand for land for irrigation purposes, one needs but to contrast this acreage with the much larger area of so-called "dry lands" which the Calgary Coloni-

---

[1] Dennis to Shaughnessy, April 30, 1907, File No. 355, Section 1, D. N. R.
[2] *Ibid.*
[3] *Ibid.*

zation Company had sold in the irrigation block in about the same length of time. Doubtless the successful sale of these lands, together with the willingness of men to gamble on the vagaries of the weather rather than assume the arduous and exacting duties of irrigation, retarded the sale of the lands tributary to secondary canal A, where Dennis hoped for thriving communities utilizing both irrigable and non-irrigable land.

Small as had been the sales by the C. P. I. C. Co., Dennis was inclined to feel that there had been certain extenuating circumstances which explained the situation. The winter and spring of 1906-7 in southern Alberta had been particularly severe and unfavorable. From early November to mid-April snow had blanketed the country, in contrast to the normal year when February alone prohibited land-selling activity. Many parties brought to Calgary in the hope of a change in the weather had been sent home without inspecting the land, while many other visits arranged for had to be cancelled, with the result that winter and spring had been virtually a total loss so far as land sales were concerned. Furthermore, Dennis solaced himself with the thought that "our project is so new and the sale and colonization of irrigable lands such an entirely different proposition to selling dry lands in the West that we must expect them to go rather slowly at first."

Despite a disposition to withhold final judgment in regard to the C. P. I. C. Co., there could be no doubt that Dennis and Whyte and Shaughnessy had really placed that company on probation, as it were. The summer of 1907 would be decisive in the history of the organization. Unless its results were far more impressive than in the previous year, Dennis was likely to avail himself of the contractual right of terminating the arrangement upon 15 days' notice.

By June, Dennis was once more voicing his displeasure with the company's pricing of the land. After reiterating his belief that the policy of the flat price was an unwise one, which inevitably retarded sales, he pointed out that the company was violating the terms of the contract as to the period of time allowed the purchaser for completing payment.[1] According to the agreement, one-tenth of the purchase price was to be paid in cash, with the balance in 9 equal installments. The company, however, was demanding one-fifth in

[1] Dennis to C. P. I. C. Co., June 1, 1907, File No. 355, Section 1, D. N. R.

cash, with 4 subsequent installments. Asserting that this practice, too, made sales more difficult, Dennis requested that the more liberal terms should be granted.[1] The objections of Dennis failed to bring the desired reforms. The manager of the C. P. I. C. Co., while admitting that there were elements of weakness in the flat price system, defended its use on the ground of its employment by all large land companies operating in western Canada. He further observed that his organization was committed to the policy and could not well break faith with existing purchasers by effecting wholesale reductions in prices at that time. This divergence in view between Dennis and the company could not endure indefinitely.

Meanwhile the C. P. I. C. Co. had entered into another contractual agreement with the Canadian Pacific. Within the confines of the irrigation block, north of the Rosebud River, was a large area of 300,000 acres of land, not included in the irrigation system. Much of it was attractive and entirely suitable for cultivation under conditions of natural rainfall. At the nearest point, however, it was about 24 miles from the main line of the Canadian Pacific and 16 miles from the Calgary and Edmonton line. Its distance from the railway would probably necessitate its sale at a fairly low price. During the early part of 1906 Dennis and Whyte gave much thought to the policy to be adopted for the sale of this area.

The Canadian Pacific Irrigation Colonization Company now offered to purchase 150,000 acres of the Rosebud tract at $6.00 per acre, subject to colonization conditions. Believing this to be a fair price in view of the remoteness of the land from the railway, Dennis recommended the sale on those terms.[2] Whyte was far from being favorably impressed by the proposal. Previous sales of dry land to the Calgary Colonization Company had netted the railway up to $6.00 per acre, and the increase in land values in the meantime more than offset the distance of the Rosebud lands from the railway. Sayre and his associates had readily retailed the lands at $11.00 per acre, which, allowing $3.00 as the cost of selling, gave them a clear profit of $3.00 per acre. On the 150,000-acre Rosebud tract the C. P. I. C. Co. would net $450,000, a large tribute, as Whyte thought, for the

[1] *Ibid.*
[2] Dennis to Whyte, November 11, 1905, File No. 436, D. N. R.

railway to pay for colonizing its lands.[1] Nor did Whyte believe the cost of selling to be $3.00 per acre in view of the fact that one of the largest land companies in Winnipeg figured the sale cost at $2.00 per acre.[2] He suggested that the railway should ask $6.50 or $7.00, which the C. P. I. C. Co. refused to pay.[3]

Thereupon Dennis suggested the possibility that the Canadian Pacific might realize $7.00 per acre by an agency agreement which would merely make the company the selling agent of the railway. His proposal was that he should be authorized to make a contract by which the railway would bear one-half of the expense of selling and receive one-half of the proceeds in excess of $6.00 per acre.[4] This suggestion met with the approval of Shaughnessy and Whyte who authorized Dennis to negotiate such an agreement.[5]

By this contract the railway made the C. P. I. C. Co. the exclusive selling agent, for a period of 3 years from July 1, 1906, of 150,000 acres in the Rosebud tract.[6] Purchasers must pay one-sixth in cash, with the balance in 5 equal annual installments. The railway company's share of the selling cost, including advertising, office expenses, and all other charges, was not to exceed $2.00 per acre. In the case of sales to actual settlers the railway was to allow the colonization company a rebate of 50 cents per acre.

The C. P. I. C. Co. entered with great vigor into the work of selling the lands in the Rosebud tract. Special effort was made to sell the lands only to those who would take up residence and develop them in person, or who would cause them to be developed. The company persistently refused to sell large tracts for speculative purposes. Particular attention was given to German families in North Dakota who had had years of farming experience there under conditions substantially the same as in Alberta.[7] These were members of the German Baptist sect, thrifty and hard-working, well supplied with live stock, implements, and machinery, and with sufficient

[1] Whyte to Dennis, December 8, 1905, *ibid.*
[2] *Ibid.*
[3] *Ibid.* Also Dennis to Whyte, January 2, 1906, File No. 436, in which he says the company will not pay $6.50 per acre.
[4] Dennis to Whyte, January 2, 1906, File No. 436, D. N. R.
[5] Whyte to Dennis, January 18, 1906, *ibid.*
[6] The contract is in File No. 436, D. N. R.
[7] A. J. Sayre, Calgary Colonization Co., to Dennis, December 16, 1908, File No. 436, D. N. R.

money to make possible the erection of suitable buildings. To December, 1908 some 40,000 acres had actually been purchased by these settlers and they were contracting for an additional 20,000 acres.[1] When complete, the colony was to number about 100 families of the generous proportions customarily found among people of that type. This group alone would constitute a most promising beginning toward the complete colonization of the Rosebud area.[2] One section of land was set aside as a demonstration farm, with 160 acres of it under cultivation.[3] On this farm several thousand trees had been planted with a view to supplying them to settlers who wished to beautify their farms.

In the sale of irrigable land, however, the C. P. I. C. Co. failed to achieve a comparable success. Increasingly, Whyte and Shaughnessy were displeased not only with the slowness of the sales but also with the return per acre sold. Believing that a more economical medium of sale could be devised, they instructed Dennis in December, 1907 to work out an arrangement for the surrender of the contract by Beiseker, Davidson and Sayre. It was evident, of course, that the ultimate success of the effort to colonize the irrigation block would depend in no small measure on a successful reorganization of the sub-agency force in the United States, and this was impossible so long as a middleman's profit had to be paid to Beiseker and Davidson. Elimination of that profit would make possible the payment of substantial commissions to the agents and sub-agents in the field, who, in the last analysis, must bring the land purchasers.

The agreement finally worked out provided that the Canadian Pacific Irrigation Colonization Company should be taken over directly by the Canadian Pacific Railway Company on January 1, 1908; and that in return for the surrender of their equity in the existing contract, Beiseker and Davidson should be paid $50,000, plus $2.00 per acre for all land covered by the contract which the railway might sell during the year 1908.[4] Thus the Canadian Pacific Irrigation Colonization Company became, for all practical purposes, the land and colonization department of the Canadian Pacific Rail-

[1] Ibid.
[2] Ibid.
[3] Ibid.
[4] Telegram, J. S. Dennis to R. B. Bennett, January 28, 1908, File No. 355, Section 2, D. N. R. Bennett was then counsel for the C. P. R. in Calgary.

way, in so far as the lands within the irrigation block were concerned. The advantage of this arrangement to the railway is apparent. Irrigable land which the C. P. I. C. Co. had sold at $25.00 per acre had netted the railway $11.00. Under the new regime, after paying Beiseker and Davidson $2.00 per acre and allowing $5.00 per acre as the cost of selling, it would net $18.00 per acre.

The Calgary staff of the company, with Peterson as manager, was retained, and new contracts were entered into with the agencies in the United States. One of the important weaknesses of the Beiseker and Davidson set-up had been the lack of coördination of the far-reaching agency organization through headquarters in Calgary. Dennis and Peterson now began the necessary reforms which within a year made the company a model of efficiency. So smoothly did it function as a land selling agency, so perfect was it compared with earlier railway machines for colonization purposes, that its methods merit careful analysis.

Under the Beiseker and Davidson regime inquiries elicited by the advertising and publicity of the company were merely forwarded to the agent in the district whence the request came. There was no attempt on the part of the main office to cultivate the client or to meet him on a common ground. That responsibility devolved on the agency, remote from Calgary. A new procedure was now adopted. Immediately upon the receipt of the inquiry at headquarters, a friendly letter was sent to the person in question, together with literature descriptive of the irrigation project.

The letter naturally contained a certain amount of advertiser's license. First of all the individual was told that irrigation farming was simple;[1] that the most successful community of irrigation farmers in southern Alberta was composed wholly of men who had never seen an irrigated field before coming to the province; that the irrigation of land required no more skill than the plowing or harvesting; that irrigation farming was not scientific farming but "business farming"—statements which represented a pardonable attempt to dispel both doubt and prejudice with respect to irrigation. Another paragraph drew a contrast between prices of irrigated land in the United States and in Alberta, a contrast which, due to the absence of engineering difficulties, was wholly favorable to the latter.

[1] Circular to Inquirers in Non-irrigation States, File No. 554, D. N. R.

The prospective client was reminded that the Canadian laws with respect to water had recently been pronounced by the National Irrigation Convention at Albuquerque, New Mexico, to be at least fifty years in advance of those in the United States.[1]

Occupying a conspicuous place in the communication was a statement accurately representing the objective of the officials of the Canadian Pacific Railway, but one which an agent in the field, with ordinary human frailty, might on occasion forget. It read: "Ours is neither a land nor a water-selling scheme. The low prices charged for both make that clear. The C. P. R. is expending millions of dollars on this project purely and simply to build up the most prosperous agricultural community in America. This sounds like philanthropy but it isn't. The railway wants a prosperous community in order to create the greatest possible volume of traffic. Therefore, we appeal to those only who will add to the prosperity of this section."[2] This was an extremely laudable purpose on the part of the railway company, but the agent, whose earnings depended on his commissions on land sold, was unlikely to distinguish between the settler and the speculative purchaser so long as the company's regulations failed to make occupation of the land compulsory.

This letter went in response to inquiries from non-irrigation states. To those from irrigation states of the Far West was sent a very similar one, except that it said nothing about experience in irrigation, or the lack thereof.[3] The letter sent to eastern Canada contained a paragraph intended to appeal especially to people in that area. It said: "While the American farmers see the money-making possibilities of and are coming into western Canada by the thousands each year, still the farmers of Ontario who have come into Southern Alberta have made the most successful irrigationists. Which fact goes to prove that irrigation is no mystery, and to meet with the greatest measure of success but requires that intelligence which has built up the prosperous agricultural class of Eastern Canada."[4]

While adjusting its appeal to the particular needs and to the peculiar situation of larger geographic areas, such as the Middle

[1] Ibid.
[2] Ibid.
[3] Circular to People in Irrigation States, File No. 554, D. N. R.
[4] Circular to Inquirers from Eastern Canada, 1907, File No. 554, D. N. R.

West, Far West, and Ontario, the company did not lose sight of the special interests of farmers in smaller areas. A circular might be prepared solely for a given state or for a particular county. Of the latter, that to the farmers in Lee County, Iowa, may be regarded as typical.[1] These men were told that "with the possible exception of the people of North Dakota . . . the people from no other state have made so much money in Southern Alberta farms as have those from Central, Western and Northern Iowa." At a recent celebration of Lincoln's birthday held in Calgary, Iowa had enjoyed a larger representation than any other state, and those present had received telegraphic greetings from the governor and bishop of their old home state. The farmer was then reminded that one-quarter to two-thirds of the price of his Iowa farm would buy land in southern Alberta which would earn 20 to 30 per cent in crops alone, and as much more in the form of appreciation in land value. He was strongly urged to communicate with the representative of the C. P. I. C. Co. in his county and to avail himself of the low-rate excursion to Alberta.[2]

The interest of people in special areas was catered to in this manner. But meanwhile a standardized procedure was being worked out to be employed in the case of every one of the thousands of names received in the Calgary office, regardless of the particular locality from which they came. Contact with the prospective settler must not be spasmodic or casual; it must be regular and systematic. To this end, four "seductive" letters, with accompanying literature, were sent at intervals to every inquirer.[3] Having in mind the great interest aroused in the United States by the periodical opening of Indian reservations to settlement, the first letter referred to the Canadian Pacific Irrigation Block as a reservation created by the Dominion Government in 1894, hitherto closed to settlement, but now at last opened up to the land hungry farmers of the United States. After describing the superior location of this area, all of it tributary to the main line of the railway and easily accessible to markets and to social and educational advantages, the letter assured the interested parties that the company was in a position to accom-

[1] Circular Letter to Farmers in Lee County, Iowa, February 22, 1908, *ibid.*
[2] *Ibid.*
[3] Copies of the four letters are in File No. 554, D. N. R.

modate every kind of land seeker. Grazing lands, winter wheat lands, all-irrigable farms, and combination farms were available. The company could satisfy the grain grower, the dairy farmer, the sugar-beet grower, and the cattle, horse, and sheep rancher.

This communication further reminded the prospective settler that the interest of the Canadian Pacific Railway in him did not cease when it had sold the land; in fact, its interest just then began. If there was any one thing which the company could not afford to do it was to sell land to the person who either would fail to occupy the land or make a failure of his effort at farming. To increase the chances of success, the letter said, the railway maintained demonstration farms for the instruction of the farmer in the best and most approved methods, while a development branch was at hand to undertake the breaking, fencing, and cropping of the land in advance of settlement.

The second letter announced that the publication, *The Staff of Life,* was being forwarded in the belief that the farmer might be interested in winter wheat growing. The non-irrigated winter wheat lands of the company were said to be, perhaps, the most fertile on the continent. The growth of this crop had proven very profitable on areas of 320 acres and upwards, and in scores of cases a single crop had more than paid for the land. Should the client be interested in mixed farming, however, attention was called to the combination farms described in detail in *Facts*, another pamphlet. He was told that the farmer on irrigable land was immune to drought, the "arch-enemy" of agriculture. With the certainty that this land would quickly increase in value, the farmer could not afford to delay.

When the farmer had had sufficient time to digest this material, the third letter was mailed to him, accompanied by the booklet, *Public Opinion*, containing press opinions and letters from purchasers of land and settlers within the irrigation block. The letter called attention to the cheap home-seekers' rates in effect and urged the man to make the trip even though he had no immediate intention of buying land. Confident that to see southern Alberta was to be convinced of its potentialities, the company reasoned that a visit might well convert the visitor and through him enlist the interest of his friends and neighbors.

With the fourth letter there went *Starting a Farm*, a pamphlet "practically edited by the settlers themselves"; in fact, as the letter stated, "it is their testimony that has made this publication possible." The letters were written by practical farmers who had actually started homes of their own in the irrigation block and who knew whereof they spoke. In the course of about forty days, the four letters, with the literature, were received by the farmer. Supplemented as this written appeal was by the personal visit of the company's local representative, the land-seeker could not lack for information with respect to what the Canadian Pacific had to offer.

While thus systematizing its relations with the land-seekers, the head office in Calgary was placing its dealings with its agency organization upon a more regular and intimate basis. One of the first steps taken to this end was the revision of the commission arrangements. So great had been the profit taken by Beiseker and Davidson that during their regime neither the amount nor the manner of payment of the commission to the agents had been satisfactory. While selling the land at a flat price, they had paid their agents a commission of $1.50 per acre on irrigable and $1.00 on non-irrigable land. Under the new arrangement, irrigable land selling for $24.00 per acre and above would command a commission of $2.50 per acre, while irrigable land priced between $18.00 and $24.00 per acre would pay a commission of $2.25 per acre. Thus, by dispensing with the middleman's tribute, the Canadian Pacific could pay larger commissions and, at the same time, receive greater returns. On non-irrigable land, the commission was to be $1.00, $1.25, or $1.50 per acre according to the price at which it was sold. The commission had been increased, therefore, on the class of land then sold in the largest quantity, irrigable land selling upwards from $18.00 per acre.

More drastic, however, was the change in the manner of paying the commission. Selling land on the deferred payment plan, Beiseker and Davidson had paid but a fraction of the commission at the time of sale, paying the agents the balance as subsequent payments were made upon the land. The inevitable result of this practice was to limit the working capital of the agent at any given time, to complicate the problem of meeting his overhead expense, and to make difficult the payment of commissions to his sub-agents. To obviate

this difficulty, so far as possible, Beiseker and Davidson had, contrary to the better judgment of Dennis, sought to reduce the deferred
installments from 9 to 4 or 5, with frequent hardship to the settler or
even at the cost of a sale. Under the new regulations the proportion
of the total commission paid the agent in cash was graded according
to the amount of the cash payment which the purchaser made at
the time of purchase. In the case of irrigable land carrying a commission of $2.50 per acre, the entire amount was paid the agent
where the buyer paid as much as one-fifth cash. For one-sixth cash
the agent would receive 80 per cent of his total commission in cash.
Upon payment of one-eighth to one-tenth of the purchase price in
cash, the agent would receive immediately 50 to 70 per cent of his
total commission. These payments were double the proportion of
the commission hitherto paid at the time of the purchase of the
land. On non-irrigable land the cash proportion was increased two
and one-half times. Nor was this all that was done to smooth the
way and ease the burdens of the agents. In future the company was
to pay 6 per cent interest on all outstanding commissions owed to
agents, and to make prompt settlement for commission certificates
upon receipt of deferred payment for land.

Not only were these reforms well-calculated to place the agents
in a pleasant frame of mind, but they unquestionably gave every
possible pecuniary incentive for them to push the company's lands
with renewed vigor. At the same time the Calgary office, by personal
and circular letters, kept in constant touch with the agency organization. Through the circulars, sent out weekly, the agents were kept
informed as to developments in southern Alberta, including land
sales, the movement of settlers, crop conditions, etc. No detail was
omitted which might enable the agents to carry on their work more
intelligently and efficiently. Not even the weather was neglected.
During the winter of 1906-7, while Beiseker and Davidson controlled
the C. P. I. C. Co., agents brought large numbers of land-seekers to
Calgary, who, because of the snow and severe weather, were unable
to inspect the land, much to the disappointment and discomfort of
the agents and the would-be buyer, and to the expense of the company. Ordinarily, however, so much of the winter season was favorable for land selling operations that the company felt it was not
warranted in suspending such activities during that portion of the

year. The problem, therefore, was to continue the work, but so to coördinate the organization that the occasional severe storm would not be coincident with the arrival of parties of home-seekers at Calgary. As the winter of 1908 approached, arrangements were made whereby the Calgary office would telegraph the St. Paul office immediately upon the occurrence of unfavorable weather in the irrigation block. The inspector of agencies at the latter point could issue a circular letter which would reach most of the agencies within twelve hours. Or, at his discretion, he might resort to the use of the telegraph in cases of emergency. The one remaining contingency to be guarded against was a storm developing while the agent and his clients were en route to Calgary. In such cases the company agreed to take care of the parties at its expense until the storm had passed, or to bear the cost of a second trip.[1]

Never were the agents permitted to lose sight of the fact that the goal of the company was the most complete agricultural development of the irrigation block, with the density of traffic which, it was hoped, that would produce. When, with this object in view, the Calgary office issued a booklet entitled *The Settlers' Guide*, intended primarily for the use of those who had purchased land from the company in the irrigation block rather than for general distribution, the agents were asked to acquaint themselves with this publication in order that they might be in a position to render every assistance possible to the prospective settler.[2] Indeed the agents were urgently requested to familiarize themselves with all the literature issued by the company.

By 1909 the number of publications had increased to the point where the gradual feeding of them to the prospect required a period of about six months. In addition, the company gave to every inquirer a six months' subscription to the *Farm and Ranch Review*, a Calgary paper devoted to the agricultural development of the southern Alberta country. In this way headquarters at Calgary could keep the inquirer interested for half the year. But, as the manager observed, the effectiveness of this appeal depended largely upon the thoroughness with which the agent mastered his material before

---

[1] Circular to Agents, November 7, 1908, File No. 554, D. N. R.
[2] Circular to Agents, September 2, 1908, *ibid.*

approaching his client. The final effort of the management to secure maximum coöperation of the agents was the preparation of a *Manual for Agents,* a step as strongly suggestive of the methods of book-selling concerns as the house-to-house canvassing of the agents in the States.

The forms of propaganda just described were supplemented by general publicity. As the Dominion Government, as well as the railways, was "booming" the Canadian West in the United States, it occurred to all parties concerned that better results might be obtained from a certain degree of union and coöperation for publicity purposes than from separate and independent action of the various agencies of colonization. In 1908 the government, the Canadian Pacific Land Department at Winnipeg, the Canadian Northern Railway, and the Grand Trunk Pacific Railway jointly entered into a contract with the advertising agency of Herbert Vanderhoof of Chicago, each contributing the sum of $5,000. For this consideration, Vanderhoof conducted an extensive publicity campaign in behalf of western Canada in American journals circulating among the rural population. The coöperative arrangement thus effected proved so satisfactory that it was continued by all parties through 1914. Although the Canadian Pacific agreement with Vanderhoof was made by the land department at Winnipeg, which had no jurisdiction over the lands in the irrigation block, Vanderhoof actively began advertising the irrigated lands, since the Canadian Pacific Railway had now taken over the Canadian Pacific Irrigation Colonization Company. In short, Vanderhoof represented the entire landed interest of the railway company.[1]

Vanderhoof had yet another medium for spreading the Canadian gospel in the States. There then existed in Chicago a magazine, *Canada West,* devoted solely to the advancement of knowledge of the prairie provinces. In 1908 Vanderhoof purchased a half-interest in this publication. The Calgary and Winnipeg land offices of the Canadian Pacific promptly availed themselves of this opportunity, each taking a full-page advertisement in the paper at $35 per issue. The magazine had a large American subscription list, built up by the publishers with the assistance of the St. Paul agent of the

[1] Griffin to Dennis, May 7, 1908, File No. 183, D. N. R.

Dominion Government, who had circulated 10,000 copies of it among American home-seekers.[1]

The circular letters to agents in that year contain frequent references to the arrival of groups of land buyers at Calgary. According to one communication "a large party from a central western State is with us today. Tomorrow a very representative delegation of magazine editors and writers from the United States will be shown over the more important parts of the Irrigation district and our system fully explained to them. While writing we have received telegraphic advice of another party of nearly eighty land seekers being on the way."[2] Another referred to a party of Hollanders sailing from Rotterdam, together with personally conducted parties from England and Scotland.[3] Still another mentioned the sale of 30 sections of land to one party of German settlers from North Dakota, all of them *bona fide* farmers.[4] The same letter recorded the arrival of personally conducted parties from England and Holland.

Beginning in January, 1909 the Calgary office launched directly in the press of the United States a publicity campaign of large proportions. Within a month it was receiving upwards of 200 letters of inquiry daily, which were "followed up" in the manner indicated above. By the end of March no less than 11,000 letters had been received, while in the same period 1,300 prospective settlers had registered at the Calgary headquarters and inspected the land in the irrigation block. These people had come from 25 different states of the United States. Land sales for the first 3 months of the year were four-fold greater than for the corresponding period of 1908. During the first 5 months 117 cars of settlers' effects had arrived at Strathmore, while large numbers had gone to other towns. So rapid was the movement of settlement that the railway deemed the time opportune for the establishment of new towns along the branch line running north from Langdon.

The rapid increase in the sale of land during the early part of 1909 was soon followed by an increase in the price of both irrigable and non-irrigable land. According to the new price schedule, the

[1] Vanderhoof to Dennis, April 8, 1908, *ibid.*
[2] Circular to Agents, August 21, 1908, File No. 554, D. N. R.
[3] Circular to Agents, July 31, 1908, *ibid.*
[4] Circular to Agents, August 7, 1908, *ibid.*

maximum for the former was to be $30.00 per acre, and for the latter $18.00. A number of considerations had contributed to this decision on the part of the company. Due to the unprecedented rush for Canadian lands during the current season, farm values in southern Alberta had risen sharply on all sides of the irrigation block, thereby justifying an advance in the price placed upon irrigable lands 4 years before. The company felt, too, that the increase was an act of justice to those who had first purchased land in the western section of the irrigation block. While strongly opposed to speculative land buying, the company recognized that this element entered into many purchases and had to be taken into consideration. Owing to unforeseen engineering difficulties, the cost of construction of the irrigation project would exceed considerably the first estimate, upon which the existing land prices had been based. Taking account of construction cost plus the large commissions paid on irrigated lands, such lands were netting the company less than the non-irrigated. This condition could be remedied only by a general increase in prices. Furthermore, as an encouragement to irrigation the company desired to extend to its purchasers the free use of water for a period of 2 or 3 years, which it could not do without an advance in the price of land. The management desired, too, to sell 40- and 60-acre tracts at the same price per acre as quarter sections, which would entail a considerable loss which had to be recouped by a general increase in prices.

Revision of the price structure, of course, required a change in commissions. In future the agent would receive $3.00 on $30.00 irrigable land, while on non-irrigable land selling at $18.00 per acre a flat $2.00 commission would be paid, which would enable the agents to meet all competition.[1] Equally important was the increase in the cash proportion of the commission to be paid to the agents under the new regulations.

Another item dealt with at this time was that of clients who appeared in Calgary with letters of introduction from agents, but unaccompanied by them as provided in the contract between the company and its agents. Usually such clients were not considered sufficiently promising by the agent to justify the time and expense of accompanying them. Although the responsibility of handling and

[1] Circular to Agents, June 4, 1909, File No. 554, D. N. R.

selling this prospect thus devolved upon the Calgary officials, the agent nevertheless expected his commission. The company now stipulated that in future it would pay only 50 per cent of the normal commission in such cases, leaving it free to pay double commission in cases where a client was claimed by two agents, as was frequently in case.[1]

Many of the company's agents in the United States, while showing parties of American buyers through the irrigation block, were in the habit of enlisting the interest of Alberta residents in Canadian Pacific lands, claiming therefor the regular commissions upon such sales. Eventually this practice became so frequent that the management was forced to take cognizance of it and to adopt regulations with respect thereto. Henceforth the agent was to receive a commission of but 6 per cent in such cases. This action, of course, was based upon the obvious fact that the organization in Calgary was entirely capable of taking care of all local business, without the payment of commission. This procedure was necessary in order to keep the average selling cost within reasonable limits.

Among the many perplexing problems which inevitably arose in connection with a campaign of such proportions as that which the company was waging for the settlement of its lands in southern Alberta was that of meeting the competition of other land companies actively engaged in the sale of land in the Canadian West. Many of these companies were American organizations. Several, if not most of them, had headquarters in St. Paul and Minneapolis, the very heart of the territory in which the Canadian Pacific was concentrating its efforts. These syndicates had been active since the turn of the century, and in the course of the years had developed a technique of land selling unknown to an earlier day. They were exclusively engaged in the sale of "dry" lands in the Canadian West, lands which either did not require or were not susceptible of irrigation. The C. P. I. C. Co., therefore, had to convince the settler that irrigable land was preferable to the cheaper lands the other companies were selling. But it had to do more than that; it had to meet the low cost of transportation which these companies provided for land-seekers.

The Beiseker and Davidson regime had first faced this problem.

[1] Circular to Agents, June 30, 1909, *ibid.*

Before the end of their first year in control of the C. P. I. C. Co. their Minneapolis agents were complaining of their inability to meet the $15.00 round trip rate between the Twin cities and Calgary, advertised and offered by the O. W. Kerr and the Stone Land companies of Minneapolis and by the Luse Land Company and the British-American Land Company of St. Paul. To compete with this rate, which was lower than the ordinary home-seeker's rate, the C. P. I. C. Co. had been able to offer nothing better than $31.00, which lost for their agents business which they had spent time and money to develop.[1]

To this problem Peterson at once gave his attention when he became manager of the C. P. I. C. Co. in December, 1906. He took the position that the company's most difficult task was to induce people to come to Alberta to look over its land. The merits of the proposition and the efficiency of the sales organization were such that it was easy to sell likely prospects once they visited Calgary. He therefore attached slight importance to the company's practice of refunding fares in case of actual purchase. When the farmer was duly impressed with the land his decision would not be influenced one way or the other by the offer to refund $30 or $40. On the other hand, agents were experiencing difficulty in convincing people that their proposition was worth risking $60 or $70 to investigate.[2]

Peterson's plan was to select a number of common points in the United States, to calculate carefully the cost of transportation of carloads of passengers, cost of berths, meals, etc., and to divide the amount into three parts, the home-seeker paying 50 per cent, the agent 25 per cent, and the company 25 per cent. This reduced rate was to apply only where a carload of prospects made the trip and where they returned in a body. Peterson believed the 25 per cent borne by the agent would tend to make him more careful and responsible in accepting his men.[3]

By this plan the agent could approach a prospective buyer with the offer of a low rate for the whole trip, including all expenses. By removing the element of uncertainty as to what the trip would

---

[1] Brubaker and Kirkwold to C. H. Davidson, December 13, 1906, File No. 2923, D. N. R.

[2] Peterson to Beiseker, December 28, 1906, *ibid.*

[3] *Ibid.*

cost, he would remove the great obstacle to successful land selling. The scheme had the added merit that, with the return trip in the company car paid for, the "prospects" would not scatter over the country to inspect other land propositions, as had about 50 per cent of those who came to Calgary in small parties at their own expense. Irrespective of its other advantages, however, the plan had the merit of enabling the company to meet a competitive situation of an acute nature.

While thus cultivating with diligence the American field for immigrants, the Calgary office had not overlooked the Canadian scene. There were, of course, in Montreal and Ontario, as well as in British Columbia, agency organizations of the C. P. I. C. Co. which were pushing the sale of land in Alberta. It occurred to Dennis, however, that besides these special agencies, the Canadian Pacific Railway had, in its station agents throughout Canada, a large force of men who might be enlisted in the cause of land sale and settlement. With large numbers of people passing daily through their offices en route to western Canada, the agents were in a position to render valuable service in the colonization of railway lands. In June, 1907 a circular letter was addressed by Dennis to all agents of the railway, advising them that a commission of 25 cents per acre would be paid them on all land sold to persons bringing a letter of introduction from one of them. To insure the presentation of the letter at the Calgary office of the C. P. I. C. Co., the holder was advised that it would be accepted as a $5.00 payment on account of any land purchased by him from the company. Failing through this first circular to achieve appreciable results, Dennis issued another in August, 1908, with greater inducements to the agents to exert themselves. The commission on land sales was increased to 50 cents per acre, and to make the system more complete it was suggested that a carbon copy of all letters of introduction issued by the agents should be forwarded to the Calgary office.[1]

Although the company sought the successful establishment of farmers of all kinds, whether individually or in groups, in the irrigation block, it quickly came to the conclusion that the community type of settlement would insure the most permanent and

[1] Circular by Dennis to agents of the C. P. R. Co., August 22, 1908, File No. 554, D. N. R.

prosperous, though probably not the most rapid, colonization of the area. The well-known group consciousness and community spirit of religious sects speaking foreign languages, the earlier success of the Canadian Pacific in the location of such colonies on government land, and the large amount of attention which American railways had given to this form of land settlement, turned the attention of the company to these people as likely colonists for its irrigable lands. By virtue of its ownership of the lands *en bloc* instead of in alternate sections, the railway was able to offer exceptional opportunities for compact settlements of the various national groups.

Mention has been made of the agency established in Buffalo with a view to cultivating the Polish population of the eastern states. A Pole, with long experience in colonization work on the Pacific Coast of the United States, was placed in charge of this office. Within a year the irrigation project had been described to more than 100,-000 members of the Polish National Alliance, whose officers had become interested in southern Alberta as a possible field for Polish settlement. One member of the colonization committee of the alliance had visited Calgary, while the company had paid the expense of at least a dozen delegates, including one of the most influential Polish Roman Catholic priests of the eastern states and the representative of a large group of Poles residing in Brazil. The agency had carried on a publicity campaign on a large scale. Advertising had been placed regularly in all the leading Polish papers and several hundred thousand circulars had been distributed. Public meetings throughout the eastern states had been addressed by special agents and attended by thousands of Poles. Activities of the Buffalo office were supplemented by those of one more recently established at New York for the purpose of contacting those arriving from Europe. The company set aside a reserve in the irrigation block for Polish settlement, and late in the summer of 1907 the colony of Krakow was located and equipped by the company with a hotel where the new arrivals were accommodated free of charge.[1]

Meanwhile the company was interesting itself in other nationalities. In the autumn of 1907 the general agent of the C. P. I. C. Co. at Council Bluffs, Iowa, J. N. K. Macalister, reported that he was in

[1] Memorandum of Peterson for Dennis, September 23, 1907, File No. 336, D. N. R.

touch with a responsible Danish gentleman in Elk Horn, Iowa, who was desirous of establishing a colony of his countrymen in western Canada. The majority of these people lived on rented farms but possessed on an average of from $2,000 to $3,000 per family in personal property and cash. The gentleman wished the company to reserve 15,000 acres, chiefly of irrigable land, to be sold by him to his people over a period of years. His compensation would, of course, be determined on a commission basis, which Macalister would arrange with him. He was further willing to show his good faith by coming to Calgary to purchase land on his own account, while any contract entered into by him with the company might contain a clause cancelling the agreement in the event of his failure to sell the land in the required time.[1]

This was the germ of the Danish colony which was successfully established in the block. The company agreed to reserve the land, but Macalister experienced some anxious moments before the colony was finally established. When it became a matter of common knowledge among land men that these Danish people were planning to emigrate to Canada, they were besieged by rival land companies who were pushing Saskatchewan lands. Macalister's job was to convince them of the superior advantages of Alberta. To make the agent's task easier, the company offered Carl Christianson, the leader of the Danish group, a sub-agency for the sale of land in his territory, and Peterson, the Manager of the C. P. I. C. Co., made a special trip to Iowa to address the Danish community. In order to clinch an excursion of the group to Alberta, the Calgary office pledged itself to refund railway fare to any one purchasing 160 acres of land. By dint of great effort, Macalister, with this assistance, was able to hold the group against the blandishments of his Saskatchewan rivals. The colony was established, within 2 years the 17,000 acre reserve was occupied, and an additional area was set aside to satisfy further accessions to the settlement.

A number of successful French Canadian colonies having been established in northern Alberta at an earlier time, it was natural that the Canadian Pacific should turn its thoughts in the direction of these people, the more so since one of the general agencies of the

[1] Macalister to C. W. Peterson, September 30, 1907, File No. 209, D. N. R.

company, that of Telfer and Osgood, of Montreal, was favorably situated for carrying on colonization work in the province of Quebec. As early as the summer of 1907 Telfer and Osgood interested themselves in a plan for a French-Canadian colony in the irrigation block. Their efforts to enlist the interest of the *habitant* met with slight success until Dennis pointed out to them that the only hope lay in securing the leadership and coöperation of the Church in the enterprise. Eventually they obtained the friendly assistance of a bishop and of Father Ouellette, who had established three of the thriving colonies of French Canadians in northern Alberta. In the summer of 1908 Father Ouellette visited Calgary, spent a week in an examination of the irrigation project, and submitted a proposition for the location of a settlement. In response to this proposal, Dennis agreed to reserve an entire township in the Cluny district for the community until December 31, 1911. He would sell the irrigable land at $22.50 per acre, and the non-irrigable at $12.50, in 10 annual instalments.[1] This somewhat lower-than-usual price was contingent upon the occupation of the land by the individual purchaser within one year of the date of sale. The land might be sold in parcels of 40 acres and upwards to any one purchaser. Forty acres were to be set aside for the establishment of the church, school, and priest's residence. Fifteen families were to be located on the land by December 31, 1909, with an additional 50 families during 1910, while the colonization of the tract must be completed in 1911.[2] The company agreed to appropriate $900 for the use of the priest whom Father Ouellette placed in charge of the project.[3]

The colony was launched under auspicious circumstances. In October, 1908 a party of 31 French Canadian farmers visited Calgary, purchased 28 quarter-sections of land in the reserve, and planned to begin the cultivation of the land in the following spring. But this was not to last. The following summer Dennis, becoming dissatisfied with the progress which Telfer and Osgood were making with the sale of land, increased the price and warned them of the possibility of cancellation of the contract. When at the close of 1910 but 32 of

---

[1] Dennis to Telfer and Osgood, July 17, 1908, File No. 221, D. N. R.
[2] *Ibid.*
[3] Copy of letter, Telfer and Osgood to Father Ouellette, July 17, 1908, *ibid.*

the required 65 families had been located in the colony, the agreement was abrogated and further efforts by the agents ceased.

It should not be inferred from this that the colony was a failure. Although the settlers experienced many of the vicissitudes of fortune peculiar to a pioneer area, they managed, with the aid of the Canadian Pacific, which supplied them with seed grain, to make steady, if not rapid, progress. The area devoted to crops increased from year to year, and within a short time the colony was considering the possibility of acquiring adjoining lands to accommodate newcomers as well as the surplus population within the colony itself.

Contemporaneously with the founding of this community there was an effort made by the company to establish the nucleus of what it hoped would become a large settlement of people from Australia. When two Australians appeared in Calgary as the advance guard of such a movement, with the request that they be sold some 2,000 acres of land at a figure attractive to them, Dennis readily acceded and recommended that Shaughnessy authorize the sale. While agreeing with Dennis as to the desirability of creating as many group settlements as possible, Shaughnessy gave his approval rather grudgingly.[1] The sale was made but no large Australian element was introduced into the irrigation block as a result of this attempt.

In its efforts to form compact communities in the irrigation block, the company did not lose sight of the Dutch as material from which successful colonies might be forged. It maintained a general agent in Rotterdam and it had sent as special agent to Holland the Reverend Father Van Aken of Helena, Montana.[2] In the spring of 1908 the latter arrived in Calgary with the first party of Dutch settlers, who were located near Strathmore, north of the main line of the railway. At that point, in a newly created irrigation district, the company set aside lands to care for the colony and to provide for its subsequent growth. Having secured this first contingent of settlers direct from Holland, it was the hope of Peterson and Dennis that Dutch colonists who had had farming experience in the United States might also be located in the reserve and thereby provide for

[1] Shaughnessy to Dennis, August 4, 1908, *ibid.*

[2] Peterson to F. Le Cocq, Harrison, South Dakota, November 11, 1907, File No. 222, Section I, D. N. R.

the others instruction in the up-to-date farming methods needed in Alberta.[1]

This colony enjoyed the watchful care and assistance of the company, which was so eager to make a success of this type of settlement. When the community was visited by a ruinous hail storm before the end of their first season, Dennis not only conveyed personally the'sympathy and condolence of the railway, but he proffered aid of a more substantial nature. He extended the time for the second payment on the land by one year and cancelled the interest for that year. He agreed also to provide at cost "five good cows" for each settler, who was to have the opportunity to pay for them with the proceeds of milk and butter sales. The company also supplied the settlers with seed grain for the planting of the second year's crop.[2] During the first year Father Van Aken brought over some 50 families, while in March, 1909, he arrived with 48 families. Augmented by further parties arriving in May and June, the Dutch colony appeared to be on its way to a successful development and was clearly indicated as one of the most satisfactory community settlements within the irrigation block.

Despite the strenuous efforts of the company to interest non-English-speaking groups in the irrigation block, it is evident that through the year 1909 the bulk of the land had been sold to individuals rather than to communities. The fault probably lay in the high price at which the land was sold. Such people were likely to be too impecunious to buy land at high prices, or, if possessed of the means, they were likely to be too comfortably situated to tackle a pioneering project in far-off Alberta. For the moment at least the best prospect seemed to be the individual farmer who might be induced to dispose of his high-priced farm in the United States, with a view to the investment of a portion of the proceeds in Canadian Pacific land.

The success of the Canadian Pacific Irrigation Colonization Company under the direct administration of the railway in 1908 and 1909 more than justified the contention of Shaughnessy and Whyte that the Beiseker and Davidson contract had not been in the best

---

[1] Peterson to A. B. Braddick, Inspector of U. S. Agencies, St. Paul, April 2, 1908, *ibid.*

[2] Dennis to Father C. M. Van Aken, August 14, 1908, *ibid.*

interests of the Canadian Pacific. Land sales in the irrigation block for 1908 were 185,000 acres,[1] while those for 1909 brought the total for the 2 years to more than 400,000 acres. Equally significant was the decreased cost of selling the land and the increased net profit to the railway. Where Beiseker and Davidson had allowed $3.00 per acre for selling, the cost to the railway in 1908 was $2.42 per acre; and where the contract with Beiseker and Davidson had netted the railway company $11.00 per acre for irrigable and $6.00 for non-irrigable land, the net for 1908 was $19.00 and $8.00 respectively.

[1] File No. 336, D. N. R.

VIII

A POLICY OF COLONIZATION

THE two years following the taking over of the Canadian Pacific Irrigation Colonization Company by the Canadian Pacific Railway Company on January 1, 1908 had removed all doubt as to the ability to sell the lands in the irrigation block. Land sales for the two years had been gratifying in the extreme. But the company, as it so often protested, was not a mere land selling organization, and it would judge itself a failure unless this large tract were settled and developed into a prosperous producing area. In manifold ways the company gave evidence of its primary concern with the occupation of the land as rapidly as it was sold.

Reference has been made to the creation of a development branch of the company at Calgary as a means of facilitating the inauguration of farming operations by land purchasers. The purpose of this service was clearly stated in the publication, *Starting a Farm in the Bow River Valley*, one of the numerous pamphlets widely circulated in the United States among prospective land purchasers and settlers.[1] In the words of the brochure, "the company, realizing that it will be of considerable advantage to many of its clients to be able to get certain preparatory work performed economically and expeditiously on land purchased by them, prior to going into occupation thereon, organized a development department as a branch of the company's service, which will take care of any such work required by purchasers of land within the irrigation block. This Department is in the hands of men thoroughly well qualified to obtain the best services for clients at the minimum cost."[2]

[1] Copies of *Starting a Farm in the Bow River Valley* (Calgary, 1909) are in the archives of the Department of Natural Resources in Calgary.
[2] *Ibid.*, p. 7.

The company stated that in undertaking work of this kind it was actuated solely by a desire to hasten the agricultural development of the lands embraced within the irrigation block and to assist new-comers to place themselves upon a profitable footing as soon as possible after going into occupation. Knowing that a great many land purchasers were unable to move to their farms at once, and would prefer to have the preliminary work done by contract, the railway was assuming this function to enable the settler to get a crop growing and to obtain a cash return at the earliest possible moment; in short, to make the lands adjacent to the railway immediately productive. The company, however, agreed merely to initiate farming operations for the settler. It undertook no further management of such lands. Once the farm had been fenced and the land prepared for crop and seeded, its responsibility ended.

All this work was done under contract with responsible parties, the contract being available in the Calgary office for any purchaser who wished to examine its provisions. By reason of being in a position to contract annually for thousands of acres of breaking, discing, harrowing, seeding, etc., the company was able to demand from the contractors the highest grade of work at the lowest possible prices. The personal services of the development staff were given to the land purchasers without charge. The company, however, found it necessary to charge a small amount to cover actual cash outlays in the way of livery, hotel bills, and travelling expenses incurred by its employees in behalf of clients. The amount of this charge, which it based upon the average expenditure for such work during a given season, amounted to about 5 per cent of the total contract price for development work. It was the invariable rule of the company that funds must be available before such work was undertaken. No development of less than 40 acres was undertaken, nor fencing of less than 1 mile.

Needless to say the assumption of such a rôle by the Canadian Pacific involved a degree of oversight and paternalism with respect to farming done by its settlers. One of the regulations governing development work read: "The Company does not encourage purchasers of lands to break the same after the end of July. The most favorable time for breaking is generally between the middle of May and the first of July. . . . The Development Department

stands for the best farming practice only. The Company's ambition
is that any work undertaken for absentee land owners should bring
as good, or even better, results than if such work were performed by
them personally. Such being the case, it positively refuses to undertake any farm development work too far out of season to serve its
purchasers."[1]

Not content with its efforts to encourage sound farming practices,
the company sought to promote intensive farming of limited areas.
Its literature reminded the purchasers that "it is a great mistake for
any person to acquire more land than his available capital will
enable him to properly develop. Eighty acres of irrigable land will
yield as much, or more, than twice that area of non-irrigable land in
regions where farming is carried on under natural rainfall. The
higher development of the dairy and sugar beet industry will further
reduce the area necessary to sustain the farmer and his family. Apart
from this, if there is any lesson in farm economics that has been
consistently and clearly proven it is the superiority, in point of production, of the small, but highly developed, farm over the cruder
methods of the large farm."[2] In a further effort to stem the tide
toward the large farm, so strong in all pioneer areas, the company
announced that it was "vastly more interested in a successful farmer
on a small farm than in a speculative buyer on a large scale. The
latter is not wanted."

During the years 1908 and 1909 the development branch confined
its activities to fencing, plowing, and seeding the land, in which
it engaged on a large scale. This was merely the beginning of a department which was to assume a larger variety of functions and a
greater importance with the passing of the years, until it became perhaps the most significant single piece of machinery maintained by
the Canadian Pacific for the colonization of its lands. Even in these
early years it attracted widespread attention when the company
briefly described its rôle as "Home Making by Contract."

Even more eloquent evidence of the Canadian Pacific's interest in
colonization rather than in mere land selling is found in another
innovation introduced in 1908. This was the plan for the sale of land
in the irrigation block on the "Crop Payment Plan." This idea

[1] *Starting a Farm in the Bow River Valley*, p. 9.
[2] *Ibid.*, p. 10.

seems to have been in the air at this time. It had been employed with some success by the Northern Pacific Railway in the nineties and it appears to have been employed in greater or lesser degree by other railways in the States.[1] Dennis and his associates in the irrigation venture seem to have had the inspiration to try the plan just at the time when certain of the company's agents in the United States were asking that they be permitted to experiment with the idea. In the opening months of 1908 Dennis was actively gathering all possible information in regard to the experience of others in the use of the method, and, at that time, he requested R. B. Bennett, the company's counsel in Calgary, to prepare a draft contract for sale by crop payment, to be shown to the Canadian Pacific management.

In presenting the proposal to Shaughnessy three months later, Dennis conceded that crop payment was a radical departure from methods hitherto employed by the Canadian Pacific in the sale of its land. He denied, however, that there was anything visionary or Utopian about it. Investigation had convinced him that the plan had worked successfully on both sides of the 49th parallel. He had found that it had been employed by the Union Trust Company of Toronto in colonizing some 200,000 acres along the Canadian Northern Railway, and by another company which had settled a large area in the Claresholm district on the Calgary-MacLeod line.[2]

Dennis contended that the idea of crop payment was entirely in harmony with the larger scheme of things which the Canadian Pacific was seeking to bring about in the irrigation block, i.e., the establishment of a "gigantic colonization undertaking" rather than mere land selling. He observed that the company was selling land in much smaller areas than was the practice in the unirrigated portions of the West and would ultimately have a much larger farming community in the irrigation block than would be found in any equal area in the West. Indulging his optimism, he pictured the purchasers

[1] See letter of John K. West, Detroit Lake, Minnesota, to Clarence F. Birdseye, New York, October 15, 1891. This letter was found by the author in 1934 while looking through a miscellaneous collection of papers belonging to Henry Villard, but then in the possession of the North American Company in New York, which Villard founded. West was an agent for the sale of Northern Pacific lands and he describes the crop payment plan. He remarked that "this is about the only way in which sales can be made at the present time."

[2] Dennis to Shaughnessy, August 13, 1908, File No. 303, Section 1, D. N. R.

of the company's lands as its tenants for all time by virtue of the water rental, which necessitated the utilization of the land and which removed "any feature of speculative buying from our scheme." The supreme virtue of the plan he expressed in this way: "Under our present system of selling land, we take the larger portion of the capital of men of moderate means in making cash payments on land sold at fairly high prices and leave him the smaller amount for development. Under the crop payment plan, we take only a very small part of his capital in the way of a cash payment and make him contract to use all the remainder in developing his farm and paying us with a portion of the crop raised. From a colonization standpoint there is no comparison between the two systems and our security for the deferred payments is absolute, while at the same time we are creating traffic and improving the value of the land."[1]

Dennis was convinced that if the scheme were given general publicity it would be the means of greatly increasing land sales and more rapidly reaching the great goal of intensive settlement and cultivation which the company had set itself. Nor was the publicity value of the plan to be taken lightly. What better proof could there be of the confidence of the Canadian Pacific that its land would pay for itself! What compelling force was possessed by the slogans, "Come to Alberta and go into partnership with the Canadian Pacific," or "No Crop, no Payment!" What could indicate more clearly the fact that the railway company was above all interested in the development of its lands, for the crop payment plan made settlement upon the land imperative.

In the autumn of 1908 approval for the plan was obtained and a special publicity campaign was planned to acquaint the farmers of the United States with the opportunities which were now offered them.[2] The plan called for the payment of one-tenth of the purchase price in cash; the balance, with interest at 6 per cent, in a portion of the annual crop. The purchaser agreed to plow and put in crop at least 50 acres during the first year, with a similar area annually thereafter, although he might by special arrangement retain

[1] Dennis to Shaughnessy, July 25, 1908, *ibid.*

[2] Dennis to Herbert Vanderhoof, Editor, *Canada West Magazine*, Chicago, November 21, 1908. Dennis stated he would be in Chicago toward the end of the week to make final arrangements for advertising the crop payment plan.

25 per cent of his holdings for pasture. No one farmer could purchase more than 160 acres of irrigable and 480 acres of non-irrigable
land. The purchaser bound himself to erect on the land a house
worth not less than $350 and a barn worth $100, to sink a good well,
and to fence his farm. Buildings were to be insured and the purchaser was to pay the taxes.[1]

It is evident that the terms of the contract gave to the company
another fairly effective control over the agricultural practices of the
farmer. The services of the development branch were, of course,
available to purchasers under this plan, but such service carried with
it the right to dictate the conduct of the farm. The whole arrangement was, in effect, a partnership between the company and the
farmer; the two prospered or failed together. The farmer covenanted
to deliver to the company annually, free of charge, at the nearest
elevator or on cars at the nearest station, one-half of the grain
grown upon the land in the course of the year, the company allowing
the market price prevailing on the day of delivery. The purchaser
pledged himself to keep an accurate account of all crops raised
on his land and to report to the company by December 1 of each
year the quantity of grain, sugar beets, alfalfa, and timothy produced
during the year.

The introduction of this plan required, of course, special regulations governing the payment of commissions to agents selling land
under it. A uniform commission of 10 per cent was paid, the agent
receiving $1.50 per acre on irrigable land when the purchaser made
the cash payment, and the remainder when the buyer paid one-
ninth of the balance of the purchase price. On non-irrigable land he
received $1.00 at time of cash payment, with balance as in the case
of irrigable land.

The whole idea of crop payment was one additional evidence of
the fact that the irrigation block had become a great laboratory
where virtually every type of experiment in land settlement was to
be tried. Only time could determine the success of the new venture
but, regardless of the outcome, there could be no doubt that this
was merely the latest proof of the desire of the Canadian Pacific to
employ any and every legitimate means to establish in southern

[1] The conditions governing the sale of land on the crop payment plan are fully
stated in *Starting a Farm in the Bow River Valley*, p. 30.

Alberta an important community providing a volume of traffic for the railway far in excess of any other area in the Canadian West.

Whatever the ultimate potentialities of the crop payment plan may have been, however, it had not at the end of its first year solved the problem of land settlement in the irrigation block. In the autumn of 1909 officials of the company began to direct their attention anew to this fundamental question. At that time it was estimated that but 10 per cent of those who had purchased land were actually in residence; and that although 75 per cent had intended to become Bow Valley residents within a year, they had, for various reasons, failed to do so.[1] One official in analyzing the situation assigned a large measure of responsibility to the company and its agents. Despite the very earnest desire of the railway company to colonize the land, by and large it had given too much attention to the sales and too little to settlement, trusting that somehow the one would lead to the other. There was the chance, too, that many had been discouraged by the campaign of slander of western Canada which certain interests launched in the States from time to time. Others might have been deterred from moving to Alberta by a mistaken idea regarding the cost, while insufficiently informed as to crops being produced in the vicinity of their land. But, regardless of the causes, the time had come when the situation must be recognized and steps taken to meet it.

Originating among lower officials of the company, the desire to solve this problem gradually took possession of those higher in authority.[2] In this way the matter came up for the consideration of Peterson, the manager of the Canadian Pacific Irrigation Colonization Company, who was convinced that his organization had been so engrossed in the work of land selling that it had given only incidental attention to colonizing it.[3] He strongly urged that the company immediately institute a vigorous campaign to persuade those who had purchased to go into occupation. The first step was to

[1] Memorandum, Rothwell to Peterson, October 4, 1909, File No. 201, Section 2, D. N. R.

[2] That serious consideration was given to this problem by those in subordinate positions is indicated by the memorandum of Rothwell and by a letter of F. W. Crandall to Peterson, October 26, 1909, *ibid.*, in which he comments favorably upon Rothwell's memorandum.

[3] Peterson to Dennis, November 5, 1909, *ibid.*

prepare a card index of the name and address of every person who had bought land in the irrigation block. He would then circularize all non-residents and endeavor to ascertain in every case the reason why they had not moved to Alberta.[1] The special requirements of every individual case should be taken up. Peterson believed that, with the assistance of the development department, it would be possible to persuade purchasers to pursue their original plan of settling on the land. If the purchasers frankly admitted that they had bought for speculative purposes, he would endeavor to obtain authority to sell the land to a settler under an arrangement which would cover the expense incurred. Peterson very properly pointed out that a policy of encouraging actual settlement should be initiated at the time of purchase rather than subsequently. Much could be done by the insertion of judicious provisions in the sales contract.

This general plan received the approval of Dennis and a special staff was established to inaugurate the campaign for increased settlement within the irrigation block. A multigraph letter was sent out every two weeks, while special correspondence was to be carried on with those indicating a desire to locate on the land.[2] Scores of items of interest to the prospective settler were to be discussed in the letters, including crop yields, towns, schools, new railroads, etc. With a view to giving the client the impression that the letters were not impersonal, perfunctory affairs, they were signed by Dennis in his capacity as Assistant to the Second Vice-President of the Canadian Pacific Railway Company, rather than by the Canadian Pacific Irrigation Colonization Company. Because this endeavor to promote the occupation of the land contrasts so strikingly with the mere land selling activity usually associated with land grant railways in North America, the first letter addressed to the purchasers is deserving of some little consideration.[3] Pertinent portions of it read:

> When you secured land from the Canadian Pacific Railway it was, no doubt, with a view to establishing a home in the Bow Valley. If I am correctly advised you have not carried out your original intention. Some obstacle has, no doubt, presented itself

[1] Peterson to Dennis, November 5, 1909, *ibid.*
[2] Rothwell to Peterson, November 16, 1909, *ibid.*
[3] See copy of this letter in File No. 201, Section 2, D. N. R. It was sent out in January, 1910.

and it is my desire to learn just what is the nature of this apparent difficulty.

The cultivation of your Bow Valley land will, I am certain, provide you with an opportunity of securing an easily and rapidly earned independence. . . .

You no doubt desire information on schools, churches, neighbors, new towns, cost of development, general development and the probable needs of the labor market in the vicinity of your Bow Valley lands. In an endeavor to provide this, I have requested the editor of *The Calgary Daily Herald* to forward to your address from time to time, issues of that paper carrying news items from the district in which you are interested. You will thus be advised regarding the prosperity of your neighbors who are in residence upon land in the vicinity of yours.

Why not write and let me answer any questions that you may wish to ask? I desire to at least attempt to assist you in determining the best method of developing your property and am prepared to do all I can to help you to obtain a return from your land. Write us and let us give you the benefit of our experience.

There was a special reason for sending *The Calgary Herald* to the client. It was to be the medium for supplying him with facts concerning opportunities and developments in the Calgary district. The Canadian Pacific Irrigation Colonization Company submitted daily to the paper copy containing material which it believed would interest the absentee owner and provide an incentive for him to settle on his land. This material, under a three-column head, on the first page of the paper, would readily acquaint the purchaser with crop statistics and general information illustrative of the prosperity of the country. The company chose this means of education, rather than sending the data direct, because of the belief that "the average farmer will more readily accept a statement appearing in a paper than a statement issued by a land company. And it will be possible to advise these clients regarding actual conditions without materially increasing the work in the office. We can provide land owners with the maximum amount of information at the minimum of labor."

It was then the custom of the *Farm and Ranch Review*, the leading agricultural publication in Alberta, to issue a special Christmas number devoted to a review of the progress and development of the year in the Calgary area, of which the irrigation block constituted such an important portion. Arrangements were accordingly made to send a copy of this issue to some 2,000 absentee purchasers of land from the Canadian Pacific in the hope that "the exceptionally good copy" would provide a renewed incentive to settlement on the land.

The first circular letter to purchasers brought a variety of responses. Some announced that the writers were shipping their effects preparatory to settlement in Alberta in the spring. Such people wanted information with respect to freight rates, customs regulations, date of opening of the Langdon branch, etc. For the benefit of these people the company delegated agents to assist them in locating their lands, purchasing lumber and seed grain, securing carpenters, and generally advising them as to the best action to take with a view to giving their holdings a maximum development. Such action by the company would not only be appreciated but it would be a guarantee that the new settler would begin farming in Alberta in an enthusiastic frame of mind.

Some of those who were unable to go into residence on their land expressed a desire to rent their holdings and welcomed whatever assistance the company might render to that end. To aid these people the company invoked the coöperation of its agency organization in the United States. Agents were asked to seek out renters in their territory who desired to move to Alberta and take a farm on shares.[1] Other absentees, who for various reasons could not settle in the irrigation block at once, availed themselves of the company's offer to perform the preliminary work through its development department. Such people, it was hoped, would be able to occupy their farms the following season.

While this campaign clearly produced results encouraging to the company, it was not permitted to run its complete course. Before its full effects had been produced the company launched itself on a program of colonization so much more ambitious that this preliminary effort was forced to assume a more modest and secondary rôle. One should not conclude, however, that it was for that reason lacking in significance. It was the first tangible evidence of the company's realization that its great objective of complete colonization of the irrigation block could not be achieved merely by selling the land. In southern Alberta the company faced a situation unlike

[1] Circular to agents, March 3, 1910, File No. 201, Section 2, D. N. R.

that encountered by it elsewhere in the West and utterly unlike that experienced by American railways. It was a situation requiring special consideration and effort, and to the study of this problem officials were now beginning to turn.

Gradually those Canadian Pacific officials, from Shaughnessy down to Peterson, who were in close touch with the problem of land settlement in the irrigation block, were increasingly concerning themselves with the idea then popular in England and termed "assisted settlement." While largely foreign to the experience and practice of land settlement agencies in North America, and hitherto unneeded amid the pioneer conditions prevailing on this continent, assisted settlement seems to have intrigued those high in command in Canadian Pacific affairs.

The original inspiration for the inauguration of such a policy by the Canadian Pacific seems to have come from a suggestion by the Salvation Army of England, which was desirous of sponsoring a program of assisted land settlement in Canada. The proposal of the Salvation Army authorities was that they should obtain English families of small means to be located on Canadian Pacific lands with the aid of the company. Contemporaneously with this proposition came the suggestion from the Reverend Father Van Aken, who had been engaged in colonization work for the company in Holland, that many Dutch farmers could be secured for the irrigation block were he in a position to put them on farms improved to the extent of a house to move into and a certain amount of land under cultivation.[1]

The Salvation Army idea appealed so strongly to Shaughnessy that he readily gave approval for the reservation of 24 quarter sections to be improved by the company for the so-called Salvation Army Colony.[2] Dennis was equally impressed by the proposal of Father Van Aken, because "these Hollanders have proved the very best settlers that we can get and I would strongly recommend that you authorize me to select, in conjunction with Father Van Aken, thirty quarter sections which we will improve to the extent of erecting a small house and barn, fencing the land, putting down a well and breaking and plowing 50 acres. Our estimate is that this

[1] Dennis to Shaughnessy, March 16, 1909, File No. 222, Section 1, D. N. R.
[2] Shaughnessy to Dennis, March 8, 1909, ibid.

can be done for $30,000."[1] Although Shaughnessy approved of this plan, neither the Holland nor the Salvation Army improved farm colony materialized. Their failure in no way diminished their importance in relation to Canadian Pacific policy, however, for they had been the means of focusing the attention of officials upon this particular type of land settlement.

During the summer of 1909 both Peterson and Dennis devoted much thought to the improved farm idea. In no way discouraged by the abortive nature of the two colony schemes, Peterson was convinced that the company must adopt the assisted settlement plan. As he observed, "from a land-selling standpoint our efforts have met with shining success. From a colonization point of view, however, I cannot say that we have been as successful as we might have been. I take the position that the whole irrigation project is designed to secure the highest possible amount of traffic. This involves the densest possible settlement. We have not succeeded in providing close settlement. Our sales have been of the quarter section, half and whole section order, more of the two latter than the former. This will not bring about the result we are striving for. . . . I like the improved farm project and think it would be the means to that end. In this way we can settle families on eighty acre tracts and make sure that this land is not being bought merely for speculative purposes, and, in working out the improved farm proposition I would not lose sight of that fact for a moment."[2]

In Peterson's opinion the improved farm plan not only was the means of securing the compact settlement of the irrigation block, so eagerly desired by the company, but also was particularly timely in view of the conditions then prevailing in Great Britain. The bulk of the land thus far sold in the Calgary district had been taken by Americans. Farmers from that country had been pouring into all sections of the Canadian West for a decade, giving rise to much talk of an "American invasion" of Canada. The American farmer with his long experience in prairie farming was ideally suited to the conditions on the Canadian prairie. The British settler, with his totally different background, had experienced greater difficulty in coping

[1] Dennis to Shaughnessy, March 16, 1909, *ibid.*
[2] Peterson to Dennis, August 7, 1909, File No. 242, Section 1, D. N. R.

with his new environment, with the result that he was in general less attracted to the West than was the American. In the face of the American invasion, might not the Canadian Pacific catch the imagination of the British and Canadian public by offering some special inducement to the British settler to locate in western Canada?

Peterson had followed with much interest the operation of the "Small Agricultural Holdings Act," passed a few years before in England, under which large estates were being subdivided and sold to small holders.[1] He had taken note of the fact that at the time of the last allotment of 2,000 holdings the Board of Agriculture had received no less than 35,000 applications. By the provisions of this act the land was sold on 29-year payments, with government loans to individual purchasers providing the means for the necessary buildings. The settler must have a capital of about 200 pounds. Peterson was convinced that the Canadian Pacific could offer a more attractive proposition to the land-hungry folk of England. In addition to the type of assistance rendered by the government over there, the company could put in a crop in advance of the settler's arrival, thereby assuring him an income from the land immediately upon the occupation of his farm. Besides, the farms would be larger than in Great Britain and the general opportunities for success vastly superior.

The 33,000 disappointed applicants for small holdings in Great Britain offered a limitless opportunity for the Canadian Pacific. The Board of Agriculture in England dealt only with selected applicants. The company could do the same; and if it could induce only 25 per cent of the disappointed applicants to entertain its proposition it would have some 8,000 agricultural settlers from whom it could choose. This would enable it to place its entire British business on a first-class foundation, obtain a high price for its land, and eliminate almost entirely the payment of commissions for the sale of land to British clients.

In response to the argument that with the existing extraordinary demand for land in the irrigation block there was no particular reason why the company should resort to heroic measures in order to attract British farmers, Peterson's contention was that there were

[1] Peterson to Dennis, August 31, 1909, *ibid.*

special arguments in favor of such a policy. The company's American buyers were preëminently half-section men, while British farmers could be settled on 80 to 120 acres.[1] Small holdings would ensure the complete success of the irrigation project and would mean much from a traffic standpoint. The company's steamship service would profit materially from the first movement of these settlers, while the project would popularize the Canadian Pacific in England and yield splendid publicity results. The imperial idea was uppermost in the British mind at the moment and Canada was popular in the British Isles. A project fathered by the Canadian Pacific with a view to the settlement of British families of small means in western Canada would readily gain official approval on both sides of the water. While the plan should be worked out on a strictly commercial basis, it could be so presented to the public that the philanthropic features would receive due prominence at all times. Every newspaper in Great Britain would gladly publish an outline of the project and much editorial comment would be secured. It would be regarded as legitimate news of considerable importance. A skillful publicity campaign could advertise the plan far and wide virtually without the expenditure of money by the company.[2] Nor would Peterson neglect to capitalize the fact that in the face of the great preponderance of Americans in Alberta, the Canadian Pacific desired to introduce a strong British element.

In the latter part of 1909 the idea so fully outlined by Peterson was sprung upon the British Isles with an avalanche of publicity, probably without a parallel in the annals of railway colonization work.[3] Peterson, who went to Europe at that time in order to lay the ground work for the execution of the plan, was at once submerged by the correspondence and interviews resulting from this publicity. The company had obtained free of cost an amount of space in the British press which could not, under ordinary circumstances, have been purchased for $10,000.[4] The London office of the company had been forced to increase its staff in order to cope with the flood of inquiries and correspondence. From London, Peterson pro-

[1] *Ibid.*
[2] *Ibid.*
[3] Peterson to Dennis, January 24, 1910, *ibid.*
[4] *Ibid.*

ceeded to Holland, Belgium, and Austria with a view to obtaining information with respect to the advisability of extending the improved farm plan to those countries.

Meanwhile Peterson's mind had also been occupied with the question of the terms and conditions governing the sale of the improved farms which the company was about to develop. While strongly of the opinion that the ready-made farm was the logical method of colonization where capital was available to carry it out successfully, he recognized that the ultimate success of the plan would depend largely upon the regulations adopted and the safeguards provided in the sales contract. Both Peterson and Dennis were at first inclined to favor the sale of such farms under the "crop payment" contract, largely because its insurance clause and the provisions with respect to the methods of farming would give the company control over the whole course of agricultural development in the improved farm colonies. In the end, however, they contented themselves with a contract containing merely the insurance features of the crop payment plan, together with a crop lien clause to protect the company's investment in the farm.

Since it was believed that $2,500 represented the minimum capital necessary for the successful inauguration of farming operations in the irrigation block, the settler had to possess at least $1,500 with which to supplement the $1,000 which the company planned to invest in each farm unit. Farms were allotted in advance to selected families and, to ensure that those receiving allotments would actually go through to Calgary, the settler must pay the passage money for himself and family before the allotment was made. The first payment on the farm was due on the date of occupation of the land.

At the time of the introduction of the ready-made farm plan the Canadian Pacific sold its land on a 10-year basis. Convinced that it was entirely consistent with the larger objectives of the company, Peterson desired to extend the period of payment on the improved farms to 15 or 20 years. While unwilling to go so far in a formal, contractual way, Dennis and Shaughnessy authorized agents in Great Britain to assure applicants that the Canadian Pacific Railway had never dispossessed a farmer on its land because of failure to pay the deferred payments, so long as he actually occupied the farm.[1] In practice this meant that the settler would have a longer period in which to complete his payments.

During 1909 the company developed as ready-made farms the 24 quarter sections originally reserved for the Salvation Army colony. It built a house and barn on each farm, fenced the land, dug a well, and prepared a portion of the land for seeding in the spring of 1910. It planned the colony as a unit and selected the lands because of their peculiar adaptability to settlement of this type. Rechristened "Nightingale," this community became the first of the ready-made farm colonies of the Canadian Pacific, about which so much was to be heard within the next few years. Settlers for the colony embarked from England in March, 1910.

The company was launching upon a program of assisted group settlement. Land selling, so long practiced by the Canadian Pacific, as well as by other railways in North America, was to become a thing of the past. Individual settlement, undirected and sporadic in nature, was to give way to community settlement of the planned and supervised variety. Regardless of its success or failure, the new plan marked such a complete break with the best practice of companies and corporations dealing in lands as to be nothing short of revolutionary.

Preparations for the extension of the ready-made farm policy engaged the attention of the company staff both in Great Britain and in Alberta throughout the year 1910. The goal for that season was 1,000 British applications from which the London office would be able to select 100 first-class families for the farms the company was preparing for settlement in 1911. As the average cost per inquiry in the United States was between $1.00 and $1.50, the British organization was authorized to expend $1,500 for special publicity with a view to obtaining the desired number of applications. This amount was materially supplemented from the advertising appropriation of the London office of the Canadian Pacific's Traffic Department. The Calgary office prepared for British distribution a special publication descriptive of the ready-made farm project, containing numerous illustrations of such farms, together with actual photographs of the 1910 contingent of British families who were located in the Nightingale colony.

[1] Dennis to Peterson, March 14, 1910, *ibid*.

Through the distribution of this booklet and through notices in selected British papers, inviting applications for the ready-made farms, the company made its initial contact with the prospective settler. He was then provided with forms to be filled out and returned to the London office. From these papers the manager of the office was able, in most cases, to decide whether or not the applicant was a good prospect. If so regarded, he was visited in his own home by members of the staff, in whose hands rested the ultimate decision to accept or reject him.

For the benefit of British settlers, agents were instructed to emphasize the desire of the company to develop in the irrigation block the intensive cultivation of small farms.[1] A special effort was to be made to secure experienced farmers from the dairying districts of England and Scotland, where the customary farming routine was substantially in line with the general policy which the Canadian Pacific was seeking to foster.

Peterson was forced to revise his original opinion that the ready-made farms could be sold in Great Britain without the payment of commissions to the company's agents scattered throughout the countryside. He recognized that as soon as the company placed any large number of these farms on the market its British business would become largely of that type, and refusal to pay commissions would soon disrupt the entire agency organization over there. The company paid the commission, however, only in cases where the agent actually initiated the business. Since the railway's publicity campaign enabled it to establish contact with many applicants direct, commission cost was reduced to a minimum, especially in view of the fact that the commission payments to English agents were 50 cents and 25 cents per acre on irrigated and non-irrigated land respectively, a mere pittance compared with the payments to American agents.[2]

If it was the job of the London office in 1910 to find the British settlers for ready-made farms, it was no less the task of Calgary to prepare the farms which they were to occupy. The latter soon discovered that because of the very large sales in the western section of the irrigation block during the two previous years, there were no longer available the areas of contiguous land necessary for group

[1] Peterson to Dennis, January 25, 1910, ibid.
[2] Ibid.

settlement. Nor had construction of the irrigation system in the central and eastern sections progressed to the point where it was possible to place large areas there on the market. To accommodate the 100 families whom the British organization was recruiting, and who would arrive in the spring of 1911, the company was forced to turn temporarily to lands beyond the confines of the irrigation block.

The region selected for this development was in the vicinity of Sedgwick, on the Wetaskiwin-Saskatoon line of the Canadian Pacific in central Alberta.[1] This was an area of sufficient rainfall for agricultural purposes, but there were certain complicating factors in the situation, so far as the development of improved farms was concerned. In this region the Canadian Pacific owned only the alternate sections, which militated somewhat against the compact group settlement which the company desired for colony purposes. Then, too, while rainfall was entirely adequate for farming, the problem of water for domestic use was a difficult one. Wells of great depth were necessary and very expensive, which increased very materially the cost of development. The result was that while the administration had allowed $1,300 per farm for the improvement of the Nightingale colony, the appropriation for the Sedgwick colony allowed $2,364.50 per farm, of which, it was estimated, $650 would be expended in well-drilling.[2] Nevertheless, the alternate sections in four townships were here available for a large-scale development of improved farms, and the Sedgwick colony became one of the largest and most prominent of such group settlements.

Continuation and extension of the ready-made farm program obviously called for a careful survey of the whole situation in the western section of the irrigation block, if land was to be found for such colonies. The company's adoption of the improved farm idea had thus far proceeded more from the heart than from the head. In a generous moment it had embraced a conception with certain philanthropic aspects well calculated to appeal to certain of the land-hungry classes in Great Britain and sure to gain for the railway widespread and favorable publicity throughout the world. The idea represented a step in the direction in which it wished to move; it was entirely consistent with the larger design of the Canadian Pacific in southern

[1] Dennis to Shaughnessy, March 2, 1910, *ibid.*
[2] Peterson to Dennis, August 12, 1910 and April 13, 1911, *ibid.*

Alberta. But Peterson and Dennis had taken up the plan without a full realization of all its implications, or of just what it meant in the way of further planning in the irrigation block.

Within a year, however, they had come to see that the further development of the improved farm plan involved a careful examination of all lands in the western section and the adoption of such a policy in dealing with them as would provide large areas adapted to arrangement in colonies. One of the first things to be considered was the disposition to be made of the cull irrigable land in that section. Contrary to the better judgment of Dennis, the original selling policy of the company had been to place a uniform price on all land and to let the buyers make the selections. When the more desirable lands in a particular area had been disposed of, it had planned to revalue the culls according to quality. With the beginning of the land rush to the irrigation block in 1909, however, officials abandoned this latter feature in the belief that it was unnecessary. They thought that the culled lands would within a reasonable time attain the same value as the superior ones. That this had been a mistake, they now freely admitted. Since irrigability depended so largely upon topographical features, the culls were likely to be left on the company's hands for years unless a special effort were made to reclassify and dispose of them.

In view of this situation, Peterson, in January, 1911, submitted to Dennis a detailed plan for dealing with the problem. As Peterson was frankly aiming at the complete colonization of the western section of the irrigation block, he brought within his purview all land in the section not already occupied, under contracts in good standing.[1] He advanced several special arguments in support of a comprehensive program of actual colonization, in which improved farms would, of course, play a large part. As he pointed out, the greatest difficulty in the operation and maintenance of the irrigation system was the unoccupied land. He had carefully investigated the water agreement and had incorporated provisions which would shift from the company to the owners the burden of maintenance, and partly of operation, thereby supplying an added incentive for the purchaser to occupy and irrigate the land. Compact settlement, district by district, would enable the company to create efficient local organization

[1] Peterson to Dennis, January 13, 1911, *ibid.*

which otherwise would be a slow process. Nor was it economical for the company to permit cull lands to lie idle. On the basis of 100,000 acres of unsold irrigable land, it was losing not merely the interest on the unpaid principal but also the annual water rental of 50 cents per acre. Should these lands be on the company's hands for 10 or 15 years it would lose more in interest and water rental alone than the reduction in price resulting from reclassification would amount to. More important was the loss in traffic resulting from the retention of this large area of unused land.

Peterson argued very cogently that by means of a complete colonization and development program, eliminating all vacant and waste lands in a district, the company would add appreciably to the value of every acre contained therein. The cull irrigable lands under existing conditions could not be sold for $20.00 per acre.[1] By judicious reclassification, with the establishment of practical farm units and an initial price reduction, the bulk of the land would ultimately net the company $30.00 to $40.00 for irrigable, and $20.00 per acre for non-irrigable land. Such a plan would also aid greatly in the adaption of better farming methods within the irrigation block. The least successful farmer usually occupied the isolated farm. Dense settlement and helpful neighbors played an important part in the general farm economy, and this was more true in an irrigated district where in the beginning the average water consumer knew little or nothing about irrigation.

As the first step in this program of reclassification, the company sent out engineers to locate the extensions to the lateral canal system. Soil examiners, practical irrigation farmers, and engineers then proceeded with the examination, district by district, of the sold and unsold, occupied and unoccupied, land. When the land was unoccupied but under contract for sale, with payments badly in arrears and without reasonable prospect of immediate occupation by the purchaser, the company promptly initiated cancellation proceedings. The examiners carefully determined the irrigable area of each farm, the advantageous ways of combining irrigable and non-irrigable land in the same farm, and the need for revision of the irrigable area. As they completed their investigation of an irrigation district, they prepared a blueprint showing all lands available for settlement. They

[1] *Ibid.*

then laid out the farm units, marking the building and well sites and indicating the area to be broken under the ready-made farm plan.[1] Farm units varied in size according to the quality of the land, but each was so constituted as to provide a good living for a family. Peterson believed that the best of the irrigable lands could be subdivided into 80-acre farms. This land examination began on the Bow River and extended to the northward, by irrigation districts, the aim being to complete the work between the river and the main line of the railway during the season of 1911. When the examiners had finished their work in a given district, they established a ready-made farm colony, which took the name of the irrigation district. The development branch then began the construction, fencing, and breaking involved in the preparation of improved farms.[2]

Two categories of land required special study and careful procedure in order to bring them into the far-reaching colonization program which the company contemplated. One was land sold, but unoccupied, with contracts in good standing. To all holders of land in this class the company addressed a letter of inquiry as to the reasons for not occupying their land. Many replied frankly that they had bought the land for speculative purposes and were holding it for the appreciation in value predicted by those whom Peterson termed the "more enterprising or unscrupulous agents" of the company. To these people Peterson pointed out the futility of such expectations in view of the water rental and interest charges on the land. The company would give these buyers an opportunity to exchange their irrigable land for central Alberta land or for non-irrigable land within the irrigation block. It even considered the possibility of selling the land for the speculators in order to be rid of them. Where none of these expedients produced the desired results these contracts were watched closely with a view to cancellation as soon as the payments were in arrears. Large numbers of replies came from men who had bought irrigable land in good faith, with every intention of settling on the land within a reasonable period of time. Because of inability to dispose of their property or to obtain additional capital, they had not found it possible to carry out their original plan. Men in this situation were to be fitted into the ready-made farm plan

[1] *Ibid.*
[2] Peterson to Dennis, February 4, 1911, File No. 201, Section 2, D. N. R.

where they had a good working outfit and a small capital, or a capital sufficient to provide the necessary farming equipment. The company would erect the buildings, and fence and break the land, adding the cost to the original purchase price of the farm.

The other class of land requiring special attention was that which was occupied with payments in arrears for various reasons. Where such a farmer occupied an entire section, the company sought to take back a portion of it, settling him on a half section or even a quarter section. The land reverting to the company was then included in the colonization scheme for the western section.[1] The existing water agreement was cancelled and the new one substituted therefor. An extension of time was allowed for completion of the payments on the land retained in view of the higher prices which the company expected to realize from the lands relinquished.

In 1911 the company entered energetically upon this program for the complete colonization of the western section of the irrigation block, a program which it was hoped would realize the high hopes with which the irrigation project was originally launched. Reclassification of irrigable land for that year was expected to yield 200 farm units, to be improved for sale as ready-made farms in 1912, with larger numbers in succeeding years. At the same time the company definitely adopted the policy of selling land in the western section only on colonization conditions, a step which it should have taken at an earlier date. With but 178,000 acres of irrigable and non-irrigable land unsold, and with the inauguration of a procedure which promised satisfactory results in the case of lands previously sold but undeveloped, it seemed that the company was in sight of the day when its major task in the western section would be completed, thus giving it an opportunity to devote greater attention to the central and eastern sections of the irrigation block.

Construction of the irrigation system in these two sections had not kept pace with the sale of land in the western. When, in 1909, land in the latter section was being disposed of at a rapid rate, and water for irrigation purposes was still unavailable in the other two, the company began to consider the possibility of selling and colonizing lands in those sections in advance of the completion of the irrigation works. Contrary as such a procedure was to the original plan of

[1] *Ibid.*

company officials, it was in harmony with the practice of the United States Reclamation Service, which required settlement before providing irrigation facilities. Nor was it inconsistent with the position which the company had taken with respect to the western section, namely, that while the rainfall frequently was insufficient for mixed farming, cereal crops could be grown successfully without irrigation. More compelling, however, as an argument in favor of the step was the fear that delay, in the face of the depletion of land in the western section, would leave the agency force in the United States with nothing to do. The policy must, therefore, be carried through.

The difficulties in the way of the adoption of such a course with respect to the central and eastern sections were very great. It meant the sale of the land without knowledge, either by the company or by the settler, of the proportion which would ultimately be irrigable. Another problem, which at first appeared almost insoluble, was the payment of commissions to agents. As the irrigable area would merely be estimated at the time of sale, hundreds of cases almost surely would arise where the percentage of irrigable land would be less than that provided in the contract, thereby rendering necessary a readjustment in commissions. An added complication appeared to be the impossibility of making the adjustment out of the deferred commissions, since the second payment would ordinarily have been completed before the revision of the irrigable area. An equally disturbing question was that of publicity. Should the lands be advertised as capable of producing cereals without irrigation or should the need for immediate irrigation be stressed? The one course seemed to run contrary to the ultimate objective of the company in the irrigation block; the other would imperil the immediate purpose of the railway.

In spite of the obstacles involved, the company pushed ahead with its plans. Blueprints were prepared of the central section, showing merely the canal system and certain large areas, portions of which were known to be susceptible of irrigation. The precise irrigable areas in a given district, however, were not indicated. The land was placed on the market at prices ranging from $30.00 to $35.00 per acre, payable in 10 years, with interest at 6 per cent. The contract provided that the company would, on or before December 31, 1910, serve written notice on the purchaser, indicating the particular portions, if any, of his land which were capable of irrigation. At the time of serving this notice the purchaser's payments were to be adjusted by giving him credit, on account of future payments, for any sum paid by him in excess of $15.00 per acre for land not irrigable.

At the time of the adoption of this policy in August, 1909, the total area included in the central section was 853,155 acres, of which the surveys thus far completed indicated that about 220,000 acres were irrigable. About 75,000 acres of non-irrigable land within the section had been sold. Land in the North Bassano, North Cluny, and East Crowfoot districts, with an estimated irrigable area of about 80,000 acres, was to be sold as rapidly as possible.

The formulation of plans for the disposal of land in the central section came at the time the company was adopting the policy of improved or ready-made farms in the western section. For two years the development of these farms was confined to that section, where the extensive program of land reclassification was being carried out. With the growing popularity of the improved farm idea, however, it was but a question of time until the policy would be extended to the eastern section of the irrigation block, where it could be introduced before any large proportion of the land had been disposed of.

The first limited application of the improved farm plan to the eastern section came in 1911, when the comprehensive reclassification work was being carried out in the western section. The program for that year called for the preparation of 100 of these farms, to be arranged by colonies, with not more than 25 farms in a given colony.[1] As officials of the company were especially desirous of encouraging the compact settlement of the eastern section, they carried out a thorough survey of the eastern section for the purpose of determining those quarter sections which were best suited to division into 80-acre farms. Naturally in the preparation of the survey maps irrigability was the governing consideration, although it was recognized that soil conditions required careful attention. As a result of this survey it was found that there were 49 townships in which ready-made irrigable farms of this size could be developed. In some townships not more than 2 such farms could be provided without a heavy extra expenditure, large decrease in irrigable area, and an unsatisfactory distribution system. In other townships as many as 30 farms

[1] Dennis to Peterson, April 8, 1911, File No. 216, D. N. R.

could be grouped together economically and efficiently. A total of 712 farms were tentatively planned for ultimate development, a number which Peterson regarded as insufficient to meet the demand which surely would arise.[1]

Experience during the course of the next year, however, revealed certain difficulties in the way of the creation of 80-acre ready-made farms. Soil conditions, topography, and drainage must be taken into careful account. Any considerable area of badly broken land, alkali sloughs, or undrainable pockets would reduce the cultivable area below the margin of safety. Another difficulty resulted from the fact that under the Dominion land surveys the road allowances contemplated farms from 160 acres up, and the provision of road allowances for smaller farms would involve additional expense. In view of these considerations, therefore, Dennis decided that the 80-acre farm was a mistake. The proposed ready-made farms in the eastern section were reclassified on the 160-acre basis.[2] In order further to emphasize the community settlement idea, the number of farms was reduced to 500 by the elimination of scattered and isolated units.

The policy of ready-made farms for British settlers was now fairly launched in both the western and eastern sections of the irrigation block. According to the intentions of officials in Calgary the greatest of care was to be exercised in selecting settlers for these farms. They were to be in every sense of the term hand picked men; the chosen few from the vast number who were expected to be applicants for the farms. The most complete information possible was to be accumulated and maintained with respect to each individual, so that the chance of mistake would be reduced to a minimum. The good intentions of Calgary, however, were no guarantee with respect to the conduct and good judgment of agents of the company in Great Britain. Knowing that the whole idea was expected to meet with an enthusiastic response throughout the British Isles, representatives there naturally lost no opportunity to recruit the desired number of settlers. Bad judgment, excessive zeal, inordinate desire on the part of agents in Great Britain to earn commissions might go far to vitiate the high resolves of those who formulated the policy.

[1] Peterson to Dennis, July 28, 1911, *ibid.*
[2] Dennis to Dawson, May 7, 1912, *ibid.*

The letters of Peterson to the manager of the Land Department of the Canadian Pacific in London illustrate the difficulties encountered. In one he wrote: "Your letter does not contain any information respecting these three settlers. You are aware of the fact that we wish to start forthwith a file for each farm as allotted by you. It surely should be clear to you that if such be the case it will be necessary for you to write a separate letter in connection with each successful applicant. Furthermore, in the said letter we want the *most complete information you have available regarding said selected applicant*, so that this will form the basis of his file and that upon this file we will have the entire history of this man set forth. . . ."[1]

Another time Peterson wrote: "I think it is good policy to attempt to get in touch with people possessing fairly large capital. At the same time, the farming class is, of course, where we would hope to draw the bulk of our men from. I notice in your list one or two people from India and other countries far removed. It seems to me you have no opportunity of ascertaining whether such would be a suitable settler or not. I also notice a Capt. A. B. Fielden. Although he seems to have abundance of capital, we are running quite a risk to settle a man of that sort, who presumably has no farming experience, on these lands. . . . I am merely again impressing upon you the absolute necessity of using the greatest possible amount of discretion in making these selections."[2]

It is clear, however, that the position of Canadian Pacific representatives in England was not an easy one. They were expected to produce settlers, but of the right sort. Agriculturists were not wanted unless they had a capital of some two hundred pounds. Urban workers with capital, but without farming experience, were in general frowned upon. These were the people most likely to be desirous of acquiring small holdings on favorable terms, but they were not welcome. Neither in Calgary nor in England could officials of the company make allowance for the human factor in a situation where, of two men with similar means and experience, one would succeed on a prairie farm while the other made a dismal failure. Frequently officers of the railway underestimated the seriousness of the process of adjustment which the British settler, regardless of his background,

[1] Peterson to G. B. Gray, October 11, 1910, File No. 224, Section 1, D. N. R.
[2] Peterson to Gray, December 14, 1910, *ibid.*

must go through to adapt himself to the changed conditions presented by the Canadian environment.

Once a ready-made farm colony had been recruited in England and the settlers were about to embark for Canada, the company was at no little pains to see that they made their new start in life under the most favorable conditions. Circular letters were distributed among them at the time of sailing and again upon arrival in 'Alberta.[1] They were warned against those who would seek to victimize them in various ways. Unless possessed of an abundant capital, they were not to purchase indiscriminately furniture and agricultural implements in excess of their needs for the first year or two. A list of necessary articles was presented to each settler, together with the current price of the same. Anything else could be purchased at a later time when the colonist was better acquainted with current values and his own needs.

It was the plan of the company, too, to send with each group of colonists, as chairman of the colony, some one who had both Canadian and British experience. Hal Carleton, who knew western Canada well and who had lectured in England in the interest of the Canadian Pacific, served as chairman of the Nightingale colony upon the departure of the colonists for Alberta. In order to give a more intimate touch to the occasion Carleton issued a detailed letter to the settlers, advising them as to the procedure which they should adopt in their new home.[2] They were not to take with them more money than would comfortably see them through to their destination. The remainder should be sent by bankers' draft to the local banker. On arrival at the colony they were to look over their house and determine the amount of furniture needed, "keeping in mind that none of us in Canada spends on this item more than is absolutely necessary for a start." They were to remember that they would be surrounded by people of all classes urging them to buy horses, cattle, implements, in fact, everything. Carleton's advice in these matters was "Be wary" and "Go slowly."

Each man required a plow for breaking, a harrow, and a wagon. According to his capital, he could pay cash and receive a discount, or pay a portion, with the balance within a year. They were told that

[1] For copies of these letters see File No. 379, D. N. R.
[2] *Ibid.*

it was unnecessary for each to have a disc, since one could borrow from his neighbor. Nor should every one have a seeder; one large seeder would suffice for two or three farmers until such time as a man had a large tract of land under cultivation. Similarly, at harvest time, one eight-foot binder would serve two or three farms. While Carleton did not "suggest that settlers should actually join in the purchase of these implements," a farmer could have an understanding with his neighbors "that one should buy, when required, a binder, another a seeder and a third a disc, grass-mower and horse-rake." They were "to be loyal to each other in the matter of lending these things."[1]

While the farmer required three horses for breaking purposes, he need not own more than two, since he could borrow from his neighbor and lend in return. While his team was away, the settler could occupy himself in various ways. To avoid jealousy and trouble, each man was to do just as much for his neighbor as the neighbor did for him, which was to expect perfection in human nature.

Carleton suggested that they purchase all supplies in bulk at wholesale prices. If a given settler lacked the knowledge necessary to the wise purchase of horses and cattle, his neighbor might give him the benefit of greater experience. Above all, they should avoid a rush to purchase these things, since that would result in a sharp advance in prices. The Canadian Pacific had laid in a supply of oats, potatoes, etc., at prices of the previous autumn, which it would retail to settlers at the cost price. The colonists should remember that "you are going into a new country where the conditions are different from the conditions encountered at home and to be prepared to take the advice of those on the spot who *know*, until you yourself have been in the country long enough to form your own opinion. Many of the land operations will seem strange, but you will soon see the value of and necessity for these things."

In conclusion, Carleton reminded them that it was mixed farming which they should develop. It was not only the most profitable, but the most dependable and best suited to the country in which they were about to settle. Officials of the Canadian Pacific demonstration farm at Strathmore were always available with their expert knowledge, of which the settlers were urged to avail themselves freely.

[1] *Ibid.*

Carleton served as chairman only until arrival in Alberta, when the settlers elected a chairman from among their number, who called weekly meetings to discuss questions and problems of common concern.

Such was the care and supervision given to British settlers for ready-made farms prior to their arrival in Alberta. We may now have a glimpse of one of the colonies as it was being put in order for the colonist. At Sedgwick, on the Wetaskiwin line of the Canadian Pacific, two colonies were established for the British, one of 50 farms, the other of 72. The first was prepared in 1910, the farms ranging in size from 160 to 349 acres. The land was priced at $13.00 to $20.00 per acre, with improvements extra. The cost of the improvements per farm varied from $1,984.42 to $2,453.92, a sum greatly in excess of the $1,000 expenditure originally contemplated for ready-made farms.

In the spring of 1911 the colonies were visited by a company inspector who described the work which was then going on. He spent four and one-half days looking over the farms of Colony No. 1, and one and one-half days locating a party of British settlers which had just arrived. In the main he found them content with their situation. The inspector wrote:[1] "On Monday April 17th ten seeders were put at work planting wheat on as many farms. Wednesday morning the number of seeders was increased to 13. The work of planting wheat on the 50 farms will be completed on the 29th inst., following which oats will be put in on seventeen acres on each farm."

This work, of course, was performed by the company's development branch. The inspector urged the settlers to harrow their fields once or twice immediately after seeding in order the better to conserve the moisture and secure a smoother seed bed. A suggestion of the problem confronting the company is found in his remark that "some of the recent arrivals have had no previous experience in farming, and those who have been engaged in agricultural work in the old country are of course confronted with new conditions here. It is therefore important that all settlers in the colony be given such attention as will enable them to acquire the knowledge necessary to successful farming here."

[1] J. E. Gustus to Peterson, April 24, 1911, File No. 224, Section 1, D. N. R.

The inspector found that in Sedgwick Colony No. 2 the preliminary work of staking out the lines of the farms had been practically completed, and that the development branch was about to begin the 1,150 acres of plowing necessary for seeding the following spring. Fencing the farms would go forward as soon as the definite size and location of each had been decided upon. Much of the land in the colony was located in a valley, pleasing in appearance, with rich soil, and with little of the brush which was found in Colony No. 1.

The eternal vigilance so necessary on the part of company officials in dealing with the ready-made farm colonists is shown by the report of another inspector who visited the Nightingale colony in September, 1910.[1] His attention was attracted to the fact that the farmers were deferring their fall work in the way of back-setting and additional breaking in expectation of the arrival of a gasoline tractor, while their teams stood idle in the fields. They were losing not only money but also valuable time at a season when the soil was in excellent condition for plowing. The inspector recommended that a memorandum be sent to the settlers "calling their attention to the fact that every day their teams are idle they are losing money; that the expense of keeping a team is just the same whether they are working or not and that whatever they do themselves with their teams will bring them just that much ahead. It is a fact that Professor Elliott and I have in every possible way tried to impress upon them the necessity for prompt and continual pushing of their work, but where they have been accustomed to longer seasons than we have here, it seems almost impossible to impress upon them the necessity for prompt action." Settlers in this colony bore good English and Scottish names such as Stuart, Campbell, Southwell, Cornwell, Goodwin, Hilton, Davis, and Carleton, in sharp contrast to the heterogeneous group of names found in most western Canadian settlements of the time.

Among those in England whose interest was aroused by the announcement of the ready-made farm program was the Duke of Sutherland. In the summer of 1910 the Duke made known to the Calgary office his desire to purchase a sufficient area of land, in close proximity to the main line of the Canadian Pacific in the irrigation

[1] F. W. Crandall to Peterson, September 12, 1910, File No. 379, D. N. R.

block, to make 12 farms, varying in size from 80 to 120 acres. He desired to erect a set of plain buildings on each farm, with a more pretentious house on a central farm. It was his plan to colonize the farms with the married sons of some of the tenants on his estates in Scotland, reserving the central farm for himself and the Duchess, who planned to spend a few weeks each summer on the land, which would be farmed under the Duke's supervision.[1] His Grace desired that the Canadian Pacific Irrigation Colonization Company should undertake the work of erecting the buildings and making the necessary improvements on the land as in the case of its own ready-made farms. He would then add the cost of the buildings and improvements to the farms as he sold them to his colonists.

The proposition of the Duke presented a nice problem to the Calgary authorities. The company had a vast responsibility on its hands in its own ready-made farm project, and to accede to this latest request was merely to add to that burden. There was the further difficulty that only in the eastern section of the irrigation block was there available adjacent to the railway an area such as was wanted. With the delay in the construction of the irrigation works in that section it would probably be some time before water would be available for irrigation.[2] Over against these disadvantages, however, was the fact, pointed out by Peterson, that if the Canadian Pacific could get the Duke of Sutherland interested in the eastern section on a basis profitable and satisfactory to him, it would be a "publicity card, the value of which it is very hard to estimate." Furthermore, the Duke's plan for the colonization of small holdings was entirely in line with the policy of the railway in the block.

Peterson realized that, while the plan had great publicity value, it was one which had to be handled with the greatest of care lest a wrong interpretation be placed upon the Duke's motives in Great Britain. Enjoining caution on J. M. Gibbon, Canadian Pacific advertising agent then in London, he wrote: "If you are able to remove the impression that the Duke is making the investment for the purpose of evading taxation in Great Britain (which I personally know he *is not*), by making it read as if it were for Imperialistic and senti-

[1] Peterson to Dennis, July 4, 1910, File No. 377, D. N. R., in which he describes the Duke's plan fully.
[2] *Ibid.*

mental reasons that his Grace is anxious to become actively identified with one of the colonies and to do his share in bringing out
good English stock to the plains of Western Canada, I am quite
certain there will be no objection forthcoming from Stafford House"
to whatever publicity the company might see fit to give his venture.[1]

Once the problem of publicity was disposed of, arrangements were
readily made for the establishment of the colony. The company sold
to the Duke two sections of land just north of Brooks in the eastern
section of the block, the price being $35.00 per acre for irrigable and
$15.00 per acre for non-irrigable land. The company agreed to con-
struct the necessary buildings on the 12 farms, expending $2,300 on
the small ones and $8,000 to $10,000 on the central farm, the Duke
paying cash for the improvements. As in the case of the company's
own ready-made farms, a portion of the land on each farm was to be
seeded to crops in advance of the arrival of the settlers, who were to
be selected by the Duke himself from his own tenants.[2]

In this way there was launched one of the most curious ventures
in the colonization of British settlers in the Canadian West. The
Canadian Pacific prepared a booklet entitled *The Duke of Sutherland's Alberta Lands: Brooks and Clyde Alberta*, which was widely
circulated in England not for the recruitment of settlers for the
colony, but by way of informing the British public concerning the
opportunities offered by Alberta to British investors.[3] With a view
to enabling the Duke to start his colony under the most favorable
auspices, the railway, at a time when it needed all its irrigation
experts in connection with its own work, loaned one of them to the
Duke's farm where he provided the newly arrived settlers with the
necessary instruction in irrigation methods and practices.[4]

Except for the Sedgwick ready-made farm colony, the work of
the Canadian Pacific Irrigation Colonization Company thus far discussed was confined to the irrigation block. From 1905 to 1910 this
had been sufficient to engross all its energies. In the latter year,
however, the scope of its activities was very materially extended
when it was entrusted with the task of selling other lands of the rail-

[1] Peterson to J. M. Gibbon, October 13, 1910, *ibid.*
[2] Peterson to Dennis, November 22, 1910, *ibid.*
[3] Copy of the booklet is in File No. 377, D. N. R.
[4] W. J. Elliott, Superintendent of Agriculture for C. P. R., to T. Heeney, November 7, 1911, *ibid.*

way in the West. So great had been the sales in the western section of the irrigation block in 1908 and 1909 that by the spring of 1910 it was apparent that insufficient land remained to keep the vast agency organization of the company busy through the year. The agencies having been built up, with great care and expense, to the point where they were models of efficiency for land-selling purposes, the company was naturally loath to see them suffer a decline in morale or a loss of interest in Canadian Pacific lands. It had been the original hope and plan of the company that by the time the bulk of the land in the western section was disposed of, that in the central and eastern sections could be placed on the market through the medium of the agency force. But when it became apparent that, because of delays in the construction of the irrigation system, sales in those sections could not begin before 1911, and even then in limited quantities and in advance of irrigation facilities, the company was brought face to face with the question as to how the organization in the United States could be kept busy during the season of 1910.

Aside from the irrigation block, Canadian Pacific lands in the prairie provinces were still handled by the General Land Department at Winnipeg. Although this office carried on extensive advertising and publicity campaigns and had disposed of millions of acres of company lands, it had in the United States no organization comparable with that which the Calgary office had built up. It had sold and settled the land in the 48-mile belt along the main line, together with the great reserves in southern Manitoba and southeastern Saskatchewan. It had also sold extensive areas tributary to the Saskatoon line of the Canadian Pacific, together with some land along the branches extending east from Lacombe and Wetaskiwin in Alberta. In the main, however, its work had been confined to the regions tributary to the main line in Manitoba and Saskatchewan and the southern reserves in those provinces. Its policy had been the eminently wise and practical one of settling the country adjacent to the older lines of the railway. It naturally had been in no haste to dispose of lands served by competing lines of railway in the West.

Along the Lacombe and Wetaskiwin lines of the Canadian Pacific in Alberta the government sections were largely taken up, indicating that the time was ripe for the railway to push the sale of its own land. If the United States agencies of the Canadian Pacific Irrigation Colonization Company were about to work themselves out of a job in the irrigation block, there was no reason why they should not bring in American settlers to purchase the railway lands in this area. The adoption of this plan would not only be advantageous to the railway company in that it would expedite the settlement of the land and increase the traffic of the lines, but it would also serve to revive the drooping spirits of the agents. A circular letter to agents under date of December 14, 1909 advised them that "an arrangement is now being perfected whereby all lands belonging to the C. P. R. Co. in the Saskatchewan Valley in Northern Alberta and Western Saskatchewan will be turned over to this company to be handled by our agents on the same basis as lands in the irrigation block. This will give us an additional area of some 3,000,000 acres of high class agricultural lands for immediate sale."[1]

This, of course, was a very sweeping statement. All lands belonging to the company in the Saskatchewan Valley in northern Alberta and western Saskatchewan were not turned over to the agency organization for sale. Only the lands adjacent to the two branch lines of the railway were included, but the brighter the picture the greater the effect upon the agents. The circular hastened to inform the agents that they would still be expected to devote their efforts to the sale of land in the irrigation block where small areas of first-class irrigable and non-irrigable land were available, but that failing to make sales there, they should seek in every possible way to interest their clients in central Alberta lands.[2]

In this way the campaign for the sale of lands along the Lacombe and Wetaskiwin lines was begun. Adequate regulations were drawn up governing the sale of these lands. Actual settlers could purchase not more than 640 acres under a 10-payment plan, with one-tenth in cash and the balance in 9 equal annual installments.[3] Within one year the purchaser must undertake to settle upon the land with his family, to break up one-sixteenth of it, and to establish, to the satisfaction of the company, proof of his settlement and cultivation.

[1] Circular to U. S. agency organization, December 14, 1909, File No. 554, D. N. R.
[2] *Ibid.*
[3] See Form o, File No. 380, D. N. R.

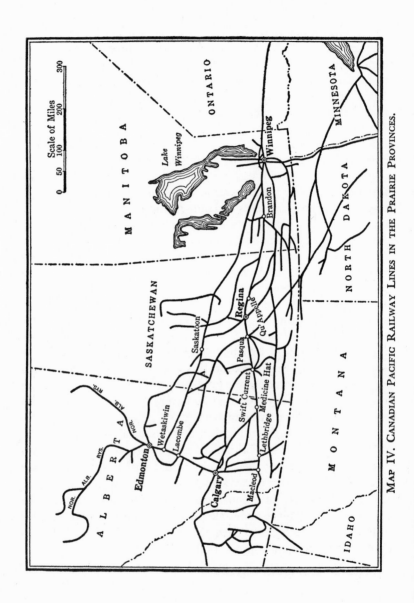

MAP IV. CANADIAN PACIFIC RAILWAY LINES IN THE PRAIRIE PROVINCES.

In the event of failure to provide such proof, he must liquidate the unpaid balance on his account in 4 annual installments. For the benefit of residents of Alberta who wished to enlarge their holdings by purchasing adjoining land from the railway, residence upon adjacent land was accepted in lieu of actual occupation or the erection of buildings upon the tract purchased. In such cases fencing of the land for grazing purposes was also accepted instead of cultivation. Non-resident or speculative purchasers must pay one-sixth in cash and the balance in 4 equal annual installments.[1] That these regulations were favorable to the settler and were designed to induce the buyer to occupy and develop the land is apparent. The speculator must pay the penalty for his absenteeism.

So actively was the sale of the land pushed that by the midsummer of 1910 some 200,000 acres had been disposed of to American settlers brought to Canada by the agents in the United States. This acreage included the best lands within a reasonable distance from the railway lines. Between Wetaskiwin and Sedgwick all desirable lands within 12 miles of the railway had been sold. From the latter point east to the Alberta-Saskatchewan boundary, over 50 per cent of the land within 18 miles of the railway had been sold.[2] Included in the area unsold was the land south of the railway between Hardisty and Hughenden, an extremely undesirable district because of its sandy and rough character. Peterson was unable to see how large parties could be brought over the line in the future with any chance of interesting them.

In the country tributary to the Lacombe extension the situation was not far different. For a distance of 18 miles east from Lacombe all land had been disposed of. A few areas remained near Alix, where the land was exceedingly rough and undesirable. South of Nevis there was still some good land which Peterson thought should be reserved for improved farms. Between Erskine and Castor all good land within 10 miles of the railway was gone. The district around Castor "had been worked to death," and while scattered sales could still be made there was nothing with which to interest large parties brought up from the United States. In the Buffalo Lake district the company could not hope to dispose of the lands for years to come.[3]

[1] *Ibid.*
[2] Peterson to Dennis, August 6, 1910, File No. 383, D. N. R.
[3] *Ibid.*

West of the Calgary and Edmonton Railway the company still had a large area of good land, especially between Okotoks and Wetaskiwin. In this region, however, the even-numbered sections had not been taken up under the homestead act, which meant that the time was not propitious for the sale of the railway lands.

The reports of Peterson as to the quality and location of unsold lands tributary to Canadian Pacific lines in central Alberta was abundantly confirmed from other sources. A representative from the Chicago office wrote that the remaining land in that part of Alberta was "not of the quality desired by people from this side of the line, either being more or less covered with brush or cut up by large coulees, or as is the case with a considerable sized strip from Hardisty east to Cadogan, running north and south, of too sandy a nature to be adaptable to agriculture." He added that he had "brought up many men having both the intention and wherewith to buy, who have been disappointed at these sections and returned without purchasing. In one instance . . . I took a carload of A number one prospects to Castor. These people were mostly prospective buyers of one section each, and I believe I am within the actual truth when I say that not one of them bought, the trouble being, in this case, the distance from the railroad as well as the brush and coulee lands, for we were taken to land lying 20 miles north of the right of way."[1] He could cite other instances where large parties, recruited at the cost of much labor by the agents in the States, were unable to find good land sufficiently close to the railway. This representative could not enthuse over the prospect of taking people to Castor, Sedgwick, and Provost to see picked over land. Yet this was the one alternative to driving long distances from the railway line.

By July of 1910 the Canadian Pacific Irrigation Colonization Company had a little land remaining in the western section of the irrigation block, a limited area of dry land in the eastern and central sections of the block, and, in central Alberta, lands which were either culled or remote from transportation facilities. If its organization was to continue to function in a high state of efficiency, additional land must be found for it to sell. In the face of this situation the officials of the company began to turn their attention in the direc-

[1] A. B. Braddick, Inspector of U. S. Agencies, to Peterson, July 19, 1910, *ibid.*

tion of Alberta lands owned by the Canadian Pacific, but tributary to the Canadian Northern and the Grand Trunk Pacific railways. Preoccupied as the General Land Department had been with the sale and settlement of the lands along the company's own lines, it had made little effort to sell these lands. In fact, if it could be said to have had any policy with respect to them it was to withhold them from the market until the surrounding country was so well settled that they would advance in price handsomely. Since the settlement and cultivation of the lands would swell the traffic of the Canadian Pacific's rivals, there had been no reason why the Winnipeg office should exert itself to sell the lands, especially since they were not yet subject to taxation. While it had disposed of some of the Alberta land adjacent to the Canadian Northern to a land company at $4.75 per acre, which in turn resold to groups holding the land for appreciation in value, it had in the main followed the course of sitting tight; and sitting tight meant placing a satisfactory price on these lands.

In the summer of 1910 the Calgary office began to scrutinize the prices at which the General Land Department had held this land. A good township along the Grand Trunk Pacific lines, embracing the well-known Viking district, largely peopled with Scandinavians, was priced at from $22.00 to $33.00 per acre.[1] A comparable township, quality of soil and location considered, in the Sedgwick district on Canadian Pacific lines had been sold at prices ranging from $13.00 to $22.00 per acre. Another township located midway between the Canadian Northern and Grand Trunk Pacific lines was listed at a flat price of $16.50 per acre, while a township of similar quality, situated between the Lacombe and Wetaskiwin branches of the Canadian Pacific, was priced at $13.00 per acre. Lands adjacent to the Canadian Northern seemed to be listed at a lower price than those tributary to the Grand Trunk Pacific. A township in the attractive Vermillion district on the former line ranged in price from $16.50 to $27.50 per acre, as compared with $22.00 to $33.00 in the Viking township on the latter line. The only apparent reason for this disparity in price was the fact that the Vermillion district was located a considerable distance to the north. The difference in price between

---

[1] Memorandum, Kirkwold to Peterson, July 16, 1910, *ibid.*

these lands and those on Canadian Pacific lines amounted to $3.50 up, averaging possibly $5.00 per acre.[1]

Calgary officials now began seriously to question the wisdom of these prices, especially in view of the fact that the agency organization in the United States required additional lands to sell. Obviously the agents would find it difficult to sell in the face of such a disparity in prices. Price, however, was not the only consideration involved in determining a policy with reference to lands served by other railways. The Canadian Pacific was now strongly committed to a policy of colonization with respect to land owned by it on its own lines of railway. To sell the land was not enough. The company was primarily concerned with development of the land with a view to traffic. Should it follow the same course with lands owned by it along other railways, or should it deal with them in a manner designed to enable it, in Shaughnessy's words, "to get our money out of them"?

Peterson conceded that, with large areas adjacent to its own lines unsettled, the company in the past had had no reason to create special facilities to sell and settle the lands in the North.[2] No one could quarrel with the course previously pursued, but the time had come when the company, in its own interest, should adopt a different policy. The lands had not sold at existing prices and there was no prospect that the demand for them would increase greatly. Assuming that the average price per acre in northern Alberta was $17.00 per acre, a conservative figure, the company was losing, at 6 per cent interest, $1.00 per acre per year by holding the land, and there was grave reason to doubt whether it would appreciate in value by that amount from year to year.[3] This was a cogent argument in favor of a change in policy.

But there were other reasons for a change. The high price attached to these lands was a product of the disappointment of the Canadian Pacific at governmental encouragement of and aid to rival railway companies in the West. The company had originally planned to develop its northern reserves by a series of branch lines, but, preoccupied with the settlement of the southern portions of the prairie provinces, it had been unable to do this prior to the appear-

[1] Ibid.
[2] Peterson to Dennis, July 22, 1910, ibid.
[3] Ibid.

ance of the Canadian Northern and the Grand Trunk Pacific. Canadian Pacific officials would have been something more than human had they not resented this outside intrusion. In their resentment they had placed upon the land a price which was all the traffic would bear. The northern Alberta lands were tributary to Edmonton, the gateway of the rival railways to the Pacific. Edmonton was to those roads what Calgary was to the Canadian Pacific. Edmonton, of course, envied the favors which the latter company bestowed upon Calgary. The irrigation development was designed to make Calgary the metropolis of Alberta, which drew Edmonton more closely to the competing railways. The Canadian Pacific, in turn, had expressed its disapproval of Edmonton by refusing to extend the Calgary and Edmonton railway, which it controlled, into the latter city, and had sought to build up the rival town of Strathcona on the south bank of the Saskatchewan River, a policy strongly reminiscent of the attempts of railways in the western states to make and break towns. The people of Edmonton felt that this was merely one attempt of the Canadian Pacific to retard their city's growth. The prohibitive price at which it held its lands to the north and east of Edmonton was also calculated to delay settlement and growth in the Edmonton district. They were bitterly hostile toward the Canadian Pacific.

The company had lately effected an entrance of the Calgary and Edmonton line into the city and was about to become a competitor of the Canadian Northern and Grand Trunk Pacific for the trade of the city. This made it important that the Canadian Pacific conciliate the Edmonton folk, and there was no better way of doing this than by adopting a more statesmanlike policy with respect to its lands. On a visit to Edmonton Peterson sought to disarm criticism of the company's policy and to refute the charge that it was motivated by jealousy of competing lines. It had merely had its hands full with the land to the south.

This territory would be served by Camrose and Edmonton wholesale houses and the Canadian Pacific in that way would obtain its fair share of the business, even though its lines did not serve the immediate territory. Peterson admitted there was no reason why the company should go out of its way to colonize the lands. It should merely endeavor to dispose of them to the best advantage finan-

BUILDING THE CANADIAN WEST

cially, which could be achieved by a slight reduction in price. The speculative element would not have to be considered; the land could be sold freely to any one who was willing to pay the price. These considerations, plus the need of keeping the agency organization in the United States intact, rendered it highly important that a vigorous selling campaign should be inaugurated.

Shaughnessy was not easily convinced by the cogency of Peterson's argument. Since the lands were not yet taxable, why should the Canadian Pacific make any effort to sell them? From the company's point of view these lands were in an entirely different category from its other land. They should be regarded and administered as an ordinary real estate proposition. Shaughnessy would place a satisfactory price on them and wait until settlement of the country created a demand for them. He would sell them over the counter to those who came, but he would not go in quest of purchasers. The answer to the views of the president was that vacated homesteads in that country were available in large numbers at $2.00 per acre less than the Canadian Pacific prices, while a Calgary land company was selling lands in the same district at prices ranging from $2.00 to $5.00 lower than the railway prices.

While not agreeing with Peterson's contention that the price of the lands must be reduced, Dennis admitted the importance of placing them on sale as a means of keeping the agency force in the States together until such time as the lands in the eastern section of the irrigation block were available for sale. He believed that the demand for land in the West would be so great in 1911 and that the company's land selling machinery was so efficient that it could dispose of the land even at the high list prices. In an effort to convert Shaughnessy to his point of view he wrote: "My suggestion is that we should now go out with a strong campaign in the effort to sell these lands. The prices, it is true, are high as compared with other lands we are offering, but I think we can dispose of them and we need them to keep up our aggressive campaign through our American agency."[1]

Dennis pointed out that on an average price of $20.00 per acre the company was losing $1.20 per annum in interest, and he doubted that the lands were increasing in value by that amount each year.

[1] Dennis to Shaughnessy, February 27, 1911, *ibid.*

He felt, too, that the company would receive a portion of the traffic which would result from their colonization. Nor did he fail to call attention to the fact that, since they would be sold chiefly to people in the United States, the purchasers would of necessity bring their effects into the country over Canadian Pacific lines. He suggested that, should the sale of the lands be authorized, certain areas adjacent to the towns be held in reserve in order that the company might receive "any increment of increased value due to the colonization of the area and the extension of such towns."[1]

In response to the plea of Dennis, Shaughnessy wrote: "Of course there is no reason why we should specially encourage settlement along these lines, or the sale of the lands for which we will not get in return anything excepting the selling price, in contrast to the lands along our own lines that become contributors to our traffic as soon as they are brought under cultivation. However, if you can get the full list price for them I do not know if we will benefit any by with-holding them from the market." While authorizing the sale of the land, Shaughnessy added the injunction that "we should carefully watch the sales . . . so that when the time comes when we can put the prices up, we may do so promptly."[2]

Dennis then sent out H. H. Honens, the sales manager of the Canadian Pacific Irrigation Colonization Company, on a tour of inspection over the Canadian Northern and Grand Trunk Pacific lines, with a view to submitting recommendations as to the points where sales headquarters could be established, to which the American agents might bring their clients.[3] Honens was none too optimistic as to the prospect of selling the lands at existing prices, even with the aid of the American organization. While the soil and topography were favorable, he felt the prevalence of brush, except in eastern Alberta, together with high prices, offered no great promise of rapid sale of the lands. He selected the towns of Viking and Chauvin on the Grand Trunk Pacific, both conveniently located to large areas of the company's land, as centers from which selling operations could be carried on, while Manville and Kiscaty, everything considered, seemed to him to be the most suitable points on

[1] *Ibid.*
[2] Shaughnessy to Dennis, February 27, 1911, *ibid.*
[3] Dennis to H. H. Honens, March 6, 1911, *ibid.*

the Canadian Northern.[1] An office was established in each of these towns, in charge of a competent man, and necessary arrangements were made with respect to livery service, hotels, etc. The northern Alberta campaign of 1911 was on!

The one question remaining to be decided was that of the terms of sale which the Calgary office should adopt. Should it place the land on the market on the 10-payment plan with settlement conditions, or the 5-year period without requirements as to occupation? As an offset to the high prices at which the land was offered, Honens had recommended the longer period without settlement conditions. Would the company be serving its best interests by forcing the speculative buyer to complete payment within 5 years? The dilemma was eventually solved by the decision to sell the lands north of a line 6 miles south of the Grand Trunk Pacific on the 10-year term, without settlement or improvement conditions. As this was the more southerly of the two competing railway lines, the regulation meant, in effect, that the very large area of fine land in eastern Alberta was to be sold without settlement conditions.

No fair-minded person, however, could well criticize the Canadian Pacific for the adoption of this course. Because of the remoteness of this land from Canadian Pacific lines, the company could not be expected to deal with it as with land in its own territory. If the railway was holding the land at a high price, it was, through its vast and expensive organization in the United States, bringing in buyers from that country, many of whom became actual settlers on the land purchased. In this way the company was actually colonizing lands which would largely benefit its competitors.

[1] Honens to Dennis, March 11, 1911, *ibid.*

IX

THE DEPARTMENT OF NATURAL RESOURCES

THE Canadian Pacific had built up at Calgary a machine for land sale and settlement so high-powered that the ingenuity of the company's officials was taxed to find the work which would keep it going in high gear. In an effort to maintain its operation at full speed the management had entrusted it with the sale of all Alberta lands of the company for the year 1911. To an acute observer this extension of the functions of the agency organization must have appeared as a mere preliminary to a further enlargement of the scope of its activities. By its success in land selling, by its aggressiveness, by the very nature of its·machinery, the Calgary office had displaced the General Land Department at Winnipeg as the most important medium of the railway for the colonization of the Canadian prairies. Originally a satellite, it had usurped the chief place in the firmament of land settlement. The time had come for official recognition to be given to this fact.

Meanwhile President Shaughnessy was becoming more and more convinced that a greater degree of coördination and centralization was desirable in the administration of the vast natural resources of the Canadian Pacific, consisting of ordinary agricultural lands, irrigable lands, coal mines, irrigation projects, natural gas, metalliferous mines and smelters, large areas of timber, numerous sawmills, improved farms, city property, and town sites. With such properties, scattered from Winnipeg to the Pacific Coast, under various and diverse agencies of administration, the need for concentration of control in the hands of one person and one office, directly responsible to the president, was increasingly manifest. And this need was emphasized by the contemporaneous acquisition of additional landed interests, with a consequent increase in responsibilities.

Through purchase of a majority of its stock the Canadian Pacific had just acquired control of the Alberta Railway and Irrigation Company, the pioneer in the development of irrigation in southern Alberta. While much of the agricultural land of this company had been disposed of, a considerable portion remained unsold. The company owned also coal and timber lands and operated an extensive irrigation project for the irrigation of much of its land, sold and unsold. It had carried on a valuable work of colonization from its Lethbridge headquarters and had in general been the most important agency for the development of that section of western Canada. To its multifarious interests throughout the West the Canadian Pacific now added the responsibility of administering the lands and the irrigation system of the Alberta Railway and Irrigation Company.

It was at this time, too, that the so-called Calgary and Edmonton security lands, amounting to 407,402 acres, were taken over by the Canadian Pacific. The Calgary and Edmonton Railway, long since leased and operated by the Canadian Pacific, had in 1890 entered into an agreement with the Dominion Government by which the railway company was to be paid a certain sum yearly, for 20 years, for transporting men, materials, supplies, and mails. As security, in the event of overpayment, the government had retained this portion of the land grant. The agreement had expired and the lands were claimed by the Calgary and Edmonton Railway, which, in reality, meant that they became part of the landed domain of the Canadian Pacific.

To administer these two grants as separate and distinct entities would mean duplication of agencies and increased decentralization of control of the land affairs of the company. To obviate this situation, a Department of Natural Resources was created at the beginning of 1912 and the administration of all the landed resources of the company was placed under its control.[1] The logical headquarters of the new department, of course, was Calgary, which was either in the center of, or in reasonable proximity to, a large number of the

[1] *Announcement of the Creation of the Department of Natural Resources*, 1912, File No. 202, Section 3, D. N. R.

manifold activities carried on in connection with land settlement. J. S. Dennis, in control of the irrigation project from its beginning, was placed at the head of the department, with the title of Assistant to the President. A better selection could scarcely have been made. Not only had Dennis been identified with the development of the West throughout his career, but he combined with genuine administrative ability, vision and imagination to a marked degree. His title of Assistant to the President was a fitting recognition both of the work he had done in the past and of the importance of the company's natural resources in the affairs of the railway.

With the formation of this department, the Canadian Pacific Irrigation Colonization Company became a thing of the past, as did the General Land Department in Winnipeg. The department was divided into Land, Engineering, Coal Mining, Treasury, and Accounting branches, each with a complete organization of its own, but reporting directly to Dennis, who, in turn, was responsible to the president. Under the Land Branch there were several offices. At Winnipeg was the Manitoba Land and Immigration Agent, in charge of land and town lots in that province, and of the forwarding of immigrants to all points west of Winnipeg. Similar offices for Saskatchewan and Alberta were established in Saskatoon and Calgary, while at Lethbridge was an agent in charge of the lands and town lots of the Alberta Railway and Irrigation Company. The British Columbia Land and Timber Agent supervised the lands and the tie and timber operations in that province. At Calgary the General Townsite Agent superintended the location of all town sites in the four western provinces and arranged with the Engineering Branch for surveys of additional town lots as required. The Lands Branch at Calgary was further divided into Agency, Sales, Publicity, and European divisions. A Superintendent of Agriculture was provided to take charge of the improved farms, together with the supply and demonstration farms of the company.

While Dennis, in his capacity as assistant to the president, was the responsible head of the Department of Natural Resources, it was recognized that an administrative officer was necessary to carry out the plans which Dennis in his policy-forming rôle was to formulate. For this purpose the company chose P. L. Naismith, General Manager of the Alberta Railway and Irrigation Company at Lethbridge, whose large experience in the land and irrigation work which that railway had carried on could be turned to good account in the post of Manager of the Department of Natural Resources.

The magnitude of the interests whose control was concentrated in the new department may be discerned at a glance. They included not only several millions of acres of agricultural lands, a gigantic irrigation project, and over 600,000 acres of timber lands, but also 137,000 acres of unsubdivided land adjoining town sites in the three prairie provinces, exceedingly valuable town properties in British Columbia, including Vancouver, 3,000,000 acres of coal rights under land sold and unsold in Alberta, to be developed on a royalty basis, 46,000 acres of coal lands, natural gas rights in 100,000 acres, petroleum rights in 50,000 acres, and extensive iron properties in British Columbia. With coal, natural gas, and petroleum rights each carried on the company's books at $1.00, these inactive assets of the railway totalled in 1914 some $133,000,000. It was indeed a veritable empire which the Department of Natural Resources was to administer.

For the first time the Calgary headquarters was entrusted with the job of administering the company's lands in Manitoba and Saskatchewan. Although but a small amount remained unsold in the former province, there was a very large area to be disposed of in Saskatchewan. Substantial portions of this were located along the Wetaskiwin-Saskatoon-Yorkton line of the Canadian Pacific, but by far the larger part was north of Saskatoon and tributary to the Canadian Northern Railway. Long known as the Battleford Block, this tract of land had been reserved for the railway in 1890, as part of the main line subsidy, and with the understanding that a line would be built north from Saskatoon to some point on the navigable waters of the North Saskatchewan River. Originally the block contained about 1,000,000 acres, to be scheduled to the company in alternate sections on either side of the proposed line to a depth of 12 miles. Later, as a reward for building the Souris branch, another million acres were reserved, which extended the land to a distance of 24 miles on either side. Before the Canadian Pacific, engrossed with construction and settlement in the South, had found time to build the line, the region was invaded by the Canadian Northern, with the support of the Laurier Government under its policy of increased railway competition for the West. Deprived of its original incentive to develop the land by its own lines, the Canadian Pacific had held it while devoting its energies to other portions of the prairie. The new Department of Natural Resources was now to direct its attention to the problem of selling and settling Canadian Pacific lands in the province of Saskatchewan.

Within two months after assuming his duties as assistant to the president, Dennis instructed W. J. Gerow, long a Land Department representative at Saskatoon, and one thoroughly familiar with the Saskatchewan situation, to make a reconnaissance of the company's lands in the province, with particular reference to the Battleford area.[1] It was the idea of Dennis that Gerow should select certain main points along the railway lines from which the company could operate in sending out home-seekers whom the agency organization in the United States would bring to Saskatchewan. This would require, of course, that provision be made for livery and hotel accommodations at those points.[2] Gerow was also to suggest terms and conditions which should govern the sale of the lands, according to their location on Canadian Pacific or rival lines of railway.

Gerow lost no time in the execution of his commission. In his comprehensive report of his findings he located and described 11 blocks of land awaiting sale. One of these was in the vicinity of Wolfe and Traynor, on the Wetaskiwin-Saskatoon line of the Canadian Pacific. There was sufficient good land in this district to make good half-section farms which he would develop under the ready-made farm policy of the company. A block north of Biggar, on the same line of the Canadian Pacific, he recommended as a desirable area for colonization with Russians, Germans, or other Continental Europeans.[3] Four blocks located respectively north and south of Maidstone, north of Lashburn, south of Marshall, and northeast of Lloydminster, all on the Canadian Northern, Gerow suggested as areas which might well be sold on the 10-payment plan, without requirement as to immediate settlement. Another large block was cut by the Canadian Northern branch extending in a

[1] Dennis to Gerow, March 1, 1912, Letter Book I, Montreal Office. Hereafter referred to as M.
[2] Ibid.
[3] Gerow to Dennis, March 8, 1912, File No. 506, D. N. R.

northwesterly direction from Battleford, and Gerow recommended that this tract be handled from Edom, in wholesale tracts of one section or more, on the 10-payment plan without settlement conditions. With the extension of this branch to the Northwest another large area could be handled wholesale. Northeast of North Battleford was a large block which, due to lack of transportation facilities, could not be disposed of to advantage at the moment. He recommended that the land be retained pending the completion of a Canadian Northern branch from Prince Albert to North Battleford, when the land could be sold through an office at the latter point.

South of the Saskatoon-Yorkton line of the Canadian Pacific, and tributary to the stations of Mozart, Elfros, and Leslie, was a large block partly covered by scrub timber, but with a good soil suitable for mixed farming. Along the Grand Trunk Pacific main line, northeast and southeast of Jasmin, there was a district of very rough land largely covered with heavy scrub, a region so unattractive as to be impossible of sale at existing prices. North of Bangor on the Grand Trunk Pacific main line was an attractive block of land in the midst of a Welsh community, a fact which Gerow would advertise extensively with a view to attracting others of that nationality to the district. Block No. 11, to the south of the Wolseley branch of the Canadian Pacific, was in the heart of a large German community and should be colonized with Russian or German settlers interested in mixed farming.[1]

Included in the survey carried out by Gerow were 4 blocks of land tributary to Canadian Pacific lines in Saskatchewan and 7 which were adjacent to the lines of the Canadian Northern and Grand Trunk Pacific. Dennis and Gerow were in agreement in the belief that the areas served by competing railway lines should be sold under the policy which had been adopted for the lands in northern Alberta along the same lines of railway, i.e., in units of moderate size, on the 10-payment plan, and without settlement conditions. The 4 tracts of land located on Canadian Pacific lines, however, were to be handled in a radically different manner. Together with all other lands of the company served by its own rails, these areas were administered under a plan which Dennis was gradually evolv-

[1] Ibid.

ing in his mind for the further extension of the policy of colonization which the railway had adopted.

The first step in the elaboration of the company's colonization program was taken when, in March, 1912, Dennis wrote to Shaughnessy a long letter in which he outlined a significant plan for the settlement of farmers from the United States. In the middle western states of the Union there was a very large number of farmers living on rented farms. While the majority of them had not much in the way of cash, they had a large capital in the form of farming experience, large families, implements, and stock. When the Canadian Pacific moved these people to western Canada they were handicapped by the fact that, while they were able to bring with them stock and implements for the development of their farms, and sufficient money to make their first payment on land purchased from the company, they lacked sufficient additional funds to provide the necessary improvements in the way of buildings, fencing, wells, and other equipment.[1]

Dennis was convinced that many of this class could be moved if the Canadian Pacific were prepared to advance a sum of money to be expended in providing the necessary improvements. He recommended, therefore, that the company make the experiment of lending $1,000,000 to settlers of that type. To protect the interests of the railway and to provide every possible guarantee of the success of the undertaking, he very carefully stipulated the conditions to be attached to the loan. The company should reserve the right to select the settler, and should accept only married men with agricultural experience and with a certain amount of cash, as well as with farm implements and live stock. The area of land to be purchased by the settler should be determined by the railway, which would then advance sums up to $2,000 on each farm, to be expended under the company's direction in erecting a suitable house and barn, fencing the farm, drilling a well, and placing part of the land under cultivation. While the building and fencing would naturally be done under contract, the company could employ the settler and his equipment in cultivating the land, paying him the ordinary rates therefor.

The proposal of Dennis was essentially that the Canadian Pacific should act as a loan company to enable the settlers to establish

[1] Dennis to Shaughnessy, March 18, 1912, File No. 507, D. N. R.

themselves as land owners. It should step into the breach resulting from the refusal of loan companies to lend money on unimproved land and of the banks to advance funds except upon chattel mortgage covering the farmer's equipment. Dennis believed the adoption of this policy would enable the railway to bring to the West large numbers of the most desirable class of actual farmers, who were otherwise forever doomed to be renters of the high priced land in the United States. With the assistance of the Canadian Pacific, they would become owners of their own farms within the 10-year period, and the loan for improvements would be a first mortgage on an improved farm, increasing in value from year to year.

While favorably impressed by the plan outlined by Dennis, Shaughnessy, with his customary caution, was inclined to proceed more slowly. He believed that the experiment could be initiated with a somewhat smaller expenditure, and he suggested $500,000 instead of the million-dollar appropriation requested by Dennis.[1] With this modification, Shaughnessy recommended the proposal to the board of directors, who promptly gave their approval.[2]

The regulations adopted for the execution of the policy stipulated that the applicant for the loan must personally visit the West and make his own selection of his farm. The construction of the house and barn was to conform to one of the standard plans provided by the company in connection with its ready-made farms, while enough of the loan was to be reserved to provide for the cultivation and cropping of at least 50 acres of land the first year. Applicants were required to have at least 4 horses valued at about $1,000, machinery to the extent of $750, cows, pigs, or other stock worth $300 to $400, and household furniture of the value of about $200.

This plan, officially termed the "loan to settlers" policy, was really the American counterpart of the "ready-made farm." The latter had been introduced as a means of colonizing British settlers in the West; the loan plan was designed to facilitate the settlement on company lands of desirable and worthy farmers from the middle western states. A farm developed under the loan to settlers plan

[1] Shaughnessy to Dennis, March 25, 1912, *ibid.*

[2] See Extract from the Minutes of a meeting of the Executive Committee of the Board of Directors of the Canadian Pacific Railway, held May 6, 1912, File No. 507, D. N. R.

became for all practical purposes a ready-made farm. The only appreciable distinction between them was that the American farmer was to do the initial cultivation and cropping, whereas the company had broken and seeded the land in advance of the coming of the British settlers.

Later in the same year Dennis submitted to Shaughnessy a plan involving even more far-reaching changes in the land policy of the company.[1] Because of its importance, this document merits examination in detail. He pointed out that the railway had about 7,000,000 acres of land unsold and about $37,000,000 outstanding as deferred payments on contracts bearing 6 per cent interest. It had built up in the United States the strongest land selling organization that had been known on this continent and could, by continuing the existing policy, dispose of the remaining lands in a comparatively short time. Although for several years the company had endeavored to discourage the speculative purchase of its lands and to encourage settlement, much of the land was still being speculatively purchased. Of the vast sum outstanding on land contracts at least 50 per cent comprised contracts for land held speculatively.

Through its ready-made farm and loan to settlers policies, the company was offering inducements to the actual settler far in excess of any other railway in America. But inducements were not enough. Dennis would adopt a policy of compulsory settlement by purchasers of company lands along its own railway lines. He suggested that the railway limit individual sales to such areas as it deemed necessary for efficient farming operations in a given locality, but in no case should it sell more than two sections to one person. The contract must contain a clause making it obligatory upon the purchaser to occupy and improve the land. With the mandatory colonization feature, Dennis coupled the significant proposal that the company should allow the settler to pay for the land in 20 annual installments instead of 10, the interest on deferred payments to remain at 6 per cent per year. He recommended that the list price of the land be increased by a sufficient amount to cover the increase of sales commissions from 10 to 15 per cent. Finally, Dennis thought the company should strengthen its colonization organization in Great

[1] Dennis to Shaughnessy, November 3, 1912, Personal Letter Book 2, August 16, 1912-March 6, 1913, M.

Britain and western Europe with the object of securing a larger number of settlers from those countries to counteract the increased movement of people from the United States which would result from the season's favorable crops in the West.

Dennis next turned his attention to lands purchased from the company but held speculatively. To deal with these he proposed that the company obtain at once, and illustrate by schedule and map, a statement showing all land held under contract for purchase which was not occupied or improved. It should insist on the prompt discharge of deferred payments and interest on contracts covering this land, and should refuse to carry over such installments, as it had done in the past. In all cases where the speculative holders of contracts were not able to meet their deferred payments and interest, the company should cancel the contracts or arrange to take them over on the best possible terms, the land so acquired to be resold at advanced prices under settlement conditions.

Dennis felt that a serious responsibility rested upon the Canadian Pacific in determining the policies governing the disposal of its remaining lands. The area already sold had realized $92,000,000. The company was now situated so that it did not need to realize an immediate financial return on the $100,000,000 which the unsold portion was worth. In conclusion he remarked that "the sale of the unsold portion on such terms as will ensure the settlement of say 30,000 farmers in the West must necessarily have a marked influence not only upon the business of the Company from a traffic standpoint, but also upon the industrial development of the West, and finally the character of the people put upon this land must inevitably have a marked influence upon the political future of the West as a portion of the Dominion and upon the Dominion as part of the Empire." This last represented an appeal by Dennis to the imperial sentiments of Shaughnessy, who, despite his American birth and his Irish name, supported enthusiastically the idea of closer relations between the Dominion and the Empire.

Several weeks later Dennis somewhat amplified the views he had previously set forth, and advanced some additional arguments in support of his proposal. By the sale of land under a 20-year term, with advances to farmers for the erection of buildings, the company could "hand pick" its settlers and ultimately place 30,000 to 40,000 selected farmers on the balance of its land grants.[1] Settlers buying land under the proposed plan would be so intimately associated with the company that it would not need to fear the competition of other roads during the life of the 20-year contract. Adoption of the policy would enable the railway to institute a publicity campaign in Great Britain, northern Europe, and the United States which would attract world-wide attention, because no landowning corporation "has ever attempted to inaugurate the policy of the sale of their land on such long terms and the loaning of money to settlers for the improvement of their farms, or the general encouragement and assistance to the farmer to make a success along the lines which I now propose." There was no better security possible for money lent than that on farms, title to which remained vested in the company (during the 20-year period), while the money lent was expended on the improvement of the farm. This policy would not only result in an ultimate return of a larger sum from the sale of the land than if sold outright under the 10-year plan, but, what was much more important, it would contribute more toward the development of the land and the provision of traffic for the railway than any other one step the company could take.

The merits of the proposal as outlined by Dennis appealed strongly to Shaughnessy and the board of directors, with the result that on December 16, 1912 the 20-year payment plan was adopted in its entirety.[2] With this action the Canadian Pacific took one additional step in the development of a policy of genuine colonization which contrasted so sharply with the mere land selling activity which had characterized American land grant railways.

Printed regulations for the sale of land under the 20-year term were accordingly drawn up.[3] They provided for the sale of the land for settlement only, with or without the loan for improvements. If the farmer elected to buy without loan, he must agree to enter into occupation of the farm within 6 months from the date of the contract, and to reside on it from the first of April to the first of November in each year for 5 years, and to continue to occupy it until

[1] Dennis to Shaughnessy, December 16, 1912, *ibid.*
[2] Extract from the Minutes of a meeting of the Executive Committee of the Board of Directors of the Canadian Pacific Railway Company, December 16, 1912, File No. 305, Section 1, D. N. R.
[3] Printed Regulations for the sale of land under the new 20-year term, *ibid.*

5 payments of principal and interest had been made. He must build a house costing at least $350 and a barn costing not less than $200 and capable of accommodating 4 horses and 4 cows. Further requirements were that he keep the buildings insured against fire, sink a suitable well, and fence the land. During the first year he must break and crop at least 25 acres on each quarter section. During the second year he was required to break and crop an additional 25 acres in each quarter section, and during each of the remaining years of his required occupancy he must cultivate and crop at least 50 acres on each quarter section. During the entire period of his required residence on the farm he must keep at least three milk cows.

No applicant for purchase with the loan for improvements could buy more than 320 acres. He must agree to go into residence within 6 months after the completion of the improvements and must reside there continuously until 5 payments of principal and interest had been made. Within 12 months following the completion of the improvements he was required to break, cultivate, and crop at least 50 acres on each quarter section. During the succeeding 12 months he must cultivate and crop an additional 50 acres per quarter section, and through the remaining years of his required occupancy he must cultivate and crop 100 acres in each quarter section. Finally, during the period of required occupancy the farmer agreed to keep not less than 3 milk cows per quarter section. The loan policy was confined to those lands of the company situated within 6 miles of a Canadian Pacific line or in the irrigation block. Thus the conditions governing purchase with the loan were substantially more onerous than those without.

While the loan policy represented primarily a genuine desire on the part of the Canadian Pacific to facilitate the settlement and development of its land by an experienced and worth-while class of farmers, officials of the company, of course, were not oblivious to its publicity value. The use of it for advertising purposes is well illustrated by this passage from one of the company's pamphlets:[1] "The $2,000 Loan to settlers is absolutely the strongest, most positive and convincing answer that any one could ask for, to any and all questions as to the quality of the Canadian Pacific lands, and as to the profits that can be made in farming these lands. Think of this—

[1] *Get Your Farm Home from the Canadian Pacific* (Calgary, 1913), pp. 2-3.

if a farmer purchases 160 acres of these lands at $20 an acre his first payment on our twenty year terms is only $1.00 an acre, or $160 on 160 acres. Now against this investment of only $160 in the land, the Canadian Pacific is willing to prove its faith in the productiveness of the land by investing $2,000 in improvements on his land. And this investment is absolutely without any security but the land itself and the positive knowledge that the land will produce great crops. In other words, for every dollar the farmer puts into the purchase of 160 acres of $20 land the first year, the Canadian Pacific stands ready to put $12.50 into improving the farm. Seeing this, can any reasonable man doubt that the soil of the lands offered is as rich or that the profits that may be made are as great as the Canadian Pacific has always claimed they are?"

It was not merely through Canadian Pacific publications that these innovations in company policy were made known to the world. The adoption of the loan to settlers plan and the 20-year, compulsory colonization requirement was followed by one of the most pretentious publicity efforts in the history of the railway. The advertising campaign was conducted on all fronts in every conceivable way. Scarcely had the loan policy been approved when Dennis instructed Herbert Vanderhoof, long in charge of the company's land and irrigation publicity in the United States, to make it the basis of the widest possible publicity. He was to present it as a marked departure from the methods followed by railway companies in the past in the sale of land, and as evidence that the Canadian Pacific had reached the colonization stage as opposed to mere land selling.[1] Sharp contrasts were to be drawn between this advanced policy and the practices of the land grant roads in the United States. Obedient to instruction, Vanderhoof wrote for use in the American press, including the agricultural, a long succession of stories in regard to the enlightened course the Canadian Pacific was pursuing. A special fund of $10,000 was placed at Vanderhoof's disposal for the purpose of advertising in the United States during the months January to April, 1913, the adoption of the 20-year payment plan.[2]

Nor did Dennis confine the propaganda to the advertising channels of the Department of Natural Resources. The traffic depart-

[1] Dennis to Vanderhoof, April 11, 1912, Letter Book 1, M.
[2] Ibid., December 19. 1912, Letter Book 6, M.

ment of the road had always maintained its own publicity bureau in which it gave much attention to western Canada and to Canadian Pacific lands. It had, in fact, always been an important agency for the promotion of immigration to the prairies. Dennis now proceeded to make the fullest possible use of this department to broadcast knowledge of what the company was doing in the West. With his aid, John Murray Gibbon, in charge of advertising for the traffic department, prepared a series of articles, under attractive titles, describing the activities of the Department of Natural Resources.[1] "The Greatest Colonization Undertaking of the Age" was a recital of facts regarding the company's land grants and a contrast between its settlement policies and those of governments and corporations. "America's Greatest Irrigation Project" described the scheme from the standpoint of engineering, permanence and sufficiency of water rights, price of lands, and terms of colonization. The mining interests of the department received attention in "One of Western Canada's Large Colliery Undertakings," which emphasized the Bankhead as the only anthracite mine in the Dominion.

"How a Railway Company Reaches the Farmer" set forth the work done through the Agricultural and Animal Industry Branch in aiding the farmer to go in for sane agriculture instead of "grain mining," the term then commonly applied in the West to the practice of growing wheat to the exclusion of other crops. "Agricultural and Animal Industry Demonstration by a Railway Company" was a full description of the company's demonstration and mixed farms and the educational work they were carrying on, together with their importance as distributing centers for good seed and live stock. One of the more subtle of the list was "How a Railway Company Bears Its Share of Taxation," dealing with a subject which had occasioned frequent criticism of the Canadian Pacific. Stress was laid on the tax exemption enjoyed by the railway on its land grants, and on the fact that, while it had defended this exemption from compulsory assessment, it had contributed large amounts voluntarily for the maintenance of municipalities in the West.

"The Owner of Six Hundred Cities, Towns and Villages" gave a full account of the company's ownership of town sites, ranging from cities such as Vancouver and Calgary down to the small villages,

[1] Dennis to Gibbon, January 30, 1914, Letter Book 10, M.

together with the efforts which the railway had made to develop them. The great exodus from the United States to the Canadian West suggested the title "Why Do Americans Emigrate?" dealing with the various points of attraction which the prairies had for American farmers. The real answer to the question, however, was found in the work which the Department of Natural Resources was carrying on. The title of the last article in the series was inspired by the remark of "an intelligent American," after visiting the West and informing himself as to the assistance given to home-seekers by the Canadian Pacific. "Providence Incorporated" was a detailed description of this colonization policy, emphasizing the fact that while there was nothing of a philanthropic nature in this work, it was far in advance of anything undertaken by other corporations, and contained an "element of soul" which was supposed to be lacking in all corporate undertakings.

The work of Vanderhoof and Gibbon thus paved the way for the agency force in the United States and for the British and European organizations of the Department of Natural Resources in finding the settlers who were to be placed on Canadian Pacific lands under the policy of compulsory colonization. Few were the prospective land buyers who were not acquainted with the distinctive features of the plan when called on by one of the multitude of agents who swarmed about the countryside of two continents. Publicity of this sort was well calculated to increase the efficiency of the railway as a means of bringing home-seekers to the West.

Once he had adopted the 20-year colonization policy, Dennis was ever ready to make whatever changes and adjustments seemed necessary to achieve the largest possible measure of success. During the first year the plan was in effect, it was the practice of the company to require that an applicant for the purchase of land must have, in addition to his live stock and farm equipment, a minimum cash capital of $1,500. This amount was deemed desirable, if not necessary, even in the case of those who availed themselves of the loan to settlers. By the end of the first year Dennis had come to the conclusion that this requirement was a mistake in that it was preventing the department from moving many desirable tenant farmers in the United States who, while having the required amount of stock, implements, furniture, etc., were unable to muster the $1,500. Nor was there any prospect that some 2,000,000 of these men would ever be able to accumulate that amount of cash. Their high rent, computed on a land value of $100 per acre, not only precluded any possibility that they would become farm owners in their own country, but also made it impossible for them to save enough to meet the requirements which the railway had laid down for their acceptance as settlers on Canadian Pacific lands.

To meet this situation Dennis proposed that the Department of Natural Resources go into the best mixed farming sections of the United States and take men with sufficient cash to defray the cost of moving and to provide living expenses for a year. These farmers he would move to improved farms of the company, which he would lease to the farmer for a term of 5 years, with option to the lessee to purchase the farm at the termination of that period.[1] A rent computed at 6 per cent of the list price of the cheaper Canadian lands, plus the cost of improvements, would enable the farmer to save with a view to purchasing the farm at the end of the rental term. To give the farmer a further advantage the rent was to begin at the end of the year the agreement was entered into. The renter assumed the obligation of keeping the buildings and improvements insured in favor of the company, and agreed to operate the farm under the supervision of the agricultural branch of the department, which would prescribe the methods of cultivation, crop rotation, raising of live stock, etc. With Shaughnessy's approval this additional feature was incorporated in the railway's land policy.[2]

The decision by the Canadian Pacific management to sell lands tributary to its own lines only to settlers necessitated a change in the machinery by which it disposed of the land. Hitherto the entire agency organization in the United States had operated on a commission basis. The general agents were the leading land or real estate companies in their territory and to them the railway paid a commission on all land sold to buyers within that area. The general agents, in turn, had their crew of sub-agents who received a share of the earnings of the former. As Dennis so frequently observed, the agency system was remarkably efficient as a medium for selling

[1] Dennis to Shaughnessy, November 30, 1913, Letter Book 10, M.

[2] Dennis to Naismith, December 10, 1913, *ibid.*, in which he says Shaughnessy has authorized him to put the policy into effect.

land, but it perhaps left something to be desired as a means of colonizing the country. Dependent as the general agents were on their commissions, they necessarily failed on occasion to use proper discrimination in the selection of settlers. To them the speculative buyer was as good a prospect as the *bona fide* farmer. In fact, the tendency of the speculator to purchase larger tracts rendered him more attractive to the agent.

To obviate this situation, the company established its own district land offices in the United States, with general headquarters in Chicago. It placed a district representative, a salaried official, in charge of each office, who appointed commission agents in his district, to whom the Canadian Pacific paid a 5 per cent commission on all sales. The term "district representative" was substituted for "district agent" because it was generally agreed that the title "land agent" placed the men at a disadvantage in dealing with people who were suspicious of all land agents.[1] The commission agent submitted to the district representative a full report in regard to all clients registered, and no client was taken to Canada without authority from the district representative. Over the entire organizaion was placed a superintendent of United States agencies with offices at the Chicago headquarters. As the placing of the district representative on a salaried basis removed his dependence on commissions, he could be depended on to curb the tendency of commission agents in his district to encourage speculative buying.

From the company's point of view the new departure was a thoroughgoing success. It reduced the cost of land selling to a marked degree. Whereas the general agents had received a 10 per cent commission, paying 5 per cent to the sub-agent, the company now paid the 5 per cent directly to the latter. The salaries of the district representatives amounted, in the aggregate, to a much smaller sum than the 5 per cent commission which the general agents had formerly retained. In this way alone the United States organization in two typical years effected a saving of more than $230,000. More important, however, was the fact that the arrangement gave to the company a more complete control over immigration work in the United States than it had previously enjoyed. A few years later the superintendent of United States agencies, in reviewing the accom-

[1] Dennis to Naismith, December 15, 1913, *ibid.*

plishments of the organization, stated that the theory back of the establishment of the district representatives was that they would "enable us to have complete control of all the United States Commission Agents and direct the immigration and stop the speculative clients. This has been accomplished. Without any doubt the United States Agency Organization, since the General Agency was abandoned, has produced a better class of settlers; with a few exceptions they have been practical farmers who have occupied their lands and become valuable settlers."[1]

The introduction of the district representatives facilitated and made more effective a practice previously employed by the company with respect to the agents in the States. As early as 1911 Dennis decided that periodical meetings or conventions of all the Canadian Pacific land agents in the United States were desirable. Not only would these get-togethers develop an *esprit de corps* among them, but they would afford an opportunity for agents to exchange views and experiences with one another and with the Calgary authorities. Common problems could be discussed, difficulties could be solved, the campaign of the previous season reviewed and that of the forthcoming one mapped. From the first Dennis attended these conventions, obtaining first-hand information in regard to the work and planning in person the lines along which the activities should be carried on. While the general agency organization lasted, his rôle at these meetings was to employ the skill and tact necessary to keep the agents in a happy and coöperative frame of mind. With the coming of the district representatives, Dennis regarded the semi-annual meeting as an opportunity to take counsel with the men in the field.

As the head of the Department of Natural Resources and assistant to President Shaughnessy, Dennis assumed a rôle of the first importance in advertising and promoting immigration to the Canadian West generally. The activity of the Canadian Pacific, the Dominion Government, the multitude of land companies and other agencies in the United States over a long period of years naturally

[1] Memorandum by M. E. Thornton, Superintendent of U. S. Agencies, June 13, 1919, File No. 110, Section 3, D. N. R., contains an excellent statement of the transition from general agents to district representatives, together with the reasons therefor and the resulting advantages.

and inevitably led to a certain sensitiveness in the States, as well as a strong anti-Canadian feeling on the part of the press and other interested groups there. Dennis now took steps to counteract this. For years he had sent press dispatches from Calgary to Herbert Vanderhoof in Chicago, who saw that they obtained the widest possible circulation in American papers, thereby keeping the American farmer constantly informed regarding developments in the West. In 1912 Dennis extended this system by appointing representatives at Vancouver, Victoria, Edmonton, Lethbridge, Regina, Saskatoon, and Winnipeg, the more important centers in the four Western provinces. From these representatives the company obtained daily items which could be used for publicity purposes. These were consolidated every night at Calgary into a single large dispatch which went east through Winnipeg and Montreal, and thence to Vanderhoof in Chicago. Although the Winnipeg and Montreal offices arranged for publication in the Canadian Press, the main effort of the company was concentrated on publication of the material in the American papers. As Dennis wrote, "in this way we hope to keep up a consistent campaign of good Western Canadian publicity, which in some measure will meet the active anti-Canadian campaign now being carried on in the United States."[1] It was just at this time that the press gave great prominence to the freight car shortage in western Canada, which the agency organization of the Canadian Pacific in the United States turned to their advantage by playing up the attractions of a country which produced so bountifully as to embarrass the railways in handling the crops.[2]

In the same year there was formed in the middle western states an association to discourage the movement of people from that section to Canada. This organization sent men to the West to travel among settlers, seek out those who were discontented, and obtain from them letters which could be published in the United States. It also arranged to pay such settlers a fixed amount for every letter which they would write to people in the United States "crying down" the Canadian West. It was the further plan of the Association, when publishing farmers' letters, to advise people contem-

[1] Dennis to C. E. Ussher, Passenger Traffic Manager, Montreal, March 1, 1912, Personal Letter Book 1, M.
[2] Dennis to Shaughnessy, March 18, 1912, *ibid.*

plating migration to the prairies that by communicating with these settlers the true facts about Canada could be obtained. This vigorous campaign of slander also drew the fire of Dennis who at once took up with Vanderhoof the matter of determining how this latest thrust might be most satisfactorily met.[1] At the same time there were articles appearing frequently in the American papers, describing the great exodus of people from Canada to the United States, in which the figures were so grossly exaggerated that Dennis was convinced they included Canadian tourists crossing over into the United States. Refutation of these reports was also dealt with through Vanderhoof's Chicago office.[2]

Another self-appointed task of Dennis was to ask the Dominion Minister of the Interior each year to renew the government's contribution of $5,000 to the maintenance of Vanderhoof's publicity bureau in Chicago.[3] Jointly supported by the Ottawa authorities and the three railways, all contributing equally to it, that bureau had proven to be such an important medium for informing the American people concerning Canadian opportunities, that Dennis was ever eager to prevent any lack of support which might impair its efficiency.

In this period the government and the Canadian Pacific revived a practice which they had jointly used earlier in the promotion of immigration from the Old Country to Canada, but which they had later abandoned. In the eighties they had sent back to Great Britain as well as to the Continent what were known as "return men," settlers who had gone to the Canadian West and who were desirous of returning to their old homes in order that they might tell their old friends and relatives of the opportunities awaiting them on the prairies. Some went in the capacity of lecturer, others merely to work quietly and unobtrusively among their acquaintances. Just when the practice was revived is not entirely clear, but in the years preceding the outbreak of the World War, the dispatch of such men across the Atlantic was a regular procedure in the winter season. Now referred to as "farm delegates," it was the custom for the Dominion

[1] Dennis to Vanderhoof, May 28, 1912, *ibid.*
[2] Dennis to Shaughnessy, January 19, 1914, Letter Book 10, M.
[3] Dennis to Dr. Roche, Minister of the Interior, March 3, 1913, Letter Book 7; March 2, 1914, Letter Book 4; February 24, 1915, Personal Letter Book 5, all at M.

Superintendent of Immigration to provide Dennis with a list of these men in the autumn, with the request that he obtain the necessary rail transportation for them to the port of sailing. While it was understood, of course, that the delegates, in return for free rail tickets over the company's lines, would book their passage on Canadian Pacific ships, there was no attempt by Dennis to limit the gratuity to delegates from Canadian Pacific territory in the West.[1] In this endeavor the railway was working in the interest of western Canada generally, with the realization no doubt that settlers secured by the delegates would take passage on the company's ships and would be accompanied by Canadian Pacific representatives to the West. Besides the men sent back jointly by the government and the railway, the company frequently selected delegates on its own account, who, with the aid of free transportation, returned to the mother country to spread the gospel of western Canada. A typical case is that of one Alex Grant, a British settler on a ready-made farm in the Sedgwick colony, who was thus aided by the company on condition that he report to the London offices of the Department of Natural Resources and carry on, under its auspices, propaganda in behalf of the improved farm program of the Canadian Pacific.[2]

Dennis coöperated in other ways with the Dominion Government. When one of its agents at Syracuse, New York, planned a trip through the West by delegates of the National Grange, Dennis was prepared to extend transportation to them in order that they might observe the "home making possibilities" of the Canadian Pacific program.[3] He made it his particular duty, too, to see that the Dominion agents were supplied with annual passes over all Canadian Pacific lines, without which, of course, the efforts of the government to promote emigration from the States would have been materially restricted as well as more expensive.[4]

While facilitating in all possible ways the emigration propaganda

[1] Dennis to W. D. Scott, Superintendent of Immigration, Ottawa, November 8, 1912, Letter Book 5, M.

[2] Dennis to Kirkwold, October 24, 1912, ibid.

[3] Dennis to J. Bruce Walker, Commissioner of Immigration, Winnipeg, January 4, 1915, Letter Book 14, M.

[4] Dennis to M. J. Power, Secretary to the President, April 12, 1912, Letter Book 1, M. In this letter Dennis asks for passes for Dominion agents at Detroit, Chicago, Milwaukee, St. Paul, Great Falls, and Spokane.

of the Ottawa authorities in the States, Dennis was of the opinion that the conduct of certain of the government agents was open to serious question. As the pioneer railway of the Canadian West, as the child and beneficiary of the Conservative Government, and as the greatest land holder in Canada aside from the government itself, the Canadian Pacific was a constant target of the opposition emanating from various sources. Regarding the Canadian Northern and the Grand Trunk Pacific as intruders, Canadian Pacific feeling toward these companies was never friendly and they cordially reciprocated the antipathy. Nor was it unnatural that the immigration agents of the Liberal Laurier Government, stationed throughout the United States, should look with particular favor upon these younger railways which had been fostered and promoted by that government, and that the Canadian Pacific should look with suspicion upon this friendship and see in it an evidence of a common hostility to it.

In June, 1912, Dennis sent J. E. Forslund, General Colonization Agent of the Canadian Pacific at Winnipeg, a Scandinavian long in the service of the general land department, where his knowledge of several languages made him particularly valuable in dealing with foreign colonies, on an extended tour through the United States. While he was to visit and observe the work of Canadian Pacific representatives there, his chief concern was to be the agents of the Dominion Government. He was to discuss fully with them the movement of people from the United States to Canada and the basis upon which they were seeking to interest people. It was to be his special duty to ascertain, if possible, whether these men were acting as agents for the sale of any particular areas of land. Dennis gave it as his opinion that "at least several of these agents" were acting under a commission arrangement with the Canadian Northern and that it was their disposition to route their people over that line and the Grand Trunk Pacific, to the exclusion, wherever possible, of the Canadian Pacific. Forslund was also to find out the basis upon which the government agents issued land-seekers rate certificates, which Dennis believed were granted freely to large numbers of people who were not *bona fide* home-seekers.[1]

The investigation thus instituted by Dennis revealed the fact

[1] Dennis to Forslund, June 26, 1912, Personal Letter Book 1, M.

that Dominion immigration agents, including the inspector of United States agencies, were engaged in selling land on a commission basis for the Canadian Northern and for land companies operating in the territory of that railway and the Grand Trunk Pacific. It further showed that the inspector, among others, had actively engaged in propaganda in the States designed to discourage settlers from moving into Canadian Pacific areas in the West.[1] This antipathy of the government agents toward the company was assumed to result from its refusal to pay them a commission for selling railway lands. It was shown, too, that on the part of certain of the agents there was gross abuse in the granting of the landseekers' rate certificates entitling the holder to the cent-a-mile rate. Obviously large numbers of people were receiving them for no other purpose than to take a pleasure jaunt or to visit relatives and friends in western Canada.[2] In conjunction with government agents, the Canadian Northern published pamphlets designed to lure the settler into that railway's territory with the promise of free homesteads, which, upon arrival of the immigrant from the States, were found to be virtually non-existent in districts served by existing lines of railway.[3] In this situation the farmer faced the choice of a return to the States or the purchase of privately owned land, but in either case he was lost to the Canadian Pacific. Although the inspector of Dominion agencies in the United States was disciplined for his zeal and indiscretion in behalf of the other railways, there was little that Dennis could do about the collusive understanding between agents and rail companies except to expose it.

It was the conviction of Dennis that much of the anti-Canadian propaganda in the States was inspired by the Hill railway lines, which naturally did not relish the idea of farmers moving from their territory to the Canadian Prairie. Since the Canadian Pacific was one of the chief instigators of this movement, the Canadian-born Hill, a member of the original Canadian Pacific Syndicate, and the American-born Shaughnessy were the leaders of contending forces. So actively did the Hill lines conduct their campaign to alarm the

[1] Dennis to Shaughnessy, February 2, 1914, Personal Letter Book 4, M.
[2] Dennis to C. E. Ussher, Passenger Traffic Manager, November 30, 1913 and December 29, 1913, Letter Book 10, M. Also Dennis to Ussher, April 27, 1914, Personal Letter Book 4, M.
[3] Dennis to Rankin, September 14, 1914, Letter Book 13, M.

public in the northwestern states over the Canadian menace that the states officially became interested in the problem. In an effort to deal with the matter a convention of governors of those states was arranged to be held in Seattle in June of 1912. Dennis shrewdly turned this occasion to the advantage of the Canadian Pacific. Representatives of the company were present in Seattle, actively distributing Canadian literature and advertising material. Throughout the convention the Department of Natural Resources carried full page advertisements in all Seattle papers, opposite the reports of convention proceedings. Dennis wrote to Shaughnessy that "we have received publicity from this Convention, for Western Canada, which could not have been purchased for a large sum of money."[1]

An incident occurring at this time illustrates very clearly the extent to which those who were giving general publicity to western Canada depended upon the Department of Natural Resources for information in regard to conditions there. An American writer, preparing an article on the Canadian West for the *Saturday Evening Post*, visited Ottawa, the seat of the Immigration Branch of the Department of the Interior, and was told to write the Calgary office of the Canadian Pacific for the materials and photographs which he desired. Not only did Dennis see that the desired data were forwarded to the writer, but he took occasion, as he often did, to suggest certain points which should be stressed in any discussion of emigration from the States to the prairie.[2] The migration was a continuation of the westward movement in the United States; people coming from south of the line found certain favorable conditions in the West, among them good soil and cheap land, higher yields of grain than in the United States, with equally good prices, a lower rate of taxation, better common schools, and a respect for the law not obtaining in any portion of the United States. These items, all good talking points in favor of Canada, were constantly stressed by the company in the campaign carried on south of the 49th parallel.

An advertising device long used by land grant railways in the United States in an effort to interest the public in their territory was the public lecture, held in the rural school house, the Grange Hall, or such other places as the local situation might provide. Later,

---

[1] Dennis to Shaughnessy, June 25, 1912, Letter Book 3, M.
[2] Dennis to E. Farrer, September 9, 1912, Letter Book 4, M.

Hill's Great Northern had introduced the idea of the lecture illustrated by stereopticon slides, which gave the prospective settler a glimpse, sometimes highly tinted, of what the railway had to offer. It remained for the Canadian Pacific, so far as the writer is aware, to employ the moving picture for publicity purposes. Under the Canadian Pacific letterhead, Dennis related to the company's agents in the United States the story of the introduction of the film as part of the railway's program for promoting settlement in the West. He prefaced his explanation with the observation that too much publicity of the "right sort" could not be given to western Canada. By the "right sort" he meant "statements of actual conditions as they are—not as some would like them to be in their imagination."[1]

He believed that, in putting western Canada on the moving picture screen in a "scenic, industrial, dramatic and comic form," the company had solved the problem of the very highest class of advertising. In order to do this the railway had entered into a contract with the Edison Manufacturing Company, by which their studio provided a troup of actors and actresses under the direction of a competent stage manager. The Canadian Pacific placed at their disposal a special train which enabled them to devote some two months to the filming of pictures at various places along the line between Montreal and Victoria. The result was thirteen attractive picture stories, which were shown in the theatres of the Edison circuit in the larger cities of the United States, Canada, and Great Britain. While the general publicity thus given to the West among the urban population was all to the good, there was need, of course, for exhibiting the films to the farming folk whom the railway especially desired to interest. Arrangements were therefore made to show them in all the smaller cities and towns where the agents of the company could use them in connection with their efforts to sell Canadian Pacific land.[2]

The wide range of interests to which the films were designed to appeal is shown by the titles: "An Unselfish Love," a purely agricultural picture; "More than His Duty"; "The Song That Reached His Heart"; "A Wedding Trip from Montreal to Hongkong"; "Riders

[1] Dennis to agents, December 1, 1910, Moving Pictures, General File, Section 2, D. N. R.
[2] Ibid.

of the Plains"; "The Little Station Agent"; "The Stolen Claim"; "The Daughter of the Mines"; "The Cowpuncher's Glove," and "The Life of a Salmon." Despite their variety, however, the agents criticized them because they lacked sufficient material relating to agriculture on the prairies and because there was too much scenery and too little farming. What was needed according to one agent was a film showing a settler and his family taking possession of a ready-made farm,[1] such as the agents were then selling. Another suggestion was that the Canadian Pacific should be played up more prominently in the pictures; otherwise, ordinary observers, after seeing them, would not know where to obtain further information regarding the lands shown. Difficulty resulted, too, from the fact that many of the halls where company lecturers attempted to show the pictures were too small for the film to be shown to advantage, while in other cases electricity was not available. Gradually these faults were corrected and the moving picture continued for many years to occupy an important place in connection with the propaganda carried on by the company in the United States. Through arrangements made with the Bureau of Economics at Philadelphia the company was able to get the pictures before several hundred thousand people per month.[2] In the winter of 1913-14 the lecture campaign, with the aid of films, covered the entire area from Boston to Seattle.[3]

In the States alone in 1913 the Department of Natural Resources spent $40,000 for the one item of general advertising, while each district representative had at his disposal $1,000 for advertising in his particular area. An additional sum of $11,000 was expended for literature circulated in the States. The general lecture campaign had cost almost $8,000, which did not include the stereopticon and moving picture campaign carried on by individual agents.[4] Salaries of the district representatives aggregated $60,000 per year, while their expense accounts amounted to an additional $30,000.[5] Add to

[1] W. H. Coyle to Rankin, January 3, 1913, ibid.
[2] Dennis to Shaughnessy, February 20, 1915, Letter Book 14, M.
[3] Dennis to K. N. Robbins, Rochester, N. Y., November 10, 1913, Letter Book 9, M.
[4] Minutes of Semi-annual Convention of American District Representatives, Chicago, June 25 and 26, 1914, File No. 44, D. N. R.
[5] Dennis to I. G. Ogden, Vice-President, C. P. R., April 24, 1915, Letter Book 15, M.

this the cost of maintaining offices, together with other items connected with the American organization, and the annual expenditure
of the department in promoting emigration from the neighboring
republic totalled some $200,000. The annual distribution of litera-
ture in that country ranged from 800,000 to 1,000,000 pieces. Publicity articles in American papers, arranged through the Chicago
office, appeared in papers with a circulation of 71,000,000.[1]

From this it is apparent that the Canadian Pacific was in full
partnership with Ottawa in making known in the United States the
attractions of the Dominion. The complete results of this effort of
the company will never be known, for there is no way of measuring
the effects of the publicity. The Calgary office had records only of
those actually brought to Canada by its organization. Many of these
purchased Canadian Pacific lands; large numbers of them bought
privately owned land or homesteaded. As for the intangible, in-
definable influence of the railway's campaign upon those who went
to Canada, unaccompanied by company representatives, one can
only conjecture. Since, however, the railway and the government
were the two chief agencies for advertising the West, it is reasonable
to suppose that Canadian Pacific propaganda interested many whom
its agents never contacted and of whom they, therefore, had no
record.

In Great Britain the headquarters of the Department of Natural
Resources was in the Canadian Pacific Building in London. There
it was assisted in advertising Canada by the traffic and general advertising departments of the railway. For the work of these allied departments the Department of Natural Resources took a debit of
$72,000 per year.[2] This, however, represented but a portion of the
total annual expenditure of the department in the British Isles,
since it maintained its own separate and complete organization,
devoting its entire time and attention to immigration work and,
particularly, to the securing of settlers for the company's lands.
Believing that the touch between the Calgary office and the British
organization was not sufficiently close, Dennis arranged to have one

[1] Dennis to Shaughnessy, February 28, 1913, Letter Book 7, M; Dennis to
Shaughnessy, January 17, 1916, Letter Book 17, M.
[2] Dennis to George McL. Brown, European Manager, January 29, 1913, Letter
Book 6, M.

member of the staff of the agency branch give special attention to
the agency in London.

Special effort was still made to push the ready-made farm program
in Great Britain, and for this purpose a special appropriation was
annually placed at the disposal of the London office. Early in 1912
that office assembled a list of names of some 50,000 British farmers
who were to be solicited in the campaign for improved farm settlers
for the following year.[1] The advertising expenditure in connection
with ready-made farms for that one year amounted to $25,000.[2]
Results of the effort, however, were anything but encouraging.
Although it had been estimated that at least 6,000 replies would be
elicited by this campaign, less than 2,000 were actually received.
In the opinion of A. Ewan Moore, the manager of the London office
of the Department of Natural Resources, the requirement that British applicants must be married men, with farming experience, plus
at least £200 in capital, rendered it increasingly difficult to secure
settlers in large numbers.[3] Moore believed it a mistake to limit
candidates to actual farmers in a country where the bulk of the
potential emigrants were urban workers. He would make eligible
any likely-appearing candidate with the prescribed minimum of
capital.

Moore went on to explain what Calgary officials had failed adequately to appreciate—that there was but a limited amount of
business to be done annually in the United Kingdom. The price of
land and stock and the cost of living had increased so materially in
Canada that it "no longer occupies the prominent position in the
opinion of homeseekers that it did a few years ago." The Australian
Government, taking a leaf from the Canadian book of experience,
had come to realize the value of aggressive advertising and was in
the market for the very class of settler that the Canadian Pacific
had been seeking all these years. Moore believed the pendulum was
swinging gradually toward Australia.

While fully aware of the limitations under which his organization operated in the British Isles, Moore in no sense felt that this

[1] Ewan Moore, Manager Land Department, London, to Dennis, June 11, 1912,
File No. 242, Section 2, D. N. R.

[2] A. Ewan Moore to Cameron, April 11, 1913, File No. 207, D. N. R.

[3] *Ibid.*

justified a relaxation of effort. On the contrary, he was strongly of the opinion that the methods employed were the right ones and should be pursued with increased vigor. Solicitation of the public by letter and circular must be followed by attendance at local fairs and markets, and, whenever possible, by visits to the farmer in his home. Since the British agents were supplied with cars there was no reason why "every village and hamlet in every county in England should not be visited by a representative of this Department during the next twelve months."

It was becoming apparent that the ready-made farm idea had not made the appeal in England which Dennis and Shaughnessy had expected. While the traffic and steamship departments of the Canadian Pacific had no difficulty in finding people prepared to move to Canada, they were not of the type, in most cases, that the company wished to establish on its lands. Reluctantly Dennis was forced to admit that in view of the impossibility of obtaining large numbers of desirable settlers from Great Britain, the Department of Natural Resources must reduce its expenditures accordingly.[1] His plans for curtailment in the British Isles, however, ran concurrently with a program of increased activity on the continent of Europe.

Dennis was particularly desirous of securing a larger number of German farmers for settlement on Canadian Pacific land. As the conduct of an active emigration propaganda in Germany was prohibited by law, it was necessary to proceed cautiously. There were, however, indirect and unobtrusive ways of getting in touch with potential emigrants from that country. Dennis established contact with a German editor, one Horst Weber, who agreed to issue a special edition of his journal devoted entirely to western Canada. Twenty thousand copies were to be issued at a cost of 20 cents per copy, plus the postage. The issue was to include 8 pages of special write-up, the manuscript to be submitted by the Calgary office and revised by Weber.[2] Dennis also agreed to provide the material and photographs for a shorter article of 1,500 words by Weber on the general subject of "Farming in Canada."[3] Newspaper material such

[1] Dennis to Moore, June 9, 1914, Letter Book 12, M.
[2] Dennis to Horst Weber, November 28, 1912, Letter Book 6, M.
[3] *Ibid.*

as this, mailed to the farming classes in Germany, constituted an indirect but not unsatisfactory substitute for a more open campaign.

The Calgary office succeeded also in getting in touch with one Kurt Thaden, whose brother was the publisher of the leading paper in Essen. In 1912 Thaden sold more than 10,000 acres of land to German settlers, and he brought 40 families from Germany in March of the following year.[1] Dennis gave every encouragement and assistance to Thaden so long as he worked quietly in Germany, but when he asked permission to open a Canadian Pacific immigration office in Berlin, the request, of course, was denied. It was agreed that Thaden should receive a 10 per cent commission on all land sold.[2]

In Denmark it was found that the Department of Natural Resources could open its own land agency, so Ole Kirkwold, a Norwegian by birth, who for several years had been in the service of the department at Calgary, was commissioned to make a trip to Denmark and to submit recommendations as to the procedure to be adopted in establishing an organization there. Equipped with letters to Canadian Pacific traffic department officials in the three Scandinavian countries, Kirkwold journeyed at once to Copenhagen where he arranged for office space in the headquarters of the traffic department, and secured as representative in charge of the office the head of the Royal Agricultural Society.[3] From Copenhagen he proceeded to Norway and Sweden where he looked over the situation with a view to advising Dennis as to the possibility of obtaining settlers from those countries without infringing upon the laws with respect to emigration propaganda.

In Holland the department had maintained the agency of Otten and Zoon at Rotterdam, who were now relieved in favor of one Baer who was established in new headquarters in The Hague. Dennis agreed to pay to Baer a commission of $2\frac{1}{2}$ per cent on all business developed by him and an equal commission to sub-agents in his service.[4] As the department was also represented in Belgium, it was now in a position to push the sale of the company's lands in all countries of northern Europe, in so far as the laws of those coun-

[1] Dennis to George McL. Brown, Europe's Manager, January 29, 1913, *ibid.*
[2] Dennis to Thaden, January 29, 1913, *ibid.*
[3] Dennis to Moore, January 9, 1913 and January 21, 1913, *ibid.*
[4] Dennis to Moore, January 8, 1913, *ibid.*

tries permitted. It is to be noted that while the traffic, advertising, and steamship departments had always advertised the Canadian West in general on a large scale, the sale of Canadian Pacific land had not been specifically sought because of the character of the restrictions imposed in the Continental countries.

With the preparation of special literature in German, Flemish, French, and the three Scandinavian languages, the Department of Natural Resources entered upon a new and enlarged sphere of activity. Before it had had a fair chance to obtain results from this effort, however, its work was largely interrupted by the outbreak of the World War. Although the Canadian Pacific was to resume immigration work at the conclusion of hostilities, it did so through its newly formed Department of Colonization and Development.

If on the continent of Europe war conditions forced an abatement in the activity of the Department of Natural Resources, that was not so in the United States, where the problem of the sale and settlement of the railway's lands was attacked with renewed vigor.

The campaign which Dennis had launched in Continental Europe was just one indication of his growing conviction that the various religious groups and sects, coming from Europe either directly or by way of the United States, offered one of the surest ways of settling the lands of the railway. Large numbers of these people living in the United States were settled in groups and communities in such a fashion as to make it difficult to reach them with the sort of advertising and publicity which the Canadian Pacific carried on. The most practical way of getting in touch with these groups was through their religious leaders or their church organization. In the early years in the irrigation block the Canadian Pacific Irrigation Colonization Company had given special attention to foreign colonies of various religious faiths, usually contacted through the church, but of late less consideration had been given to this type of settlement. Dennis now resolved to renew the effort to secure such colonies.

The Lutheran church in the United States, with its millions of adherents among Germans, Norwegians, Swedes, Danes and German-Russians, was clearly indicated as a medium through which to work. This church had a large number of missionaries working among its people in the provinces of Saskatchewan and Alberta, for whom the American church organization had to supply annually large sums of money, since the scattered nature of population on the prairie made it impossible for the communicants there to maintain an adequate religious service. Dennis got in touch with the church authorities and during one of his tours of the district offices of the Department of Natural Resources he had a conference with the head of the church in Chicago. As a result of this discussion an arrangement was made by which the superintendent of missions on the prairie was to obtain from local pastors lists of friends and relatives of their parishioners living in the United States or in Europe. Through the pastors, in turn, the railway planned to get in touch with those who wished to emigrate, with a view to locating them on its lands in districts where there were opportunities for settlement. In this way the mission would be rendered self-supporting and the American organization of the church relieved of the necessity of extending further financial aid. This latter aspect of the matter appealed strongly to the church authorities, who promised full coöperation.[1]

As a result of this plan there was brought into the service of the department a Lutheran minister of the United States, T. O. F. Herzer, who was so successful in colonizing members of his faith on Canadian Pacific lands that he was later made special agent of foreign colonies in the United States.[2] Meanwhile contact was being made with the Luthern church through other channels. At the meeting of the Synod of the church in Chicago in 1912, the Reverend L. P. Bergstrom of Winnipeg was elected chairman of the Colonization Committee of the Synod. Plans were laid to establish a main office in Chicago, with branch offices in the different conferences in the United States and Canada.[3] The pressure of population upon the older Scandinavian Lutheran settlements in the two countries was such as to require the acquisition of new lands into which to expand. Bergstrom asked Dennis to set aside two townships east of Traynor on the Wilkie-Saskatoon line of the railway as a reserve to be colonized by him with Scandinavians of his own faith. He desired merely such commission for the lands thus sold as would cover the

[1] This whole question is discussed fully in letter, Dennis to Shaughnessy, December 19, 1914, Personal Letter Book 5, M.

[2] Dennis to Thornton, February 3, 1916, Letter Book, October 10, 1916—February 3, 1917, M.

[3] Bergstrom to Dennis, December 5, 1912, File No. 208, D. N. R.

expense incurred in carrying on the work. The fact was stressed by him that his settlers would not be inexperienced people from Europe but "up-to-date American farmers who in a short time will show what this wonderful country can do." Although unwilling to withdraw two townships from sale by the United States organization of the company, Dennis agreed to reserve one township exclusively for the work of Bergstrom.[1]

In August, 1914, the irrigation block was visited by a delegation of German-Russians representing about five hundred farmers living in central California, where they were engaged in fruit growing, partly on land owned by them, partly on rented land. They were not entirely happy in fruit growing and desired to come to southern Alberta where the conditions of soil and climate were more similar to those in south Russia, and where they could engage in mixed farming. The delegation made a very favorable report and selected land northeast of Bassano in the eastern section for colonization.[2] This marked the beginning of what Dennis hoped would be a large migration of those people into that section. The Danish Peoples Society of the United States was another organization through which the department sought to win the foreign settler. In 1916 the Land Committee of this society visited western Canada, accompanied by Canadian Pacific representatives, with a view to the selection of locations for additional colonies of Danes on railway lands.[3]

It was not merely through religious channels, however, that Dennis sought to reach the foreign settler in the United States. Early in 1915 he reported that after a great deal of negotiation he had been able to effect an arrangement under which the agents of the Scandinavian-American and Russian-American steamship lines in the United States would distribute the department's literature in foreign languages and supply the district representatives of the department with names of prospective settlers in their districts. These lines had more than 2,000 agents in the United States and had, under contract with various railways, been instrumental in turning a strong

[1] Notation by Dennis on letter, Cameron to Dennis, January 13, 1913, *ibid.*

[2] Dennis to Shaughnessy, August 23, 1914, Letter Book 5, M.

[3] Dennis to Thornton, December 27, 1916, Letter Book, October 10, 1916–February 3, 1917, M., in which he refers to the visit of Jens Gregerson of the Land Committee of the society.

tide of immigration into the northwestern states.[1] They had been especially important in settling large numbers of Scandinavians along the line of the Northern Pacific. Besides promising to augment materially the flow of foreign settlers from the United States into western Canada, the plan had the added merit that at the close of the war it would make it possible for the Canadian Pacific to get into direct touch with emigrants from northern Europe.[2] While the steamship lines would undertake this work only for a consideration, the colonization campaign of the Department of Natural Resources would not be rendered more expensive by the arrangement, since it would be possible to close two of the district offices in the United States. In order that the plan might be handled intelligently and aggressively, the department issued for distribution in the States a condensed folder regarding the company's land and colonization policies, printed in German, Russian, Polish, Norwegian, Swedish, Lithuanian, Ruthenian, Hungarian, and Flemish. While the company had always widely distributed its publications in foreign tongues, this was the first time such material had been printed for dissemination among immigrant groups in the United States.[3]

All in all, Dennis believed this the most important colonization contract the company had ever entered into.[4] To facilitate the operation of the arrangement, the department closed its New York and Kansas City offices and centralized the work in the remaining offices. The Chicago office was provided with a corps of additional inspectors, speaking foreign languages, to handle the settlers which the new agreement would provide. The department supplied to the New York offices of the Scandinavian-American and Russian-American lines a Russian experienced in immigration work, while another Russian, with wide experience in Alberta, was engaged as a special

[1] Dennis to Shaughnessy, February 9, 1915, Letter Book 14, M.
[2] Ibid.
[3] 250,000 copies of these pamphlets were printed; the numbers in the various languages were:

Russian	75,000	German	70,000
Norwegian	30,000	Swedish	20,000
Lithuanian	20,000	Polish	10,000
Ruthenian	10,000	Hungarian	5,000
Bohemian	5,000	Finnish	5,000

Dennis to Vanderhoof, February 24, 1915, ibid.
[4] Dennis to Shaughnessy, March 4, 1915, ibid.

agent to visit colonies of Russian people in the United States and to accompany delegations of them to the West.[1]

Meanwhile, Dennis had become interested in the possibility of moving German Mennonites from Russia to western Canada. Descended from members of their sect established in Russia in the time of Catherine the Great, these people had prospered in the land of the Tsars. Upon the outbreak of the World War, however, their pacific inclinations caused them to be singled out for expulsion from the country. Although the efforts of Dennis to move them during the war proved unavailing, his interest in them at that time is important, since it culminated after the war in the removal of thousands of the Mennonites from Russia to the Canadian prairies by the Canadian Pacific.

When the report first reached Dennis, late in 1914, that the Mennonites were actually to be expatriated, he suggested to Shaughnessy that the Canadian High Commissioner in London be asked to ascertain from the Foreign Office the truth of the rumor. If true, Dennis would seek, through the British Ambassador in Petrograd, to make an arrangement with the Russian Government which would permit the Canadian Pacific to send representatives who would distribute literature among the Mennonites.[2] He thought it of the utmost importance that every effort be made to move them, since they were excellent farmers and would undoubtedly have sufficient capital to make an auspicious start in the West.

While Shaughnessy was corresponding with Sir George Perley, the Canadian High Commissioner, on this subject, Dennis was busy opening up other channels of negotiation. Through A. W. Perelstrous, the Russian whom the Department of Natural Resources had attached to the Scandinavian-American and Russian-American steamship agencies in New York, Dennis had been brought in touch with one A. M. Evalenko, a Russian of large experience and influence, through whom he believed a successful plan could be worked out. Evalenko had owned and published the Russian-American magazine in New York, had served as Immigration Commissioner for the Atchison, Topeka and Santa Fe Railway in the United States in the colonization of Russians along its lines, and had acted as

[1] Dennis to Shaughnessy, August 27, 1915, Letter Book 16, M.
[2] Ibid., December 31, 1914, Letter Book 5, M.

commissioner in the settlement of differences between the Dukhobors and the Dominion Government.[1] Upon the outbreak of the World War Evalenko had returned to Russia, offered his services to the government, and had been sent back to New York as the special representative of the President of the Duma, who was also Chairman of the Committee of National Defense in Russia.[2]

Exaggerating his influence with the Russian Government, perhaps, Evalenko submitted to Dennis a proposition with respect to the colonization of the Mennonites on Canadian Pacific lands. In reply to this, Dennis asked Evalenko to return to Russia and present to the proper authorities the proposal made to the company. If these authorities would officially constitute Evalenko as their representative to deal with the matter, Dennis would, in behalf of the Canadian Pacific, enter into a contract with him. In that event the Mennonites were to be brought directly from Russia to western Canada, given an opportunity to purchase land from the railway and settle in colonies along its lines, and allowed to pay for the land in bonds issued by the Russian Government to indemnify the Mennonites.[3] The Department of Natural Resources was prepared to assume the expense of bringing a delegation of representative Mennonites to western Canada to observe conditions and prepare a report for their friends and relatives in Russia.[4]

Although Evalenko made a tentative arrangement with the Russian Minister of the Interior for bringing the delegation to Canada, Dennis insisted that any action the Canadian Pacific might take must have the sanction of the full Russian Government. This Evalenko failed to obtain, with the result that Dennis terminated negotiations with him the following year. Dennis then turned to A. Ross Owen, who represented the Canadian Pacific at Vladivostok.[5] Throughout the latter part of 1916 Owen labored faithfully in an effort to arrange for the dispatch of the necessary Mennonite delegation to inspect the land in the West, but before a definite arrangement could be effected the Russian Revolution of March,

[1] Dennis to Shaughnessy, August 31, 1915, Letter Book 16, M.
[2] Ibid.
[3] Dennis to Evalenko, August 26, 1915, ibid.
[4] Ibid.
[5] Dennis to A. Ross Owen, May 3, 1916, Letter Book 18, and Dennis to Owen, October 17, 1916, Letter Book 19, M.

1917, brought all further negotiation to an end. We shall see in a later chapter how Dennis, with conspicuous success, returned to the idea at the conclusion of the World War.

While losing no opportunity to make contact with foreign colonies, whether in the United States or Europe, Dennis did not neglect to use colonies of the various nationalities located along Canadian Pacific lines in the West as media through which new settlers could be obtained. Special maps of Saskatchewan and Alberta were prepared showing the districts occupied by different nationalities, with a view to colonizing the unsold lands of the company in those areas with people of the same nationality.[1] Special booklets were then prepared, descriptive of those districts and their settlers, and distributed widely in foreign settlements in the United States. This procedure, of course, was based upon the essentially sound theory that the prospective settler in the West would prefer to locate in a community inhabited largely by people of his own kind, with the same church affiliation and speaking the same language.

Potentially, one of the most practical ways of facilitating settlement was to interest the people of a given community in the settlement of unoccupied land in their locality. With this end in view, the Department of Natural Resources selected colonies of all the different nationalities along Canadian Pacific lines in the West and formed them into "Extension of Settlement Clubs," with a suitable local name.[2] The department prepared and printed a short leaflet for each club, containing a general description of the district and letters from each of the members giving his experience in the West and the results he had obtained there. The members of the club then furnished the secretary with the names and addresses of any of their relatives and friends in the United States or their home country who might be induced to emigrate and take up land in the colony. Copies of the leaflet were then mailed to the persons on the list, with an invitation to correspond directly with the relative or friend whose letter was published in the leaflet. Copies of the lists of names were filed with the Department of Natural Resources, which paid a commission on sales of land to persons interested in this way.[3]

[1] Dennis to Cameron, May 6, 1915, Letter Book 15, M.
[2] Dennis to Shaughnessy, December 18, 1914, Letter Book 5, M.
[3] *Ibid.*

The "Extension of Settlement Clubs" were a recognition by the company of the fact that the best immigration agent it could have was the satisfied settler on its lands in the West.

The clubs thus organized appear to have coöperated with the Department of Natural Resources with considerable enthusiasm. Fairly typical of their attitude was the protest of the Danish Extension of Settlement Club at Standard, Alberta, against inadvertent plans of the department to establish a ready-made farm colony so close to the Danish colony as to limit the latter's opportunity for expansion through further Danish settlement in the district. To this protest the department readily acceded by reducing the number of farms in the Improved Farm Colony from 100 to 25.[1]

While working so earnestly to bring people from the United States, Great Britain, and northern Europe to western Canada, the Canadian Pacific was not entirely neglectful of the older provinces of Canada itself. We have seen that in the early days the company endeavored with all the resources at its command to promote an exodus of eastern farmers to the West. Through agents of the General Land Department and the traffic department this movement was stimulated. The home-seekers' excursions, inaugurated by the railway in the eighties, had for years been the most important single factor in moving people from Ontario, Quebec, and the Maritimes to the prairie. These had continued into the boom period in the West after 1900. With the inception of the irrigation project and the organization of the Canadian Pacific Irrigation Colonization Company in 1905, agencies had been established in Montreal and Toronto for the sale of the company's lands. Upon the formation of the Department of Natural Resources, however, the agency organization in those provinces was soon withdrawn and from that time on no campaign was carried on in eastern Canada.[2] Repeatedly Dennis expressed the belief that as a transportation system, nation-wide in its scope, extending from the Atlantic to the Pacific, the Canadian Pacific had nothing particularly to gain by moving people from one part of the Dominion to another. In effect, the railway would not exert itself and would not spend large sums of money in

[1] Dennis to Arthur M. Rasmussen, Standard, Alberta, May 3, 1916, Letter Book 18, M.
[2] Dennis to Naismith, March 4, 1913, Letter Book 7, M.

such an effort. The fact remained, however, that there were people in the East who were disposed to move to the West or who were at least desirous of examining the possibilities of the country, and the company had nothing to lose by catering to the wishes of those people. For their benefit, special weekly home-seekers' excursions, with a low second-class round trip rate, were continued throughout the year.[1]

The long discussion of Canadian Pacific activities centering at Calgary during the years from 1905 to 1914 may well give the impression that in the making of plans, in the formulation of policies, in the devising of experiments, and in the resourcefulness of its methods the Calgary office had few equals and no superior in the annals of land settlement under corporate auspices. The plans and policies, however, were but the means to the attainment of the ultimate objective of the company—the disposal of the land in a manner which would best serve the larger interests of the railway. Undeniably, substantial progress had been made in this direction.

Between January 1, 1908, when the company terminated the arrangement with Beiseker and Davidson for the sale of land in the irrigation block, and December 15, 1913, net sales through Calgary amounted to 2,485,669 acres for $38,749,226.[2] The cost of selling was $4,853,522, an average of $1.84 per acre. The disparity between this last figure and $3.00 per acre, the alleged cost of selling under the Beiseker and Davidson regime, bears out the contention of the Canadian Pacific as to the efficiency of its land-selling organization. The results of those years appear the more notable when it is recalled that they were achieved without resort to the sale of large tracts, and in the face of the determined effort of the company to exclude the speculative element and to sell to actual settlers only. The figures, in short, represent the net area disposed of after the reversion to the railway of large amounts of land through cancellation of contracts speculatively held.

[1] Dennis to C. E. Ussher, November 4, 1913, Letter Book 9, M.
[2] File No. 39, Section 1, D. N. R.

X

LATER LAND POLICIES

IT WILL be recalled that, in the face of the delays in the construction of the irrigation works, land in the central and eastern sections was offered for sale in limited amounts in advance of the completion of the canal system. Under this plan the company sold during the years 1911-13 a small area which ultimately proved to be irrigable and a much larger acreage which was not capable of irrigation. The latter class of lands was situated mainly in what had originally been termed the central section. The realization, however, that this region was unsuited to irrigation led to the abandonment of plans for its development as a separate unit in the irrigation scheme and it came to be considered as part of the eastern section.

Under the spell of the "dry farming" idea, so compelling and so pervasive throughout western America in the years preceding the World War, much of this land had been sold to so-called "dry land" farmers who, it was hoped, would be able to utilize the "dry farming" technique in the cultivation of this district. Nor, under the existing circumstances, did this hope appear illusory. In the western section the development of irrigation was being retarded by the fact that in an ordinary season grain crops could be grown successfully without the artificial application of water. If that could be done in the western section, why was it not possible farther east? Unfortunately this view left out of account two important factors which placed the eastern section in a different category. Not only did the average annual rainfall decrease as the distance from the mountains increased, but the average temperature during the growing season was considerably higher. This made irrigation essential in the eastern section for all kinds of farming except stock growing.

By 1913 it was apparent that this attempt at dry-farming was a failure. Dennis then estimated that the company would have to take

back at least 100,000 acres. Although much of this had been purchased speculatively and was unoccupied, a large area had been cultivated without success. The company would not attempt to recolo-
nize these lands because to do so would merely be to invite the
same disaster as before; to make the mistake which had been made
in Nebraska and Colorado. In the eastern section, therefore, Dennis
would concentrate on the irrigable land of which there were some
450,000 acres. That section must be developed by intensive farming
of the irrigable land and by stock raising on the dry land, with a
combination of the two types wherever possible. Dennis reasoned
that when the irrigable land was colonized the dry land would have
a distinct value and would be in demand for grazing purposes.[1]

The immediate problem, therefore, was the sale of the irrigable
land, and as to the difficulty of that problem Dennis had no illusions.
From 100,000 to 150,000 acres in the eastern section were classified
and ready for sale.[2] Two ready-made farm colonies, Bassano and
Rosemary, were awaiting settlers. Could the land be sold, and where
were the colonists to be found? The doubtful success of British
settlers on ready-made farms largely removed them from further consideration as potential colonists for irrigable land. From the inception of the irrigation project the company had realized that there
was slight hope of moving experienced irrigation farmers from the
far western states in numbers. Successful irrigationists in that part
of the country had once been dry-land farmers in the middle west,
who had later learned the use of water. The company had believed it
could teach irrigation methods to Mississippi Valley farmers but it
had been unable to convince them, once they were established in the
western section, of the obvious advantages of irrigation. Dennis
hoped that those settling in the eastern section would increasingly
realize that irrigation was indispensable.

The difficulty of selling the lands in the eastern section was increased by the fact that the American organization was expected to
sell at the same time the vast area owned by the Canadian Pacific in
northern Alberta and in Saskatchewan, some of it adjacent to the

[1] Minutes of Annual Convention of American Land Agents, Chicago, November
24 and 25, 1913; also Semi-annual Convention of American District Representatives, Chicago, June 25, 1914. Before both of these gatherings Dennis explained
the situation in great detail. These are in D. N. R.

[2] *Ibid.*

company's lines, some remote therefrom. Undeniably it was hard for an agent to push the sale of the two types of land with equal enthusiasm and with complete impartiality. Land in the North sold readily but its lower price meant smaller commissions. That in the eastern section was harder to sell but its higher price yielded handsome commissions. Such was the dilemma of the commission agent. Yet there was no alternative. The two classes of land must be offered. Experienced irrigation farmers must be taken when obtainable; when not, ordinary farmers conforming to the requirements of the company's colonization policy must be secured in the hope that, with the aid of the ready-made farm, the loan to settlers, and other forms of assistance the railway was prepared to extend, they would develop into successful irrigationists. Buyers not interested in irrigable land must be taken to the lands in the North.

By 1914 construction had advanced sufficiently to warrant the inauguration of a vigorous campaign for the colonization of irrigable lands in the eastern section. Water was taken from the Bow River at the Horseshoe Bend, about 3 miles south of Bassano. The works comprised a concrete spillway dam of the Ambrusen type, 720 feet long, together with an earthen embarkment 7,180 feet in length, which raised the level of the river 50 feet. Water was diverted through 5 steel sluice-gates into the main canal whence, by an elaborate system of canals, reservoirs, and flumes, it was distributed throughout the area to be irrigated. The reservoir had a storage capacity of 186,000 acre-feet of water, while the aggregate length of the canals was in excess of 2,500 miles. Such great care was taken in the classification of the irrigable land that only a slight revision by the Department of the Interior was necessary.[1] With the further approval of the Ottawa authorities a new form of water rental was adopted. Because of the greater cost of operation in the eastern section the company felt obliged to charge an annual water rental of $1.25 per acre. Provision was made, however, that with the formation of water-users' associations among the settlers to take over the maintenance of the secondary canal system, the rental should be reduced to 75 cents per acre, as in the western section.[2] From the company's point of view this latter plan had the merit of limiting

[1] Dennis to Shaughnessy, July 28, 1913, Letter Book 8, M.
[2] *Ibid.*

its responsibility to the maintenance of the main canal system and the delivery of water at the upper end of each water district. To facilitate the sale of land in the eastern section special terms of payment were offered. While it was to be sold on the 20-year plan, the settler was excused from the second payment on the principal until the end of 3 years of residence and was exempted from the payment of the water rental for 2 years.[1]

For the season of 1914 the Department of Natural Resources devoted particular attention to the settlement of the ready-made farm colonies available in the eastern section, and the successful establishment of 23 Colorado families in the Bassano colony seemed to provide an auspicious beginning. This inspired Dennis and his associates with the idea of establishing another colony from the States at Brooks. At Scotts Bluff, Nebraska, there was a community of German-Russians engaged in the cultivation of sugar beets on rented land. Although very poor, they were hard working and experienced in irrigation, which made them excellent prospects for the Canadian Pacific. Because of their poverty, however, they could not be moved except by dint of great effort, and it was out of the question for them to purchase irrigable land even under the liberal colonization policy of the railway, with its loan for improvements and 20-year period for payment. So important did the Calgary office deem the acquisition of this colony to be, however, that it felt justified in making an exception to the accustomed policy governing the sale and settlement of the company's land.

Arrangements were made by which these settlers, after paying one-twentieth of the purchase price at the time of application, should be excused from all further payments for three years, at which time one-seventeenth of the unpaid balance would be due. Water rental was to be remitted for two and one-half years. The company would erect a house and barn on each farm, and supply materials for other structures to be built by the farmer himself; it would dig a well and supply posts and wire for the fencing to be done by the settler himself.[2] But even these favorable terms were not sufficient to move the colony. The farmers put forth the plausible argument that in their existing location they could somehow muddle through, and

[1] Circular to district agents, March 7, 1914, File No. 554, D. N. R.
[2] Thornton to Cameron, November 6, 1915, File No. 764, D. N. R.

were doing reasonably well on a rental basis. The cost of moving to Canada, they averred, would be an absolute loss to them. To this the Department of Natural Resources countered with the offer to credit the amount expended in freight and transportation on the cost of the land.[1]

When these terms proved unavailing, it became apparent that nothing short of heroic measures would suffice to move this group, and the question which naturally arose at the Calgary office was how far the company could afford to go in its inducements. The feeling was unanimous among officials at Calgary that this colony must be established in the Brooks district as a nucleus for further settlement in that area, and the belief was equally unanimous among company representatives in the United States that these people could not be moved as ordinary American settlers, but must be transplanted in a body, the poorest along with the more well-to-do. To meet this situation, therefore, Dennis gave approval to a plan by which the Department of Natural Resources advanced from $500 to $1,000 per family to the poorer members of the colony to enable them to purchase stock, machinery, and other equipment.[2] For these people, then, the company combined the ready-made farm with a loan for live stock. This clinched the bargain and in February, 1916 the vanguard of the colony arrived at Brooks, where T. O. F. Herzer was temporarily stationed to help them in getting started.[3] Pending the arrival of their own teams, the services of the Agricultural Branch of the Department of Natural Resources were placed at their disposal.

By 1916 the recovery from the shock occasioned by the outbreak of the World War was apparent. The demand for land increased, with the result that by the end of 1918 the company had sold in the eastern section the bulk of the irrigable land close to the railway lines. The drought of 1918 offered ample opportunity for object lessons in the value of irrigation. Dry crops in the Brooks area were total failures, while irrigated lands brought excellent returns.[4]

[1] Ibid.
[2] Cameron to Naismith, November 26, 1915, ibid.; Dennis to Naismith, December 1, 1915, ibid.
[3] Kirkwold to Rev. H. J. Eggold, Scotts Bluff, Nebraska, February 25, 1916, ibid.
[4] Annual Report of the Department of the Interior for the year ending March 31, 1919, Part IV, p. 11.

Because of failure to irrigate, the Bassano colony suffered a general crop failure, while the Duchess colony obtained fine results from irrigation, even in the face of inadequate advance preparation for irrigation. The Duke of Sutherland colony, by virtue of greater age and better preparation, produced excellent crops by the use of water. In the St. Julien colony, south of Tilley, the company itself undertook the irrigation of 40 acres on each of 25 farms. Despite a late start and insufficient preparation, a satisfactory crop was produced in every case. The results obtained were regarded as indicative of what an energetic settler might accomplish in his first season by settling on the land in early spring. All told some 24,500 acres were irrigated in the eastern section during the season of 1918.

The summer of 1919 saw a repetition of the hot, dry weather of the previous year. With the aid of irrigation the Bassano and Duchess colonies produced excellent crops.[1] Phenomenal yields of alfalfa and clover were obtained. Dry farming in the eastern section was again generally disastrous. The St. Julien colony was again farmed by the company with gratifying results. A definite area on each farm was seeded to alfalfa. Within the eastern section about 43,500 acres were irrigated.

By 1924 the irrigation system in the eastern section had been in operation for a decade. Out of a total irrigable area of some 400,000 acres the company had sold about 124,000 acres.[2] The area actually irrigated fluctuated greatly from year to year, according to the annual precipitation. In 1922 over 93,000 acres were irrigated, while in the following year the area had declined to about 43,000 acres.[3] This disparity was due entirely "to the unusually heavy rainfall which led many farmers to trust to natural conditions instead of irrigating." Obstinacy and inertia were proving powerful deterrents to the whole-hearted and intelligent practice of irrigation farming. Farmers had not yet come to a realization of the amount of water their crops required for maximum returns. On 10 typical farms within the section the average yield of wheat per acre with only one irrigation was 19½ bushels per acre, a figure corresponding closely

[1] *Annual Report of the Department of the Interior for the year ending March 31, 1920*, Part IV, p. 9.

[2] *Annual Report of the Department of the Interior for the year ending March 31, 1924*, Part IV, p. 122.

[3] *Ibid.*

with the results obtained at the Brooks Experiment Station, under similar soil and climatic conditions, and with one 4-inch irrigation. With two 4-inch irrigations the yields at Brooks ranged from 30 to 35 bushels, while three 4-inch irrigations produced yields as high as 43 bushels per acre.[1] These results pointed clearly and unmistakably to the need for greater use of water by farmers within the section.

During the years 1924-26 inclusive, the irrigated area in the eastern section ranged from 73,000 to 84,000 acres, while the number of water users reached the figure of 733 in 1924.[2] In the middle twenties the officials of the Department of Natural Resources put forth strenuous efforts to increase settlement within the section. Special devices and incentives were resorted to. "Prospective purchasers were examined and if found to be likely settlers, farms not priced were leased to them . . . on the understanding that our share of the crop would apply as the cash payment, providing it met the required 7 per cent of the purchase price and the applicant was satisfied with the price when submitted."[3] That his bid to the man of small means was attractive would seem to be indicated by the fact that at the end of 1927 the department had applications for purchase from 80 of the leaseholders.

As a further means of keeping purchasers on the land, the department in 1927 began the adjustment of outstanding contracts in the section. It offered to the settler a downward revision in the purchase price of his farm, together with a new water agreement containing provisions for the formation of a canal company. A substantial reduction in the price of the land, of course, met with general approval and seemed to augur well for the future. Department officials reported that at the end of the year the farmers seemed more eager to meet their obligations to the company than at any previous time in the history of the project. Only in exceptional cases were the settlers likely to require further extension of time to meet their arrears.

Another encouraging feature was the decline in 1927 in the number of farmers lost to the section either through voluntary abandon-

[1] *Ibid.*

[2] *Annual Report of the Department of the Interior for the year ending March 31, 1926,* p. 125, and *Annual Report of the Department of the Interior for the year ending March 31, 1927,* p. 112.

[3] *Land Branch Report, Eastern Section,* 1927, p. 3.

ment of their farms or through cancellation of contracts because of utter non-fulfillment of obligations to the company. In that year the railway more than held its own in this respect. An optimistic tone prevailed as a result of the reclassification and readjustment of lands and contracts, and officials expressed the belief that the near future would see a marked increase in improvements and settlement within the section.

Conditions on the project could never be ideal or even satisfactory until a large number of new settlers with a fair amount of money were placed in the section. The various districts comprising the project were so sparsely settled that school and telephone facilities were maintained with great difficulty. Community life and spirit could be adequately maintained only with increased settlement. "This sparse settlement with some abandoned farms and with the present settlers normally farming more land than they can take good care of is neither conducive to good crop yields nor to the control or eradication of weeds."[1] A 20 per cent increase in the farm population was urgently needed.

Distinct progress was made in 1928. A total of 199 farms in the eastern section were disposed of, representing an aggregate of 31,426 acres, an average of 152 acres per farm.[2] Of the 199 purchasers, 55 were contract holders who were increasing their holdings, while 30 were renters of farms under the leasing scheme developed a few years before. The balance were new settlers in the eastern section. In that year the Department of Natural Resources, in conjunction with the Canada Colonization Association, conducted an intensive study into the feasibility of settling 100 Mennonite, Lutheran, and Catholic families on the eastern section, without exacting a first payment at the time of settlement. While the colonization association existed primarily for the purpose of settling privately owned lands tributary to the Canadian Pacific lines, there seemed to be no reason why its machinery should not be used on occasion to secure settlers for company lands; and by virtue of its contacts with the various religious sects named it was especially well equipped to

[1] *Annual Report of Irrigation Investigation Branch,* Department of Natural Resources, for 1927, p. 3.
[2] *Annual Report of Irrigation Development Branch,* Department of Natural Resources, for 1928, p. 53.

obtain such families for the project. After careful consideration of all aspects of the plan the department decided not merely to omit the first payment on the land but also to advance to each family an average of $1,000 worth of equipment, live stock, feed, and seed. An arrangement was entered into with the Canada Colonization Association to select the families, to each of whom the company would sell a quarter section of land under a contract requiring the settler during the duration of the agreement to turn over to the company one-half of all crops produced on the land. Up to the end of 1928, a total of 29 families had been selected, of whom 12 had already gone into occupancy. It will be noted that this scheme combined the loan for live stock, employed by the Canadian Pacific before the war, with the crop payment plan also used by it in that period, but more extensively applied in the twenties by the railway in connection with its own lands and by its subsidiary, the Canada Colonization Association, in the settlement of Mennonites and others on privately owned lands in the West. An essential feature of the plan was the requirement that these settlers must farm under the direction of the Department of Natural Resources. Farming under the supervision of the department meant a balanced, diversified agriculture, such as Dennis had envisaged when the irrigation project was first undertaken, and for which the company had so largely worked in vain.

By 1928 the department was convinced that more mixed farming and more careful farming would prove the salvation of numerous contract holders in the eastern section who had fallen badly in arrears. And the low price of wheat then prevailing seemed to make the moment auspicious for the transition from grain farming to the more diversified type. The Irrigation Development Branch of the Department of Natural Resources recommended the appointment of a man whose entire time should be devoted to assisting contract holders greatly in arrears in their payments. It was believed that "if this can be done they can be induced to put some of the methods that we suggest into practice and to take us into their confidence in connection with their financial obligations; and that . . . such advice and assistance should go a long way toward putting them on their feet in the next few years."[1]

[1] Ibid., p. 62.

The department had long hoped that diversified farming in the eastern section might in part take the form of sugar beet production. The sugar beet was not only an excellent cash crop but it was well suited to conditions prevailing in the project. Its production, however, required a special type of labor. The average Canadian, British, or American farm family would not submit to the arduous labor which sugar beet growing entailed. The agreement with the Canada Colonization Association for selecting Mennonite and other Continental European families seemed a step in the right direction. The additional need was a sugar factory, and it was the earnest hope of the department that the railway company would "take every legitimate means to foster the early construction of a factory on the Project."

Despite the heroic efforts of the Canadian Pacific, all was not well in the eastern section before the depression. Payments on land contracts were in arrears, water rates were unpaid. The company had spent money lavishly on the Brooks Experimental Farm in an effort to sell irrigation to the settlers. It had maintained a corps of irrigation experts for the same purpose. What it had not done was to recognize that the back of agriculture was being broken by the weight of capital costs. The irrigation project had been a costly venture. In its efforts to pay the cost of construction and to realize a profit from the land, the company had priced the land at a figure which was more than the average purchaser could manage. With the onset of the depression in 1930 a bad situation in the eastern section became progressively worse. Many farmers abandoned the land; others became subsistence farmers. Operating revenue of the section shrank alarmingly. For 5 years the railway spent money to the tune of $470,000 annually in an effort to breast the storm. Twice it revised the contracts of settlers. Under the existing capital set-up, the eastern section had become a white elephant for the Canadian Pacific. Obviously the company could not continue indefinitely to bear the burden of operating costs and of taxation upon the unsold land in the section.

Through a plan brought forward by settlers, a way out was found in 1935. The railway transferred the irrigation works, together with 1,233,812 acres of land, to the farmers on the eastern section, organized as the Eastern Irrigation District. The company further agreed to contribute over a period of 2 years the sum of $300,000 toward the operating expenses of the system. Control of the project was vested in a democratically elected Board of Trustees, who sensibly cancelled about four-fifths of the debt against the land, the average being reduced from $45.00 to $9.00 per acre. Current operating costs were cut from $2.00 per acre to 70 cents. None of the Canadian Pacific fund for operating costs was used the first year.

If with this reduced load of capital charges the Eastern Irrigation District should be successful, as now seems likely, the Canadian Pacific will be twice blessed: first, through the increased traffic to the railway resulting from the extension of settlement; and, second, through relief from operating costs and the taxes upon the land. To offset the mistakes of the past it will have the knowledge that the success of the future must rest upon the foundation of irrigation which it laid in Alberta a generation ago.

Meanwhile, the western section had not been without its problems. The comparative ease with which the company had sold the land in that section did not mean that it was not to experience difficulty with some of the purchasers. By 1912 it was involved in a first-class controversy with certain of those who held contracts covering irrigable land within the section, and, to make matters worse, the situation was aired in at least two annual conventions of the Western Canada Irrigation Association. In one of them the President of the United Farmers of Alberta pointed an accusing finger at the Canadian Pacific policy which he alleged had precipitated the disagreement.[1] According to President Speakman, the railway had organized a "very large irrigation and settlement scheme . . . at great expense, in good faith, but with insufficient knowledge." It had brought in a large number of settlers by what he characterized as "real estate boosting methods." Soon there developed difficulties unforeseen by either side. First there was the impossibility of obtaining water in sufficient quantity, which in turn necessitated a system of crop rotation not provided for in the water agreements and inconsistent with their terms. Much of the land which the company had classed as irrigable proved too uneven for

[1] *Department of the Interior, Irrigation Branch; Report of the Proceedings of the Ninth Annual Convention of the Western Canada Irrigation Association, held at Bassano, Alberta, November, 1915* (Ottawa, 1916), p. 65.

irrigation. This led to reclassification on the basis that all land which could be levelled at a cost of not more than $8.00 per acre should be considered irrigable, thereby increasing the price of the land. Some of the land was of such a "heavy, impervious nature that it became water-logged, spoiled by alkali, and unfit for vegetation," a condition which could be remedied only by drainage, at further expense to the settler. Added to these difficulties was the fact that when irrigation was applied to grain crops, maturity was retarded sufficiently to result in heavy damage by frost. Finally, seepage from the canals was changing large patches of land to alkali swamps. Seep-holes were forming "which on the farms have to be fenced and on the prairies are becoming death-traps for cattle and horses." All told, it was a forbidding picture which this farmers' organization official painted of conditions in the western section of the block.

The facts with respect to the situation were substantially these. Once the investigations of the company and the government had shown that water was available and could be brought to the land in the irrigation block, the railway proceeded with the construction of the necessary works. Against the better judgment of Dennis, who realized the heavier nature of the soil in the western section, its greater elevation, and its somewhat shorter growing season, construction was begun in the West instead of in the Bassano district. The reason for this was obvious. The western section was immediately tributary to Calgary, a Canadian Pacific town and the metropolis of southern Alberta. To have disregarded Calgary and started elsewhere would have created an unfortunate situation. Water was taken, therefore, from the Bow River at Calgary and the development of the western section was begun.[1]

Once the canals in that section were completed, the company began to colonize the land. As no large immigration of experienced irrigation farmers was possible, it was forced to go where it could obtain people to settle in the block, regardless of their experience or lack of it. It went to the United States, Great Britain, and to northern Europe, but more largely to the country first named. Although the agents of the railway in certain instances made misrepresentations, despite efforts to control them, nevertheless virtually every buyer personally inspected the land he purchased. The first

[1] *Department of the Interior, Irrigation Branch* (1916), p. 77.

colonization was carried on in the district between Strathmore and Gleichen, during the years 1906 to 1908. Here was a fine piece of country, with easy slopes, capable of a high state of development. This area was soon sold out and the company went quietly on with the work of construction.[1]

The period to 1910 was one of ample rainfall in which the settlers farmed without irrigation. Many neither levelled the land nor prepared the ditches necessary to make irrigated farms. The summer of 1910 was a dry one which caught the farmers without facilities for distributing water. This led to dissatisfaction. A further source of discontent in that year was inability of the company to deliver the desired amount of water to those who had prepared their land for irrigation. This was due to "bad engineering necessitated by lack of money." After the water was brought to the highest point in the district, it was dropped into a coulee, whence it was distributed to the land. In passing through the coulee the water carried silt into the ditches which resulted in the admitted inability of the company to supply the necessary amount of water.[2]

There was recurring dissatisfaction. Settlers complained that some of the land was too rough to be irrigated economically. Others charged that the water supply provided for in their contracts, approved by the government, was insufficient and that they should have a larger amount. The company offered to reclassify the land and to amend the contracts accordingly. Some accepted, others rejected, this offer. Meetings were held, resolutions passed, and complaints filed. Doubts were cast on Dennis's knowledge of irrigation and it was freely charged that settlers had been "flimflammed." Unable to arrive at an agreement with the company, the settlers appealed to the Minister of the Interior who, under the Canadian Irrigation Act, had jurisdiction in the case of such disputes. Representatives of the railway and the settlers met with the minister, where the company, after hearing the statement of the farmers' case, suggested that the Department of the Interior reclassify the land, on the basis used by the Canadian Pacific in the eastern section. This was recognized as a fairer method than that employed in the western section, where the company had been hampered by lack of funds with which to make

[1] Ibid., p. 78.
[2] Ibid.

complete contour surveys, with resulting mistakes in classification. This proposal was accepted by both the settlers and the Minister of the Interior.

The Department of the Interior began the work of reclassification in June, 1913. Field work was carried on until the approach of winter, when the task of analyzing the reports of the field force was undertaken. The sheer magnitude of the job and the accuracy required of the engineers made progress slow. The company submitted topographical plans for the entire area. The department tested the accuracy of the plans by a resurvey of selected areas, and in cases of appreciable inaccuracy it asked the railway to submit new plans. Each quarter section was carefully examined by an engineer who convinced himself of the accuracy of the plan before determining the amount of irrigable and non-irrigable land therein.[1]

The settlers having questioned the capacity of the canal system, an examination of the entire plan was made with a view to defining the capacity of each canal and lateral in the western section. Reclassification involved, of course, an investigation of the soil and climatic conditions. Soil samples were taken from areas which seemed to be impregnated with alkali, as well as from those sections which were alleged to be or suspected of being potentially alkaline in quality. Samples of soil were taken at varying depths down to six feet, and alkaline land was classed as non-irrigable regardless of topographical features conducive to irrigation. Climatological data were gathered at various points in the western section. These included evidences as to the character of crops best adapted to the prevailing conditions of soil and climate, length of the growing season, volume and distribution of the annual precipitation, and the dates of killing frosts.

The work of reclassification in the western section continued through the seasons of 1914 and 1915 at which latter date it was finally completed. The Minister of the Interior was able to report that "it is satisfactory to note that the decision in almost every case, involving the revision of about 1,600 water agreements has apparently proved acceptable both to the company and to the water users." The field force had examined in detail about 454,000 acres, of which 223,500 acres were classed as irrigable. Of the remainder,

[1] Annual Report of the Department of the Interior for the year ending March 31, 1914, p. 3.

the bulk had been rejected on account of topographical conditions, although soil defects had led to the classification of some 13.6 per cent as non-irrigable.[1]

Reclassification of the land in the western section necessitated, of course, a readjustment of contracts and a new schedule of prices to fit the changed situation. Land originally sold as irrigable, but now classed as non-irrigable, had to be priced accordingly. Irrigable land was now divided into the three categories of arable, meadow, and gumbo, and priced at $35.00, $20.00, and $10.00 per acre respectively; non-irrigable was sold as arable, grazing, and meadow or slough land at $25.00, $15.00, and $10.00 per acre respectively.[2]

Despite the difficulties recounted above, the development of the western section went steadily forward. By 1920 the company's work in that part of the irrigation block was virtually completed. The land was sold and largely under cultivation. By dint of great effort the company had, since 1905, recruited, largely in the United States, the settlers who were in occupation of this large area. The colonization of such a large, compact block constituted a notable achievement in the development of the Canadian West.

The success attained in selling and settling the land in the western section could in no way remove the fact, however, that the company had only in part realized the objective it had in mind when the project was launched. Mixed farming and live stock growing, based on the practice of irrigation, had been the goal of Dennis and his associates. Only in this way could a maximum be achieved either in density of settlement or volume of traffic for the railway. Unfortunately for the attainment of the company's ends, the precipitation and temperature in the western section were such in many seasons as to make possible the growth of satisfactory crops without irrigation. This fact, combined with the obstinacy, inertia, and inexperience of the settlers, militated against the general acceptance of the idea of irrigation. At the beginning of the season the settler usually assumed that irrigation was unnecessary. The result was that the onset of drought found him largely unprepared to irrigate his land.

The Report of the Department of the Interior for 1919 accurately

[1] *Annual Report of the Department of the Interior for the year ending March 31, 1916*, pp. 9-10.
[2] Dennis to Cameron, May 3, 1915, Letter Book 15, M.

described the situation which has largely prevailed in the western section. "The settlers have never made any general use of the irrigation water from year to year, and as a consequence the land has not generally been prepared for irrigation, and the smaller ditches have lacked care. When the season developed so extremely dry, many of the farmers called for water, and during the height of the irrigation season there was a very heavy demand on parts of the system. The call on the company's operation staff was very great and for a considerable time they were working 'night and day' in order to meet all demands. It is believed that the situation was handled very efficiently, and that satisfactory delivery was made to all water users. . . ."[1] In that year the area irrigated amounted to 25,191 acres out of a total irrigable area of 220,000 acres. In the middle twenties the area irrigated annually varied from 3,000 to 19,000 acres. Yet the total cropped area on water right land was as much as 209,000 out of a possible 220,000 acres.[2] This meant that for all practical purposes the distinction between irrigable and non-irrigable land was wiped out. As the Department of the Interior reported in 1921, the "larger part" of the western section was under cultivation, with the two types of land largely lumped together and farmed under conditions of natural rainfall. In 1920 grain and flax were practically the only crops grown. With but 3,000 acres under irrigation in 1923, the average yield of wheat throughout the section was 35 bushels per acre, while the yield on summer fallowed land varied from 40 to 60 bushels per acre. Oats under similar conditions yielded as much as 130 bushels per acre.

Although every year was not so favorable, the western section experienced generally satisfactory conditions through the decade and underwent a steady development. As an evidence of the prosperity enjoyed by the farmers in the area, the Department of the Interior cited the large expenditure for buildings during the 1926-27 season.[3] What was even more encouraging from the point of view of

[1] *Annual Report of the Department of the Interior for the year ending March 31, 1919,* Part IV, p. 12.
[2] *Annual Report of the Department of the Interior for the year ending March 31, 1924,* Part IV, pp. 121-22. Also *Annual Report of the Department of the Interior for the year ending March 31, 1926,* p. 125.
[3] *Annual Report of the Department of the Interior for the year ending March 31, 1927,* p. 112.

the Canadian Pacific was the indication that farmers were gradually being weaned away from their old-time devotion to grain growing. The live stock situation had greatly improved, an increased interest in hog and sheep raising was noticeable, and alfalfa was growing in favor. There was reason to hope that, with the increasing popularity of diversified agriculture, the farmers would more and more make use of the water which was available for irrigation.

The remaining irrigation interests of the Canadian Pacific centered about the Lethbridge district where the Alberta Railway and Irrigation Company had developed its irrigation project in the early years of the century. With the acquisition of this company by the Canadian Pacific in 1912, the latter took over the unsold portions of the land grant together with the irrigation system. That same year the new owners developed the Coaldale colony of 17 ready-made farms. The company also undertook promptly the extension of the irrigation system north of Lethbridge, and for the selling season of 1914 it had there between 20,000 and 25,000 acres of excellent irrigable land ready for the market.[1] Thus the Lethbridge system became the third unit of the Canadian Pacific irrigation project in Alberta.

The Lethbridge section extends from a point on the St. Mary's River, 5 miles north of the international boundary to the Oldman River on the north, and from the St. Mary's and Oldman Rivers on the west to a point on the Crows Nest Branch of the Canadian Pacific 37 miles east of Lethbridge. Practically all the land in this district has been sold and more than 80 per cent of the area under the canals is under irrigation. Development of the area has been retarded, however, by the presence of numerous large holdings, in many cases controlled by absentee owners. The gross area covered by water agreements is approximately 114,500 acres.[2] Of this area about 25,000 acres in townships 5 and 6 in the Magrath and Raymond districts are covered by fractional water rights, with more land ordinarily under irrigation than is provided for in the water right.

[1] Minutes of the Third Annual Convention of American Land Agents, Chicago, Novmber 24 and 25, 1913. File No. 44, D. N. R. Statement by J. S. Dennis at the convention.

[2] In this I have followed the MS. account by Sam G. Porter and Charles Raley, *A Brief History of the Development of Irrigation in the Lethbridge District*, pp. 38 and 39, Appendix E.

The total number of water agreements is 940, while the estimated irrigable area commanded by the canals is 163,405 acres.

Besides the operation and extension of the Lethbridge system, the Canadian Pacific has served the cause of irrigation in that district in other ways. In 1913 the farmers in the Taber area began negotiations with the railway company with a view to securing a water supply for their lands. The company had constructed reservoirs in Chin Coulee for the storage of the waste and surplus water from their Lethbridge system, and surveys had shown that this water could be economically applied to the lands around Barnwell and Taber. The farmers proposed that the Canadian Pacific should build the irrigation works and accept contracts from the individual landowners, the contracts to be secured by mortgages on the farm lands. When this was found impracticable the Alberta Government was asked to enact legislation which would enable the farmers to organize a district with authority to issue bonds to cover the cost of the irrigation works. The Irrigation District Act was passed by the Alberta Legislation in 1915, and in the same year the Taber Irrigation District was organized. After numerous delays, negotiations with the Canadian Pacific were completed in the spring of 1919, and in July of that year the landowners voted unanimously for the issue of bonds for the construction of the canals. The railway company accepted the bonds for the actual cost of the construction of the work, which amounted to $16.50 per irrigable acre, and it agreed to deliver water for the irrigation of 17,000 acres for an annual operation and maintenance charge of 50 cents per acre. Construction was completed in October, 1920. Although the system is operated by the farmers themselves, it is dependent, of course, upon the Canadian Pacific's Lethbridge system for its water supply. It has been successful from the beginning.[1]

Future expansion of irrigation throughout southern Alberta is closely linked with the existing system of the Canadian Pacific. Large areas south of Raymond could be served by developing the reservoirs south of that town, while other large areas further south and east, already surveyed by the Dominion Government under the name of the Lethbridge Southeastern Project, can be brought under irrigation only through the utilization of the Canadian Pacific's irrigation

[1] *Ibid.*, pp. 38-39.

facilities. Thus the railway has not merely been an indispensable factor in the important developments throughout southern Alberta; it will largely determine the progress which will be made in the future.

As for Canadian Pacific lands outside the company's irrigation projects, the war years brought new developments. In 1915 renewed attention was given to the sale of the large areas in the north tributary to competing lines of railway. The Department of Natural Resources reduced the prices of these lands to bring them more in line with those of similar land elsewhere in Alberta and Saskatchewan. At the same time, Dennis sought to enlist the aid of the officials of those railways, which would chiefly benefit by the sale and settlement of the land. His proposal was that Canadian Northern and Grand Trunk Pacific agents, especially in Great Britain, should undertake the distribution of Canadian Pacific literature descriptive of the land along their lines.[1] He made it clear that he would expect them to route the prospective settlers over their railway lines, and he asked only that the Department of Natural Resources be kept carefully informed as to arrivals, in order that its agency force might endeavor to make sales of the land. The plan came to naught, unfortunately, because of the refusal of the rival railways to cooperate except on the condition that the Department of Natural Resources should prepare special literature for distribution, which Dennis politely, but firmly, refused to do.[2]

In the meantime the Canadian Pacific was giving increased attention to the possibility of settling and developing the lands in the north by means of branch lines which would guarantee to the company the benefit of the resulting traffic. As a result of a petition of the Battleford Board of Trade, it was considering the possibility of a line from Saskatoon to Battleford. In March, 1914, Dennis advised Shaughnessy that the next year, in order to keep up the average of sales of the Department of Natural Resources, it would be necessary that the agency organization in the United States devote a greater degree of attention to the northern areas so largely served by rival

[1] Dennis to M. Donaldson, Vice-President and General Manager, Grand Trunk Pacific, April 30, 1915, Letter Board 15, M.

[2] Dennis to W. P. Hinton, Passenger Traffic Manager, Grand Trunk Pacific, June 8, 1915, *ibid.*

companies than in the previous two years.[1] He included maps on which he had indicated various branch line extensions which he believed imperative "if we are to get the traffic from colonization of our lands in the districts affected." Under the 20-year payment plan, with loans for improvements, Dennis observed, the settler became more closely allied with the company than under a mere land-selling policy, which made it reasonable to suppose that it could expect the larger part of the traffic in districts colonized by it, provided, of course, that it had the facilities to handle the business. Dennis believed that in the large area north and northwest of Battleford the department could establish flourishing colonies of northern Europeans, devoted to mixed farming and prepared to give their business to the company.[2] This required, as it foreshadowed, the branch line extensions which the railway ultimately built in this region but which the war temporarily delayed.

By the close of the World War the bulk of the unsold lands of the company outside of the eastern section of the irrigation block were concentrated largely in three areas. One was the so-called Battleford Block, north and west of Battleford, for which the town of North Battleford was the natural administrative center. A second was the Lloydminster Block, a large area north and west of the town of that name, which was the logical headquarters for any selling campaign designed to dispose of these lands. The remaining area was termed the Calgary and Edmonton Block, comprising the large area west of the Calgary and Edmonton line of the Canadian Pacific. The larger portion of this area lay tributary to the town of Wetaskiwin and belonged to the railway by virtue of the great northern reserve set aside for it in 1882.[3]

Shaughnessy believed the time had come for the company to undertake an active campaign for the sale of these blocks of land. The Battleford and Lloydminster blocks contained large areas of attractive, open prairie or slightly wooded land for which it was reasonable to suppose there would be a ready demand from land buyers in

[1] Dennis to Shaughnessy, March 5, 1914, Letter Book, January 13—March 31, 1914, M.

[2] Ibid.

[3] The term Calgary and Edmonton applied to this block should not lead one to the conclusion that these were the Calgary and Edmonton security lands acquired by the C. P. R. in 1912, but which were now largely sold.

the United States.[1] As the branch lines which Dennis so much desired had been delayed by war-time conditions, these lands were not yet tributary to Canadian Pacific lines. For this reason the lands were placed on sale without settlement conditions, except where purchasers desired to avail themselves of such provisions in order to obtain the 20-year term for payment instead of the straight 10-year period which would otherwise prevail. Dennis assumed that most of the settlers for these blocks would have to be obtained in the United States.

The Calgary and Edmonton area presented a problem. Most of this land was covered with timber, which repelled the American farmer accustomed to the prairie. It was obvious that this area would have to be disposed of gradually to colonies of Europeans who would clear the land slowly and bring it under cultivation. A special scheme of colonization must be worked out for that block, which was not turned over to the United States organization for sale. Under what were termed "brush-land" contracts various settlements of European colonists were established there during the twenties.

But even for the sale of the Battleford and Lloydminster blocks by the organization in the States adjustments had to be made. For several years, ever since the irrigable land in the eastern section of the irrigation block was placed on sale, the district representatives in the United States and their commission agents had been engaged largely in the sale of those lands. By dint of hard effort they had been successful in starting a movement into that section which promised to continue into the future. The commission agents working under the district representatives were devoting their energies chiefly to the sale of the irrigable lands at prices ranging from $40.00 to $60.00 per acre on a 5 per cent commission basis. Naturally, they would rather sell these lands than those in northern Alberta and Saskatchewan at $12.00 to $20.00 per acre, with the same rate of commission. Obviously the company had to meet this situation if it hoped to interest American agents in the sale of the land.

Dennis was ready with a plan designed to solve all difficulties. In

[1] Dennis to Chairman, Advisory Committee, August 24, 1919, File No. 3506, M. When in 1916 the Department of Colonization and Development was formed, with headquarters in Montreal, and with Dennis as Chief Commissioner, an Advisory Committee was created to supervise and coördinate the new department with the Department of Natural Resources.

the autumn of 1919 a huge advertising and publicity campaign was launched in the United States to acquaint the farming classes with the Battleford and Lloydminster areas. In order to interest the agency organization in the sale of these lands, as well as to increase the number of commission agents, the commission for the sale of this land was increased to 10 per cent, the increase to be taken care of by a blanket increase of 10 per cent in the list price of the land. The commissions were to be payable, 5 per cent from the first payment, 5 per cent from the second.

This provision with respect to the manner and time of payment of the commission was based on the assumption that the lands, not being tributary to Canadian Pacific lines, could be sold on the 10-payment plan. All the literature of the Department of Natural Resources since 1913, however, had emphasized the colonization policy of the company, with the 20-year period for payment. So well known was this policy that settlers brought from the United States, to the surprise of company officials, assumed they could purchase on the 20-year plan, provided, of course, that they complied with the settlement requirements.[1] Feeling that it could not withdraw the privilege of the 20-year payments in view of the widespread publicity given it, the company was placed unwittingly in the position of actually colonizing its lands along the competing lines of railway, a situation which supplied an additional incentive to the construction of Canadian Pacific branch lines into the territory.

Preponderance of sales to actual settlers under the 20-year plan necessitated a change in the manner of paying the 10 per cent commission to agents in the States. Payment in equal amounts at the time of the receipt of the first and second installments on the principal was satisfactory under the 10-year plan, where the second payment came at the end of the second year. But when the concession, originally limited to the eastern section of the irrigation block, exempting the settler from the second payment on the principal for a period of 3 years was extended to all settlers on company lands, the agent found himself at a disadvantage. Since the settler paid his second installment on the principal at the end of the fourth year, the agent must forego the receipt of the balance of his commission for that period of time. Believing this to be unfair to

[1] Cameron to Naismith, February 3, 1920, File No. 3506, M.

the agents and not calculated to secure maximum coöperation from them, the Department of Natural Resources made provision for the payment of the second installment of the commission upon the careful performance by the purchaser of the settlement conditions applicable to the first year which, in practice, meant one year from the date of the completion of the sale.[1]

Although after 1920 the company ceased to emphasize ready-made and loan farms as features of the land policy then in force, throughout the post-war period it granted such assistance in special circumstances and under different names. More and more it became evident that the sale of the remaining lands must be a long, slow process, calling for the use of special inducements in increasing degree. Recognizing in the middle twenties that the best of its lands had been disposed of, the Department of Natural Resources revalued its unsold lands in the light of existing land values in different parts of the West. As this step meant in general a lower schedule of prices it made a substantial appeal to the prospective buyer. At the same time, however, it created something of a problem for the department. Many contract holders saw in it a means of escaping accrued interest and arrears in principal by surrendering their contracts with a view to repurchase of the land either by themselves or their relatives.[2]

In 1923 the 20-year payment plan was discarded by the company in favor of an exceedingly liberal, 34-year amortization plan for the sale of the company's lands. While offering this inducement to the man of small means the department encouraged the settler with capital by offering a 10 per cent discount for payment in cash, a provision which it called to the attention of all persons making inquiry at land offices. Under the amortization plan, department officials sought to obtain the largest possible first payment, the theory being that the larger the stake of the settler in the land the greater would be his industry and his fidelity to his obligations.

Of the lands unsold at the middle of the decade, outside the irrigation block, a large portion was covered with a growth of brush and

[1] Extract from the Minutes of the meeting of the Advisory Committee of the Department of Natural Resources and the Department of Colonization and Development, February 6, 1920, *ibid.*

[2] *Annual Report, Land Branch,* Department of Natural Resources, for 1928.

timber. While well watered and possessed of unquestioned fertility, the presence of trees increased the difficulty of the settler in bringing it under cultivation. With a view to facilitating the settlement of such land, the department devised a special brush-land contract, embodying liberal provisions designed to appeal to certain types of settlers. Assuming that British and American immigrants would be repelled by the brush covering of the land, the officials of the railway relied chiefly upon Continental Europeans, with large families equal to the arduous task of clearing the land. The first area selected for the brush-land experiment was located west of Leduc, on the Calgary and Edmonton line. There, 170 families from Hungary were established under conditions which promised well for the success of the community. This experiment was watched with interest by company officials, who hoped that by its application to other areas there might be found a solution to the problem of disposing of the rather inferior unsold land of the railway.

The practice of leasing land, which was employed so freely in the irrigation block, came to be widely applied with respect to the lands of the company generally. During the decade of the twenties the crop and grazing leases averaged about 2,000 annually and produced an annual revenue as high as $247,000.[1] This income was of substantial importance to the company. As the unsold land of the railway was now subject to taxation, the funds derived from this source went far toward meeting the demands of the tax gatherer. At the same time the leasing policy was conducive to the sale of company lands (since many leaseholders later purchased the land) and served as an aid in the control of the noxious weed situation on lands once under contract and cultivation, but which had subsequently reverted to the company.[2]

A significant development during the period was the quiet but steady extension of the crop-payment policy. This plan had been adopted with a flourish back in the early days of the irrigation block but was soon overshadowed by the ready-made farm policy. Although never entirely abandoned, it was not until the post-war years that it came into general use. The increasing popularity of

[1] *Annual Report, Land Branch,* Department of Natural Resources, for 1927. *Ibid.,* for 1928.
[2] *Annual Report, Land Branch,* Department of Natural Resources, for 1927.

the policy enabled the Land Branch of the Department of Natural Resources to say in 1927 that "this matter of securing payments by way of crop shares is one of the most important of our activities." In that year the department administered 4,084 crops in widely scattered parts of Alberta and Saskatchewan. As an interesting and practical way of fostering the sale of company lands the policy was important. It was more noteworthy, however, by virtue of the control which it enabled the company to exercise over farming methods and techniques throughout the prairie region. It placed the Department of Natural Resources in the position of landlord in relation to many western farmers. Although an absentee landlord in a sense, the department's interests were vitally bound up with those of the farmer and its corps of inspectors stood constantly at the service of the settler.

In 1930 settlers on Canadian Pacific lands, as upon most lands in the West, entered upon a difficult and trying period, the end of which is not yet. Depression, repeated drought, poor crops, and low prices brought many farmers to the verge of disaster. Beginning in 1932, the company repeatedly made concessions designed to ease the burden of these stricken settlers. In February of that year it remitted one year's interest on the total amount outstanding on land contracts throughout the West. It also agreed to remit a second year's interest where the settler had paid one year's taxes, had paid one installment on his purchase, or had delivered to the company one-third of his crop. It made further allowance on arrears of interest by granting the settler dollar-for-dollar additional credit for all payments in cash or by delivery of crop. These concessions were continued during the years 1933-36, inclusive, except that the share of crop was reduced to one-fourth. To obtain the benefit of the concession, the farmer merely needed to enter into the covenant and deliver the share of his crop. If his crop were a complete failure, he still enjoyed the remission of a year's interest. In this way, settlers on company lands between 1932 and 1936 received remission of payments amounting to more than $10,000,000.

New regulations governing the sale of land were introduced in 1934. The 34-year amortization plan was abandoned. Lands once under contract for sale but which had reverted to the company, and which had 50 acres of improved land to a quarter section, were sold on the crop-payment plan. Eight per cent was due with the application, the balance being payable by delivery of one-third of the crop annually over a period of 21 years, with interest at 6 per cent. Unimproved land was sold with a cash payment of 8 per cent, plus 21 annual cash installments, with 6 per cent interest. Heavily brushed lands were available in quarter sections to those prepared to occupy them, upon a cash deposit of $25. After an interest-free period of 4 years the purchaser paid 17 annual installments, with interest at 6 per cent.

With the continuance of depression and drought in the West the problem of the company more and more became that of escaping the burden of taxation entailed by the possession of sub-marginal lands. In the words of one official, the unsold land had of necessity to be viewed "in an entirely different light than was the case when the company was favored with tax exemption." It quietly adopted, therefore, the policy of gradually relieving itself of such areas, where it was felt that the carrying charges would leave little or nothing to be realized. In 1936 it transferred free of charge a total of 126,679 acres to a holding company (especially organized to deal in such land), to the province of Alberta, and to the rural community of Carmichael, Saskatchewan. This, together with the transfer of the large area to the Eastern Irrigation District in 1935, reduced the unsold area at the end of 1937 to 2,039,239 acres. Of this, a very large portion was better adapted to pasturage and mixed farming than to grain growing. With the return of normal business and climatic conditions in the West, the exceedingly liberal terms offered by the company would undoubtedly make possible the early sale of much of this land.

As the company approached the depletion of its great land subsidies in the West, the work of its Department of Natural Resources in Calgary did not diminish correspondingly. Its inspectors in 1937 were entrusted with the administration of more than 16,000 land contracts scattered through the three prairie provinces, together with some 12,000 leases and crop-share agreements. The sum outstanding as deferred payments on land contracts still amounted to $34,000,000. After 56 years of ceaseless effort, the company's land grants were far from liquidated.

XI

PROMOTING BETTER
AGRICULTURE

THE railways of North America serving territory predominantly
rural have ever been interested in improving the methods and
condition of agriculture in areas tributary to their lines. The land
grant roads, frequently built so far in advance of settlement as to
force upon them the rôle of colonizers, have been especially active
in their efforts to show the farmer how to improve the quality of his
live stock and his grain crops, and how to adapt his technique of
farming to the conditions of soil and climate prevailing in his
locality. Students of history have generally regarded James J. Hill,
the builder of the Great Northern Railroad, as the pioneer in the
field of railway encouragement to agriculture, and supposedly his
methods were widely copied by railways in the western states. It is
now known, however, that the Illinois Central, the first land grant
railway, was very active in its efforts to promote a well-rounded
agriculture in central Illinois. Especially was this true of President
Osborn of that company, who took a personal interest in the problem and whose Illinois farm functioned as something of an experimental unit for the railway. Railways farther west took up the idea,
carried it to greater lengths, and applied it in a variety of ways
unknown to Osborn. As in the case of railway land policies in general, the Canadian Pacific fell heir to all the knowledge and experience of its predecessors in fostering agricultural improvements. But,
just as in its land and colonization policies, it was not content to
follow in the steps of others, so in relation to agricultural progress
it adopted novel methods and policies. While its efforts in this regard
were conceived and carried out in the grand manner which characterized its other ventures, it was not mere scale alone which distinguished the company's work from that of other railways.

Those who projected the Canadian Pacific Railway did not await the completion of the road to evince their interest in the agricultural possibilities of the Canadian West. As the rails crept steadily westward toward the mountains the company began to investigate the potentialities of the country traversed by its lines between Swift Current and Medicine Hat. To the extent that this quest for agricultural data was prompted by a desire to have criteria as to soil and climate which would guide the land department in the intelligent application of the "fairly fit for settlement" clause in the selection of land, it represented enlightened self-interest on the part of the company. It must be remembered, however, that no railway has been influenced by philanthropic motives in the formulation of its policies, and in attempting to ascertain the agricultural fitness of the region beyond Swift Current the Canadian Pacific was actuated by the same considerations of intelligent selfishness that have governed other railways. In its search for knowledge of this area the company established some 10 experimental farms along the line in the eighties, in which it experimented with crops of all kinds. It was upon the basis of results there obtained that the land department rejected much of the land in the 48-mile belt west of the 3rd meridian. In doing a service to the company, these farms may also have rendered a kindness to numberless settlers, for had the railway accepted these lands, it would, of necessity, have sought to sell and settle them, with the resulting heartbreaks suffered by thousands of farmers who followed in the wake of the railways into the land of semi-aridity in the United States.

Van Horne, who served as general manager of the company prior to succeeding George Stephen in the presidency, took a strong personal interest in agricultural development. By inviting American cattlemen to come in and avail themselves of the grass which covered the prairies, he encouraged a new industry and secured the benefits of cattle shipments for the road. Together with his associates in the company he established milling and elevator companies, with a view to profit to the railway, the farmer, the community, and to himself.[1] Before he became identified with the development of the Canadian West, flat warehouses were used there for the storage of grain. With

[1] Walter Vaughan, *The Life and Work of Sir William Van Horne* (New York, 1920), p. 139.

his background of experience in Minnesota, he realized the necessity of establishing the most approved type of warehouse on the prairies, in order to make possible the cleaning and grading of the grain. Due largely to his influence, the first modern elevator in Canada was built at Fort William with a capacity of one million bushels. Despite the prophecy that it would never be filled, similar structures were soon located at Port Arthur and Owen Sound, while small receiving elevators soon dotted the prairie for hundreds of miles along the line west of Winnipeg.[1]

Van Horne early became a convert to "Red Fife" wheat, imported into Upper Canada by David Fife in the middle of the 19th Century, and well suited, by virtue of its early maturity, to the short growing season on the prairie. While supporting the doubtful thesis that the softer varieties could be grown successfully in the West, he constantly reminded people that they should seek to grow a harder, finer type. He was convinced that the soil and climate of the prairie were peculiarly adapted to the growth of Red Fife.[2] Perhaps he should have said that the other varieties were susceptible to frost damage! On March 11, 1882, the *Manitoba Daily Free Press* printed an "Important C. P. R. Circular" which was being widely disseminated among farmers throughout Manitoba. After quoting the warnings of various milling companies against the growth of soft grades of wheat, the circular pointed out that the production of such grain would injure the reputation of the "New Northwest." In an effort to dissuade farmers from a continuance of their evil ways, the document announced the readiness of the Canadian Pacific Railway Company to "transport seed wheat westward free of charge, provided it is unmixed dark Scotch Fife; all other varieties of mixed wheat will be charged full tariff rates." When later the company turned its attention to the development of southern Alberta, where many people believed the climatic conditions were well suited to the growth of winter wheat, it encouraged the farmer by importing Turkey Red wheat, developed in Kansas, from Kansas City. It charged no freight on this wheat over its lines from Portal to Calgary.[3]

[1] *Ibid.*
[2] *Ibid.*
[3] *Manitoba Free Press*, August 17, 1905.

In the early period the efforts of the company to divert the attention of farmers from the exclusive growing of grain crops to the development of animal husbandry assumed various forms. Not only did it import high grade sires which it located at designated points where they could be of service to the farmers of the community, but it systematically extended free transportation to all those who would bring thoroughbred sires into the northwest territories and Manitoba. At fairs and exhibitions it offered handsome cash prizes for thoroughbred cattle, bred and raised in the West.[1] Beginning this policy with respect to the live stock industry in Manitoba, the company extended it into other parts of the West as settlement moved in that direction. By the turn of the century this work of the railway in Alberta had assumed an importance which attracted the attention and elicited the favorable comment of an immigration agent of the Liberal Laurier Government, whose servants were usually sparing in their words of commendation of the Canadian Pacific. Writing from his station at Edmonton he said: "The action of the C. P. R. Co. in importing thoroughbred cattle and hogs for the improvement of the live stock in Alberta is commendable. Spirited enterprise, such as this, following the reduction in transport rates, is likely to go far to convince the settlers of the Company's good will, and that its management clearly recognizes the fact that the prosperity and contentment of any region are the best basis upon which to rest the railway shareholders' hope of future traffic and profits."[2] He added, incidentally, that the existing prosperity of Alberta was due largely to the "intelligent action" of the railway in reducing the rate on farm produce shipped to British Columbia.

Important as were the contributions just mentioned to the development of a sounder agriculture in the Northwest, it was, of course, in connection first with its irrigation project in Alberta and later with its Department of Natural Resources that the Canadian Pacific exercised its most far-reaching influence upon the course of agricultural development in Canada. The mere idea of constructing a great irrigation system was born both of a desire to shape the farming practices in a large area, and of the belief that those practices could be so shaped. There the railway would develop a form of

1 *Manitoba Morning Free Press*, April 2, 1900.
2 *Sessional Papers* (No. 13), 1900, p. 171.

agricultural life radically different from that found elsewhere between the Red River and the Rocky Mountains.

In its efforts the Canadian Pacific had the example of the Alberta Railway and Irrigation Company in the Lethbridge area of southern Alberta. This company not only pioneered in irrigation in the Canadian West, thereby determining in no small measure the trend of agricultural development in its territory, but it had also taken definite steps to insure the cultivation of desired crops. One of the crops well adapted to growth under conditions of irrigation is the sugar beet. But unfortunately its profitable production requires the presence of a sugar factory close at hand. Resolved to encourage sugar beet production on its lands, the company in 1901 entered into an agreement with an energetic and resourceful Mormon, Jesse Knight, for the establishment at Raymond, Alberta, of what came to be known as the Knight Sugar Factory.[1] By the terms of the contract, Knight undertook to spend $300,000 in erecting and equipping a factory for the manufacture of beet sugar and other products, the work to be completed by September 1, 1903. He agreed to break and plow 3,000 acres by December 31, 1901. As a guarantee for the faithful performance of his obligations, Knight deposited $50,000, to be forfeited in the event of default on his part. The railway company agreed to hold 52,000 acres of land for sale at prices to be determined from time to time by agreement with Knight, who, provided the factory was completed within the allotted time, was to receive two-thirds of the proceeds of land sales in excess of $5.00 per acre. The railway further agreed to lease to Knight 226,000 acres until completion of the factory, when it would sell to him the entire area at $2.00 per acre, or one-half of it at $2.25 per acre. The terms of the agreement, so mutually advantageous, were carried out and the Raymond Sugar Factory became one of the important auxiliaries of the Alberta Railway and Irrigation Company for the development of its country.

The Alberta Railway and Irrigation Company was equally alert to other ways and means of promoting the formation of a healthy and prosperous agricultural community in that district. In 1901 it established a model farm to encourage and instruct its settlers, and to demonstrate what could be accomplished with the aid of irriga-

[1] See the text of the agreement, File No. 4291, D. N. R.

tion.[1] The farm of 300 acres was placed in charge of Professor W. H. Fairfield, then superintendent of the State Experimental Station at the University of Wyoming.[2] He arrived in April, 1901, and immediately prepared the land for irrigation. An expert in irrigation matters and a great enthusiast for alfalfa, Fairfield became a figure of genuine importance not merely in the Lethbridge area, but in the Calgary sector as well, where the Canadian Pacific frequently drew upon his knowledge and experience. By the work which he carried out on the model farm as well as by the aid and counsel he gave to the farmers throughout the district, he for years wielded an important influence upon southern Alberta agriculture.

By a curious turn of events the Canadian Pacific, which was promoting the largest irrigation project in the Northwest, was also a most important instrument for the propagation of the dry farming idea. And yet it was entirely logical that this should be so. Adjacent to its main line from Moose Jaw to Medicine Hat was a sparsely settled region, in which the company had not accepted land but in which the government land could be rendered productive provided some practical system of dry farming could be developed. Within the irrigation block, as well, much of the land was incapable of irrigation and would be made more valuable and attractive by dry farming technique. None of the Rosebud tract was to be irrigated, yet it was a fertile area, with a rainfall normally sufficient for arable farming. With the assistance of dry farming methods crops would be grown with greater certainty.

Just where, when, and by whom dry farming was discovered is one of those puzzling questions which so frequently confront the student of history. The practice is undoubtedly as old as agriculture itself, but the term originated in the western states in the nineteenth century. Dry farming, the growing of crops in regions of sub-normal rainfall without the aid of irrigation, was practiced with more or less success in California and Utah in the fifties and sixties. With the occupation of the Great Plains area, between the 98th meridian and the Rocky Mountains, the pioneer settlers first employed the methods of cultivation they had known in the humid regions, with

[1] Sam G. Porter and Charles Raley, *A Brief History of the Development of Irrigation in the Lethbridge District*, MS., D. N. R., Calgary, p. 25.
[2] *Ibid.*

disastrous results. Gradually, as repeated waves of settlement swept into that region, it became recognized that the technique of farming must be adapted to the prevailing climatic conditions. In this way there developed a body of knowledge and a code of farming practice which better enabled the farmer to cope with this situation. This obviously was dry farming, but as yet it was not a religion, and the memory of earlier disasters in the plains still tended to discourage settlement. What was needed was someone who would preach the gospel of dry farming, and such a person ultimately appeared.

In the first decade of the twentieth century the term "dry farming" came to have a definite and peculiar connotation. It was the method of soil culture advocated by Hardy W. Campbell of Lincoln, Nebraska, who became the most conspicuous propagator of the faith. So closely did Campbell become identified in the public mind with dry farming that the term itself became interchangeable with "the Campbell system." Campbell, a native of Vermont, where he had been brought up on a farm, went west in 1878. The following year he took up a homestead and tree claim near Aberdeen, South Dakota. After a few successful seasons, drought completely destroyed his crops in 1884. Succeeding dry seasons set him thinking and by 1893 he had grasped the "fundamental principle" of dry farming.[1] In that year he raised a good crop. The following year he produced bountiful crops of wheat, corn, and potatoes, while his neighbors experienced complete failure. Campbell then turned missionary, going about the country, talking to farmers and explaining his theories.

How much Campbell could have achieved single-handed one cannot say. But he was not to go unaided. No other interest had so much at stake in the plains area as the railways. Some of them had vast areas of land there, while the others would naturally profit from the increased productivity which dry farming promised. And they had the means with which to foster and promote the idea. It was no accident, therefore, that the railways traversing the plains country became the chief sponsors of, and largely sold, Campbell's dry farming system. The first to take up the idea appears to have

[1] See statement by Campbell of his early career and experiences printed in *Chicago Record-Herald*. Unfortunately the date is missing from the copy in the D. N. R.

been the Northern Pacific. In 1895 Campbell was conducting four experimental farms for that company in North Dakota and by 1896 the number had increased to twelve. The general manager of the road was enthusiastic about the plan and gave it generous support. Next it was the Soo Line, the Canadian Pacific subsidiary, running from St. Paul across Minnesota and North Dakota to Portal, which engaged him to operate experimental farms in its territory. From there he went to Nebraska where the general manager of the Burlington system, George W. Holdrege, arranged for him to conduct farms at Otis and Holdrege in that state. Like a great prairie fire the idea seems to have swept across the plains from north to south. Campbell was next invited to carry on demonstration work for the Union Pacific in Kansas, and by 1905 he was supervising two model farms in the Texas Panhandle, one on the Chicago, Rock Island and Pacific Railway, the other on the Santa Fe. While the railways in question did not actually own these farms, Campbell received their enthusiastic support at all times. It was the hope of the railway companies that, as a result of Campbell's demonstration, settlers in the Panhandle would turn to arable farming, with a resulting extension of settlement and an increased volume of traffic.

Meanwhile, Campbell had codified his ideas in *Campbell's Manual of Soil Culture*, which was widely distributed by the railways in the plains country. At the same time he was much in demand as a contributor to agricultural papers, including the *Nebraska Farmer*, published at Omaha, to which he contributed regularly. The basic principle of dry farming is the conservation of water in time of rainfall for use in time of drought. This is done not by the storing of the water in reservoirs, as in irrigation, but by storing in the soil itself. The dry farmer uses capillary water which affords the moisture for growing plants. By deep plowing, which increases the capillarity and raises the water level, by packing the soil with a sub-surface packer, by constant cultivation which preserves a dust mulch over the surface of the ground and minimizes evaporation, the capillary water is conserved and made to last for a maximum period of time.

Campbell frankly admitted that dry farming required much greater effort, care, and patience than ordinary farming; but the added labor meant the difference between bountiful crops and none at all. Not only did he develop his system of soil culture, but he perfected tools and equipment for dry framing which required a capital outlay in excess of what many farmers were willing to make.

By 1905 the fame of Campbell had spread to Canada. In that year Dennis made inquiry of the Department of Agriculture in Washington in regard to him.[1] Further investigation of the results achieved by dry farming so impressed Dennis that he sought to interest high officials of the Canadian Pacific in it.[2] Dennis proposed the purchase and distribution by the railway of a thousand copies of Campbell's *Manual,* and the company coöperated with the province of Saskatchewan in the distribution of a publication entitled *Hints to the Grain Growers,* issued by the Provincial Department of Agriculture. This pamphlet was an adaptation of Campbell's *Manual* to Canadian conditions.[3]

During the next few years the interest of company officials in the dry farming idea continued. In the summer of 1909 Campbell was brought to the irrigation block on a speaking tour to defend his method among the farmers there.[4] When in September of that year the budget of the Canadian Pacific Irrigation Colonization Company's agricultural demonstration work was prepared for the following year, there was included an appropriation for two "dry land" demonstration farms.[5] While it would, of course, be fallacious to conclude that this step resulted directly from Campbell's visit, one's eyes should not be closed to the coincidence. One thing is certain: it was due to the appeal of the dry farming idea that the company decided to dispose of large areas in the central and eastern sections of the irrigation block as "dry land" farms in advance of the completion of the irrigation system in those parts. And "dry land" demonstration farms were established and equipped by the company with a view to teaching the technique to those who purchased such lands. Large areas were thus sold for dry farming purposes, but, as Dennis later confessed, few of those who tried the experiment in the eastern section were successful. Whether due to the perversity of

[1] R. T. Teele, Acting Chief of Irrigation and Drainage Investigation, U. S. Department of Agriculture, to Dennis, June 10, 1905. File No. 3251, D. N. R.

[2] Dennis to Sir Wm. Whyte, July 22 and November 28, 1905, and May 30, 1906, File No. 3251, D. N. R.

[3] Whyte to Dennis, June 4, 1906, *ibid.*

[4] Peterson to Rothwell, July 21, 1909, *ibid.*

[5] Shaughnessy to Dennis, September 2, 1909, *ibid.*

human nature, to the speculative element in so many of the purchases, or to adverse natural conditions, the company was wholly unsuccessful in its efforts to encourage the formation of a successful dry farming community in the eastern part of the block.

Despite its efforts to promote dry farming in southern Alberta, the main interest of the Canadian Pacific in its agricultural work in the irrigation block during the period from 1905 to 1911 was the development of irrigation farming. As we have seen, so eager was it to promote the rapid settlement of its irrigable lands that it organized a Development Branch of the Canadian Pacific Irrigation Colonization Company to break and seed the land for the settler in advance of his occupation. The work of this branch assumed large proportions and, while early settlement and development was its primary objective, the company made admirable use of the opportunity which it gave to dictate and determine agricultural practices and methods. Thousands of acres were brought under cultivation with the aid of the branch before its sphere of activity was greatly enlarged by the adoption of the ready-made farm policy.

The first of the demonstration farms within the irrigation block was that at Strathmore, opened in 1905 when the sale of irrigable land was begun. Here experiments of all sorts were tried under irrigation conditions. In one year plots of land were planted to two-rowed barley, flax, millet, banner oats, Sonora wheat, Prussian blue pea, Northwestern dent corn, rape, Longfellow corn, Seredella, Kubanka wheat, Swedish select oats, Preston wheat, and white hulless barley. Special attention was given to grasses for pasture purposes.[1] The farm was under the supervision of a trained agriculturist, Professor W. J. Elliott, was supplied with the best of equipment, and was provided with a special irrigation instructor, who not only had charge of irrigation operations on the farm itself, but was available for service throughout the block.

That the company was prepared to spend money liberally in its effort to promote a sound agriculture in that area is indicated by the budget for 1910. For demonstration purposes alone, which do not include salaries of the staff, it allotted $18,850.[2] This included such

[1] Report of Experimental Plots conducted on C. P. R. Demonstration Farm, Strathmore, 1910, by Prof. W. J. Elliott, File No. 3265, D. N. R.

[2] Shaughnessy to Dennis, September 2, 1909, File No. 3271, D. N. R.

items as a lecture campaign within the block, prizes for agricultural products at exhibitions, educational publicity in regard to the care and handling of crops, experiments with malting barley, and rainfall statistics. That year the actual expenditure was $460 in excess of the appropriation. The budget for the following year included allowances for seed selection work, meteorological records, and the introduction and encouragement of alfalfa.[1] With the growth of settlement in the western section of the irrigation block the function of the Strathmore farm as an educational agency diminished and more and more it became a supply farm where the company provided the dairy, poultry, and garden produce for its Hotel and Dining Car Department. Additional demonstration farms were established in the eastern section of the block, however, and by 1914 experimental work was being carried on at the Tilley, Brooks, Cassils, and Latham farms.[2]

Believing the extension of settlement in the irrigation block, with the resulting fencing of the land, would soon make an end to the free grass on the range, the company appreciated the importance of encouraging the growth of fodder or forage crops by the farmers on its land. As a means to this end it not only preached alfalfa, but it imported alfalfa seed and retailed it at cost to the farmer, and provided an alfalfa expert to give advice and counsel with respect to its growth.[3]

While farmers did not require encouragement to grow grain crops, officials of the Canadian Pacific Irrigation Colonization Company came to the conclusion that they needed special guidance in growing pure specimens of the various crops. The best way to insure that was to see that they were provided with pure seed grain. Peterson was greatly concerned because much of the newly broken ground in the irrigation block was being "systematically seeded down" with noxious weeds which would require years to eradicate. This resulted, of course, from the use of impure seed. He also deprecated the fact that he had not seen a crop of winter wheat which did not contain two or more varieties of grain maturing at

[1] Peterson to Dennis, February 6, 1911, *ibid.*

[2] *Annual Report of the Canadian Pacific Railway Company for the Fiscal Year ending June 30, 1914,* p. 18.

[3] Dennis to C. W. Rawley, November 15, 1909, File No. 3264, D. N. R.

different times.[1] Peterson took immediate steps to correct this latter situation. Knowing that Professor Fairfield, whom the Alberta Railway and Irrigation Company had brought to Canada, had introduced at the Lethbridge Experimental Farm the pure Kansas Turkey Red seed wheat, grown from a hand-selected foundation at the Kansas Agricultural College, Peterson obtained from Fairfield a quantity of this approved seed, sowed it in specially prepared ground on the Strathmore farm, and obtained a pure variety of seed grain free from noxious weeds. This seed grain the company then sold to farmers at the cost of production.[2]

The company officials did not confine their effort to improvement in the quality of grain grown in the irrigation block. They were equally desirous of introducing live stock and promoting thereby a better balanced agriculture. An illustration of the railway's work in this respect is the assistance extended to the first of the ready-made farm settlements, known as the Nightingale colony. Composed of English settlers, unacquainted with conditions in southern Alberta, this colony had a hard fight in 1910 and 1911 to keep going. At the instance of Professor Elliott, the company imported from Ontario in the autumn of 1911 several carloads of 2-year-old heifers, due to freshen in the following spring. Each member of the colony was supplied with some 7 or 8 of these, the company paying the settler $2.00 per head per month for their keep during the winter. The cost of the cattle was added to the land contract of the settler, to be paid in installments, but carried for 2 years without an interest charge.[3] As Elliott pointed out, this plan offered numerous advantages. It recognized the real purpose of a farm given over to intensive agriculture; it insured to the colonists a more abundant living during the winter season; it guaranteed them a living during the following summer; and it laid the basis of a successful animal husbandry within the colony.

Outside of the irrigation block in these years the Canadian Pacific was also actively promoting better farming. While it naturally did not assume toward prairie farmers in general the paternalistic atti-

[1] Peterson to Dennis, August 27, 1908, File No. 3226, D. N. R.

[2] Peterson to Dennis, September 10, 1908, *ibid.*

[3] Elliott to Dennis, October 19, 1911, File No. 244. In this letter Elliott outlines his plan. On October 21, 1911 Dennis endorsed his approval on the letter, D. N. R.

tude maintained with respect to those in the block, it did whatever it could to help the cause along. With the coöperation of the provincial departments of agriculture it operated "seed trains" and "agricultural trains."[1] Manned by the staffs of the provincial departments, a given train would visit all points in a province located on Canadian Pacific lines. Lectures were given in large numbers, pamphlets distributed in quantity, and demonstrations held wherever possible.

With the formation of the Department of Natural Resources at the beginning of 1912, the agricultural work of the railway was greatly enlarged, not only in the irrigation block but throughout the prairie provinces. Professor Elliott, hitherto stationed at the Strathmore farm, was brought to Calgary and placed in charge of the Agricultural Branch of the department. Dennis, as the responsible head of the Department of Natural Resources, with the title of Assistant to the President, assumed a position of leadership in agricultural betterment throughout the West, just as he played a similar rôle in advertising the prairie and promoting immigration. Not only did he lead in this work so far as the Canadian Pacific was concerned, but he succeeded in focusing the attention of all interests upon the problem of improved farming, and in enlisting their aid and coöperation.

As in all the work of the Canadian Pacific on the prairie, company officials, in their efforts to improve agricultural methods, followed with great care the policies which the railways in the United States employed in this regard. By the spring of 1912 George Bury, Vice-President and General Manager of the railway, had come to the conclusion that the seed trains operated by the company in Manitoba and Saskatchewan were not enough.[2] While it was generally admitted in the West that the trains were productive of great good, Bury felt that the three-hour stop at a given station along the line allowed insufficient time for the lessons to be grasped thoroughly. They were soon forgotten by a great many farmers. What was needed was a more permanent form of demonstration, which would

[1] Whyte to Dennis, June 4, 1906, File No. 3257, in which he refers to the "seed train" of 1905 in Saskatchewan. George Bury, Vice-President and General Manager, C. P. R., to Dennis, May 7, 1912, File No. 3276, in which he refers to the "agricultural train" in Manitoba in 1911, D. N. R.

[2] George Bury to Dennis, May 7, 1912, File No. 3276, D. N. R.

remain after the train had gone. Bury had investigated the work which the railways in Minnesota and North Dakota were doing in this connection. He had found that the Soo Line, in addition to operating demonstration trains, had contributed extensively to the support of "The Better Farming Association" in North Dakota.[1] This association had been formed by various interests in the country tributary to the Soo Line, and had in each of 13 counties from 50 to 100 farmers working under its supervision. The farmer entered into a 3-year contract with the association, which supplied him with advice and supervision, while he in turn allowed his farm to be used for the demonstration of the farming methods best adapted to the particular district in which he lived. The farms were well balanced, with good farm buildings and a substantial amount of live stock. Dairying and gardening occupied a prominent place in their routine. The idea was not merely to clear the farm of weeds, but by showing the farmer that diversified farming would pay, to overcome his tendency to grow grains to the exclusion of other things. The Soo Line had also printed a set of pamphlets, written by the best available authorities on the different lines of agriculture, and distributed them widely and with beneficial results.

The Great Northern and Northern Pacific Railways coöperated in retaining the services of Professor Thomas Shaw, an acknowledged authority on agriculture. With three assistants, Professor Shaw supervised 40 small farms on the Great Northern and 10 on the Northern Pacific. The farms were located at accessible points and were operated in such a way as to make clear the advantages of diversified farming. The railway paid the farmer $10 per acre for the use of his land and allowed him the produce, except where required by the railways for exhibition purposes. This work cost the railways about $12,000 per year. Bury recommended that the Canadian Pacific establish such farms in the Portage Plains and in the Mennonite Reserve in Manitoba, where the advantages of good soil had been lost through poor farming methods.

In Montana, although no "Better Farming Association" had been formed, the Northern Pacific had for several years contributed as much as $7,500 per year to enable the Montana Agricultural Experiment Station to carry on demonstration farms in various parts

[1] *Ibid.*

of the state along its line of railway.[1] The Great Northern and the Chicago, Milwaukee, St. Paul and Pacific roads had contributed somewhat less liberally for the same purpose.[2]

Dennis was in complete agreement with Bury as to the need of follow-up work in the wake of the agricultural trains the company was operating in the prairie provinces. But quite independently of Bury's information regarding the work of the railways south of the 49th parallel, Dennis, with the approval of Shaughnessy, had decided upon a procedure designed to achieve the same end. His plan was to establish "mixed farms" on railway land in the prairie provinces with a view to proving by demonstration that diversified farming was "the style of agriculture that should be adopted."[3] Five of these farms were to be located in Manitoba, with 10 each in Saskatchewan and Alberta. Shaughnessy had approved the expenditure of $250,-000 for this purpose, a generous allowance, quite in keeping with the scale on which the company commonly embarked on a new undertaking. Dennis would make of each farm a mecca for the farmers of its particular locality. The farmers, in turn, he would organize into Better Farming Associations, committed to acceptance of the methods employed on the mixed farms. To reinforce the lessons conveyed by the mixed farms, Dennis made provision for the issuance of monthly bulletins by the Agricultural Branch of the Department of Natural Resources in Calgary, to be widely distributed among prairie farmers.[4] For guidance in the preparation of the bulletin the Calgary office obtained samples of the literature issued by the railways and Better Farming Associations of the northwestern states.[5]

Dennis was careful to make clear that it was not his intention to establish "fancy demonstration farms." He merely desired to "conduct them on such a basis as to show the possibilities from 160 acres stocked and equipped in an intelligent manner."[6] He would start the farms "at the point of development that would be reached by

[1] F. B. Linfield, Director, Montana Agricultural Experiment Station, Bozeman, Mont., to Elliott, May 21, 1912, File No. 3265, D. N. R.
[2] Ibid.
[3] Dennis to Bury, May 13, 1912, Letter Book 2, M.
[4] Ibid.
[5] Dennis to Elliott, May 13, 1912, ibid.
[6] Dennis to Shaughnessy, August 20, 1912, Letter Book 4, M.

a man of small capital after he had been in occupation from . . . five to seven years." That would make possible a comparison of a 160-acre farm, running under full pressure as a diversified farm, with a farm of similar size operated merely as a grain producing unit. He also planned to conduct the farms as an object lesson regarding barns and equipment on farms "quite within the reach of any man with moderate means," starting in a small way and working toward a well-defined objective.

Of the 25 mixed farms originally contemplated, only 13 were actually established, of which 3 were located in Manitoba, 4 in Saskatchewan, and 6 in Alberta, the allocation among the 3 provinces being roughly in proportion to the distribution of the company's landed interest in the West. It will be observed that while the American railways used privately owned farms to teach the lessons of better farming, the Canadian Pacific carved the farms out of its unoccupied land, an entirely natural procedure in view of the possession of large unsold areas by the company.

With the opening up of these farms, the Agricultural Branch of the Department of Natural Resources became not only one of the most important agencies of the railway for western development but one of the significant forces for agricultural improvement in the West generally. Commenting upon its work for the year 1912, Dennis said: "The Agricultural Branch of the Department has dealt with all our demonstration and mixed farms and all matters of agricultural development on our 'ready-made' or improved farms. This service during the past year necessitated the breaking, cultivation and seeding of 9,800 acres on our 'ready-made' farms, the harvesting and threshing of 7,000 acres of crops on these farms, breaking and cultivation of 5,000 acres on 'ready-made' farms for 1913, and on the mixed demonstration farms in Manitoba, Saskatchewan and Alberta."[1]

Calling attention to other activities of the branch, Dennis listed answers to inquiries regarding agricultural methods, the preparation of articles on agriculture for publication, the operation of agricultural and mixed farming educational trains in coöperation with provincial governments, and the eradication of noxious weeds within the irrigation block. His conclusion was that "our Agricultural

[1] Dennis to Shaughnessy, February 28, 1913, Letter Book 7, M.

Branch is doing very valuable work through our demonstration and mixed farms and along general educational lines, and is being conducted on as practical a basis as possible so as to bring us closely in touch with farmers in the Western provinces with the object of improving agricultural methods along all lines."

The decision to encourage diversified farming by the establishment of mixed farms, however, necessitated further expansion of the services of the Department of Natural Resources. There could, of course, be no diversified farming without live stock. In large part the development of mixed farming meant increased attention to the live stock industry. Realizing this fact and appreciating its importance, Dennis created the Animal Husbandry Branch of the department. As head of this service he secured Dr. J. G. Rutherford, a man of large experience and complete professional equipment.

The live stock situation in the West, and in Alberta in particular, was a matter of very genuine concern to Dennis. In 1906 there were some 900,000 head of cattle in Alberta, as compared with something more than 500,000 in 1912.[1] While some decrease was to be expected in view of the transition from ranching to farming in the southern part of the province during that period, Dennis felt the decline was far too sharp. In the face of these unpleasant facts Dennis inaugurated a campaign to arouse influential and responsible parties to a realization of the need for action. The most influential and widely circulated farm paper in the West at that time was the *Farm and Ranch Review*, published in Calgary. Appreciating the influence of this publication among farmers, Dennis sought to enlist the aid of its editor, F. S. Jacobs. "You could strengthen our hands materially if you will keep pounding at this subject," he wrote to Jacobs, after explaining what the Department of Natural Resources hoped to do.[2]

His next appeal was to Duncan Marshall, Minister of Agriculture in Alberta. Explaining that the Canadian Pacific hoped to effect an arrangement for importing good stock from eastern Canada for distribution in the West, Dennis asked the minister to make plans for

[1] Dennis to F. S. Jacobs, Editor of *Farm and Ranch Review*, May 28, 1912, Letter Book 2, M.
[2] *Ibid.*

an annual live stock census of the province.[1] This he thought was necessary in order to gauge the results of efforts to improve conditions. Meanwhile, he had approached the Alberta Stock Yards Company and secured its coöperation in the stock importation plan. That company would serve as a general distributive depot for all cattle the Canadian Pacific might bring into Alberta, and would work with the Dominion and provincial demonstration and experimental farms, as well as with the mixed farms of the railway, in effecting local distribution.[2] The Canadian Pacific would purchase the cattle, bring them to Calgary, and sell them at cost to farmers equipped to handle them. All it asked of the other agencies was their aid in distributing the stock.

Dennis lost no opportunity to further the cause of live stock improvement. When informed by George Bury, the Vice-President and General Manager of the Canadian Pacific, that he had promised the Minister of Agriculture an educational train for Alberta in the fall of 1912, Dennis promptly wrote the minister asking that the train be devoted chiefly to the encouragement of stock and poultry production.[3] And Dr. Rutherford, the superintendent of the Animal Husbandry Branch, was to accompany the train.[4]

Perhaps the most eloquent testimony to the leadership of Dennis in the cause of better agriculture for the prairie at that time was the conference which was arranged by him and held at Winnipeg in the latter part of July, 1912. At his request, there assembled the Dominion Minister of Agriculture, the Ministers of Agriculture of the three prairie provinces, the general manager of the Canadian Northern Railway, as well as representatives of Swift and Company of Chicago.[5] At this meeting the live stock question was thoroughly discussed and all interests represented promised their wholehearted coöperation in efforts to improve conditions. From the time of this meeting there was no longer any doubt in the public mind of the initiative which the Canadian Pacific was taking in regard to the stock situation. Up to this time, both Dennis and Shaughnessy,

[1] Dennis to Duncan Marshall, May 25, 1912, *ibid.*
[2] Dennis to Duncan Marshall, May 27, 1912, *ibid.*
[3] Dennis to Duncan Marshall, June 27, 1912, Letter Book 3, M.
[4] Dennis to Shaughnessy, August 2, 1912, Letter Book 1, M.
[5] See letters by Dennis to all these people, dated June 27, 1912, Letter Book 3, M.

while assuming an aggressive attitude in the matter, had desired
to keep the company somewhat in the background, feeling that
advice and aid might be more cheerfully accepted by the farmers
if it emanated from Dominion and provincial authorities rather
than from a great corporation, sometimes referred to as "the
benevolent despot of the West." Shortly after the meeting, Dennis
wrote to Shaughnessy: "After having considered the matter very fully
and particularly after the result of our meeting with the government
officials, representatives of the other railway companies and of the
packers at Winnipeg, I have come to the conclusion that it would
be much better for us to come out in the open in connection with
our interest in the live stock industry in the West. . . ."[1]

The plan set forth by Dennis for the importation and distribution of cattle among the farmers on the prairie was all very well for
those who possessed the means to pay for them. But unfortunately,
in new communities such as prevailed generally in the West, most
farmers, after the initial outlay necessary at the start, had little
capital left to invest in stock of any sort. While the Canadian
Pacific obviously could not undertake to supply the necessary means
to enable settlers on government land to purchase cattle, it could
assist materially those who had purchased land from it. The company which had introduced ready-made farms and the policy of
loans to settlers to provide the necessary buildings on their farms,
the company which, in short, had adopted a policy of selling its land
to settlers only, would likely find a way of rounding out and perfecting that policy by facilitating the acquisition of live stock by its
settlers. To meet this situation, the Department of Natural Resources
lent money to the farmer with which to purchase cattle. The amount
of a given loan was limited to $1,000, secured by lien notes, payable
at the convenience of the settler.[2] Naturally the department selected
with some care the beneficiaries of this policy, and of course it
claimed the right to have some voice in determining the manner in
which the farmer handled his cattle. But in so far as it asserted this

[1] Dennis to Shaughnessy, August 2, 1912, Letter Book 1, M.
[2] Thornton to Cardell, Superintendent of Agencies, May 15, 1913, File No. 507,
D. N. R. Also *Saskatchewan Handbook,* 1913, p. 4. The loans to farmers for the
purchase of live stock are not to be confused with the "loan to settlers" policy,
under which the company advanced money to the settler for buildings and improvements on the land.

right it contributed to better agriculture on its lands. The policy was not philanthropy, but enlightened selfishness on the part of the company. The department dealt leniently with those receiving the loans. Evidence of good faith and an honest effort to meet the obligation within a reasonable period were all that was asked.

While the loan-for-live-stock policy provided for the distribution of cattle to farmers on Canadian Pacific lands, those residing on other lands were still uncared for. Dennis, however, did not lose sight of them. He was interested in the live stock industry of the West in general, not merely on company lands. As a result of a persistent campaign carried on by him for more than a year, local associations were formed at Winnipeg, Regina, Saskatoon, Battleford, Edmonton, Calgary, and Lethbridge for the distribution of stock among farmers, the associations being financed by the banks. These organizations functioned in this regard much as the Department of Natural Resources in respect to Canadian Pacific settlers, and they became important agencies for agricultural betterment throughout the Northwest.

The prominence of the railway in this work on the prairie soon led to calls from British Columbia for assistance. There, settlers in the various river valleys had made the mistake of farmers in the prairie provinces; they had concentrated on one crop, theirs being fruit instead of grain. Those in the Okanagan Valley now appealed to Shaughnessy and Dennis for assistance in the introduction of cattle into their territory.[1] This request placed Dennis in a difficult position. On the one hand he believed strongly that the Okanagan settlers must abandon the single fruit crop in favor of a more diversified agriculture, including live stock, poultry, and dairying. On the other hand, under conditions then existing the farmers had no pasture or fodder crops, and no creameries at which to market dairy produce. An added difficulty was the policy of the Department of Natural Resources of limiting advances of live stock entirely to purchasers of company lands. Should this policy be departed from in British Columbia it would set an awkward precedent east of the mountains. The solution first proposed by Dennis was the formation by valley towns of an association such as existed on the prairie.

[1] This whole matter is fully discussed by Dennis in his letter to Shaughnessy, December 21, 1914, Personal Letter Book 5, M.

When this suggestion failed to bear fruit, he circumvented the difficulty by advancing money not to the settlers directly but to the Okanagan Loan and Investment Company, which was in a position to speak with respect to the reputation of the farmers making application for loans. He further made the advance contingent upon the completion of arrangements for the establishment of a creamery and cold storage plant within the valley. On these conditions the company advanced $25,000 toward the purchase of cattle for the Okanagan Valley settlers.[1] Dennis estimated that this amount would make possible the purchase of 300 cows, a number sufficient to warrant the establishment of the creamery.[2]

Hand in hand with the company's efforts to improve the live stock situation in the West, went renewed emphasis upon the encouragement to alfalfa culture which it had given for the past decade. With the aid of the Department of Natural Resources and of Professor Fairfield, steady progress was made in the growth of this crop in the company's Lethbridge system, until in 1913 some 10,000 acres of alfalfa were harvested in that area. In the western section of the irrigation block an annual alfalfa growing contest was held, which stimulated interest and extended the area devoted to the crop.[3] Loans by the department for the purchase of live stock gave added incentive to the growth of alfalfa. As a further encouragement, the company distributed alfalfa seed in both the eastern and western sections, the total for 1915 amounting to more than 12,000 pounds.[4]

The leadership of Dennis in behalf of agriculture was made apparent in other ways. When he received from the Agricultural Extension Department of the International Harvester Company in Chicago an offer of their coöperation in the Canadian Pacific campaign for better farming and more live stock in the West, Dennis wrote in reply: "We appreciate your offer to coöperate with us in this very important work, but might I be permitted to say that one of the most effective methods which can be adopted by your Company in furthering the work that we have in hand is to exercise some patience with settlers who have purchased farm implements

[1] Ibid.
[2] Dennis to Shaughnessy, February 3, 1915, Letter Book 14, M.
[3] Ibid., September 22, 1913, Letter Book 9, M.
[4] Ibid., September 18, 1916, Letter Book 17, M.

from your Company and owing to crop or other conditions have been unable to meet their payments. I make this suggestion owing to the fact that in several cases which have come to my notice, what would seem to be rather harsh treatment has been taken towards the collection of amounts due for excessive quantities of agricultural machinery sold settlers by your representatives."[1] In other words, the International Harvester could help by exercising restraint in salesmanship and forbearance in collections.

The menace of noxious weeds to sound farming was an ever present one on the prairie. Alert to this danger, Dennis kept a watchful eye out for areas in which the evil was especially pronounced. When the weed situation in the Lethbridge district was particularly bad, he appealed to the Premier of Alberta for drastic action by provincial authorities: "It is quite evident that unless prompt and effective steps are taken that very serious consequences are going to follow, and it would be lamentable that that exceptionally fine area should be destroyed for agricultural purposes owing to failure on the part of land owners to eradicate weeds. As you know, we are doing everything we possibly can to overcome the situation, but what is really needed is prompt and vigorous action on the part of weed inspectors in compelling people who own infested lands to get busy and destroy the weeds."[2]

A cause ever close to Dennis's heart was that of irrigation. A firm believer in its efficacy, even its necessity, in portions of southern Alberta, he never lost faith in it because of momentary discouragements and he never missed an opportunity to further its development. He was convinced of the need of education with respect to irrigation and had confidence in the value of meetings at which the subject was discussed. For years he had followed with interest the meetings of the International Irrigation Congress, and in 1914 he was instrumental in securing its meeting for Calgary. With his solicitation the city, as well as the provinces of Alberta and British Columbia, each contributed $5,000, the Canadian Pacific appropriating a like sum. He looked upon the Congress as a means of giving the

[1] Dennis to International Harvester Company, Agricultural Extension Department, February 25, 1913, Letter Book 4, M.
[2] Dennis to A. L. Sifton, Premier of Alberta, July 24, 1913, Letter Book 8, M.

company's irrigation project some valuable publicity among the 4,000 delegates who would be in attendance.[1] When the province of Alberta was somewhat remiss in the payment of its contribution, Dennis wrote the Premier: "We have not yet heard anything from the Provincial Treasurer relative to the grant to the International Irrigation Congress. From present indication the Congress will be eminently successful in spite of the War situation. We are particularly anxious to make this Congress a success, in view of the necessity for Irrigation made apparent by this year's climatic conditions, and in addition we are going to have a very creditable exhibition of products with a prize list running into several thousand dollars. I trust you will be able to give us a grant of at least $5,000 to help on this important work."[2]

Another organization which received his wholehearted support was the Dry Farming Congress, which held annual meetings in the United States and Canada and which had been an important medium for the intelligent extension of the system of dry farming. For the 1912 meeting of the congress, held in Lethbridge, the Canadian Pacific, at the request of Dennis, contributed $5,000, and an additional $1,000 to clear up the deficit.[3] When a federation of the International Irrigation Congress and the Dry Farming Congress was projected, Dennis took the initiative in enlisting the support of interested and influential persons in both the United States and Canada. Asking the aid of the President of the Soo Line Railway he said: "Both of these Congresses are doing valuable work along the lines of improving agricultural methods whether it be by more intensive cultivation in so-called dry farming districts or the proper method of using water when irrigation is practised, but as they are both dealing with primary matters of agriculture there is no sound reason why as federated Congresses they should not carry more weight and achieve better results."[4] He wrote similar letters to the same general effect to the Ministers of Agriculture of Alberta and Saskatchewan, and to the Presidents of the Great Northern, Northern

[1] Dennis to Shaughnessy, January 30, 1914, Letter Book 10, M.

[2] Dennis to A. L. Sifton, September 14, 1914, Personal Letter Book 5, M.

[3] Dennis to Shaughnessy, November 29, 1912, Letter Book 6, M.

[4] Dennis to E. Pennington, President, Soo Line, November 2, 1914, Personal Letter Book 5, M.

Pacific, Chicago, Burlington and Quincy, Chicago, Milwaukee and St. Paul, and the Spokane International Railway companies.[1]

Better grain selection was encouraged by the Canadian Pacific through prizes offered to boys and girls in schools in a wheat selection contest.[2] The Forestry Branch of the Department of Natural Resources offered $2,400 in cash prizes to farmers raising the best wind-breaks in certain districts.[3] A steer feeding contest for farmers' sons was annually carried on. In the autumn each boy was furnished by the company with eight head of prime feeder steers, to be fed according to his own methods. In the spring, when the steers were sold, the boys received the advance in price. Prizes offered in the various competitions held under the company's auspices aggregated several thousand dollars yearly.[4] At various central points the company still maintained high-grade bulls for service.

When crop failures came, as they sometimes did in young communities, as well as in older ones, the farmers were likely to be short of seed for the next year's planting, and they were apt to be short of cash as well. The year 1914 was such a year in portions of the West. The Dominion Government recognized its obligation to supply seed grain to settlers on homestead land, but it, of course, did not construe this obligation to extend to those who had purchased land from the Canadian Pacific. The Department of Natural Resources, therefore, appropriated $50,000 for the purchase of seed, which was distributed among the farmers by the Agricultural Branch of the department.[5]

In the irrigation block where both odd- and even-numbered sections had been granted to the railway, the company felt itself more than ordinarily responsible for the development of the institutions and agencies of community life. Besides donating land for churches and schools, the railway was asked to make a contribution toward the water supply of one town or the establishment of a creamery

[1] All these letters are to be found in Personal Letter Book 5, M. With the exception of the one to L. W. Hill, of the Great Northern, which is dated October 31, 1914, they bear the date of November 2, 1914.
[2] S. E. Greenway, University of Saskatchewan, to Dennis, March 2, 1914, in which he thanks the Canadian Pacific for sponsoring these contests. File No. 379, D. N. R.
[3] *Saskatchewan Handbook*, 1913, p. 4.
[4] *Ibid.*
[5] Dennis to Shaughnessy, February 3, 1915, Letter Book 14, M.

in another.[1] Especially great was the obligation to support schools in the block in the formative period when settlement was still scattered. In 1913 a grant of $700 was made to each of fourteen school districts. Of this Dennis wrote: "I have recommended that this should be made in the form of a loan, not that I expect we will ever get it repaid, but if we make a straight grant it will soon be forgotten all about, whereas if we make it in the shape of a loan it will be continually before them."[2]

Realizing that those residing on irrigable land were in a somewhat different relationship to the company than the purchasers of other lands, that they were in fact life-tenants of the railway by virtue of the annual water rental, Dennis felt keenly the importance of maintaining a close touch with those settlers. They must be made aware of the company's interest in them, of its partnership with them, as it were. The more intimate the contacts between them and the company, the greater would be the chances that a significant influence could be brought to bear in the agricultural development of the block. To foster closer relations, Dennis instituted meetings during the winter months at various points within the block where short addresses were given by officials of the Department of Natural Resources on the care and feeding of stock, the growth of alfalfa, and other important and timely subjects of interest to the settlers.[3]

At the end of the year 1915 Dennis, in a report to Shaughnessy, reviewed the agricultural policy of the railway for the preceding years.[4] Speaking of the mixed farms he said: "These farms were originally established for the purpose of illustrating, by an object lesson, supplemented by printed bulletins, the fact that mixed farming would pay better than the prevalent system of one-crop farming. The reports submitted, together with the balance sheet for each farm, indicate that this is being amply proved and there is no question that the farms are doing a valuable educational work in encouraging a more sane system of agriculture in all three Provinces." Eleven of the thirteen farms returned a profit, after charging them with 6 per cent interest on the value of the land and improve-

[1] Dennis to Cameron, May 13, 1912, Letter Book 2, M.
[2] Dennis to Naismith, December 6, 1913, Letter Book 10, M.
[3] Dennis to Rutherford, December 29, 1914, Letter Book 14, M.
[4] Dennis to Shaughnessy, January 18, 1916, Letter Book 17, M.

ments and providing a proper amount each year for depreciation of buildings and implements. Of the Animal Husbandry Branch of the Department of Natural Resources, he expressed the belief that no more valuable work was being carried on in the West than the distribution of live stock through that branch.

To December 31, 1918, the department through the Animal Husbandry Branch had expended $468,602 in advances of live stock to settlers and in the promotion of a better live stock situation. Up to that time a total of 16,438 head of live stock had been distributed.[1] By 1921 the expenditures for this purpose had increased to $514,366, while expenditures on agricultural demonstration and experimental work amounted to $971,527, a total of approximately $1,500,000 expended in the cause of improved agriculture.[2] The advances for live stock were, of course, repaid, but the money spent for demonstration and experimental work brought no immediate or direct return and, except for the buildings and improvements on the experimental and mixed farms, was not recoverable by the company. In 1914 the 5 demonstration farms and the 13 mixed farms were carried on the company's books at a figure of $218,000, representing the value of the land, buildings, and other improvements.[3]

This discussion of Canadian Pacific aid to agriculture has been confined to the company's organized activities in that connection. No attempt has been made to include the countless instances of individual assistance which a pioneer railway, built largely through unsettled country and concerned primarily with the rapid development of a profitable traffic, was called upon to make to settlers. The evidence of this form of assistance is extensive, but, because of the scattered nature of it, it has not seemed worth while to attempt to bring it together in this place.

[1] Recapitulation of Land Settlement Work to December 31, 1918, File No. 110, Section 4, M.

[2] *William Pearce Report:* Activities of the C. P. R. in connection with land settlement in western Canada from 1881 to 1921, M.

[3] *Annual Report of Canadian Pacific Railway Company for the fiscal year ended June 30, 1914,* p. 18.

XII

THE DEPARTMENT OF
COLONIZATION

IN THE main, the advent of the World War in 1914 marked the
end of an era in the development of the Canadian West. The
period of the competitive building of railways in advance of settlement was practically over. Virtually all habitable portions of the
prairie had been made accessible to the railway and to markets.
At least a beginning of settlement had been made throughout the
three prairie provinces. Villages and towns, the future centers of
trade and industrial growth, had been laid out, banking facilities
had been extended throughout the West, and wholesale and retail
business had been established.

The significance of what had happened, and was happening, had
not escaped Dennis and Shaughnessy.[1] Dennis realized that for a
decade before the outbreak of the war, developments on the prairie
had been accompanied by a degree of speculation and inflated values
which had resulted in a superstructure built on an insecure foundation. As he expressed it, "the growth of urban centers, cities, towns,
villages, construction of railway mileage, banking facilities, wholesale and retail trade and industrial extension are all in advance of
what is justified by the foundation of agricultural development."[2]
While much effort and vast expenditures by the government and
landowning corporations had produced a large immigration into
the West, with a resulting increase in population, Dennis believed
this increase had not run parallel in urban and rural areas. The
business and laboring classes had increased more rapidly than the

[1] In a long letter to Shaughnessy, December 23, 1914, Personal Letter Book
5, M., Dennis discussed in great detail the existing state of settlement and development in the three prairie provinces.
[2] *Ibid.*

agricultural. As a consequence of this situation, Dennis thought, the West imported a large share of its foodstuffs, except grain, and with the cessation of government, municipal, and railway construction, a serious condition of unemployment in urban centers was inevitable. This necessitated a period of "marking time" until agricultural development could be brought into line with that of the towns and cities. Surrounding every urban center were large areas of unoccupied land, lying unproductive and held at speculative values. Much of the land adjacent to larger centers had been subdivided into town lots and speculatively sold. While this land would not be needed for town extension for years, it was used to swell fictitious assessments and to assist in borrowing money to provide the towns with improvements and facilities of older and larger cities. Industrial development in some of the cities was far in advance of what conditions warranted. Instead of confining manufacture to the raw products of the country, especially those of agriculture and animal industry, plants for the fabrication of imported raw materials had been established, in many cases with evil consequences.

Per capita, the prairie provinces had a greater railway mileage than any similar area in the world. Built largely in advance of settlement, the mere movement of immigrants and their goods, the rapid growth of towns and cities, and governmental and municipal public works had thus far provided traffic for the railway lines. With the inevitable slowing down which was at hand, traffic losses were certain to follow until rural development caught up with urban growth.

Undeniably rural settlement and development had not kept pace with the alienation of land by the government and the sale of it by private corporations. Between 1896 and 1914 the Dominion Government had given away millions of acres, supposedly to homesteaders and settlers; the Canadian Pacific had sold millions more; various land companies had acquired and disposed of vast areas; but western Canada was still far from settled from the point of view of a sane and well-developed agricultural life. Conditions on the prairie at the close of the boom period in 1914 were not unlike those which had prevailed in various portions of the American West at earlier times. There, too, settlement had repeatedly jutted out into the great sea of unoccupied land in periods of boom. There, too, the wily speculator had all too frequently preceded the actual settler, securing title to large areas of the best lands by one device or another, promoting embryonic towns which he hoped would assume metropolitan proportions, and generally inflating values of all forms of property. Too often the land grant railways west of the Mississippi found that after much of their land was sold and the bulk of the government land along their lines had passed into private hands, their territory was but sparsely settled. Large areas of land had been held for appreciation in value, without improvement or cultivation. Many homesteaders had not been *bona fide* farmers. Large numbers of them mortgaged their homesteads to loan companies immediately upon acquiring title. Undoubtedly there was much truth in the remark of the land commissioner of an American road that after title to the land had passed from the railway and the government, the railway's job of settling its territory really began.

The impression of Dennis with respect to prairie conditions was completely confirmed by a report which William Pearce submitted to the Department of Natural Resources in the spring of 1915.[1] Equipped with experience accumulated in the service of both the government and the Canadian Pacific in the West, Pearce was commissioned to make a tour of central Alberta, primarily with a view to examining conditions obtaining on railway lands held under contract for sale, and making recommendations in regard thereto. His mission was designed to supply information which would enable the department to deal intelligently with outstanding contracts, especially those which were badly in arrears. As he proceeded with his investigation of company lands, however, Pearce became more and more convinced that the chief problem in improving the conditions of rural settlement was that presented by lands alienated by homestead right or by half breed or other scrip. He reported that 50 per cent of such lands were unoccupied. Of the remaining lands, only a small portion showed a substantial amount of cultivation and development. The degree of settlement on homestead lands varied greatly from district to district. Some areas were fairly well occupied, while others, equally attractive, were almost wholly without inhabitants. This latter condition was particularly pronounced

[1] Memorandum by William Pearce to P. L. Naismith, May 21, 1915, File No. 804, D. N. R.

around Bawlf, Vegreville, Innisfail, Vermilion, and Lloydminster. In the vicinity of Vegreville the situation was especially bad because the even-numbered sections had been scripped, while the railway sections, originally the property of the Canadian Pacific, were being held by a syndicate with a view to their appreciation in value.

Upon inquiry as to what had become of the homesteaders, Pearce found that "probably one-third of the men who made entry to the land never intended to become permanent agriculturists. They 'earned their patent,' as it was termed, with the least possible delay. As soon as they had title, they either sold or mortgaged it for what they could get, and a large portion of them left the country. Many are reported to have gone to the north to repeat the operation, others drift to the large urban centers." The lax administration of the homestead act was, in Pearce's opinion, responsible for this situation. Pearce found, too, that the country had suffered from the "wave of insanity" with respect to town lots which had swept over the prairie. Many men had traded their farms for town lots in Saskatoon, Edmonton, and Vancouver, only to wish that they were now back on the land. The unoccupied land was largely in the hands of mortgagees or was destined soon to be there. In most cases the mortgages were held by large mortgage companies.

The problem confronting the Canadian Pacific was that of correcting the unsatisfactory conditions analyzed by Dennis and described by Pearce. Dennis believed the company, by its land policy, its system of demonstration and mixed farms, its ready-made and improved farms, and its advances of live stock, was doing more than its share to remedy the existing evils. But it could not do the job alone. Coördination of effort and the closest possible coöperation between governmental agencies and private interests were necessary. Fortunately there was a growing realization among municipalities, banks, boards of trade, and provincial governments of the urgent need for action. In February, 1915, the provincial authorities of Alberta called a convention which met at the town of Olds to consider the question of vacant lands within the province.[1] As a result of the meeting the Alberta Rural Development League was organized. The league planned to form committees in all the urban

---

[1] This is fully described in a letter of Dennis to Shaughnessy, February 13, 1915, Personal Letter Book 5, M.

centers and to interest them in the colonization of the unoccupied lands adjoining the towns and cities. According to Dennis the plan was very similar to that employed by the Soo line in settling the unoccupied areas tributary to its lines in North Dakota.

Dennis endeavored to enlist the interest and support of men of influence and official position, among them C. A. Magrath, who had been an officer in the West with the Alberta Railway and Irrigation Company and who was now a member of the International Joint Commission.[1] He also discussed the question at length with Sir Robert Borden, the Prime Minister, who expressed the belief that increased settlement of the West was the most important single problem confronting the government, since on its solution depended the future of the newer railways in the West.[2] Dennis forwarded to the Premier a number of memoranda and statistical tables bearing upon the question.[3] He urged upon Sir Robert "in the strongest possible manner" that a new department of immigration and colonization should be created by the Dominion Government to deal with the problem of western settlement at the close of the war.

Various officials of the company were becoming increasingly convinced of the evil effects of unoccupied land in the West. In September, 1916, President Shaughnessy in a speech at Calgary suggested that instead of sending immigrants to distant regions, remote from transportation facilities, the government should commandeer the vacant land held by corporations and individuals for speculative purposes near existing lines of railway.[4] Professor W. J. Elliott, who had played such a prominent rôle in connection with the company's agricultural work in the West, observed that the railway's policy of hand-picking settlers applied only to its own lands; that the railway mileage affected by this policy represented but a small fraction of the total Canadian Pacific lines in the three prairie provinces; and that along the bulk of the company's lines in the West virtually no

[1] Dennis to C. A. Magrath, June 2, 1915, File No. 379, Immigration and Colonization, M., in which he relates in detail his conference with Sir Robert Borden, the Prime Minister, in regard to the problem of western settlement.
[2] *Ibid.*
[3] Dennis to Sir Robert Borden, June 7, 1915, *ibid.*
[4] Referred to in *Report of Samuel Altman on Foreign Colonies in Western Canada*, 1916, M. This report consists of a series of letters and lists of names by Altman, together with a special report on prepaid business.

effort was being made to encourage and direct the settlement of land adjacent to the railway.[1] He suggested the creation of a "Free Bureau of Agricultural Information" to provide data respecting the district surrounding every town served by the Canadian Pacific on the prairie. This would provide the machinery for placing a desirable settler on every parcel of vacant land within 10 miles of the company's lines.

In the same year Samuel Altman, formerly a representative of the Canadian Pacific in Europe, was engaged by the Department of Natural Resources to make a survey of the possibilities of an extension of settlement in foreign colonies in the prairie provinces. Altman estimated the land held by speculators as about twice that actually occupied. He recommended the listing of the vacant lands in the offices of the department. After interviewing and listing the names and addresses of some 1,540 farmers of Continental European origin, he suggested that the department should get in touch with them, obtain the names of friends and relatives in Europe or the United States who would like to come to Canada, and endeavor to move them to the West. He believed that many of the farmers listed by him would gladly provide prepaid tickets for friends and relatives.[2]

Realizing the important rôle which prepaid business played in immigration from Europe, Altman urged that the company give increased attention to it, that it be thoroughly organized, and that agents be appointed in all foreign settlements in the West to secure this form of assistance to prospective settlers. All in all, the report submitted by Altman was another indication of the imminent change by the Canadian Pacific to a broader and more comprehensive settlement policy, in which an effort would be made to encourage and promote the occupation of privately owned lands.

In 1916 this growing interest of company officials in the problem of settling the privately owned lands in the West resulted in the organization of the Department of Colonization and Development, with headquarters at Montreal, and with Dennis as the Chief Com-

[1] Elliott to Dennis, December 26, 1916, File No. 110, Section 2, M.

[2] *Report of Samuel Altman on Foreign Colonies in Western Canada*, 1916. This is a MS. account in the archives of the Department of Colonization in Montreal.

missioner. Although the new department was intended to supplement the work of the Department of Natural Resources at Calgary in the cause of land settlement, the line of demarcation between the two agencies was not yet sharply defined. They were under the supervision of an advisory committee of company officials and worked in close coöperation, but whether the Montreal organization would do more than to secure purchasers for Canadian Pacific lands administered by the Calgary office was as yet undetermined. The Department of Colonization and Development, however, took over immediately the agency force in the United States and thus became the chief medium of the Canadian Pacific for the recruiting of settlers for western Canada.

The new department quickly showed that it was to be no mere paper organization. Knowing that the Railway Lands Branch of the Department of the Interior had complete lists of all absentee owners of unimproved land in the three western provinces, company officials planned to obtain duplicate copies of these lists, from which they would prepare a mailing roster of owners who were *bona fide* farmers living in the United States.[1] With these men the Canadian Pacific would communicate and offer them its services in locating on their lands in the West. Although the Ottawa authorities at first demurred to the railway's request for this information, they readily complied when Dennis assured them the Canadian Pacific would not show preference to lands tributary to its own line in the West. In this way the Department of Colonization and Development secured the names and addresses of some 50,000 absentee owners of land in the Canadian West. From these the department prepared a list of 7,000 names of the more likely prospects residing in the United States. In the early months of 1917 it sent letters to these owners, telling them the Canadian Pacific had recently created a new department with the primary object of assisting them in locating on their Canadian farms. The letters further advised them that if they would answer certain questions, the department would not only do everything possible to assist them, but would have a representative call on them at their convenience.

[1] Dennis to F. C. C. Lynch, Superintendent, Railway Lands Branch, Department of the Interior, December 9 and 21, 1916, Letter Book, December 1, 1916–February 27, 1917, M.

It would be interesting to know the results which would have attended this first concrete and definite attempt on the part of the Canadian Pacific to promote the settlement of privately owned lands in the West could it have been made under normal conditions. As it was, the confusion of the war period, and particularly the entrance of the United States into the war in April, 1917, so completely disrupted the plan that it was productive of no appreciable result. Nevertheless, the idea is significant as showing that the Canadian Pacific was no longer concerned merely with general immigration to western Canada, combined with the sale and settlement of its own lands. It was now clear that the company appreciated thoroughly the importance of settling the vast area held by absentee owners, some of whom were mere speculators, while others were actual farmers who for various reasons had been unable to occupy their holdings.

Meanwhile, Dennis had not permitted the Dominion Government to lose interest in the problem of settling the privately owned lands in the West. He had been active in impressing upon Sir Robert Borden the importance of creating a Dominion Department of Immigration and Colonization, and, following the formation of the department, he maintained a friendly contact with James Calder, the first minister to preside over it. In February, 1918, Dennis forwarded to Calder copies of existing regulations covering the sale and colonization of Canadian Pacific lands, a pamphlet relative to returned veterans colonies planned by the railway company, and a publication dealing with abandoned farms available for colonization in the eastern provinces of Canada.[1] At the same time he arranged for William Pearce to go to Ottawa, with a full set of charts which he had prepared illustrating existing conditions with respect to land settlement in the West. Pearce was to remain in Ottawa for a time, in order that he might be available to the minister for interpretation of the charts. With the concurrence of Shaughnessy, Dennis also forwarded to Calder a proposal for a "Holding Company" in whose hands the lands available for settlement in the western provinces could be placed, together with an outline of the terms upon which the lands should be sold for colonization.

[1] Dennis to James Calder, Minister of Immigration and Colonization, February 6, 1918, File No. 110, Section 2, M.

Although Calder was unable to secure the enactment of legislation embodying the essential features of this proposal of Dennis, the minister did arrange an Interprovincial Conference at Ottawa in November, 1918, at which provincial cabinet ministers and members of the Dominion Government were in attendance.[1] At this conference Calder presented a plan for coöperative land settlement, the purpose of which was the development of a national sentiment in favor of increased production; the encouragement of a movement from urban to rural districts; the securing of a large movement of settlers to vacant lands; and the creation of conditions under which small holders might become owners.

Calder's plan included provision for the holding company suggested by Dennis earlier in the year, but it differed from the proposal of Dennis in certain important respects. It contemplated the compulsory fixing of a price upon all unoccupied and unimproved land, as well as a tax thereon, regardless of the willingness of the owner to sell. That this latter idea was in the air at the time is shown by the enactment of so-called wild land taxes by Alberta and Saskatchewan. To the Calder proposal the Canadian Pacific could not be indifferent. Its application would not only require the company to place a price on its land, but it would materially increase the tax burden of the railway after 1924 when the tax exemption expired on the remaining portion of the land grant. The Ottawa conference of Calder is important, however, not by virtue of any definite and concrete steps to which it led, but because it indicated a widespread realization of the fact that unoccupied privately owned land constituted something of a national problem.

With the termination of the war the Canadian Pacific was confronted with the necessity of deciding upon the colonization policy it should adopt under peace time conditions. What proportion of its energies and its means should it employ in the promotion of general immigration to Canada, what to the sale and settlement of its remaining lands, and what to the colonization of vacant lands in the West owned by private parties? Before the war it had confined itself to the first two of these activities. It had contributed in an important degree to the tide of immigration which had poured into

[1] Montreal *Gazette*, November 21, 1918. Also Memorandum by E. G. White for President Shaughnessy, December 10, 1918, File No. 110, Section 2, M.

Canada; it had sold millions of acres of land and had actually colonized a large area. But years of tireless effort by the company had not brought the degree of settlement which it had hoped for in the territory tributary to its lines. As a consequence, company officials had throughout the war years given much thought to the question of increased settlement. With this situation in mind, too, they had created the Department of Colonization and Development in 1916.

The return of peace in 1919, however, found division of counsel among those of the company whose duty it was to determine the scope of the colonization campaign to be waged by the railway. Especially was there difference of opinion as to the use to which the United States organization should be put. Should it be confined to the recruiting of settlers for Canadian Pacific lands or should it also devote its energies to the settlement of all vacant lands tributary to the main and branch lines of the railway? Against the latter course several objections were urged. The company should not dissipate its energies between the sale of its own lands and the settlement of those privately owned. Since a large proportion of the unsold lands of the railway would soon become taxable, effort should be concentrated solely on the sale of those lands.[1] A colonization staff devoted to the settlement of vacant lands would be tantamount to the duplication of the sales branch of the Department of Natural Resources. The United States commission agents would not have the same incentive to sell Canadian Pacific lands if they also had the opportunity to sell other and possibly more desirable land. Finally, it was contended, the enforcement of settlement conditions on privately owned lands would be impossible.

Dennis, with his customary support of a vigorous policy, dissented emphatically from the views expressed above. Answering the specific objections to the colonization of privately owned lands, he felt the large area of this land tributary to the company's lines rendered its settlement as vital to the interests of the railway as the sale of Canadian Pacific land remote from the company's lines. As

[1] Memorandum by Dennis for Shaughnessy, July 7, 1919, File No. 110, Section 3, M. In this Dennis sets forth in detail the various objections advanced by P. L. Naismith and Sir Augustus Nanton to the use of the company's agency force for the colonization of other than railway lands.

for the taxation of the railway's lands, Dennis observed that, because
of inferior quality, a large area of the remaining lands would still be
unsold in 1924 when they became liable to taxation, even if the
company concentrated its attention on the sale of its own land.
Duplication of organization was not to be feared since the colonization staff in western Canada would deal only with clients from the
United States, whom the sales staff of the Department of Natural
Resources was unable to interest in railway land. To obviate the
possibility of loss of interest by the commission agents in the United
States in the sale of railway land, Dennis would pay a smaller commission on the sale of privately owned land. Under these conditions
they would have every incentive to endeavor to sell company land.
Only when unsuccessful in that regard would they sell other lands
at a lower commission.

Dennis, however, did not confine himself to a refutation of the
views of others. In his opinion there was one compelling argument
in favor of the use of the agency organization in the United States
to secure settlers for privately owned lands along the railway. During
the two previous years that organization had not been particularly
successful in securing buyers for railway lands. Between January 1,
1917 and May 31, 1919 they had brought about 5,000 clients to
western Canada, of whom only about 1,200 had purchased Canadian
Pacific land. Some had fallen into the hands of local realtors who
had sold them other lands, but many had returned empty handed.
Dennis doubted whether the interest and morale of the commission
agents could be maintained in the face of the declining proportion
of sales they were making. An agent who spent money and time in
interesting a client, only to lose him in the end, could not be
expected to retain his enthusiasm for the sale of railway land. The
danger was that, in the face of continued discouragement, agents
would ask to be released from their contracts, with the resulting
disintegration of the agency organization.

Acting as arbiter of the conflicting views, Shaughnessy decided
that for the season of 1919 at least the organization in the United
States must confine itself to the sale and settlement of Canadian
Pacific lands.[1] A special effort was to be made to sell the Lloyd-

[1] Dennis to M. E. Thornton, Superintendent of U. S. Agencies, July 17, 1919,
ibid.

minster and Battleford blocks.[1] Special advertising matter was carried in the agricultural press of the United States; leaflet literature devoted solely to those districts was prepared; brief stories descriptive of the blocks were issued from the Chicago and New York offices; short films were distributed among district representatives; and a commission agents' excursion to the blocks was conducted as part of the campaign for the disposition of those areas.[2] In this way the Canadian Pacific launched its last great drive to sell its land to American farmers.

Not for long, however, was the Department of Colonization and Development to devote its energies chiefly to the sale and settlement of the company's land. With the depression which settled upon American agriculture after 1921, the western states ceased to play the important part they had once enjoyed in swelling the tide of immigration to the prairies. In the face of this changed situation, the American organization of the department diminished in importance, and the chief scene of the company's activities, as well as the main source of immigrants, became the British Isles and Continental Europe. Gradually, the department became primarily concerned with the settlement of privately owned lands.

During this post-war period the railway had, of course, to adapt its colonization activities to the immigration policy of the Dominion Government. At the close of the war it was apparent to the government that new conditions called for new policies with respect to immigration. The country's first obligation was to re-absorb into its economic life the thousands of returning soldiers. The remaining government lands were largely remote from railways, and the public, now fully aware of the folly of excessive railway building during the pre-war years, was in no mood to sanction further construction designed to open distant areas of the West to settlement. Free land, therefore, largely ceased to absorb immigrants. As a result, the Dominion Department of Immigration and Colonization for several years confined its efforts to those able to purchase land, to agricultural workers and to domestics. This policy, combined with high costs of transportation and depreciated currencies abroad, brought about a sharp decline in the movement of people into Canada as

[1] *Ibid.*
[2] Memorandum of W. J. Gerow for Dennis, September 4, 1919, *ibid.*

compared with the years before 1914. The total immigration for 1923 was only 72,887 souls.

By that year, however, returning prosperity and the absorption of surplus labor had produced a change in sentiment with respect to immigration. While there was no popular demand for letting down the bars to Europeans indiscriminately, there was widespread opinion in favor of the admission into Canada of those who could be readily assimilated to the Canadian population. The exclusion of such people, it was thought, resulted in an economic and social loss to the Dominion. Especially strong was the feeling that thousands of British families would make desirable settlers if only the means could be found of meeting the costs of transportation to Canada.

The new immigration policy adopted by the government was selective in character. Gone were the days when just any person of sound body and mind, with money sufficient for his passage, was admitted in the confident belief that he would make a place for himself in the rural economy of the country. Either the immigrant must convince the authorities that a position awaited him in Canada, or he must have sufficient funds to prevent him from becoming a public charge while seeking employment. The corollary of this was that the gates would open and close with the swing of the economic pendulum. In periods of prosperity increasing numbers would be admitted; with the onset of depression, numbers would be restricted.

British immigrants received distinct preference and encouragement. Under the Empire Settlement Agreement assisted passage was provided in 1923 for married farmers and their families, for single agricultural laborers, for domestics, and for juveniles between the ages of 14 and 17. Adults received a loan to cover the cost of transportation, while the juveniles enjoyed free passage.[1] In 1926 a new passage agreement substituted for the loan a low ocean rate, first of £3, later of £2, a figure so nominal as to be within the reach of virtually every potential immigrant. This arrangement was made possible by the contributions and rebates of the British and Dominion Governments and the steamship companies.

Not only did Dominion policy give preferential treatment to

[1] *The Canada Year Book* (1926), pp. 182-83.

British subjects emigrating to Canada, but it included, as a further encouragement, various plans for land settlement. Under the 3,000 Family Scheme, British families brought to Canada at the special steamship rates were located on lands designed originally for soldier settlement. The British Government provided each family with $1,500 for stock and equipment which, with the price of the farm, was to be repaid in yearly installments extending over a 25-year period. The Dominion Government supplied, free of charge, additional assistance in the form of selection, settlement, and supervision.[1] Under this agreement 500 British families came to Canada the first year and more than 1,000 the second. Another plan for fostering British settlement was the British-Dominion-Provincial Land Settlement Scheme. Under this, the Provincial Government provided the farm, the British Government made available $1,500 for stock and equipment, and the Dominion Government recruited the settler and supervised his settlement on the land.[2]

Particular attention was given to the training and placement of boys, for whom "training farms" were maintained in Canada. The Dominion and Provincial Governments each contributed $10 per boy toward the operation of these farms, while the British Government provided $20 per boy. Still another scheme was designed to establish on their own farms British boys with the necessary Canadian farming experience and with savings of $500. The British Government lent $1,250, the Dominion Government, $1,000, and the Provincial Government, $250, which with the boy's nest egg made $3,000 available for settling him on a farm.[3]

British settlers coming forward under these schemes were located on privately owned land rather than on homesteads. To facilitate the successful establishment of them in their new homes, the gov-

[1] *Ibid.*

[2] *Select Standing Committee on Agriculture and Colonization, Minutes of Proceedings and Evidence and Report* (Ottawa, 1928), p. vii; hereafter referred to as *Select Standing Committee on Agriculture and Colonization.* This is the record of an exhaustive hearing before the Dominion House of Commons on the subject of immigration and colonization, conducted in 1928. Twenty-nine witnesses, including high officials of the Canadian Pacific, appeared before the committee. The first six pages of the report contain a statement of the conditions under which people of the various countries were admitted to Canada, in accordance with the immigration laws.

[3] *Ibid.*

ernment converted the machinery of the Soldier Settlement Board
into the Land Settlement Branch of the Department of Immigration
and Colonization.[1] This branch directed new settlers to desirable
lands and safeguarded "them from exploitation in the purchase
price of their farms." The Land Settlement Branch enjoyed the
assistance in various districts of advisory settlement boards composed
of mortgage and loan men, as well as farmers, who gave advice with
respect to the quality and the fairness of the price of privately
owned lands listed with the branch. Especial encouragement was
given to the settlement of families and groups of friends and
kinsfolk.

This aid to immigrants from Great Britain reflected the desire of
Canadian public opinion that the country should remain primarily
British in the make-up of its population. It was recognized, however,
that the industrious and thrifty people from northern Europe were
excellent material for the building of a nation. Government immigration policy classified Norway, Sweden, Denmark, Finland, Germany, Switzerland, Holland, Belgium, and France as "preferred
countries." All citizens or subjects of these countries were admitted
if mentally and physically fit, and capable of supporting themselves
until employment was obtained.[2] The average minimum ocean rate
from these countries was $120 and there were neither special rates
nor assisted passages from them to Canada.

It was the people from eastern and southern Europe whose admission into the Dominion provoked the chief discussion on the part
of the Canadian public. On the one hand was the fear that these
people, settled in large colonies in the West, would become but
slightly assimilated to Canadian ways and habits of thought. On the
other hand was the view, voiced a generation earlier by Sir Clifford
Sifton, that what Canada needed was the "man with the sheep-skin
coat and the big, broad wife." Regardless of the merits of the controversy, Austria, Hungary, Poland, Roumania, Lithuania, Esthonia,
Latvia, Bulgaria, Jugoslavia, and Czechoslovakia were classed as
"non-preferred countries." From them the government admitted
only agricultural and domestic workers, and those of a prescribed
relationship to persons already legally admitted from those coun-

[1] *The Canada Year Book* (1926), p. 183.
[2] *Select Standing Committee on Agriculture and Colonization*, p. vi.

tries. Exceptions, however, might be made in special cases where the Minister of Immigration was convinced of a definite need in Canada for the labor or service of these people. The average minimum ocean rate from these countries was $135, with no special rates or inducements of any sort.

All citizens of the United States were privileged to emigrate to Canada, if in good physical and mental health and possessed of sufficient funds to prevent them from becoming public charges. No passports were required of American immigrants.

Beginning in 1923 the government, the railways, and other private agencies actively solicited immigration from Great Britain and the preferred countries. Organizations were maintained in those countries and Canadian propaganda was carried on, in so far as the laws of those states permitted. Prior to 1925 no particular effort was made to solicit immigrants from the non-preferred countries. If agricultural workers and domestics came of their own volition, or with the aid of relatives or friends in Canada, they were received. By 1925, however, the evident fact that only a limited immigration from the British Isles and the preferred countries could be expected brought a change in attitude and policy with respect to emigrants from eastern and southern Europe.

On September 1, 1925, the Dominion Government, through the Minister of Immigration and Colonization, entered into the so-called "Railways Agreement" with the Canadian Pacific and the Canadian National Railways. Designed to avoid all duplication of effort as between the government and the railways in the conduct of immigration work in the non-preferred countries, the railways agreement was a recognition by Ottawa authorities of the fact that the railway companies had a "special interest in the settlement of available unoccupied lands" and by reason of their "transportation facilities by land and sea" were specially "qualified to procure, select and settle immigrants" on the land. The government authorized the railways for a period of two years to invite citizens or residents of the non-preferred countries to emigrate to Canada and to settle there as "agriculturists, agricultural workers and domestic servants."[1] The railways, on their part, agreed to invite only persons of the specified classes, and to transport to the countries of origin all those

[1] *Ibid.*, p. 733, for the agreement.

who, refusing to engage in agriculture or domestic service, became public charges within one year from their admission to Canada.

The agreement was subsequently renewed for a period of three years from October 1, 1927, but in a somewhat revised form.[1] Cash nominations and prepaid applications for the admission of single men and men unaccompanied by their families must come from persons actually engaged in farming in Canada, who desired to bring relatives or friends to join them in employment on the land. As an additional safeguard, nominations and applications must be made on forms provided by the Department of Immigration. The railways were so to restrict the issuing of occupational certificates as to prevent agricultural families and workers from arriving at seasons when they could not be successfully placed on the land.

Such, in brief, was the immigration policy of Canada in the postwar years. Into this framework the Canadian Pacific was forced to fit its own plans. As the policy was a selective one, emphasizing placement of the immigrant in employment on the land, the railway must maintain an elaborate machinery not only for recruitment but also for establishing the newcomers in gainful pursuits. It could ill afford to risk governmental disapproval by bringing forward persons who became public charges. Merely to transplant the immigrant to Canadian shores was not enough. As these people were largely without either the means or the experience which would make them desirable settlers on the company's lands, it sought to secure agricultural employment for them or to facilitate the location of them in groups on privately owned lands.

The necessary machinery the company provided through its Department of Colonization and Development. Attached to the Montreal office was a superintendent of colonization, whose desk served as a clearing house for settlement opportunities, nominations of colonists, and applications for farm laborers.[2] He also had charge of the port staff, composed of capable linguists who met incoming ships, assisted colonists in going through the customs, boarding the proper

[1] *Ibid.*, pp. 732-33, for the modifications in the agreement.
[2] The abundant records of the Department of Colonization and Development in Montreal reveal very clearly the organization and operation of the department. For an excellent statement in brief compass see the testimony of E. W. Beatty, J. S. Dennis, and J. N. K. Macalister before the *Select Standing Committee on Agriculture and Colonization, passim.*

trains, and other details connected with the last lap of their journey to the new home.

At Montreal the department maintained a Publicity Branch, responsible for the preparation and issuance of all literature and the placing of advertising in Canada, the United States, and Great Britain. The branch issued *Agricultural and Industrial Progress in Canada*, a monthly publication devoted to the dissemination of the latest information regarding agricultural and business opportunities and developments in the Dominion.[1] Individual industries were dealt with in a comprehensive way in articles of about 700 words, which the press was free to copy with or without credit. A weekly supplement of the bulletin was issued in a convenient form for use by newspapers as "fillers." A daily news sheet of ten items was compiled and sent to certain newspapers and periodicals, as well as to press correspondents in Canada, London, New York, and Chicago.

The department maintained a large library of motion picture films, illustrative of Canadian conditions and opportunities, with branch libraries in London and Winnipeg. The films, covering 35 topics, were available for schools, theaters, clubs, societies and boards of trade, and were extensively used, of course, by the department staff in lecturing campaigns. A Bureau of Information at Montreal, with branches in London and Chicago, had for its slogan "ask the Canadian Pacific about Canada." This elicited thousands of inquiries which were answered through the up-to-date data and statistics kept on file. An Exhibits Branch maintained 17 permanent agricultural exhibits in Canada, 13 in the United States, and 3 in Europe, together with large numbers of portable display cases used by the staff in the British Isles.

Supplementing these various means of acquainting the world with Canadian opportunities was the Development Branch, with a staff of expert geologists, mining engineers, and other specialists devoting their time and talent to the gathering of data and the preparation of reports on mining and manufacturing developments and possibilities. This information was furnished free of cost to those unable to secure professional advice through other channels. Up to 1928 reports had been prepared and published on 59 different subjects, the reports being revised up to date each year.

[1] *Ibid.*, p. 231, testimony of Macalister.

In Canada, the Department of Colonization and Development maintained sub-headquarters at Winnipeg, with district offices at Montreal, Toronto, Winnipeg, Saskatoon, Edmonton, Calgary, and Vancouver. Each of these offices was in charge of an assistant superintendent of colonization, a man of long experience in the land settlement work of the Canadian Pacific. Attached to each of the district offices was a staff of travelling colonization agents. Through their own efforts, combined with those of affiliated organizations and of Canadian Pacific station agents, they sought out and developed the settlement opportunities in Canada.

The affiliated organizations were among the most distinctive, as well as the most important, parts of the company's colonization machinery. Before the war, Dennis and his associates in the Department of Natural Resources had realized that existing settlements, particularly of foreign nationalities, constituted one of the most effective media through which the railway could extend settlement in the West. As a result of this conviction, the department had organized the various foreign settlements into "Extension of Settlement Clubs," whose function it was to encourage and aid their friends and relatives in coming to the Canadian West. In the post-war period these clubs appeared in the old rôle but under new names.

There were certain organizations or societies of a general character whose activities were either inter-provincial or coextensive with a particular province. There were some 25 of these, conspicuous among them being the Scottish Immigrant Aid Society, the Lutheran Immigration Board, the Canadian Mennonite Board of Colonization, the German Catholic Board, the Danish Immigrant Aid Society, and the Atlantis Hungarian Board. Of the total, 19 were situated in the 3 prairie provinces. More nearly resembling the "Extension of Settlement Clubs" were the local colonization boards which in 1928 numbered some 170, a large majority of them located on the prairie. These local boards were formed by public-spirited citizens of the locality, largely upon the initiative and with the encouragement of the Department of Colonization. They were composed of farmers, merchants, and bankers who realized the need of increased settlement upon the unoccupied or partially developed lands of their community. In some cases they were able to finance themselves; in others, they received financial assistance from the Department of Colonization and Development. In the words of a high official of the department, "they make a survey of the settlement opportunities in their district, farms which are available for sale or for rent, or on assisted settlement terms. They carry on a campaign amongst the residents of the district and get them to get in touch with their friends or relatives in the United States, in the British Isles, or on the Continent, who may be induced to come forward and settle in their community or district." The boards obtained from the farmers the applications for farm and domestic help, as well as the nominations of friends and relatives in Europe who were desirous of emigrating to Canada. The data thus gathered was sent to the district office of the department, whence it passed through the Montreal headquarters to the European organization.

Closely associated in the work were the station agents of the railway in the West and the Steamship Department of the Canadian Pacific. In 1928 there were in the province of Saskatchewan alone some 215 station agents actively coöperating by accepting and forwarding to the Department of Colonization applications for farm labor and nominations of prospective immigrants. The rôle of the steamship department was an especially important one. On all nominations which resulted in the movement of the designated person from Europe to Canada by way of the company's ships, the steamship department paid a commission to the society or local colonization board through which the nomination came. Funds derived in this manner defrayed in part the expenses incurred by the various organizations in the cause of increased settlement in their communities. The commissions ranged from $2.50 on settlers from the British Isles to $5.00 for continental immigrants. This discrepancy, however, was in no way indicative of the relative value placed upon the two types. In view of the substantial contribution made by the Canadian Pacific to effect the £2 rate on British immigrants, the $2.50 commission was proportionately larger than the $5.00 for continentals who paid from $125 to $140 for their passage. In either case, however, the steamship division served as an important adjunct to the Department of Colonization and Development.

The machinery thus far described served effectively to recruit immigrants, to place them in agricultural employment in Canada, and to find settlement opportunities for them on vacant and unimproved land in the communities where their friends or relatives resided. There was still needed, however, an organization which could aid in the location of families, singly or in groups, on improved lands in the West requiring more careful and intensive cultivation than they had received in the past. Upon the return of Dennis from military service in Russia in 1919, a meeting was held in Calgary of those interested in the larger question of land settlement in western Canada generally.[1] When asked to express his views on this occasion, Dennis stressed the need for an organization which would systematically undertake the settlement of the undeveloped areas tributary to existing lines of railway. This need was the more imperative, he asserted, because of the excessive railway mileage on the prairie in proportion to population. As a result of a memorandum prepared by Dennis, a committee was formed for the purpose of creating a Western Canada Colonization Association. Provided with a charter, this committee appealed to people throughout Canada for support of the undertaking. Dennis insisted it should be a citizens' movement, in which Canadians, without respect to section, should interest themselves. Participation by the Dominion and Provincial Governments and by the railways was to be definitely excluded.

The association was launched on this basis and promptly began to solicit funds from individuals and organizations, the goal being a million-dollar war chest. Successful in its efforts to secure subscriptions in the West, it turned to eastern Canada, where individuals and banks swelled the total to $1,200,000. Within a year or so, many of the subscribers became displeased with the manner in which the organization was being administered. There was strong objection to the extravagant claims made with respect to the financial prospects. Equally pronounced was the disapproval of the participation of the provincial governments in the administration of the concern, which was denounced as a breach of agreement jus-

[1] *Address by Col. J. S. Dennis, Delivered at Opening of New Offices of Canada Colonization Association, at Winnipeg,* 1927 (Winnipeg, 1927), p. 4. In this address, Dennis reviewed the early history of the Canada Colonization Association.

tifying withdrawal of private subscribers from further support of the organization.

With the release of the subscribers, the Canadian Pacific, the Canadian National Railways, and the Dominion Government took it over, with Sir Augustus Nanton as President. During the year in which this agreement was in effect the government bore 50 per cent of the expense while the railway companies assumed equally the responsibility for the remainder. This arrangement, however, was of brief duration. After one year the Dominion Government withdrew to form its own Land Settlement Branch. The two railways then carried on for another year, when the Canadian National abandoned the project in order to establish a Land Settlement Association.

This crisis in the affairs of the organization naturally raised the question whether the Canadian Pacific should assume single-handed the financial responsibility which its continuance would involve. Doubt on this score, however, was dispelled when Dennis was able to show President Beatty figures indicating that some 25,000,000 acres of land tributary to existing lines of railway were available for immediate settlement. Beatty decided to continue his support for at least a year. T. O. F. Herzer, American-born, of German-Danish descent, with a wide knowledge of western Canada gained from long connection with the Canadian Pacific, was appointed manager, and the Canada Colonization Association entered upon a new and active phase of its career.

Proceeding slowly for a time, the association's first objective was to efface the unfavorable impression of it which leading men in western Canada had formed as a result of its earlier policies and practices. Through the elevation of Dennis to the presidency and the selection of a board composed entirely of Canadian Pacific representatives of long interest and experience in western Canada, it won the confidence of influential elements, east and west. In the middle of the decade of the twenties, therefore, this agency was prepared to play an important rôle in the settlement of the privately owned lands in Canadian Pacific territory throughout the Canadian West.

While the Canada Colonization Association was thus evolving as an adjunct of the Department of Colonization and Development, that department itself was paving the way for an important movement of people from Continental Europe which was to give the association ample opportunity to test its machinery for land settlement. We have seen that in the early part of the war Dennis was greatly interested in the prospect of moving large numbers of German Mennonites from Russia to western Canada. After prolonged negotiations the plan came to nought in the confusion and uncertainty attending developments in Russia during the year 1917. The close of the war found the Mennonites in Russia in such a pathetic state as to enlist the sympathy of their brethren in Canada, who promptly sought to devise ways and means of rescuing their Russian co-religionists from their sad plight.

In March, 1922, the Dominion Minister of Immigration and Colonization in Ottawa was waited upon by three prominent representatives of the Mennonite church, who asked the government to lift the ban upon Mennonite immigration to Canada and requested assistance in moving the distressed people from Russia. The Prime Minister promised to remove the restrictions upon Mennonite immigration, while the Minister of Immigration gave the Mennonite representatives letters of introduction to Dennis, the Chief Commissioner of the Department of Colonization and Development of the Canadian Pacific.[1]

More than 100,000 of the Mennonites in Russia were reported to be desirous of emigrating to Canada. The problem was how to finance the movement of such a group. It was the hope of the Mennonite representatives that the immigrants might be located on lands which the old-colony Mennonites were vacating in Manitoba. These lands, it was alleged, could be purchased, with their improvements, at $25.00 per acre. With the sum of $150,000 a village could be purchased.[2] They would then mortgage the land at the purchase price, which was about one-half its real value, and sell the mortgages to Mennonite people in Canada and the United States.

---

[1] See two letters from Charles Stewart, Minister of Immigration and Colonization, both dated March 30, 1922, introducing to Dennis, Gerhard Ens, of Rosthern, Saskatchewan, H. H. Ewert, Gretna, Manitoba, and A. A. Friesen, Bluffton, Ohio, File No. 218, Section 1, M. See also Memorandum by Col. Dennis for President Beatty, March 31, 1922, in which he describes the visit of the three Mennonites and the promise of the Prime Minister to lift the ban on Mennonite immigration.

[2] H. H. Ewert to J. S. Dennis, April 13, 1922, *ibid.*

Having realized the original investment on the first village, they would buy another and repeat the process. The problem was to obtain the initial $150,000.

Of greater concern at the moment was the item of transportation cost. To meet this situation the spokesmen of the Mennonites sought from the Canadian Pacific a low through rate from a Baltic or Black Sea port to a point in western Canada. After considerable negotiation the company granted a through rate of $140 for adults and $90 for children under ten years of age, to Saskatoon.[1] Late in 1922 arrangements were completed for moving some 3,000 of the Mennonites from Libau to Canada. To facilitate this work, Dennis dispatched to England T. O. F. Herzer, of the Department of Colonization and Development, who spoke the language of the immigrants. Herzer was to travel back and forth between Southampton and Libau until the entire contingent of people had been assembled in England, preparatory to embarkation for Canada.[2]

With the conclusion of these arrangements it seemed that all was in readiness for the first phase of the important Mennonite immigration to Canada under the auspices of the Canadian Pacific. Difficulties soon arose, however, which delayed the departure of these folk for Canada. Refusal of the Soviet authorities to admit to Russia Canadian medical and civil examiners, combined with the unwillingness of the Canadian Pacific to bring the immigrants forward merely with a Russian medical examination, necessitated the temporary abandonment of the entire plan. After several months of negotiation a satisfactory plan was evolved by a Mennonite representative in Russia. The people were to be moved to the Latvian border for examination by Canadian medical officers. Since those who were rejected were denied readmission into Russia, a Mennonite organization was to care for them in Germany. By July, 1923, the first party of 760 Mennonites embarked at Libau for Southampton.[3] By October some 2,400 of these people had been

[1] Dennis to Rev. David Toews, Rosthern, Saskatchewan, June 20, 1922, *ibid.*
[2] Dennis to T. O. F. Herzer, November 13, 1922, *ibid.*
[3] Dennis to Rev. David Toews, July 4, 1923, File No. 218, Section 2, M. Subsequently the Soviet Government allowed prospective Mennonite emigrants to be examined in their homes. In the years 1924 to 1927 inclusive, Dr. Edward Drury of the Canadian Pacific Medical Services at London travelled 25,000 miles by rail, apart from other forms of transportation in Russia, in pursuance of

brought to Canada by the Canadian Pacific.[1] Not only had the
company provided a very low rail and steamship rate for them, but
it had actually brought them on a credit basis, under which a Mennonite organization in Canada was to assume responsibility for the
liquidation of the debt by installments.

The agency in western Canada which was to see the Mennonite
immigrants through the winter and to aid them in finding their
place in the economic life of the Dominion was the Canadian Mennonite Board of Colonization. But while this organization was
entirely capable of providing temporary care for the newcomers,
its potentialities for settling them upon the land were distinctly
limited by the slender means of the Mennonite communities in the
West. Although a thrifty and industrious farming folk, these people
lacked the large resources, the prestige, and the machinery necessary
for the successful colonization of the new arrivals in the prairie
provinces. What was really needed was the union of the Mennonite
Board of Colonization with some agency of the Canadian Pacific,
the company which had made possible the coming of the immigrants
into Canada. The railway was maintaining the Canada Colonization Association as a medium for the settlement of privately owned
land. The Mennonite board was eager to locate its people on such
lands. In recognition of Canadian Pacific assistance, the board was
desirous, so far as possible, of placing them on lands in Canadian
Pacific territory. This situation indicated the importance of a working arrangement between the Mennonite organization and the
Canada Colonization Association.

During the winter and spring of 1924 the Canadian Mennonite
Board of Colonization, in coöperation with the Colonization Association, busied itself with the settlement on the land of the Mennonites brought forward during the preceding year. The importance
of locating them promptly was apparent. Consent of the Dominion
authorities to a further movement of Mennonites would naturally
be contingent upon the satisfactory disposition of the first comers.
Yet midsummer found many of them unplaced. The lack of progress

this work. The purpose of the new medical arrangement was, of course, to
lessen possible hardship which might have resulted had the Mennonites been
permitted to leave without such examination.

[1] Dennis to Rev. A. D. Klochin, October 15, 1923, *ibid.*

seemed to result from an insufficient liaison between the two organizations. To bring them into closer harmony and more active coöperation, a Mennonite Land Settlement Board was now formed, with three representatives from the Canadian Mennonite Board of Colonization, three from the Canada Colonization Association, and three from the Mennonite newcomers.[1]

These steps, of course, were taken upon the initiative of Dennis in behalf of the Canadian Pacific. The company, through its Department of Colonization and Development, had assumed responsibility for the movement of the Mennonites to Canada and for their placement on the land. In effecting this close coöperation between the Mennonite organization and the Canada Colonization Association, Dennis sought to secure for the company a degree of control and oversight commensurate with the responsibility it had assumed. The Canadian Pacific would be the guiding spirit in a partnership which existed for the mutual benefit of the railway and the Mennonite people. But while keeping his hand on the throttle, Dennis was careful to make his control as unobtrusive as possible. To this end, one of the three representatives of the Canada Colonization Association on the Land Settlement Board was himself a Mennonite.

Under the new arrangement, substantial progress was made during the latter part of 1924 in the settlement of Mennonite families. The primary functions of the Land Settlement Board were to find owners of improved land who were disposed to sell their holdings, to bring such owners together with Mennonite immigrants, to see that contracts for the sale of such lands were fair to all concerned, and to provide after-care and supervision for the new settlers. The day was gone when the settler was placed on the land and promptly forgotten, while he shifted for himself as best he could. The aim and purpose of immigration promotion now was to build the settler into the economic life of the country. Every precaution must be taken, therefore, to guard against failure of the newcomer; care must be taken to prevent the immigrant from becoming a public charge. With a strong public opinion which was at best merely tolerant of Continental immigration, Mennonite colonization must be a success.

Since the Mennonites were meagerly provided with funds, and since they were being settled on lands which sold at a substantial

[1] Dennis to Rev. David Toews, July 19, 1924, File No. 218, Section 6, M.

price, particular care was necessary in evolving a practical plan by which they could acquire title to land. There were in western Canada many large farms, survivals of the bonanza days when wheat farms of great proportions were a common sight. With the passing of the prosperous conditions which had prevailed in agriculture during the pre-war and war periods, many of these farms had lost their attractiveness to their owners. The depressed prices of farm products after 1921 made these men receptive to proposals that they dispose of their holdings. But the mere willingness of them to sell offered no solution of the problem. There remained the question of the buyer; and in the face of the prevailing farm situation there was no demand for the large farms. The obvious solution was either to divide these large holdings into small units for sale to individual families or to sell them intact to groups of families who would operate them on a community basis.

By virtue of their traditional devotion to the community form of settlement, the Mennonite immigrants whom the Canadian Pacific was bringing to Canada were clearly indicated as the ones who would make a success of group settlement on the large farms. But while the Mennonites were good human material, they were so largely without means as to preclude the possibility of their purchasing the lands in the ordinary way. In working out special arrangements for purchase by the Mennonites there was needed some responsible organization commanding the confidence of both the vendor and the buyers. As the chief sponsor of the Mennonite immigration, and as the agency which had made it possible for them to come forward, the Canadian Pacific was the logical intermediary; and in its Canada Colonization Association it had an instrument at hand for such work. Not only could the latter cooperate with the Mennonite Land Settlement Board in locating the lands available for purchase, but, what was more important, through its agents it could guarantee a just appraisal of the land and devise contracts for sale which would safeguard the interests of all parties concerned.

The particular form of contract evolved to meet this situation was one calling for purchase on a crop-payment basis. Where groups of Mennonite families were settled on the large farms, additional buildings and equipment must be provided by the vendors and added to the price of the land. The total cost was then to be liquidated by the annual delivery to the vendor of one-half of all crops and live stock produced on the land. In this way every incentive was given to the settlers to achieve maximum production as a means of effecting the most rapid payment for the land. Once a community of Mennonites had been settled on a large farm the inspectors of the Mennonite Land Settlement Board and of the Canada Colonization Association provided supervision and after-care in order to reduce the possibility of failure to a minimum.

In this way the Canadian Pacific effected not merely a solution of the problem of establishing the Mennonites on the land, with reasonable assurance of their success, but it also inaugurated something in the nature of a revolution in land holding in portions of the Canadian West. Extensive cultivation, a marked feature of the early development throughout the wheat belt on the American and Canadian prairies, was to be replaced in a measure by a more intensive cultivation by the hands of a thrifty and industrious people long accustomed to unremitting toil. And intensive agriculture meant balanced farming in which diversified production would supplant the exclusive grain production which had attended the operation of the large farms. The new system was a recognition, too, of the fact that the Mennonites were more likely to succeed through community effort than when each family was left to work out its own salvation.

The following letter from the manager of the Canada Colonization Association to Dennis affords an excellent illustration of the process of group settlement on the large farms in the West:[1]

Since your visit a deal for the Sheldon farm at Hanley has been closed up, locating 35 families thereon. The Big Four Farm at Flaxcombe, Saskatchewan, is all arranged for, terms of contract agreed on, and only awaits the owner from London, England, to complete the contract.

At the same time the Pidgeon Lake Farm on your line at Meadows, Manitoba, of 9,200 acres, under the same ownership as the Flaxcombe farm, we expect will be closed up. In addition to this the Sir William Van Horne Farm, situated at East Selkirk on your line, has been inspected, and a proposition submitted to the Royal Trust Company, Winnipeg, which Board has approved the

[1] W. T. Badger to Dennis, August 9, 1924, File No. 218, Section 7, M.

sale and now awaits confirmation from the Montreal Office. This farm would take care of twenty families. We have also inspected the Lyman Farm on your line at Arnaud, Manitoba, 10,720 acres, and owing to the fact that the owner lives in California there will be some delay in negotiating, although the prospects are very good. This block will take care of forty-four families. The Bean Farm on your line at Springstein, Manitoba, is being inspected and reported on favorably; it is now a matter of carrying on further negotiations with the Bean interests in Minneapolis, as they will require to erect buildings to take care of ten families. . . . Arrangements are made to make inspections of four other large blocks next week on your lines in Manitoba.

As a result of the adoption of this plan for Mennonite settlement, the Canadian Pacific was soon able to show gratifying results from its efforts, which warranted it in seeking authorization from Dominion authorities for a further movement of these people from Russia. The encouraging prospects for Mennonite success on the land in the West had the effect, too, of predisposing President Beatty of the Canadian Pacific toward a continued movement of the Mennonites on a credit basis, care being taken at all times, however, to guard against the granting of excessive credits to the Canadian Mennonite Board of Colonization at any given time. Through the decade of the twenties the immigration of the Mennonites and the work of the Canada Colonization Association went hand in hand. The Canadian Pacific continued to move Mennonites on both a cash and credit basis. By the summer of 1926 it had been authorized to move some 16,000 of them, of whom more than 12,000 had already arrived in Canada. Of this latter number, it had brought 8,790 on credit, as compared with 3,484 who were cash or prepaid arrivals.[1] To March, 1927, the Canada Colonization Association had settled on privately owned land a total of 1,138 Mennonite families, not to mention some 203 families of other nationalities.[2] By the close of the 1928 season it had placed more than 3,000 Mennonite families, representing over 16,000 souls.[3] The area of land thus colonized was in excess of 700,000 acres, with a contract price of almost $30,000,000.

[1] File No. 218, Section 14, M, Memorandum of number of Mennonites authorized to be moved from Russia as of July 7, 1926.
[2] Herzer to Macalister, March 11, 1927, File No. 294, Section 11, M.
[3] *Report of the Canada Colonization Association for 1928.*

Through experience the Canada Colonization Association gradually evolved certain definite principles governing its procedure with respect to this type of land settlement. It refused to accept for assisted settlement any families who could not be personally interviewed and inspected by the prospective vendors. In order to interest the seller, particularly financial corporations, assurance must be given that some organization would provide oversight and direction of the immigrants purchasing the land. For the performance of this function among the Mennonite settlements there were, of course, the Canadian Mennonite Board of Colonization and the Mennonite Land Settlement Board, both of which functioned in close harmony with the Canada Colonization Association.

The financing of this type of settlement was a problem of no mean proportions. As a non-profit-making organization, the Canada Colonization Association received an annual appropriation of from $60,000 to $90,000 from the Canadian Pacific, which it used to cover its operating expenses, including compensation for officials of the Mennonite Land Settlement Board. Then the latter organization, as the immediate agency which brought the vendor and vendee together, was to receive a commission on the land sold, payable as deferred payments were made by the purchasers. The proceeds defrayed the cost of guidance and counsel to the settlers.

The primary concern of the Canadian Pacific in this work was, of course, the increased settlement of the country tributary to its own lines in the West. On occasion, however, the lands thus settled were tributary to both the Canadian Pacific and the Canadian National Railways. As a protection to its interests in such cases, the company, through the Canada Colonization Association, insisted that there be inserted in the contract a clause requiring the parties purchasing the land to deliver their crops to Canadian Pacific stations.

Until 1927 the activities of the Canada Colonization Association were confined almost wholly to the three prairie provinces. In the earlier years Manitoba had been the scene of greatest activity, but in 1928 both Saskatchewan and Alberta were far ahead of Manitoba in number of families as well as area of land settled. By that time most of the large farms in Manitoba had been colonized on a community basis, and now the same process was being extended to the other provinces. In 1928 some 120 families were located on lands in Ontario, marking the initial appearance of the association in the rôle of colonizing agent in that part of the Dominion.

Although the settlement of Mennonites engaged the major portion of the time and energies of the colonization association, various other nationalities and groups were represented in the total number of families settled under its auspices. Officials of the association were at particular pains to establish and maintain with organizations of other nationalities the close and friendly relations which existed with the Mennonite Colonization and Land Settlement Boards. When the association moved to new headquarters in Winnipeg, it provided office facilities not merely for the Mennonite board but also for the Lutheran Immigration Board, the Danish-Lutheran Immigration Board, the Baptist Board, the Association of German-Canadian Catholics,[1] the Norwegian-Lutheran Immigration Board, and the Swedish-Lutheran Immigration Board. As the manager of the Canada Colonization Association expressed it, "I am desirous of having these boards associated with the C. C. A. because they furnish us the people whom we can accept for assisted settlement under our present scheme."[2]

Indicative of the results achieved through coöperation with organizations of this type was a colony of 30 German Catholic families whom the Canada Colonization Association was instrumental in locating on the "Bennett Lands," a tract of about 30,000 acres near Winnipeg. This group deposited $30,000 with the association, to be expended for the additional buildings and equipment necessary to accommodate such a community. The families were met at St. John by a priest who was secretary of the V. D. C. K., the association of German-Canadian Catholics on the prairie. The importance which the Canada Colonization Association attached to the colony is illustrated by the statement of the manager: "All possible care will be taken to insure the success of this settlement, which is the largest settlement attempted of a group other than Mennonites, and will be

[1] Commonly referred to as the V. D. C. K., "Verein Deutsch Condischer Katholiken," a cultural society organized in 1909.
[2] Herzer to Dennis, May 7, 1927, File No. 294, Section 11, M.

closely watched by many people in western Canada, since the settlement is so close to Winnipeg."[1]

The relative importance of Mennonites, as compared with other nationalities, in the settlement work of the Canada Colonization Association is illustrated by the figures for the year 1928. Of a total of 667 families, representing 3,668 souls established on the land in that year, 393 were Mennonites. German families numbered 178, of whom 135 had been settled through the aid of the Lutheran Immigration Board, while the remaining 43 families were Catholics in whose settlement the V. D. C. K. had played an important part. Of 13 other nationalities included in the year's total, 47 British families were the largest group.

By 1927 the Canada Colonization Association had achieved a degree of success in the colonization of privately owned land which attracted increasing attention among various interests and elements in the Dominion. Especially was this true of the financial community, where insurance and mortgage companies holding large areas of land were struggling with the problem of finding a workable plan for the settlement of their land. Although the Canada Colonization Association had been functioning for a number of years during which its activities became increasingly known, it was only gradually that the earlier skepticism with respect to it, conceived in its formative stages, began to disappear; and the doubts of financial interests were not finally dispelled until it became thoroughly understood that the association was really a subsidiary of the Department of Colonization and Development of the Canadian Pacific.

It was in September, 1926, that the assistant manager of the association addressed the convention of the Dominion Mortgage and Investments Association at Edmonton on the work of the association.[2] At that time the mortgage and insurance group fully realized the connection of the organization with the Canadian Pacific. Shortly afterward, certain influential financiers called upon Canadian Pacific officials in Winnipeg to secure confirmation of this connection

[1] Minutes of Meeting of Executive Committee of C. C. A., March 18, 1927. Report of Manager, *ibid.*

[2] See Report by Herzer on Proposed Financial Corporation, having for its object the giving of Financial Assistance to the New Settler in acquiring land in Western Canada, 1927, *ibid.*

and also to invite T. O. F. Herzer, the manager of the Canada Colonization Association, to address the board of directors of the Mutual Life Assurance Company at Waterloo, Ontario. This in turn led to an appearance of Herzer before the annual meeting of the Dominion Mortgage and Investments Association at Montreal in March, 1927, where he spoke on the subject of colonization and land settlement. Herzer outlined the history of the Canada Colonization Association, asserted that the time had come for organized coöperation between it and the investment association, and suggested that a committee be appointed to whom he might submit a detailed plan for a land settlement corporation. Later, at a luncheon in Toronto, Herzer discussed this plan before representatives of fourteen of the largest insurance and mortgage companies in Canada. It was there agreed that his scheme for "Financial Assistance for new settlers on the Land" was feasible and a committee was appointed to work out the details.

The advantages to be gained from coöperation by the loan and insurance companies were obvious. The cost of management of the individual properties would be materially reduced through the use of one inspector or manager to supervise a number of properties in the same district. Land of different companies in a given area could be settled simultaneously with an appreciable saving of money and effort. The possibility of failure could thus be reduced to a minimum. In this way not merely would the lands in the possession of the loan and insurance companies be settled, but the surplus holdings of western farmers and the properties of absentee owners could be rendered increasingly productive, to the advantage of the entire community.

As a result of these preliminary steps there was formally launched in September, 1928, the Colonization Finance Corporation of Canada, which, with the machinery of the Canada Colonization Association, was to apply to the settlement of the lands in question the methods which the association had so successfully employed during the preceding years.[1] The Canadian Pacific signified its constructive interest in the undertaking by a promise to advance up to $85,000 annually for five years as an aid in the administration of the project. The member companies represented in the new corpora-

[1] Montreal *Gazette*, September 20, 1928.

tion were to advance additional funds for buildings and to provide equipment and live stock for sale on long amortization terms to settlers.

Thus far our discussion of group settlement in western Canada in the decade following the war has been confined chiefly to people from Continental Europe. That period, however, was marked by several important steps taken by the Canadian Pacific with a view to locating colonies of British settlers on the land. The earliest of these was the Clan Donald settlement established near Vermilion in northern Alberta in 1925. Projected by Father MacDonnell, a Scottish priest, for the purpose of settling Scotch Catholics, this colony owed its success largely to the friendly interest and support of President Beatty of the Canadian Pacific. Convinced by Father MacDonnell of the soundness of the plan, Beatty advanced the $100,000 necessary for locating some 100 families in the colony. Despite the very real difficulties under which the settlers labored, the settlement achieved a degree of success which by 1928 warranted an enlargement of the colony, with further financial assistance from the Canadian Pacific. Through the funds advanced by the railway company the necessary buildings and improvements were provided for the colonists, who were to liquidate the indebtedness by a long-term amortization plan. The scheme, therefore, was essentially a return to the ready-made farm program which the Canadian Pacific had developed before the war.

Another plan for British settlement was the Askew Scheme, sponsored by Mr. W. H. Askew, for the settlement in Canada of people from the mining areas in Great Britain. Askew placed certain funds at the disposal of the Canadian Pacific for assisting settlers, while with the approval of the Dominion Government an agreement was made with the company under the Empire Settlement Act by which these funds were to be supplemented by a grant from the Overseas Settlement Committee.[1] The first contingent of 200 settlers embarked under this plan in June, 1929.

In 1928 a ready-made farm plan for British settlers was launched jointly by the British Government, the Hudson's Bay Company, and the Canadian Pacific. In the spring of 1929 more than 100 families

[1] *The Oversea Settler,* June, 1929, issued by the Overseas Settlement Department of the Dominions Office, London.

were established in a colony near Vermilion, in Alberta. Each family was allotted 160 acres of virgin land, of which a few acres had been broken by the companies. The corporations also provided a cottage, with necessary furniture, farm buildings, and wells, together with advances for the purchase of stock, equipment, seed, and other essentials. The total cost of the farms, including the loans, was to be repaid over a period of 20 years, at which time the settler would receive a freehold title to the land.

The families selected for this colony had an average of three children, while the parents were possessed of farming experience. Travelling at assisted passage rates, an entire family was able to make the trip from Great Britain to Vermilion for the small sum of £11. At the latter point farm supervisors of the companies met the settlers and advised them regarding the selection of a team of horses, a cow, a new wagon, all of which could be purchased at wholesale prices. The settlers were assured in advance of the friendly assistance and coöperation of the company supervisors during the difficult period of getting started. Care was exercised to provide farm employment during this stage as a means of supplementing the farm income pending the time when the farm was a going concern.

The most ambitious plan for the settlement of British families on the land in the West was that adopted by the Canadian Pacific at the time of the visit of Lord Lovat, of the Overseas Settlement Committee, to Canada in the summer of 1928. Indeed, the scheme was appropriately described as the "first fruits" of Lord Lovat's visit. The first feature of the program worked out at that time was that which called for the construction by the company of 100 cottages at various points in the West for use by British families whom the railway was to bring to the Dominion after selection by agents of its Department of Colonization and Development.[1] The families were to be located in the cottages and provided with farm employment to enable them to acquire experience with Canadian farming conditions. When sufficiently acquainted with the ways of the new land, the settlers would be aided through Canadian Pacific facilities in acquiring farms of their own on the prairie, thus making room for new families to occupy the cottages. The provision for farm training was a frank recognition of the fact that British settlers

[1] Montreal *Gazette*, September 4, 1928.

adapted themselves to prairie conditions less readily than did families from the continent of Europe. With the aid of supervised apprenticeship the process of adjustment was to be made easier, with a corresponding increase in the chances of success.

By a second agreement with the Overseas Settlement Committee, the Canadian Pacific was authorized to select, through its Department of Colonization and Development, and bring to Canada during a period of 5 years 1,000 British families.[1] The company agreed to provide agricultural employment for these people, to supervise their progress, and ultimately to establish them on farms of their own. This last duty was to be performed through the Canada Colonization Association and it would represent essentially an extension to British families of the type of settlement which the association had so successfully employed with respect to Mennonites and other peoples from Continental Europe.

The announcement of this plan was hailed by the Montreal *Gazette* as a significant event in British settlement in Canada. Especially important in the opinion of this journal was the assurance "that the settler-families will be recruited, brought to Canada, and their progress supervised through the same agency until they are finally established as producers on the land. This means continuity, which is a factor of first-rate value to the settler."[2]

Under yet another agreement with the Overseas Settlement Committee the Canadian Pacific undertook to prepare 100 farms for British settlers, the company supplying the land and $1,200 to be expended on each farm, the Overseas Settlement Committee providing $800.

While cultivating so assiduously the British and Continental European fields during the twenties, the Canadian Pacific by no means ignored the United States as a source of desirable settlers for western Canada. Having been for so long a chief theatre of the company's activities, the western states continued for years to figure prominently in the calculations of the officials of the railway. In the post-war decade, of course, the Department of Colonization superseded the Department of Natural Resources as the agency through which the company worked in the States. The headquarters office

[1] *Ibid.*
[2] *Ibid.*

of the organization in the United States was at St. Paul, with sub-offices in Chicago, Spokane, Portland, Oregon, Billings, Montana, Omaha, and Minot, North Dakota.[1] Unlike the company organization in other parts of the world, the representatives in the United States were still primarily interested in bringing to Canada likely prospects to whom the Department of Natural Resources at Calgary might sell Canadian Pacific land. Their function was not to secure settlers for the privately owned land in the prairie provinces.

Despite unflagging effort, however, the company found it impossible to revive the old-time interest of the American farmer in the Canadian West. Compared with the wave of immigration which rolled in from the middle western states before the war, the movement in the twenties was a mere trickle. In the early years of the decade it all but ceased entirely. Through persistent work, the American organization brought 538 land-seekers to Canada in 1925, while the following year this number had increased to 820, a mere fraction of the figures for pre-war years.[2] Even these meager numbers, however, accounted for virtually all the land sold by the Department of Natural Resources to settlers whom the railway brought to Canada in those two years. Buyers from the United States accounted for some 13,000 acres in 1925 and about 25,000 acres in 1926.[3]

Notwithstanding the improvement in these years as compared with those which preceded, the Chief Commissioner of the Department of Colonization and Development, in his report for 1926, felt constrained to comment at length upon the unfavorable situation prevailing among farmers in the western states, which was not conducive to emigration to Canada. In fact, the commissioner thought that serious consideration must soon be given to the matter of closing most of the United States agencies until conditions should improve. With the continued depression of middle western agriculture in the later twenties, which culminated in the crash of 1929, the movement of American farmers to the prairie never again assumed important proportions.

If the results obtained in the United States were deeply disap-

---

[1] *Annual Report of the Department of Colonization and Development for 1926*, p. 3.
[2] *Ibid.*
[3] *Ibid.*

pointing, those elsewhere were more encouraging. Within the limits imposed by the regulations of the Dominion Government, the company, through its Department of Colonization and Development, was able to maintain a substantial flow of settlers into the country. While British immigration never measured up to expectations, and that from the preferred countries of the Continent was not all that had been hoped for, the aggregate result was not to be despised.

Of this total result, the movement of some 20,000 Mennonites to western Canada was, of course, the most spectacular feature and perhaps the most notable contribution of the Canadian Pacific to the increased settlement of the West during the post-war period. This achievement was rendered the more noteworthy by virtue of the fact that the company moved such a large portion of these people on a credit basis. On numerous occasions the Mennonites have publicly acknowledged the vital part which the railway played in transplanting them to the western prairies. The latest of these was in September, 1937, when Sir Edward Beatty and Col. J. S. Dennis visited the Mennonite colony at Coaldale, Alberta, where 267 families were successfully established on 17,000 acres of land. As a token of their appreciation of Canadian Pacific coöperation the Mennonite leaders presented Sir Edward Beatty with an illuminated address acclaiming their "land of adoption," where they had "found peace, security, daily bread and a home." That Canadian Pacific confidence in the essential honesty of the Mennonites was not misplaced is shown by the unfailing promptness with which they have repaid the large sums advanced to them by the railway company.

Aside from the Mennonite migration, the achievements of the early twenties were distinctly less impressive than those in the latter part of the decade. As late as 1925 the department moved but 14,000 people to Canada.[1] With the inauguration of the Railways Agreement in 1926 there followed a sharp increase in the numbers from the non-preferred countries. In that year the total number of colonists moved to Canada by the company was 31,272, while in the following year the figure was 32,749.[2] Of the total for 1926, Great

[1] *Ibid.*, p. 1, which gives the figures for 1925 as well as for 1926.
[2] *Ibid.*, 1927, p. 1.

Britain supplied 4,229, and the preferred countries accounted for 2,293.[1]

In accordance with Dominion regulations and with the railways agreement, the Department of Colonization and Development was under obligation to find places for these immigrants in the economic life of western Canada, and it was required to place them on the land. It was to meet this situation that the department had encouraged the formation of the local colonization boards as well as those larger organizations whose activities covered larger areas in the West. These societies, whether local or general, through the nomination system, placed company officials in touch with the prospective immigrant and provided employment for him upon his arrival in the West. The important part played by some of these is well illustrated by the figures for 1928. In that year the Canadian Pacific placed 2,585 settlers through the Colonist Service Association in Calgary, with branches in Lethbridge and Raymond. Through the Confederation Land Corporation in Edmonton locations were secured for 3,706. In Winnipeg the Lutheran Immigration Board provided for 2,012 colonists, while the V. D. C. K., the German Catholic Board, accounted for 1,264. The Atlantis Hungarian Board in Regina placed 1,304, and the Ukrainian Colonization Board at Saskatoon absorbed 2,434.[2]

These results were achieved only by the expenditure of very large sums of money. In 1925 the budget of the Department of Colonization and Development was $685,000; in 1926, $734,000; in 1927, $724,000.[3] Yet this outlay was not without its compensations. Unlike other railways which had engaged in immigration and colonization work, the Canadian Pacific was also a steamship company, with the attendant facilities for recruiting and transporting immigrants across the water. Immigrant traffic was not an unimportant item in its business. In 1925 the ocean and rail fares of colonists moved to the West amounted to $1,371,000, a sum which was $686,000 in excess of the expenditure for the Department of Colonization. With the increased immigration of 1926, the ocean and rail revenue amounted to $3,341,000, with only a slightly smaller

[1] *Annual Report of European Organization for 1926*, p. 10.
[2] *Annual Report of the Department of Colonization and Development, 1928.*
[3] *Ibid.*, 1926, p. 1; 1927, p. 1.

figure for 1927.[1] From this it is apparent that without its steamship facilities for the transport of the settler from Europe, the Canadian Pacific could not have afforded to indulge in the luxury of selected immigration. The expense of selecting and placing and supervising colonists was justified only because of the ocean and rail traffic produced by such work. This is not to say, however, that the Canadian Pacific was interested in the promotion of immigration purely from a traffic standpoint. Its chief concern was increased settlement and traffic for its rail lines in the West. The expenditure in the cause of increased settlement was made possible only by the immigrant traffic.

The Department of Colonization and Development served a threefold purpose in the decade of the twenties. It was a medium by which the company sought settlers for railway and privately owned lands in the West; it enabled the company to carry on immigration work within the framework of Dominion regulations; and it was an important adjunct to the ocean service of the Canadian Pacific. It was distinctly a product of the post-war era in the Dominion, when opportunities were no longer considered limitless; when the government wanted, preferably, British settlers; and when the immigrant, regardless of the country of his origin, must be assured that employment was awaiting him in the new country.

For the Department of Colonization, as for all other agencies engaged in western settlement, the depression and drought years following 1929 brought an anticlimax. With thousands joining yearly the army of the unemployed in Canada, there was little disposition on the part either of public opinion or Dominion authorities to sanction immigration. The number of new arrivals declined almost to the vanishing point and settlement schemes which the Canadian Pacific had worked out in the late twenties were held in abeyance. Perhaps the most notable feature of its work in the depression was the continued success of the Canada Colonization Association in the placement of families on privately owned land. Working quietly, but nevertheless effectively, it had by January 1, 1938, placed a total of 6,416 families on the land and provided supervision for them. At a conservative estimate, it had thus enabled more than

[1] *Ibid.*

30,000 persons to establish themselves in agricultural pursuits within the Dominion.

It was obvious that the future of the Department of Colonization was uncertain. In any event its status would be determined primarily by Dominion policy with respect to immigration. With an agriculture which, even before the crisis, was suffering from the depressed price of wheat, and with large portions of the West so devastated by drought as to create a serious problem of providing for stricken settlers, the country might well hesitate to encourage further immigration of the agricultural classes of the Old World. Meanwhile, the company's organization for the recruiting and placement of settlers could do little more than mark time.

XIII

SUMMARY AND CONCLUSION

CANADIAN PACIFIC lands were sold through the Winnipeg and Calgary offices, and in each case two distinct periods are discernible. The first era at Winnipeg includes the years from 1881 to 1896, while the second begins in 1897 and continues to the abolition of the General Land Department in 1912. At Calgary the two epochs extend from 1905 to 1920 and from 1921 to 1937 respectively.

At all times the volume of land sales depended mainly on two factors, i.e., the prevailing economic conditions and the policies maintained by the company. In periods of prosperity and business confidence sales greatly increased; with each recurring era of depression the demand for land declined sharply. In periods of expansion, however, company policy exercised an important influence in determining the extent of the boom.

The signing of the syndicate contract in 1881, with its assurance that the railway was finally to be constructed, was the occasion for a land boom in the West. Land buyers, large and small, appeared in surprising numbers, ready to stake their all on the speedy development of the prairie country. As a result of the rush of small buyers and colonization companies, 3,631,640 acres had been sold by December 31, 1883. Then came the evil times. From 1883 to 1886 the prairie was cursed with almost complete crop failures. The lack of effective means for marketing grain at remunerative prices, the uncertainty resulting from frequent changes in Dominion land regulations, the heavy frost of August 28, 1885, the half-breed and Indian rebellion of the same year, and the popular opposition to the alleged monopoly privileges of the Canadian Pacific served as added deterrents to immigration and land settlement. The boom collapsed as suddenly as it had developed. Hundreds of settlers deserted their farms, while the colonization companies found them-

TABLE I

LAND SALES BY YEARS TO 1920[1]

YEAR	AREA IN ACRES	AMOUNT	AVERAGE PER ACRE	CANCELLATIONS
To Dec. 31, 1886.........	3,943,522			696,254 acres
1887....................	47,243		$ 3.39	21,762
1888....................	138,001			11,300
1889....................	142,661	$ 494,402	3.46	10,253
1890....................	73,941	276,586	3.76	4,988
1891....................	72,674	294,875	4.05	6,040
1892....................	230,308	748,618	3.25	144,739
1893....................	93,184	295,288	3.17	21,341
1894....................	43,155	131,628	3.05	33,683
1895....................	55,453	176,950	3.19	99,548
1896....................	66,624	220,360	3.30	234,744
1897....................	135,682	431,096	3.18	46,898
1898....................	242,135	757,792	3.13	33,093
1899....................	326,280	1,016,081	3.11	19,841
Jan. 1, 1900–June 30, 1901.	537,379	1,663,234	3.10	19,232
1902....................	1,362,852	4,442,136	3.26	17,224
1903....................	2,260,731	8,473,573	3.75	23,802
1904....................	857,474	3,516,864	4.10	64,347
1905....................	411,451	2,045,800	4.97	33,092
1906....................	1,012,322	6,015,060	5.94	97,301
1907....................	923,252	5,496,371	5.95	50,960
1908....................	130,378	1,400,349	10.74	33,957
1909....................	363,085	4,974,017	13.70	34,621
1910....................	925,260	14,021,316	15.15	55,952
1911....................	628,092	9,391,459	14.95	54,006
1912....................	666,699	10,653,198	15.98	59,046
1913....................	471,756	7,433,135	15.76	100,829
1914....................	259,371	4,618,420	17.80	not given
1915....................	231,297	3,747,115	16.17	
To June 30, 1916.........	390,715	6,126,108	15.68	
To Dec. 31, 1916.........	328,574	5,295,345	16.12	
Dec. 31, 1917............	789,055	14,330,811	18.16	
1918....................	842,191	15,375,996	18.25	
1919....................	681,763	13,668,443	20.05	
1920[a]....................	471,669	9,431,613	20.40	

[a] Cancellations by years are not given in the Annual Reports for the period June 30, 1914–December 31, 1920. By deducting the unsold area as of December 31, 1920 from the corresponding figures for June 30, 1914, we get the net area sold in the period. By subtracting this figure from the gross sales we get the cancellations—1,263,778 acres.

[1] For the years to 1912 these figures include only the sales from the main line grant and the Souris branch. After that date they include sales from all grants of the company. The figures are from Annual Reports of the Canadian Pacific.

selves unable to comply with the settlement and development provisions of their contracts. Wholesale cancellations resulted, and for several years lands reverting to the company almost balanced those sold.

A good crop in 1887 offered a ray of hope which was not to last. The heavy frost of early August, 1888, brought renewed discouragement and failure from which there was momentary recovery in 1892. With the panic of the next year the West settled deeply into the depression. A new low for land sales was set in 1894, when the net sales from the main line grants amounted to but 9,482 acres. In the next two years cancellations greatly exceeded sales.

Although the company had by the end of 1896 sold 3,623,066 acres net from the main line grant, and 171,958 acres of Manitoba Southwestern lands, the large tract of 2,200,000 acres purchased by the Canada Northwest Land Company accounted for about 60 per

TABLE II

LAND SALES MADE AND CONTRACTS CANCELLED DURING THE YEARS 1921 TO 1937 INCLUSIVE[1]

YEAR	SALES		CANCELLATIONS	
	Acres	Amount	Acres	Amount
1921	160,941.62	$ 2,790,420.81	158,199.96	$ 2,798,188.45
1922	116,804.33	1,698,460.76	266,138.67	4,019,386.05
1923	54,033.64	918,378.66	205,924.26	3,672,831.74
1924	99,484.82	1,698,947.36	252,185.61	4,595,511.13
1925	173,979.55	2,535,828.12	275,652.94	5,202,559.73
1926	367,054.43	4,621,291.51	291,717.18	5,103,036.42
1927	430,453.23	4,962,142.77	294,972.97	5,031,682.00
1928	664,559.86	7,516,008.93	153,374.20	2,946,609.54
1929	408,666.90	4,788,370.47	156,812.82	3,049,592.33
1930	202,138.72	2,883,280.78	211,398.56	3,665,390.82
1931	88,222.47	1,104,474.82	166,829.60	2,804,092.52
1932	59,933.92	723,347.28	154,317.26	2,302,260.96
1933	68,383.71	675,596.58	116,627.71	1,975,180.31
1934	120,380.50	1,250,776.28	102,627.32	1,911,503.71
1935	147,519.27	1,178.735.51	89,383.65	1,775,151.59
1936	156,972.31	912,972.51	95,363.01	1,747,196.37
1937	167,882.50	1,276,559.70	64,879.33	1,565,888.03
	3,487,921.78	$41,535,592.85	3,056,405.05	$54,166,061.70

[1] Figures supplied by Department of Natural Resources, Calgary.

cent of the total. Nevertheless well over a million acres had been sold in small parcels and the land department had placed 5,770 settlers on company lands.

The beginning of the second period in the history of the General Land Department at Winnipeg is coincident with the business upturn which began late in 1896 as a result of the conjunction of a number of favorable factors. Beginning with large sales in the late months of 1896, the net area disposed of increased yearly through 1903. Between January 1, 1900 and June 30, 1903, sales from all grants amounted to 4,800,000 acres, much of which was sold in large tracts to colonization companies. With the continuance of flush times in the West, sales at Winnipeg remained large for several years. After 1907, however, the importance of Winnipeg as the center of the land-selling activities of the company gradually waned as Calgary emerged into a position of first importance.

With the beginning of the first Calgary period in 1905 there appeared a new emphasis in the land policy of the company. While it had not yet definitely banned sales to land companies, it increasingly stressed sales to actual settlers, with cultivation and development of the land as its objective. Having disposed of the bulk of its land in Manitoba and southern Saskatchewan, it was now prepared to concentrate upon the irrigation block and the northern reserves. It was in this period that the Calgary office developed in the United States the agency organization which functioned so effectively as a medium for the recruitment of American settlers. Between 1905 and 1914 the bulk of the purchasers of company land undoubtedly came from the United States.

Although the outbreak of the war in 1914 brought a recession in sales, the good crops in the West in 1915 and 1916, combined with high prices for agricultural products, greatly stimulated the demand for lands. While American buyers continued to be numerous, settlers from the States were relatively less important than in the pre-war years. In increasing degree the purchasers were drawn either from the ranks of resident farmers enlarging their holdings or from Canadians lured to the land by the agricultural boom of the war years. Between June 30, 1914 and December 31, 1920, the net sales from all grants were 2,468,207 acres.

The second Calgary period extending from 1921 through 1937

TABLE III

LAND SALES FROM MANITOBA SOUTHWESTERN GRANT BY YEARS[1]

YEAR	AREA IN ACRES	AMOUNT	AVERAGE PER ACRE	CANCELLATIONS
To Dec. 31, 1896.........	171,958			
1897...................	63,800	$234,644	$ 4.17	12,529 acres
1898...................	106,473	363,982	3.42	2,540
1899...................	90,526	311,586	3.44	5,084
1900 to June 30, 1901.....	131,098	458,996	3.51	4,735
1902...................	206,412	713,366	3.46	2,194
1903...................	250,452	699,610	2.79	2,544
1904...................	29,522	113,303	3.84	23,201
1905...................	80,342	296,936	3.70	481
1906...................	83,418	360,889	4.33	1,440
1907...................	67,086	344,428	5.13	1,728
1908...................	33,256	160,069	4.81	2,495
1909...................	12,314	98,838	8.11	872
1910...................	49,357	441,985	8.95	21,206
1911...................	20,711	128,178	6.19	15,996
1912...................	2,140	40,308	18.03	14
1913...................	2,241	38,668	17.25	161

TABLE IV

LAND SALES FROM GREAT NORTHWEST CENTRAL GRANT BY YEARS[2]

YEAR	AREA IN ACRES	AMOUNT	AVERAGE PER ACRE	CANCELLATIONS
To June 30, 1902.........	19,804			
1903...................	128,434	$522,490	$ 4.07	14,946 acres
1904...................	41,858	177,081	4.07	
1905...................	17,593	103,564	5.89	1,440
1906...................	20,003	137,503	6.87	
1907...................	4,502	46,578	10.35	
1908...................	816	8,747	10.72	
1909...................	647	11,662	18.02	322
1910...................	413	5,263	12.74	
1911...................	2,071	38,790	18.73	160
1912...................	800	16,640	20.80	417
1913...................	801	15,465	19.31	479

[1] Figures are from Annual Reports, Canadian Pacific Railway.
[2] *Ibid.*

was the most trying of all. With the best of its lands already sold, with the West in the grip of the post-war depression in agriculture, and with the onset of the great depression, followed by the most disastrous series of crop failures the prairie had known since the eighties, the net accomplishments of the company in the 17-year period were far more meager than in any other. Net sales amounted to but 431,007 acres.

If the volume of land sales varied greatly in the different periods that was no less true of the acre price. Lands in the main line grant declined from an average $4.05 per acre in 1891 to $3.05 per acre in 1894. Even in the face of the upturn in the business situation in the late nineties the price had advanced only to $3.11 per acre in 1899, and to $3.12 per acre in the 18-month period ending June 30, 1901. The strong tide of settlement which began to pour into the West in 1902 brought an advance in prices, which had reached $4.10 per acre in 1904 and $4.97 per acre in 1905. In view of the sale of large areas to colonization companies at $2.50 and $2.75 per acre, the average price of land in small units was about $6.00 per acre. The average price of $5.94 per acre in 1906 marked the beginning of a sharp advance which continued without interruption until 1910, when the figure of $15.15 was attained. This situation was due not merely to the rapid growth of settlement in the prairie provinces, but also the sale of irrigable lands at high prices. The average of $17.80 for 1914 declined to $15.68 in 1916, only to rise steadily until 1920 when the average was $20.48 per acre, an all-time high. As these figures include the irrigable lands which sold at prices ranging from $42.94 to $66.93 per acre, the average for dry lands was substantially below the general average.

Prices for the period 1921-37 reflect not only the generally depressed state of agriculture in those years but also the inferior quality of the remaining lands of the company. The downward trend, broken by occasional advances, reached a low of $9.79 per acre in 1935.

A glance at Table V reveals significant facts with respect to the prices received for different portions of the land grant. The largest single area is the 10,574,276 acres of the main line subsidy, sold at Winnipeg between 1881 and 1912, for $42,600,000, an average of $4.00 per acre. While this acreage represents 55.6 per cent of the

TABLE V

Land Sales, Acreage, and Sale Price, and Acreage Unsold as at December 31, 1937[1]

		Land Sales		Unsold Acreage
Land Grant		Acres	Sale Price (Land Only)	
Main Line:				
	C.P.R. (Winnipeg)	10,574,276.718	$ 42,600,869.93	
	Manitoba........	149,752.55	562,134.53	60,205.41
	Saskatchewan.....	820,275.422	9,595,567.10	472,235.077
Dis-posed of at Cal-gary	Alberta..........	2,276,364.118	29,572,118.77	816,991.765
	Irrigation Block:			
	Irrigable.......	196,324.108	7,749,726.90	
	Non-irrigable...	1,398,662.333	18,391,219.96	209,095.086
	Transferred to Eastern Irrigation District[a]..	1,172,370.053		
Total Main Line[a]......		16,588,025.302	$108,471,637.19	1,558,527.338
Hudson's Bay: (Purchased)				
Irrigable...............		5,181.97	206,287.23	
Non-irrigable...........		24,730.315	412,350.11	10,469.125
Transferred to Eastern Irgation District........		61,441.93		
A. R. & I.				
Irrigable...............		32,194.47	1,990,123.17	3,168.53
Non-irrigable...........		100,067.843	1,514,378.41	41,826.997
Souris Branch............		1,268,791.216	11,374,166.32	334,747.164
Manitoba Southwestern.....		1,342,034.727	5,446,728.79	45,188.993
Great Northwest Central....		285,400.17	1,950,150.19	33,185.91
Calgary & Edmonton.......		395,408.602	4,788,284.32	11,993.398
Manitoba & Northwestern..		1,888.48	19,700.84	131.95
Saskatchewan & Western...		98,880.00	296,640.00	
		20,204,045.025[b]	$136,470,446.57	2,039,239.405

[a] *Summary—Main Line Grant:*

	Acres
Sold and transferred to Eastern Irrigation District.............	16,588,025.302
Unsold...	1,558,527.338
Transferred back to the Dominion Government (Year 1886)....	6,793,014.00
Reserved for Town Sites.................................	60,433.36
	25,000,000.00

[b] Deducting from this figure the 1,172,370.053 acres from the main line grant and the 61,441.93 acres of Hudson's Bay lands transferred to the Eastern Irrigation District, we have the 18,970,233.042 acres actually sold by the company to December 31, 1937.

[1] Figures supplied by Department of Natural Resources, Calgary.

18,970,233 acres sold to date, its sale price accounts for only 31 per cent of the total of $136,470,446. These comparatively modest returns are due in part to the fact that the sales at Winnipeg were made relatively early in the settlement of the prairie, and in part to the purchase of large areas of this land by colonization companies at bargain prices.

Another area chiefly sold through Winnipeg was the Manitoba Southwestern grant, of which 1,342,000 acres brought $5,446,728, an average of $4.06 per acre. Winnipeg disposed of the Saskatchewan and Western subsidy of 98,880 acres in a block to the Saskatchewan Valley Land Company, at $3.00 per acre. The same office sold the bulk of the Great Northwest Central lands at an average price of $6.48 per acre. If, to simplify matters, we allocate to Winnipeg one-half of the acreage and the returns from the Souris Branch subsidy (a proportion which is probably somewhat excessive), we have a grand total of approximately 13,000,000 acres sold at Winnipeg to 1912, for $56,000,000, or an average of $4.30 per acre.

The Calgary organization, therefore, between 1905 and 1937 sold approximately 6,000,000 acres for $80,000,000, an average of $13.33 per acre. While it accounted for but 31.6 per cent of the acreage disposed of, it provided roughly 59 per cent of the total sale price of all Canadian Pacific lands sold to date.

On the surface this would seem to indicate that the lands sold at Calgary were much more profitable than the Winnipeg area. Because they were sold at a later date and included irrigable lands they naturally brought substantially higher prices. Yet it is doubtful if the net profit at Calgary was as great as that at Winnipeg. Lands at the latter place were sold at a minimum of expense to the company. While the General Land Department advertised liberally and although the railway carried on an active immigration propaganda in the British Isles and Continental Europe in the early days, the Winnipeg office maintained no expensive land-selling organization such as Calgary built up in the United States. Furthermore, by selling large areas to colonization companies, Winnipeg largely shifted to others the expense of selling and settling the land. Nor is it to be forgotten that the Winnipeg lands were in the main disposed of before they became taxable. Of the more than $48,000,000 which the Canadian Pacific has spent merely for the administration and sale of its lands, a great deal less than half is to be charged against the General Land Department at Winnipeg.

At Calgary very little land was sold in large blocks, and for years it was sold chiefly to settlers recruited in the United States by an expensive agency force. The cost per acre of operating the machinery of land selling at Calgary was in excess of $2.00 per acre, and in 1908 it was $2.42 per acre.[1] The $32,000,000 expended by the company on the irrigation project represents an added charge of more than $5.00 per acre against every acre of land sold at Calgary in the 33-year period which began in 1905. Taxes which have been paid on all unsold land of the railway since 1923 are an additional charge against this land.

TABLE VI

TOWN-SITE SALES, AMOUNTS OUTSTANDING, AND EXPENSE,
AS AT DECEMBER 31, 1937[2]

| LAND GRANT | SALES | AMOUNTS OUTSTANDING | | EXPENSE |
		Principal	*Interest*	
Canadian Pacific Ry.	$12,652,748.86	$374,629.46	$65,350.36	$6,252,842.99
Irrigation Block....	478,799.09	18,225.93	3,929.87	191,024.62
A. R. & I.........	241,092.14	841.55	47.93	551,929.16
Lacombe & North-western........	792.13	14.55		782.70
Manitoba South-western........	537,520.18	8,281.34	541,76	176,723.56
Great Northwest Central........	41,299.60	7,042.89	2,788.30	31,229.59
Manitoba & North-western........	66,054.88			37,989.35
	$14,018,306.88	$409,035.72	$72,658.32	$7,242,521.97

The difference between Winnipeg and Calgary was the difference between mere land selling and the actual settlement and development of the land. Calgary sold a smaller area by dint of great effort and large expenditure, but its achievement of actually colonizing 6,000,000 acres of land constitutes the more enduring monument to

[1] Statement of Expenditure in connection with the sale of lands in the Irrigation Block for the year ending December 31, 1908, File No. 336, D. N. R.

[2] Figures supplied by Department of Natural Resources, Calgary.

the Canadian Pacific's part in the building of the West. The work of Calgary, however, has undoubtedly returned a smaller net profit to the company from land sales and has contributed less to the traffic of the railway than the lands sold at Winnipeg.

From Tables V, VI, and VII it is evident that the sale price of the agricultural lands and town lots disposed of from the subsidies received from the Dominion Government totals $150,000,000, of which somewhat more than $34,000,000 was outstanding in deferred payments on December 31, 1937.[1] Over against this amount the company had incurred expenses of $59,719,268.65 for land administration and settlement, town-site development, colonization and immigration promotion; $32,899,882.79 for irrigation construction and maintenance; and $24,124,599.93 for taxes on lands; a total of $116,743,699.37. While it is impossible to determine the precise proportion of this latter sum which was expended on account of the subsidies in the three prairie provinces, it seems likely that $100,-000,000 would be a reasonable estimate, which would leave a balance of $50,000,000 on the approximately 19,000,000 acres sold from the Dominion land subsidies to the end of 1937. This balance, however, does not accurately represent the profit made by the company on the subsidy lands. Judging from past experience of the railway, especially in the years since 1921, it is likely that a substantial proportion of the $34,000,000 outstanding on deferred payments may never be collected.[2] Furthermore, before final payment is made, if ever, the company's expenditure for land sale and administration will have materially increased. It would appear, therefore, that if the

[1] The total cash receipts from land and town-site sales up to the end of 1937 were approximately $160,000,000, of which approximately $122,000,000 were from land sales in the prairie provinces. The balance consisted of $10,000,000 received from the acreage returned to the Dominion Government in 1886, while $28,000,000 represents receipts from sales in other provinces, largely British Columbia. If to the $122,000,000 in cash receipts from land and town-lot sales in the Prairie Provinces, we add the more than $34,000,000 outstanding on sales in the same area, the potential receipts amount to more than $156,000,000, compared with the sale price of $150,000,000 for land and town-lots disposed of to date. This discrepancy is accounted for by payments on cancelled contracts through the years.

[2] Table II shows that in the period 1921-37 cancelled contracts aggregated $54,166,061.70, while the sale price of land sold in the same period amounted to only $41,535,592.85, a difference of more than $12,500,000.

company is fairly successful in collecting the outstanding sums due on land contracts it may realize a net profit of something more than $2.00 per acre on the 19,000,000 acres sold to date.

In Canada, as in the United States, there has been much discussion as to the value of subsidy lands granted to railways by the government. The Canadian Pacific subsidy did not, of course, represent the equivalent of $150,000,000 granted by the Dominion. Without the railway the land had little value, for otherwise the government would have been unwilling to grant it. The construction of the railway and the exertions and expenditures of the company contributed to the value represented by the sale price of the land. An important governmental agency has recently estimated the value of railway subsidy lands in the United States at 97 cents per acre.[1] This figure was arrived at by taking as the value of subsidy lands the average price received by the United States Government for all lands sold by it between 1785 and 1871, when the last railway subsidy was granted.

For Canada the value would possibly be somewhat higher because the Canadian Pacific subsidy came later when land values generally had advanced, although the average quality of the land was probably not appreciably better. While by the terms of its contract with the government the company was entitled to lands "fairly fit for settlement," in the final apportionment it accepted areas of inferior quality, as in the "semi-arid" belt west of Medicine Hat, where heavy expenditures for irrigation were necessary. Although the company may ultimately realize a profit in excess of $2.00 per acre on the land sold to the present time, this does not represent its value as a subsidy in 1881. Significant in its bearing on the point of value is the fact that when in 1886 the Canadian Pacific relinquished 6,793,014 acres of its subsidy by way of satisfying a debt owed the government, the latter allowed it a credit of only $1.50 per acre on the land. Probably this is a fair estimate of value, although the Royal Commission on Railways and Transportation, in its report published in 1932, set a value of $1.00 per acre on lands granted to all

[1] *Report on Land Grants, Contributions, Loans and other Aids to Railroads,* Federal Coordinator of Transportation, Section of Research. This study, prepared in 1933-35, when Mr. Eastman of the Interstate Commerce Commission was Coordinator of Transportation, has not been published. I am indebted to Mr. John B. Rae, who examined the manuscript, for this information.

Canadian railways. In 1881 Canada believed a railway to the Pacific was a national necessity. The large land subsidy was part of the price which the country had to pay for that necessity.

One of the difficult and perplexing problems attending the sale of the company's land grants was that of dealing with the purchaser who was seriously in arrears in his payments. Contract holders who found themselves in this situation were generally one of two sorts. One was the *bona fide* settler who promptly occupied the land or who purchased with every intention of so doing. The other was the speculator who, to secure a stake in the land, made the necessary first payment in the hope and expectation that he might delay further payments until the appreciation in the value of the land enabled him to dispose of it at a profit. Regardless of the reasons for the arrearage, however, the situation called for careful thought by officials of the company; and out of this situation there resulted the necessity of cancelling periodically contracts covering a very large acreage of land.

The Land Department first found itself confronted with this embarrassing problem when the collapse of the land boom of 1882 was followed by a series of poor crops. This disaster weighed heavily upon those pioneers who were in the process of establishing themselves as prairie farmers. Hundreds of settlers deserted their farms during those years, but the Land Department persuaded a goodly number to remain and to look forward to better times. Every conceivable effort was made to keep on the land the settler who showed promise of making good. No concession was too great if it meant the difference between success and failure. Nuclei of settlement must be established on the prairie at all cost. In many cases where the settler's ambition was greater than his purse, he was allowed to relinquish a portion of his acreage, and to apply the payments already made to the land which he retained.

But it was not merely short crops that plunged the settler into debt. More than once in the period before 1896 depressed prices for farm products rendered the farmer incapable of meeting his payments to the company. By carrying over the purchasers' accounts, by rearranging contracts, by cancelling interest, and by reducing prices which the farmers had contracted to pay for the lands, the railway kept on the land many who were trying to carve out homes for themselves. When the price of wheat declined to 37 cents per bushel the company accepted large quantities of it at 50 cents per bushel. When settlers were unable to pay their municipal taxes it advanced sums of money for that purpose, thereby aiding materially in the maintenance of municipal farms during a period of crisis.

Despite all efforts of the company, however, contracts cancelled to 1896 covered 1,284,652 acres, of which about one-half had been held by colonization companies unable to comply with the settlement conditions imposed by the Canadian Pacific.

Generally speaking, purchasers of land experienced little difficulty in meeting their payments during the years of expansion and prosperity which began in 1897 and continued to the World War. Although the company sold 3,623,583 acres in 1902 and 1903, cancellations for the 2 years amounted to only 40,000 acres. Only in 1913 did cancellations reach the 100,000 figure. Almost without exception the colonization companies discharged their indebtedness promptly, while comparatively few actual settlers were in trouble.

As the war approached, however, it became apparent that large numbers of small speculative purchases had been made, in the irrigation block and elsewhere. Although the individual holdings of this character were small, they represented in the aggregate a large area. By 1912 the problem of the arrears on the lands had become so acute that the company was forced to take steps to deal with it. The policy then laid down was:

1. In all cases where the purchasers of land are in occupation and are endeavoring to make homes, we will not press them unduly for payment of outstandings on their contracts, but will endeavor, as far as possible, to have the interest kept up and to collect the principal after we see that we are going to have a good crop this year.

2. On all contracts where the purchaser is not in occupation, if he indicates that he is going to occupy it at an early date we will be as lenient as possible with reference to his payment of overdue amounts, but, in this case, we should also endeavor, as far as possible, to collect outstanding interest.

3. Our general policy will be not to cancel contracts except where they have got so much in arrear that there is no hope of collecting the amount, or, in case where there is no indication on

the part of the purchaser to go into occupation of the land and it is clear to us that it is being held for speculative purposes only.[1]

When arrears continued to mount steadily during 1913 it became necessary to resort to more extreme measures. A policy of cancellation was adopted, but with a proviso designed to enable the purchaser to salvage his equity in the land.[2] Where land was held unoccupied and unimproved, cancellation notices were to be issued promptly. The contract holder, however, was to have the opportunity of surrendering his contract, with reimbursement by the company of the amount paid on the contract, minus the commission paid by the company, together with unpaid accrued interest. Where contract holders were unwilling to surrender on that basis, cancellation was carried through. Where the land was occupied and improved, arrears of interest must be paid and an effort was to be made to secure some payment on account of arrears of principal.

Between October, 1913, when this procedure was adopted, and April 30, 1914, contracts covering 61,181 acres of irrigable land and 201,059 acres of non-irrigable land in the irrigation block were cancelled.[3] Payments made on these contracts amounted to $458,788 on account of principal and $54,540 on account of interest, which would indicate that in the great majority of cases only a first payment had been made. Commissions paid by the company for the sale of this land were $312,034. Meanwhile, a careful examination of contracts covering lands unoccupied and unimproved, with payments of principal and interest 2 or more years in arrears, indicated that a large additional area would have to be cancelled. Of a total of 1,577,459 acres sold in the irrigation block to that date, 577,922 acres were in one or the other of these two categories, leaving net sales of almost exactly 1,000,000 acres. Slightly more than one-third of the area disposed of within the block was covered by delinquent contracts.

The situation described above reflects the effects of the speculative fever engendered by the pre-war expansion in the West. The spirit of optimism had caused many purchasers to overreach themselves, to their subsequent disillusionment. Under the stimulus of high prices

[1] Dennis to Frank W. Russell, March 18, 1912, Letter Book I, M.
[2] Dennis to P. L. Naismith, October 28, 1913, Letter Book 9, M.
[3] See statements in File No. 336, D. N. R.

during the war years, the speculative element continued to enter into land sales, despite efforts of the company to exclude it. This fact, coupled with the failure of the dry farming experiment in the eastern section of the irrigation block, made it necessary for the railway to take back large areas. Between June 30, 1914 and December 31, 1921, cancellations amounted to 1,263,778 acres, out of gross sales of 3,731,985 acres.

As was inevitable, the years 1921-37 were the most notable era of land cancellations. For 25 years the West had enjoyed a prosperity spree. For the next 17 years it gradually sobered up. Ambitious plans collapsed overnight; fair prospects suddenly vanished. Western agriculture was ground down by price deflation and crop failure. Only with difficulty did land sales keep ahead of reversions. In some years cancellations actually exceeded sales. Table II tells the sorry tale.

Not from choice, but for reasons of necessity, the company cancelled contracts for 3,056,405 acres in this period. This large area represents a gradual clean-up of outstanding contracts, inherited from the prosperous days. When price reductions, adjustments of contracts, scaling down and writing off of interest, and other concessions failed, the company resorted to cancellation. Much of the cancelled area represented surplus holdings of farmers occupying more land than they could cultivate, and of which they were glad to be relieved. Although farmers in the eastern section of the irrigation block suffered from the excessive capital charges resulting from the high prices paid for the land, their difficulties were due to mistaken judgment by the company rather than to severity in its dealings with them. Before it transferred the region to the eastern irrigation district in 1935 the company had made repeated concessions and adjustments designed to ease the burden of contract holders.

The story of the twenties and thirties is anything but heartening, but certainly at no other time in its history did the company accord to its contract holders more considerate treatment. The cancellations of this period were the product of the attempt to sell and settle the inferior lands of the company in a time of economic adversity and climatic perversity.

In retrospect, the most distinctive feature of Canadian Pacific land policy, the one which differentiated it most sharply from that of

TABLE VII
LAND CONTRACTS, ACREAGE, AND AMOUNTS OUTSTANDING
AT DECEMBER 31, 1937[1]

LAND GRANT	CONTRACTS IN FORCE		AMOUNTS OUTSTANDING	
	Number	Acres	Principal	Interest
Main Line:				
C.P.R. (Winnipeg).	84	15,917.79	$ 78,973.80	$ 12,303.78
Manitoba........	174	28,838.18	118,532.86	22,892.34
Saskatchewan.....	3,013	542,835.18	4,750,203.18	763,883.45
Alberta..........	7,184	1,312,891.78	12,854,809.23	3,077,058.14
Irrigation Block...	2,165	516,958.08	7,726,461.33	1,934,698.53
Total—Main Line.	12,620	2,417,441.01	$25,528,980.40	$5,810,836.24
Hudson's Bay.......	62	13,814.91	193,561.71	66,064.55
A. R. & I.........	470	85,197.31	2,204,664.19	113,259.77
Souris Branch.......	2,512	465,126.36	4,494,123.48	921,479.11
M. S. W.........	135	31,846.30	206,251.91	65,454.06
G. N. W. C.........	252	45,389.26	475,211.29	99,581.09
C. & E............	318	66,307.05	850,593.85	150,726.22
M. & N. W........	1	159.50	1,548.84	
	16,370	3,125,281.70	$33,954,935.67	$7,227,401.04

other land grant railways on the American continent, was its program of assisted settlement which officials of the company commonly referred to as "colonization." The distinguishing characteristic of this policy was the extraordinary effort made to guarantee the actual occupation and the successful cultivation of the land, as opposed to a primary preoccupation with the sale of the land, with the hope and trust that settlement and development of the land would follow. The latter was the method employed by other railways, and while many of them achieved a notable success in settling and developing their lands, this result was due to their good fortune rather than to intelligent planning on their part. The Canadian Pacific itself had sold land for almost 30 years before it finally resorted to a program of assisted and supervised settlement.

The essential features of this program were ready-made farms, loan farms, and the advance of funds for the purchase of live stock by the farmer. Ready-made farms were introduced in 1909, while

[1] Figures supplied by Department of Natural Resources, Calgary.

the loan farm idea was adopted in 1912. The one was designed to stimulate the flow of British settlers to the company's lands; the other represented the most notable effort of the railway to locate on its remaining lands thousands of the experienced, but impecunious, occupants of rented farms in the middle western states of the neighboring republic. The following table shows the number of developed farms at the end of each year from 1909 through 1919.

TABLE VIII[1]

YEAR	No. of Farms Developed		TOTAL	FARMS UNSOLD	
	Ready-made	Loan		No.	Percentage
1909............................	24		24		
1910............................	102		102		
1911............................	279		279	193	69.2
1912............................	333	1	334	146	43.7
1913............................	404	123	527	133	25.2
1914............................	480	173	653	175	26.8
1915............................	521	165	686	186	27.1
1916............................	652	185	837	264	35.1
1917............................	691	229	920	213	23.2
1918............................	744	277	1,021	192	18.8
1919............................	762	419	1,181	124	10.5

The original plan of development called for the grouping of the ready-made farms in colonies. While a majority of the 762 farms of this type were to be found in the 24 colonies, a substantial number were without a colony connection. It seems to have been in the latter years of the colonization experiment that the departure was made from the colony or group plan of settlement. The Nightingale colony of 24 farms was developed in 1909. Other colonies, ranging in size from 5 to 122 farms, came rapidly to the outbreak of the World War, which momentarily interrupted the program. In 1915 but 41 farms were prepared. Meanwhile the Department of Natural Resources was giving serious thought to a plan which would combine sentiment with business. At the close of the war there would be thousands of demobilized Canadian veterans seeking once more to find their niche in the economic life of the Dominion. The Canadian

[1] *Annual Report,* Development Branch, Department of Natural Resources, 1919, p. 6.

Pacific might well make its contribution to the solution of the veterans' problem by providing ready-made farms to be sold to them on easy terms. In 1916 the department developed the Anzac, St. Julien, and Van Horne colonies for the veterans. The St. Julien colony contained 50 farms of 160 acres each, while the other two were limited to 25 farms each. The Van Horne farms were 80 acres; those in the Anzac colony averaged 246 acres. Each of the three colonies was equipped with a large central farm where agricultural experts were to offer practical lessons in farming for the benefit of the veterans.

The ready-made farm was first conceived in connection with the irrigation block and the majority of these farms were located there. A notable exception was the Sedgwick colony, numbering 122 farms. This settlement, centering about the Alberta town of that name, was begun in 1910 and enlarged the following year. At first the loan farm policy was applied to Canadian Pacific lands generally, but subsequently it was limited to the irrigation block. As a result, of the 418 loan farms which had been sold up to 1919, all but 7 were situated in the province of Alberta.

After 1919 no ready-made farms were developed for several years, but the loan farms were continued until by 1924 there were 580 of them, making a total of 1,342 farms of the two types. If we add the 120 farms in the Clan Donald colony, the 100 farms provided for by the joint project of the Canadian Pacific and the Hudson's Bay Company, and the 100 farms which the company undertook to prepare under the agreement with the Overseas Settlement Committee, we have a total of 1,662 farms sold and settled by the Canadian Pacific under the assisted settlement policy. As was befitting to a planned type of settlement, the farms under the two policies were of moderate size. Care was necessary to counteract the tendency of the settler in a new country to buy more land than he could advantageously use. Farms varied in size from 80 to 250 acres, with the great majority of them averaging from 150 to 160 acres.

The 1,181 farms developed under the ready-made and loan farm plans up to 1919 had a combined area of 232,069 acres. The 481 farms subsequently developed on an assisted settlement basis bring this total to approximately 300,000 acres. In a compact block this area would represent more than 13 townships developed by the railway under the ready-made and loan farm plans. Compared with the total acreage which has passed through the hands of the company, this area is not large. Yet, when viewed in comparison with other ventures in a similar type of settlement, its colonization stands out as a conspicuous achievement. Up to our own day no governmental agency in the United States had undertaken such a program of colonization. In Canada it compares favorably, as regards magnitude, with the Soldier Settlement and Three Thousand Family Schemes of the British and Dominion Governments. No private agency or corporation on the continent had undertaken such an ambitious project in colonization as opposed to land selling. Among land grant railways of North America this achievement of the Canadian Pacific stands unique.

Despite the interesting and significant character of this experiment in colonization, neither the ready-made farm nor the loan farm achieved the degree of success for which officials of the company had hoped. The one failed to dot the irrigation block with prosperous colonies recruited from the landless classes of the mother country; the other left the thousands of tenant farmers of the middle western states undisturbed in their drab existence. Immediate responsibility for the lack of expected success with the ready-made farms must rest squarely on the officials of the company charged with the duty of selecting the colonists. The optimistic belief of those officials to the contrary, there were only a limited number of experienced farmers in Great Britain who were potential settlers. This fact dictated the utmost care to see that only the right sort of people were chosen. Too often the one important consideration was not that of experience and character but the possession of sufficient funds to carry the colonist and his family to Calgary, where their farm with the necessary improvements awaited them. Even with company assistance there was no substitute for the spirit of enterprise, adaptability, and the will to succeed. By 1914 it was evident that British settlers on ready-made farms had largely failed. Many abandoned their farms, which the company later sold, in many cases, to settlers from the United States. In 1914 the recruitment of colonists for ready-made farm colonies began in the United States, when the initial group of farmers for the Bassano colony were brought from Colorado.

Throughout the war such colonies were prepared with an eye to either Canadian veterans or American farmers.

One of those who followed this experiment with keen interest was F. H. Newell, head of the Reclamation Service in the United States, and a noted authority on irrigation. Writing to Newell in 1914, Dennis frankly confessed his disappointment with the results obtained and diagnosed the reasons for the limited success achieved. He said:

> We, as you know, in the effort to obtain colonists have been going to the limit in assisting them. We have prepared "ready-made" farms, have given loans for improvements, have made advances of live stock and extended the terms of payment to twenty years. In addition, we have made advances of seed-grain and have established some seventeen farms of our own, which we operate as object lessons in the particular districts in which they are located.
>
> I am not going to say that our results have been altogether unsatisfactory, but I frankly admit they have not been what I hoped for and I have come to the conclusion that it is possible for a company or a government to do too much for settlers; and in this way rob them of the personal initiative which is so necessary for success.
>
> From now on we are going to exercise a great deal more care in the selection of men to whom assistance is to be given and we are going to insist on a larger initial payment being made where the man buys a "ready-made" farm or takes advantage of our loan policy with the object of trying to create a greater "stake" and thus keep him on the land.
>
> We have had a much larger percentage of success with men of small means than with men who apparently had ample capital.[1]

It was upon the ready-made farm policy as applied to British settlers that Dennis was pronouncing a verdict of failure. That was the policy which had been tried and found wanting. The loan farm policy for American farmers had not at that time received a sufficient trial to warrant a judgment. As Dennis had intimated, lack of care in the selection of British settlers had militated against the success of the ready-made farm plan. The loan farm policy received its trial during the war period when conditions were anything but normal and when the movement of American settlers to the Canadian West was seriously impeded. As a result the sales under

[1] Dennis to F. H. Newell, November 26, 1914, Personal Letter Book 5.

the policy to the close of 1919 were less numerous than had been anticipated. Yet of the 419 farms sold to that time, 418 were occupied by the original purchasers, a quite extraordinary record of success for any policy in any period.

The unsatisfactory nature of the company's experience with ready-made farms in the early stages of the experiment had by the close of the war cooled the ardor of officials for assisted settlement. While the loan farm policy was kept alive in the early twenties, it obviously was not pushed. In the latter part of the decade, however, the idea seems to have grown in favor. Not only were four separate projects launched involving the advance of company funds for the improvement of farms, but more and more those administering the lands of the railway were coming to realize that in an age of restricted immigration the less attractive lands remaining on the company's hands could be sold and settled only by the adoption of novel and extraordinary measures. Except where railway land was being taken by settlers enlarging their holdings, the offer of specific inducements of one sort or another was necessary. The increased use of the loan policy, the 34-year amortization plan, the brush land contracts, were variant forms of the recognition which the company gave to this fact.

To December, 1919, the Canadian Pacific had expended under the ready-made and loan farm policies a total of $2,959,713.[1] While the company's interests were amply protected through the addition of this sum to the cost of the land, the execution of the policies entailed a vast expenditure of thought and energy on the part of the Department of Natural Resources, as well as the maintenance of a special branch of the department for the supervision and performance of the work. This was no less true of the loan than of the ready-made farms, for the settler receiving the loan selected buildings from the standard plans provided by the department. However great the disappointment of the company over this experiment in assisted settlement, there probably exists in the annals of railway land subsidies no finer example of a railway's attempt to administer its landed estate in the interests of a sound development of the country.

At the close of 1918 the Department of Natural Resources for its

[1] *Annual Report, Development Branch, Department of Natural Resources,* 1919, p. 48.

own information, and not for public consumption, made a recapitulation of the work of the company in the interest of land sale and
settlement in the West. Since 1905 it had issued 5,600,920 pieces of
literature, had developed 14 motion picture films illustrative of
conditions in western Canada, and had given 1,256 illustrated lectures on opportunities in the West before audiences aggregating
841,741 persons. Its circulation of newspaper and magazine articles
relating to Canada was 887,434,893. This publicity effort had elicited
769,540 inquiries and had led to the registration by company agents
of 322,690 prospective purchasers of Canadian Pacific land. Its
agency force had brought 51,563 of these prospects to the western
land offices of the railway. The total number of sales since 1881
(after deducting cancellations) was 68,694, while the number of new
families placed on company lands was 45,856.

While between 1918 and 1937 the number of net sales probably
increased to 85,000, the number of new settlers was not correspondingly augmented because land sold in those years went largely to
farmers already residing in the West. A conservative estimate of the
number of new families located on Canadian Pacific land between
1881 and 1937 would be 50,000.

In proportion to acreage the number of sales by the company was
much smaller than by the Illinois Central. The latter made between
30,000 and 35,000 sales from an acreage of 2,595,000 acres, an
average of about 80 acres per sale. Actually much of the Illinois
Central land was sold in 40-acre tracts. The Canadian Pacific has
made 85,000 sales from approximately 19,000,000 acres. Had the
company sales averaged 160 acres the total would have been 118,000.
Its relatively smaller number of sales was due to two principal
factors: first, some 4,250,000 acres were included in 15 sales to land
companies; second, its land was located in a region primarily devoted
to grain growing which, owing to labor-saving machinery, was conducted on a larger scale than was farming in Illinois when the Illinois Central was selling land. In western Canada a quarter section
was the minimum area for a farm.

The figures given above as to the land settlement work of the
Canadian Pacific are in no way the full measure of its contribution
to the building of the Canadian West. They take no account of
general immigration work in behalf of Canada conducted by the

company in Great Britain and on the continent of Europe; of the contribution of Canadian Pacific steamship agents; of the people from the United States who went to the West on the land-seekers' rates certificates to settle on homesteads or to buy privately owned land; of those brought from eastern Canada and the States on low rate excursions and who failed to buy railway land; of harvesters who came to reap and who remained to sow; of those brought to the West in the post-war years under the auspices of the company's department of colonization. Nor do they include the thousands of Mennonites and other settlers established on privately owned land by the Canada Colonization Association, a subsidiary of the railway.

There remains the question as to whether the land subsidy to the Canadian Pacific was justified on grounds of national interest. It was one of the principal means of bringing to the task of railway building a group of men who completed in 5 years the railway about which the country had talked for 10. It was the means also of making the railway company an agency of land settlement second in importance only to the government itself. In 1881 the Liberal *Manitoba Free Press*, never an apologist for the Canadian Pacific, remarked that the vigorous encouragement of immigration and land settlement in the West weighed far more heavily than the number of dollars and acres given for the construction of the railway. A few thousand settlers more or less each year, it said, would have a greater effect upon the future of the Northwest than "the granting of a few million dollars or acres more or less to a syndicate."[1] To the *Free Press*, the speedy settlement of the West would justify the land subsidy. Judged by that test, the Canadian Pacific certainly was not found wanting.

To every young country speed of development seems essential. To none did it appear more necessary than to Canada in 1881. Without government aid the completion of the Canadian Pacific might well have waited for 20 years. From the point of view dominant in the Dominion in 1881 such delay was unthinkable. Looking back from the vantage point afforded by the lapse of 57 years, however, one might well conclude that in the Canadian, as in the American, West speed was sometimes unwise and made for waste of

[1] *Manitoba Daily Free Press*, January 13, 1881.

national resources, human and material. A calmer and more considered course might well have averted the mistakes of the pre-war period and spared the people of the West some of the untold heartaches and the cruel disillusionment of the post-war years. Unfortunately the world moves forward without the benefit of hindsight!

BIBLIOGRAPHICAL NOTE

This book has been written mainly from manuscript materials, of which the most important, of course, are in the archives of the Canadian Pacific Railway Company. These records are housed in the Office of the Secretary, Montreal; in the Department of Immigration and Colonization, Montreal; and, more particularly, in the Department of Natural Resources, Calgary. The last seven chapters are based almost wholly upon these documentary collections. Because of the destruction of much of the correspondence of the General Land Department at Winnipeg for the years prior to 1900, the author has been forced to draw more heavily upon other materials for Chapters IV, V, and VI.

For Chapters II and III the author had the benefit of the manuscript records in the Dominion Lands Branch, Department of the Interior, Ottawa.

The *Statutes of Canada, Sessional Papers, Debates of the House of Commons, Journals of the House of Commons,* and *Debates and Proceedings of the Senate of Canada* yielded data supplementary to the manuscript collections.

The files of the *Manitoba Free Press* for the years 1881-1905 are rich in material relating to the settlement and development of the Canadian Northwest. Heavy reliance was placed on the *Free Press* because it was not only the best informed newspaper with respect to the prairie, but, as a Liberal paper, it was fair without being too sympathetic toward the Canadian Pacific.

Among the published works bearing upon the subject are:

Dafoe, John W., *Clifford Sifton in Relation to His Times,* Toronto, 1931.
Dawson, C. A., *Group Settlement: Ethnic Communities in Western Canada* (Volume VII in Canadian Frontiers of Settlement), Toronto, 1936.
England, Robert, *The Colonization of Western Canada,* London, 1936.

Gibbon, John Murray, *Steel of Empire,* Indianapolis, 1935.
Hedges, James B., *The Federal Railway Land Subsidy Policy of Canada,* Cambridge (Mass.), 1934.
Innis, H. A., *A History of the Canadian Pacific Railway,* London, 1923.
Innis, H. A., and Plumptre, A. F. W. (Editors), *The Canadian Economy and Its Problems,* Toronto, 1934.
Innis, Mary Quayle, *An Economic History of Canada,* Toronto, 1935.
Knowles, L. A. A., *The Economic Development of the British Overseas Empire,* Vol. II, London, 1930.
MacBeth, R. G., *Sir Augustus Nanton: A Biography,* Toronto, 1931.
Mackintosh, W. A., *Prairie Settlement: The Geographical Setting* (Volume I in Canadian Frontiers of Settlement), Toronto, 1934.
Mackintosh, W. A., "Some Aspects of a Pioneer Economy," *Canadian Journal of Economics and Political Science,* November, 1936, pp. 457-63.
Marchbin, Andrew A., "Early Emigration from Hungary to Canada," *Slavonic Review,* XIII, 127-38.
Mavor, James, "Report to the British Board of Trade on the Northwest of Canada," *British Parliamentary Papers,* 1904, Cd. 2628, Appendix A.
Morton, A. S., and Martin, Chester, *History of Prairie Settlement and "Dominion Lands" Policy* (Volume II in Canadian Frontiers of Settlement), Toronto, 1938.
Newton, A. P., Rose, J. H., and Benians, E. A. (Editors), *The Cambridge History of the British Empire,* Vol. VI, New York, 1930.
Parkin, George A., *Sir John A. MacDonald,* Toronto, 1920.
Pope, Joseph (Editor), *Memoirs of the Right Honorable Sir John MacDonald,* 2 Vols., Ottawa, 1894.
Pope, Joseph (Editor), *Correspondence of Sir John MacDonald,* London and Toronto, 1921.
Pope, Joseph, *The Day of Sir John MacDonald,* Toronto, 1920.
Saunders, E. M. (Editor), *The Life and Letters of the Rt. Hon. Sir Charles Tupper,* New York, 1916.
Shortt, Adam, and Daughty, Arthur G. (Editors), *Canada and Its Provinces,* Vols. XIX and XX, Toronto, 1914.
Skelton, O. D., *The Life and Times of Sir Alexander Tilloch Galt,* Toronto, 1920.
Skelton, O. D., *The Railway Builders,* Toronto, 1920.
Vaughan, Walter, *The Life and Work of Sir William Van Horne,* New York, 1920.

INDEX

Aberdeen, South Dakota, 114

Aberdeen Star, Canadian immigration material in, 115

Adamson, A. J., and Saskatchewan Valley Land Company, 144-145

Agents, Dominion, Immigration propaganda of, in United States Alberta and Saskatchewan Colonization Company, 163

Alberta Central Land Corporation, 163

Alberta, creation of Province of, 168; sale of Canadian Pacific lands in central and northern, 245-254

Alberta Irrigation Company, 171

Alberta Railway and Irrigation Company, 60, 154, 171ff., 310, 324

Albert Rural Development League, formation of, 349

Alberta Stock Yards Company, distribution of live stock by, 337

Alfalfa, distribution of seed by Canadian Pacific, 340

Allan, Sir Hugh, and plan for Pacific Railway, 18; elected President of Canadian Pacific, 19; and Pacific Scandal, 20

Along the Line, pamphlet, distribution of in England, 96

Altman, Samuel, report of, on foreign colonies in Canadian West, 351

American Immigration Association of the Northwest, organization of, 165

Anderson, George C., report of, on irrigation in the West, 173

Angus, R. B., member of Canadian Pacific Syndicate, 24; elected to Directorate of Canada Northwest Land Company, 75; trustee for Canadian Pacific town sites, 86

Animal Husbandry Branch of Department of Natural Resources, organization and work of, 336-337

Anzac, Veterans' colony of, 404

Armstrong, L. O., report of, on immigration propaganda in Michigan, 113

Army, Salvation, of England, and plan for colony in Irrigation Block, 222, 227

Askew, W. H., and financial aid to settlers, 379

Association of German-Canadian Catholics, coöperation of, with Canada Colonization Association, 376

Atchison, Topeka and Santa Fe Railroad, 30, 289

Atlantis Hungarian Board, coöperation of, with Canada Colonization Association, 384

Australia, publicity for, in England, 282

Australians, land sales to, in Irrigation Block, 209

Austrians, settlements by, at Egg Lake and Beaver Lake, 92

Austria-Hungary, immigration activities in, 121, 132

Baker, Archer, report of, on British and continental emigration to Canada, 99ff.

Balgonie, Roumanian colony of, 123

Baptist Board, coöperation of, with Canada Colonization Association, 376

Bassano, ready-made farm colony at, 295

Battleford Block, origins of, 48; sale of lands in, 258ff., 313-316, 357

Beatty, Sir Edward, and support of Canada Colonization Association, 367; and movement of Mennonites to Western Canada, 374; and aid to Clan Donald colony, 379; and Mennonite colony at Coaldale, 383

INDEX